BARRON'S

HOW TO PREPARE FOR THE

PRAXIS I PPST/CBT

BARRON'S

HOW TO PREPARE FOR THE

PRAXIS I
PPST/CBT

PRE-PROFESSIONAL SKILLS TEST
AND COMPUTER-BASED TEST

Dr. Robert Postman
Professor
Mercy College

To my wife Liz
A joy to behold
This book is dedicated to you.

All inquiries should be addressed to:
Barron's Educational Series, Inc.
250 Wireless Boulevard
Hauppauge, NY 11788
http://www.barronseduc.com

Library of Congress Catalog Card No. 00-031207

International Standard Book No. 0-7641-1443-3

Library of Congress Cataloging-in-Publication Data

Postman, Robert D.
    Barron's how to prepare for the PPST and CBT pre-professional skills test and
computer based test / Robert D. Postman.
        p. cm.
    ISBN 0-7641-1443-3
    1. Pre-Professional Skills Tests—Study guides.   I. Title: How to prepare for the PPST
and CBT pre-professional skills test and computer based test.   II. Barron's Educational
Series, Inc.   III. Title.

LB2367.75 .P66 2000
378.1'662—dc21   00-031207

PRINTED IN THE UNITED STATES OF AMERICA

9 8 7 6 5 4 3 2 1

CONTENTS

Preface   ix

PPST 2000–2001 Test Dates   xi

PART I: TESTS AND STRATEGIES

1. Praxis I Tests   3
Read Me First!   4
Praxis I—The Inside Story   4
What Are the Tests Like?   5
Should I Take the PPST or the CBT?   6
Registering for the Praxis Tests   7
Other Praxis Tests   9

2. Test Preparation and Test-Taking Strategies   11
Preparing for the Tests   12
Proven Test-Preparation Strategies   12
Proven Test-Taking Strategies   14
   Multiple-Choice Strategies   15
   CBT Strategies   16
   Essay Strategies   17

PART II: SUBJECT MATTER PREPARATION

3. Writing   27
English Review Quiz   28
   Part I—Sentence Correction   28
   Part II—Essay   30
   Study Checklist   32
English Review   35
   Nouns and Verbs   35
   Pronouns   40
   Subject-Verb Agreement   43
   Adjectives and Adverbs   45
   Comma Splices and Run-on Sentences   49
   Sentence Fragments   50
   Parallelism   52
   Diction   53
   Punctuation   56
   Strategies for Taking the Multiple-Choice Writing Test   67
   Strategies for Taking the Essay Writing Test   72
   Targeted Writing Test   73

4. Mathematics   80
Mathematics Review Quiz   81
Study Check List   85
Using the CBT Mathematics Calculator   88

Mathematics Review   90
  Whole Number Computation   92
  Positive Exponents   94
  Square Roots   95
  Order of Operations   96
  Understanding and Ordering Decimals   97
  Rounding Whole Numbers and Decimals   99
  Add, Subtract, Multiply, and Divide Decimals   100
  Understanding and Ordering Fractions   101
  Multiply, Divide, Add, and Subtract Fractions and Mixed Numbers   104
  Subtract Fractions and Mixed Numbers   105
  Number Theory   106
  Ratio and Proportion   109
  Percent   111
  Three Types of Percent Problems   113
  Percent of Increase and Decrease   115
  Probability   117
  Statistics   119
  Permutations, Combinations, and the Fundamental Counting Principle   121
  Integers   122
  Scientific Notation   124
  Equations   125
  Geometry   127
  Coordinate Grid   131
  Measurement   134
  Formulas   138
  Time and Temperature   142
  Graphs   145
  Stem-and-Leaf and Box-and-Whisker Plots   148
  Flow Charts   150
  Logic   152
  Problem Solving   153
Strategies for Taking the Mathematics Test   168
Targeted Mathematics Test   170

5. **Reading   183**
Vocabulary Review   184
  Context Clues   184
  Roots   184
  Prefixes   185
  The Vocabulary List   185
Strategies for Taking the Reading Test   192
  Reading About Reading   192
  Five Steps to Taking a Reading Test   192
  Author's Purpose   195
  Applying the Steps   196
  Practice Passage   198
Targeting Reading Test   204

PART III: PRACTICE TESTS

6. **Practice PPST 1**   211

7. **Practice PPST 2**   257

8. **Practice CBT**   297

PART IV: SCORES AND CAREERS

9. **Praxis I Test Scoring and State-by-State Certification**   359

10. **Getting Certified**   389

11. **Getting a Teaching Job**   393

PREFACE

This book shows you how to do your absolute best on the Praxis I Teacher Certification examinations and helps you get started in a teaching career. Hundreds of prospective teachers field-tested preliminary versions of this book and dozens of experienced teachers and subject-matter specialists reviewed the book to ensure that it provides you with the subject-matter preparation and practice tests you need.

The practice tests in this book have the same question types and the same question-and-answer formats as the real tests. The practice tests also have the look and feel of the real thing—complete with uneven margins, open space, and the single and double columns found on the actual tests.

My wife, Liz, a teacher, was a constant source of support and she made significant contributions to this book. My children, Chad, Blaire, and Ryan, have also been a source of support as I worked on this and other books over the years.

I can attest that Barron's is simply the best publisher of test preparation books. The editorial department spared no effort to assure that this book is most helpful to you, the test-taker.

Max Reed, senior editor at Barron's, did an amazing job with a complex manuscript. Max and I have worked on four other books. As usual, many of the special touches in this book are due to her caring attention. I also appreciate the contributions of Virginia Monaco.

Special thanks to the undergraduate and graduate students and those changing careers who field-tested sections of this book. I am particularly grateful for the contributions of Ryan Postman. I am also grateful to experts at state education departments and colleges throughout the country for talking to me about teacher certification requirements.

You are entering teaching during a time of tremendous opportunity, and I wish you well in your pursuit of a rewarding and fulfilling career. The next generation awaits. You will help them prepare for a vastly different, technological world.

Robert D. Postman
September 2000

PPST 2000–2001 TEST DATES

Test Date	Regular Registration Deadline
November 18, 2000	October 17, 2000
January 20, 2001	December 19, 2000
March 10, 2001	February 6, 2001
April 21, 2001	March 20, 2001
June 23, 2001	May 22, 2001

For details, late registration dates, or additional test information, check the ETS Praxis Bulletin, call ETS at 609-771-7714, or visit the Praxis Web site at
www.teachingandlearning.org/licnsure/praxis/

PART I

Tests and Strategies

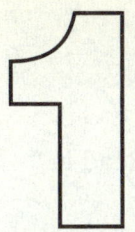

PRAXIS I TESTS

READ ME FIRST!

This section explains the steps you should take in beginning your test preparation. Read it before going on.

WHAT'S GOING ON WITH PRAXIS I?

Teacher certification examinations have been around for years. Until recently, most states relied on the National Teacher Examinations (NTE). Recently, states have focused on the reading, writing, and mathematics skills tested by the Praxis I test.

THE GOOD NEWS

The good news is that Praxis I tests focus on a central core of reading, writing, and mathematics skills. In this book, you learn how to prepare successfully for each test.

At the end of the book we show you how to begin your career in teaching, get certified, write your perfect resume, and look for your first job.

PRAXIS I—THE INSIDE STORY

Praxis I is a name for the paper and pencil PPST and the computer-based CBT. The Praxis Series was developed by the Educational Testing Service (ETS), an educational testing organization that administers over 6,000,000 tests yearly all over the world. Praxis I consists of three separate tests: (1) Reading, (2) Mathematics, and (3) Writing—multiple choice and essay. The test is available in two forms: the paper-and-pencil PPST and the computer-based test (CBT). The CBT generates questions based on your previous responses.

PRAXIS I SUMMARY

	PPST	CBT
Reading	40 multiple-choice questions— 50 minutes	36 multiple-choice questions— 95 minutes
Writing		
Multiple choice	45 multiple-choice questions— 50 minutes	35 multiple-choice questions— 30 minutes
Essay	1 handwritten essay— 30 minutes	1 typed essay—40 minutes
Mathematics	40 multiple-choice questions— 50 minutes	29 multiple-choice questions— 65 minutes

WHAT ARE THE TESTS LIKE?

The PPST and the CBT each assess reading, writing, and mathematics skills. However, they are very different tests. The PPST is a straightforward pencil and paper multiple-choice test with one handwritten essay. The CBT is a computer-adaptive test with one typed essay. On the CBT the computer generates an item based on your previous response. On the CBT you may be asked to choose one or more answers, highlight information, move information, mark a response, complete a graph, or enter a numerical answer.

The PPST and the CBT tests are described below.

PRE-PROFESSIONAL SKILLS TEST—PPST

You take the PPST on scheduled test dates. You may also take the test on a special date because of religious beliefs or a disability. The multiple-choice items are all prepared in advance. You mark your answers on a standard answer sheet and handwrite your essay. You can skip items and come back to them and you can change your answers to items you have already answered.

Reading

The 60-minute reading test has 40 multiple-choice items. Each item has five answer choices. There are some long passages of about 200 words, some shorter passages with about 100 words, and some statements of a few sentences. According to ETS, test items are partitioned as follows: literal comprehension 55%, critical and inferential comprehension 45%.

Writing

The 60-minute writing test is partitioned into a 30-minute multiple-choice section and a 30-minute essay section. There are 45 multiple-choice items with four answer choices. There are 25 usage items and 20 sentence correction items. You are given a topic to write your essay about. Each section contributes 50% to the final score.

Mathematics

The 60-minute mathematics test has 40 multiple-choice items. Each item has five answer choices. The test measures a wide range of mathematics topics primarily from the pre-college curriculum. According to ETS, test items are partitioned as follows: conceptual knowledge 15%, procedural knowledge 30%, data representation 30%, geometry and measurement 15%, and reasoning 10%. You may not use a calculator.

COMPUTER-BASED TEST—CBT

You take the CBT almost any day of the week and almost on demand. You sit in a cubicle in front of a computer screen while a television camera mounted overhead records your every movement. You use a mouse and a keyboard to enter your answers and you type your essay. You must answer each item as it is presented. You can't come back to an item, and you can't change your answers to items you have already answered.

CBT tests are computer-adaptive. That is, the computer generates an item based on your previous response. Each test starts out with items of average difficulty. Then the computer generates items based on your previous responses. If you miss an average item, the computer gives you an easier item. Get that one correct and the computer gives you a more difficult item. The more difficult the item, the more it contributes to your final score. You don't spend time answering items that are too difficult for you, or that are too easy for you.

Reading

The 95-minute reading test has 36 computer-generated items. There are 200-word passages, 400-word passages, and passages with graphs, charts, and other diagrams. You indicate your answer by highlighting one or more answers, by highlighting other information, by moving information around, or by clicking boxes. According to ETS, test items are partitioned as follows: comprehension 60%, analysis and application 40%.

Writing

The 70-minute writing test is partitioned into a 30-minute section with 35 computer-generated error recognition items and a 40-minute essay section. You indicate your answer by highlighting the part of a sentence that contains an error, or by highlighting "No error." You choose one of two topics for your essay, and you type your essay. Each section contributes 50% to the final score.

Mathematics

The 65-minute mathematics test has 29 computer-generated items. You indicate your answer by typing a numerical answer in an answer box, moving numerals or other symbols, marking a scale, completing a graph, or checking boxes. According to ETS, test items are partitioned as follows: numbers and operations 25%, mathematical relationships 25%, data interpretation 25%, geometry and measurement 20%, reasoning 10%. There is an on-screen calculator to add, subtract, multiply, divide, and find square roots. The calculator display can be transferred directly to an answer box.

SHOULD I TAKE THE PPST OR THE CBT?

Most states let you take either the PPST or the CBT. There are a few exceptions, such as Connecticut, which only accepts the CBT. Let's look at the advantages and the disadvantages of each test.

PPST

The PPST is given on six preset dates, but it is given at many more locations than the CBT. PPST items use a simple multiple-choice format. The PPST does not require you to use a computer. You have less time for each item than on the CBT. The PPST, most notably the mathematics test, is probably easier than the CBT, but the score scaling makes up for much of the difference. See page 359 for more information about scale scores. You can go back and change your answers. You're not videotaped while you take the PPST. You wait a month for your PPST scores.

CBT

The CBT can be taken 300 days out of the year, but you can only take the test once every 60 days. That's a maximum of six times a year. CBT items have more complex ways to show an answer. You must use a computer for the CBT and you have more time for each item than on the PPST. The CBT is probably more difficult than the PPST, but the score scaling makes up for much of the difference. See page 359 for more information about scale scores. You must answer each item as it is presented and you can't go back to change your answer. You are videotaped while you take the CBT. You get CBT scores immediately, except for the writing score, which takes about a week.

THE VERDICT

Apply these rules in the order given.

1. If your state accepts only one test, take that test.
2. If you're more than 90 minutes from the nearest CBT site, take the PPST.
3. If you're uncomfortable with computers, take the PPST.
4. If you want to take the test on your schedule, take the CBT.
5. If you like to have a calculator for the mathematics test, take the CBT.
6. If you are comfortable with computers, take the CBT.
7. If you like to skip items and come back to them or if you like to change your answers, take the PPST.
8. If you want to see your scores immediately, take the CBT.
9. If you hate being videotaped from above, take the PPST.
10. If you like taking a test with lots of people, take the PPST.

REGISTERING FOR THE PRAXIS I TESTS

PPST Registration

The Praxis Bulletin contains registration forms for the PPST. The Praxis Bulletin is available in late July for the following school year. If you are attending college, you can usually find copies of the bulletin in the school or department of education. If not, you can call 609-771-7395 to obtain the bulletin and other information or go to *www.teachingandlearning.org*.

You can also get a bulletin by writing to:

Praxis Bulletin
Educational Testing Service
Princeton, NJ 08541-6051

When you get the Praxis Bulletin, check the location and schedule for the tests you want to take. Complete the registration form and send it in with the correct fee.

CBT Registration

The Praxis I Computer-Based Test (CBT) is offered at over 200 Sylvan Key Learning centers and at colleges. To register call

(800) 853-6773
(800) 529-3590 (TTY)

ON THE WEB

The Educational Testing Service has a web site with comprehensive information about Praxis I tests (*www.teachingandlearning.org*). You can register for the PPST through the web site and get up-to-date information about test dates and state-by-state testing requirements. You can also download the Praxis Registration Bulletin. Test scores are not available through the web site.

PPST TEST LOCATION

Where you take the Praxis is very important. Check the bulletin for locations near you and list as your first choice the location in which you feel the most comfortable. Remember to list acceptable alternative locations but never list any alternates you really don't want to go to.

Send in the registration form as soon as possible. Early registrants are more likely to get their first choice location. Each test date has a cutoff usually one month before the test is given. You may still be able to register at Ticketmaster or other computerized ticketing agencies after the deadline has passed.

You will receive a registration ticket from ETS several weeks before the test. If you don't like your test site, you can call the numbers on the previous page and try to have it changed.

If you are too late for regular registration or computerized ticketing, don't give up. Most Praxis sites accept walk-ins if they have space. Call sites until you find one that can accept you. If you still have no luck, go directly to a site early on the test day and hope for the best; some registrants may not show. With persistence, you should be able to take the test somewhere.

CBT TEST LOCATION

You must take the CBT at one of the 200 centers. Go to *www.etsist.ets.org.tcenter.lst.cfm* for an up-to-date list. You may be able to register for a test and take the test that same day.

WHERE TO SEND YOUR SCORES

The Praxis Bulletin lists a code for each organization that can receive scores. You should list the code for each certification agency or college you want to receive your scores. The scores must usually be sent directly to the agencies from ETS.

You may feel that you should wait until you know you have gotten a passing score before sending it in, but that's not necessary. You will just slow down the process and incur extra expense. Certification agencies do not use these scores for evaluative purposes. They just need to see a passing score, and ETS reports only your highest score.

You will receive your own report and you are entitled to have four score reports sent to the certification agency or colleges you choose. Any extra reports will be sent to you.

SPECIAL TEST ARRANGEMENTS

ETS offers special arrangements or considerations for the following categories. If you qualify for special test arrangements, take advantage of the opportunity. Special arrangements can be made for both the PPST and the CBT. Go to *www.ets.org/disability* for complete documentation.

Do You Have a Disability (a Learning Disability or a Physical, Visual, or Hearing Impairment)?

You may qualify for additional time to complete the test, for someone to read the test to you, or for other special circumstances to accommodate your disability. You must use the Certification of Documentation form from the Registration Bulletin or write directly to ETS to receive these special considerations. Your letter should describe your disability and the special arrangements you desire. Also enclose a note from a school counselor or employer to verify that these arrangements have previously been made for you, or a note from a health professional documenting your disability. Contact ETS if you have any questions.

Do You Celebrate Your Sabbath on Saturday? Do Your U.S. Military Duties Prevent You from Taking the Test on a Saturday?

You may qualify to take the test on the Monday following the Saturday administration. Complete the Praxis I registration form indicating this special situation. If you are unable to take a test for religious reasons, include a note from the head of the religious group where you worship, on that group's letterhead, stating that your Sabbath is on Saturday. If you cannot take a test for military reasons, include a copy of your orders.

Do You Live More Than 100 Miles from a PPST Test Site?

You may qualify for an alternative test site. Send in the registration form with a note explaining your circumstances. There is an additional fee for taking the test at an alternative test site. Contact ETS if you have any questions.

OTHER PRAXIS TESTS

NTE CORE BATTERY TESTS

The NTE Core Battery tests consist of the Test of General Knowledge (GK), the Test of Communication Skills (CS), and the Test of Professional Knowledge (PK). Refer to *Barron's How to Prepare for Praxis*.

NTE CORE BATTERY SUMMARY

Communication Skills Core Battery (Four 30-minute tests)	General Knowledge Core Battery (Four 30-minute tests)	Professional Knowledge Core Battery (Four 30-minute sections)
Reading 40 multiple-choice questions	**Social Studies** 30 multiple-choice questions	35 questions in each section. Questions are on planning, implementing, evaluating, and managing instruction and on professional foundations and functions.
Listening 40 multiple-choice questions	**Mathematics** 25 multiple-choice questions	
Writing 45 multiple-choice questions	**Lit./Fine Arts** 35 multiple-choice questions	
Writing-Essay 1 essay question	**Science** 30 multiple-choice questions	

PRINCIPLES OF LEARNING AND TEACHING (PLT)

The PLT consists of three separate tests, Elementary (K–6), Middle School (5–9), and Secondary (7–12). Each test has three scenarios that describe teaching situations. Each scenario is followed by seven multiple-choice and two short-answer (constructed response) questions based on that scenario. In addition, there are 24 multiple-choice questions that are not based on any of the scenarios, making a total of 45 items. Test questions cover four broad areas: organizing content for student learning, creating an environment for student learning, teaching for student learning, and teacher professionalism.

Refer to *Barron's How to Prepare for the Praxis.*

SUBJECT ASSESSMENTS

Subject Assessments are the revised form of the old Specialty Area tests. Subject Assessments have been extensively revised and all are based on a job analysis. These tests feature a modularized format that usually includes modules for Content Knowledge, Content Essays, and Pedagogy (a combination of multiple choice and short answer). States may require some or all these modules for certification.

Refer to *Barron's How to Prepare for the Praxis.*

MULTIPLE SUBJECT ASSESSMENT FOR TEACHERS (MSAT)

The MSAT is used primarily in California and Oregon but is being reviewed for adoption by other states to replace the Test of General Knowledge.

The MSAT is designed to measure knowledge comparable to that found on the NTE General Knowledge test in Language/Literature, Mathematics, Science, History/Social Studies, Visual and Performing Arts, Physical Education, and Human Development at an introductory level. You have five hours to complete this test, which consists of a two-hour multiple-choice test and two short-answer (constructed response) tests lasting two hours and one hour, respectively. Both the multiple-choice and the short-answer tests measure knowledge in eight areas.

Refer to Barron's *How to Prepare for the MSAT*.

# TEST PREPARATION AND TEST-TAKING STRATEGIES

This chapter shows you how to set up a test preparation schedule and shows you some test-taking strategies that will help you improve your score. The important strategies are discussed below.

MULTIPLE CHOICE

Eliminate and then guess. There is no penalty for wrong answers. Never leave any answer blank.

Suppose a multiple-choice test has 40 items with four answer choices. Eliminate two incorrect answer choices on all the items, guess every answer, and, on average, you would get 20 correct.

ESSAY

Write an outline first, then write the essay. Handwrite your outline for the CBT.

Topic Paragraph: Begin the written assignment with an introduction to orient the reader to the topic. The first paragraph should clearly state the main idea of your entire written assignment.

Topic Sentence: Begin each paragraph with a topic sentence that supports the main idea.

Details: Provide details, examples, and arguments to support the topic sentence.

Grammar, Punctuation, Spelling: Edit sentences to conform to standard usage.

Avoid passive construction: Write actively and avoid the passive voice.

Conclusion: End the written assignment with a paragraph that summarizes your main points.

PREPARING FOR THE TESTS

This section describes how to prepare for certification tests, and the next section describes test-taking strategies. Before we go on, let's think about what you are preparing for.

WAIT! WHY TEST ME? I'M A GOOD PERSON!

Why indeed? Life would be so much easier without tests. If anyone tells you that they like to take tests, don't believe them. Nobody does. Tests are imperfect. Some people "pass" when they should have failed, while others "fail" when they should have passed. It may not be fair, but it is very real. So sit back and relax. You're just going to have to do it. And this book will show you how.

WHO MAKES UP THESE TESTS AND HOW DO THEY GET WRITTEN?

Consider the following scenario. It is late in the afternoon in Princeton, New Jersey. Around a table sit teachers, deans of education, parents, and representatives of state Education Departments. In front of each person is a preliminary list of skills and knowledge that teachers should possess. The list comes from comments by an even larger group of teachers and other educational professionals.

Those around the table are regular people just like the ones you might run into in a store or on the street. They all care about education. They also bring to the table their own strengths and weaknesses—their own perspectives and biases. What's that? An argument just broke out. People are choosing up sides and, depending on the outcome, one item on the list will stay or go.

This goes on for a few days until this group has drawn up a final list. Thousands of teachers and national teacher organizations receive the list. Each rates the importance of every item. The items rated important will be measured by the test.

The final list goes to professional test writers to prepare test items. These items are tried out, refined, and put through a review process. Eventually the test question bank is established, and a test is born. These test writers are not geniuses. They just know how to write questions. You might get a better score on this test than some of them would.

The test writers want to write a test that measures important concepts. They try not to ask silly or obscure questions that have strange answers. For the most part, they are successful. You can count on the test questions to cover concepts that you should know.

You can also be sure that the test writers will ask questions that will make you think. Their questions will ask you to use what you know and apply it.

Keep those people around the table and the test writers in mind as you use this book. You are preparing for their test. Soon, you will be like one of those people around the table. You may even contribute to a test like this one.

PROVEN TEST-PREPARATION STRATEGIES

Here are several strategies and steps to follow as you prepare for the test. These strategies take you right up to test day.

GET YOURSELF READY FOR THE TEST

Most people are less tense when they exercise. Set up a *reasonable* exercise program for yourself. The program should involve exercising in a way that is appropriate for you 30 to 45 minutes each day. This exercise may be just as important as other preparation.

Prepare with another person. You will feel less isolated if you have a friend or colleague to study with.

FOLLOW THIS STUDY PLAN

Begin working four to ten weeks before the test. Review the description of each test you have to take and then take each appropriate review quiz. Use the answer key to mark the review quiz. Each incorrect answer will point you to a specific portion of the review.

Use the subject matter review indicated by the review quiz. Don't spend your time reviewing things you already know.

Take the targeted test after the review of each chapter is complete. It will let you know what further review may be necessary. Complete your review two weeks before the test. Then, complete the practice test. Take the test under exact test conditions. We recommend that you take the practice test on the same day of the week and during the same time period that you will take the actual test.

Grade your own test or have someone do it for you. Either way, review each incorrect answer and read all the explanations. Every answer is explained in detail.

Two Weeks to Go

During this week look over those areas you answered incorrectly on the practice test. Go over the answer explanations and go back to the review sections. For the CBT, practice using a computer mouse, a keyboard, a word processor, and a calculator.

One Week to Go

Get up each day at the time you will have to get up the following Saturday. Sit down at the time the test will start and spend about one hour answering questions on targeted tests or practice tests even if you've answered these questions before.

Follow this schedule for the week leading up to test day.

Five Days to Go (Monday for the PPST)

Make sure you

- have your admission ticket.
- know where the test is given.
- know how you're getting there.

Four Days to Go (Tuesday)

Visit the test site, if you haven't done so already.

Three Days to Go (Wednesday)

Get some sharpened No. 2 pencils, a digital watch or pocket clock, and an eraser.

One Day to Go (Friday)

- Complete any forms you have to bring to the test.

- Prepare any snacks or food you want to bring with you.

- Talk to someone who makes you feel good or do something enjoyable and relaxing.

- Have a good night's sleep.

Test Day (Saturday)

- Dress comfortably.

- Eat the same kind of breakfast you've been eating each morning.

- Get together things to bring to the test including: registration ticket, identification forms, pencils, eraser, and snacks.

- Get to the test room about 10 to 15 minutes before the start time. Remember to leave time for parking and walking to the test site.

- Hand in your forms.

- Follow the test-taking strategies in the next section.

PROVEN TEST-TAKING STRATEGIES

Testing companies like to pretend that test-taking strategies don't help that much. They act like that because they want everyone to think that their tests only measure your knowledge of the subject. Of course, they are just pretending; test-taking strategies can make a big difference.

However, there is nothing better than being prepared for the subject matter on the test. These strategies will do you little good if you lack this fundamental knowledge. If you are prepared, then these strategies can make a difference. Use them. Other people will. Not using them may very well lower your score.

BE COMFORTABLE

Get a good seat for the PPST. Don't sit near anyone or anything that will distract you. Stay away from your friends. If you don't like where you are sitting, move or ask for another seat. You paid money for this test, and you have a right to favorable test conditions. For the CBT, make sure that your chair is comfortably adjusted and that the computer is working properly.

YOU WILL MAKE MISTAKES

You are going to make mistakes on this test. The people who wrote the test expect you to make them.

YOU ARE NOT COMPETING WITH ANYONE

Don't worry about how anyone else is doing. Your score does not depend on theirs. When the score report comes out it doesn't say, "Nancy got a 661, but Blaire got a 670." You just want to get the score required for your certificate. If you can do better, that's great. Stay focused. Remember your goal.

MULTIPLE-CHOICE STRATEGIES

IT'S NOT WHAT YOU KNOW THAT MATTERS, IT'S JUST WHICH ANSWER YOU MARK

No one you know or care about will see your test. An impersonal machine scores every item except the essay. The machine just senses whether the correct answer is marked. That is the way the test makers want it. If that's good enough for them, it should be good enough for you. Concentrate on marking the correct answer.

YOU CAN BE RIGHT BUT BE MARKED WRONG

If you get the right answer but mark the wrong answer, the machine will mark it wrong. We told you that marking the right answer was what mattered. We strongly recommend that you follow this strategy.

On the PPST, write the letter for your answer big in the test booklet next to the number for the problem. If you change your mind about an answer, cross off the "old" letter and write the "new" one. At the end of each section, transfer all the answers together from the test booklet to the answer sheet.

DO YOUR WORK IN THE TEST BOOKLET (PPST) DO YOUR WORK ON SCRAP PAPER (CBT)

You can write anything you want in your test booklet. The test booklet is not used for scoring and no one will look at it. You can't bring scrap paper to the PPST but it's available for the CBT.

SOME QUESTIONS ARE TRAPS

Some questions include the words "not," "least," or "except." You are being asked for the answer that doesn't fit with the rest. Be alert for these types of questions.

SAVE THE HARD QUESTIONS FOR LAST ON THE PPST

You're not supposed to get all the questions correct, and some of them will be too difficult for you. Work through the questions and answer the easy ones. Pass the others by. Do these more difficult questions the second time through. If a questions seems really difficult, draw a circle around the question number in the test booklet. Save these questions until the very end. Remember, though, you can't skip items on the CBT.

THEY SHOW YOU THE ANSWER

Every multiple-choice test shows you the correct answer for each question. The answer is staring right at you. You just have to figure out which one it is.

SOME ANSWERS ARE TRAPS

When someone writes a test question, they often include distracters. Distracters are traps—incorrect answers that look like correct answers. It might be an answer to an addition problem when you should be multiplying. It might be a correct answer to a different question. It might just be an answer that catches your eye. Watch out for this type of incorrect answer.

ELIMINATE THE INCORRECT ANSWERS

If you can't figure out which answer is correct, then decide which answers can't be correct. Choose the answers you're sure are incorrect. Cross them off in the test booklet on the PPST. Only one left? That's the correct answer.

GUESS, GUESS, GUESS

If there are still two or more answers left, then guess. Guess the answer from those remaining. Never leave any item blank. There is no penalty for guessing.

CBT STRATEGIES

TAKE YOUR TIME

This is the single most important strategy for the CBT. When you see an item, stop and think. Take your time. Come up with your best answer.

Let's compare the amount of time you have for each item on the PPST and the CBT.

PPST–CBT TIME COMPARISON

	PPST			CBT		
	Time in Minutes	Items	Time per item	Time in Minutes	Items	Time per item
Reading	50	40	1.25 minutes	95	36	2.64 minutes
Writing	30	45	0.67 minutes	30	35	0.86 minutes
Mathematics	50	40	1.25 minutes	65	29	2.24 minutes

You have twice as much time for each CBT reading and mathematics item. Overall, you have about 50% more time for each CBT item. Take your time.

YOU CAN'T COME BACK TO CHANGE ANSWERS, SO MAKE EVERY ANSWER COUNT

Once you have answered an item and moved on to the next item you cannot go back. Concentrate on each item and make every answer count.

DON'T SKIP ITEMS

Don't just skip an item without answering it. If you don't know the answer, guess.

DON'T TRY TO FIGURE OUT HOW DIFFICULT AN ITEM IS

Just do your best on each item. Trying to decide how difficult an item is will just distract you. Even if you could figure it out, it wouldn't help.

ESSAY STRATEGIES

The PPST and CBT writing tests each have an essay. You have 30 minutes for the PPST essay and 40 minutes for the CBT essay.

YOUR RESPONSES ARE GRADED HOLISTICALLY

Holistic scoring means the raters assign a score based on their informed sense about your writing. Raters have a lot of answers to look at and they do not do a detailed analysis. The Educational Testing Service gets together groups of readers. These readers typically consist of teachers and college professors. At first, representatives of ETS show the readers the topics for the recent test and review the types of responses that should be rated 1–6. The rating guidelines are on page 34. The readers are trained to evaluate the responses according to the ETS guidelines.

Each written assignment is evaluated twice, without the second reader knowing the evaluation given by the first reader. If the two evaluations differ significantly, other readers review the assignment.

Readers have a tedious, tiring assignment. Think about those readers as you write. Write a response that makes it easy for them to give you a high score.

STEPS FOR WRITING PASSING ESSAYS

Follow these steps to write a passing essay. Remember, you have 30 minutes for the PPST essay or 40 minutes for the CBT essay.

1. **Understand the topic** (2 minutes).

   A topic is introduced and then described in more detail. Read the topic carefully to ensure that you understand it completely.

2. **Choose a thesis statement. Write it down** (2 minutes).

   Readers expect you to have a point of view about the topic. Choose yours; make sure it addresses the entire topic, and stick to it.

3. **Use the PPST test booklet or the CBT scrap paper to write a brief outline** (4 minutes).

   Write a brief outline summarizing the following essay elements.

   • Thesis statement

   • Introduction

   • Topic sentence and details for each paragraph

   • Conclusion

   Use this time to plan your essay.

4. **Write or type the essay** (18–22 minutes).

   Essays rated in the upper third typically have three or four paragraphs totaling 150 to 250 words. Writing an essay this long does not guarantee a passing score, but most passing essays are about this long. Use this time to write well.

5. **Proofread and edit** (4 minutes).

   Leave four minutes to read your essay over and correct any errors in usage, spelling, or punctuation. The readers understand that your essay is a first draft and they expect to see corrections on the PPST essay.

APPLY THE STEPS

Let's see how to apply these steps for a particular essay topic. Remember, there are many different thesis statements and essays that would receive a passing score.

Essay Topic

Some people say that machines cause difficulty for people. Others say that machines help people.
   Choose one of these positions. Give a specific example of a machine that causes difficulty or one that helps people. Write an essay that explains how the machine you chose causes difficulty for people or helps people.

1. **Understand the topic.**

   The topic is about machines. I have to decide whether to write about machines that cause difficulty for people OR about machines that help people. I have to give a specific example of a machine that causes difficulty or a machine that helps.

   I've got to stick to this topic.

   For this essay, I'm going to choose machines that help people.

   A complete response to the topic is an essay about a machine that helps people. There are many machines to choose from. An incomplete response will significantly lower the score.

2. **Choose a thesis statement. Write it down.**

   This important step sets the stage for your entire essay. Work through this section actively. Write down the names of several machines that help people. There is no one correct answer, so it does not have to be an exhaustive list.

Computers

Escalator

Car

Heart-lung machine

Fax machine

Add your own machines to this list.

_____

_____

_____

_____

I'll choose <u>heart-lung machines</u>.

Now I write how, what, and why heart-lung machines help people.

How: Circulate blood in place of the heart.

What: Replaces the heart during heart surgery.

Why: The heart is unable to pump blood when it is being operated on.

Write the choice from your list of machines. _____

Write how, what, and why the machine you chose helps people.

How: _____

What: _____

Why: _____

Thesis statement

My thesis statement is:

Heart-lung machines are machines that help people by taking the place of the heart during heart surgery.

The thesis statement identifies the heart-lung machine as a machine that helps people and explains the basis for my choice of the heart-lung machine. Both parts are needed for an effective thesis statement.

3. **Write a brief outline.**

Here is my outline.

• Introduction, including the thesis statement

• A heart-lung machine saves lives.

• People would die if the machines were not available.

• The machine circulates and filters blood during operations. Special membranes filter the blood, removing impurities.

• The heart can literally stop while the heart-lung machine is in use. Doctors have to restart the heart.

• Conclusion

My outline consists of an introduction, topic sentences and supporting details for three paragraphs, and a conclusion. That's five paragraphs in all.

Now write your own thesis statement and an outline on the heart-lung machine and how it helps people.

_____

_____

_____

_____

4. **Write the essay.**

I wrote an outline to plan my essay. I am going to rely on that plan as I concentrate on writing well.

Use a separate piece of paper, or a word processor.

Write your own essay about the heart lung machine—a machine that helps people.

5. **Proofread and edit.**

Revise, proofread, and edit your essay.

Remember that readers expect to see changes on the PPST essay.

REVIEW SAMPLE ESSAYS

You will find five rated sample essays on this topic on pages 20–23. Compare your essay to the samples.

PRACTICE

Write, proofread, and edit an essay on this topic, but for the machine you chose on page 19. Show your essays to an English professor or an experienced essay evaluator. Ask that person to evaluate your essay using the samples on pages 20–23 and make recommendations for improving your writing.

SAMPLE ESSAYS

ESSAY 1

> Heart-lung machines are a medical miracle. Heart-lung machines are used in hospitals all over the country. Doctors rely on this machine during surgery. Heart-lung machines keep alive during surgery and they use them to do open heart surgery. Lots of people can thank the heart-lung machine for keeping them alive. Some people say that there are too many bypass surgeries done every year and this may cause more problems than it fixes. However lots of people would die without the machine. It is a good thing that the heart-lung machine was invented.

Total final score: 1 or 2

ESSAY 2

Heart-lung machines are use in hospital all over the world. They get use every day. People are hook up to them when they are having surgry like if they are in open heart surgery.

I will now present one of way heart lung-machines are use. Once we did't have heart-lung machines to help a doctor. When the machine was invent we see lots of changes in surgry that a doctor can do. The doctor can oprate during the person heart not work. My granmothr when to the hospital for have surgry and they use the machine. Where she would have been without the machine.

And the machine keep blood move through the body. The doctor can take their time to fix a person heart while they are laying their on the operating room. I know someone who work in a hospital and they said don't know how it was possible befour the machine.

Last, that machine clean a bodies blood as it foes through. The blood won't poison the person who blood it is. But it wood be better if the body could clean it's own blood. A body is better than a machine.

I did tell about how the machine work and what it did. The machine can save a lifes.

Total final score: 2 or 3.

ESSAY 3

Heart lung machines are a medical miracle. They are used in hospitals all over the world. Heart lung machines are used during open heart surgery to circulate a patients blood and clean the blood. These machines can save lots of lives.

Heart-lung machines have made open heart surgery possible. Before they were invented, many people died because of disaese or during surgery. Surgery would not have been possible before then. And many people are alive today because of them. Besides surgery can now go on for hours. Sometimes the surgry can last as long as 12 hours. The heart lung machine makes things possible and saves lives.

Heart-lung machines circulate blood through the body. It pumps like a heart. The heart can stop and the heart lung machine will pump instead. Then the blood moves through the body just like the heart was pumping. So the blood gets to all the viens. It is unbelievable how the heart-lung machine can work and to keep people from dying.

The heart-lung machine can clean a persons blood. All the bad stuff gets taken out of the blood before it goes back into the body. That way the body won't get poison. I know of someone who had their blood cleaned by the machine while they were operated on. The person was unconscience. The doctor fixed his heart. Since the machine was going the persons heart was stopped. The doctor had to start it up again. It was pretty scary to think about that happening to a person. But the machine took all the bad stuff out of the blood and the person lived.

To conclude, I believe that the heart lung machine is great for people who need open heart surgery. It pumps and cleans their blood too. They are a medical miracle.

Total final score: 4 or 5.

ESSAY 4

Every day the heart-lung machine saves someone's life. Each day we walk by someone who is alive because of a heart-lung machine. Each day in hospitals throughout the world, skilled surgeons perform difficult surgery with the aid of a heart-lung machine. Some day, we may be kept alive by a heart-lung machine. The heart-lung machine is a wonderful machine that makes open-heart surgery possible by pumping and cleaning a person's blood. Surgeons use the machine during open heart surgery.

The heart-lung machine makes open-heart surgery possible. Open-heart surgery means the doctor is operating on the inside of the heart. In order to operate on the inside of a heart, the flow of blood through the heart must be stopped. But without blood flow, the patient will die. Researchers worked for decades to find a way to keep a person alive while the heart was stopped. Many of their early attempts failed; however, during this century the researchers and inventors were successful. They named their invention the heart-lung machine. The first heart-lung machines were probably very primitive, but today's machines are very sophisticated.

The heart-lung machine circulates blood while the heart is not pumping. The machine is hooked up to a person's circulatory system and acts just like a heart. The blood is taken from the body into one side of the machine and pumped back into the body through the other side of the machine. Blood returning to the heart is taken into the machine. The blood pumped out travels to every part of the body. The heart-lung machine helps the patient by replacing blood while the heart is stopped during open-heart surgery.

However, just pumping blood is not enough. As blood passes through a person's body, the body takes oxygen stored in the blood. Blood starts through the body full of oxygen and returns from the body without much oxygen. Normally, the lungs would take in oxygen and place that oxygen in the blood. But since the person's heart is stopped, the lungs are not working. The heart-lung machine does the lung's work and places oxygen in the blood as the blood passes through the machine.

The heart-lung machine makes open-heart surgery possible. The machine circulates and oxygenates a person's blood while their heart is stopped. Without the machine, many people would die from heart disease or would die during surgery. The heart-lung machine is a machine that helps people by keeping them alive and holds the promise for even more amazing machines to come.

Total final score: 6

Handwritten PPST Essay

This is what Essay 3 looked like in handwritten form. This is the essay that the PPST raters would actually see. Note the editorial changes that the student made during writing and editing. The raters expect to see these changes and marks on the PPST essay.

Heart lung machines are a ~~medicine~~ medical miracle. They are used in hospitals all over the world. Heart lung machines are used during open heart surgery to circulate a patients blood and clean the blood. These machines can save lots of ~~lifes.~~ lives

Heart lung machines have made open heart surgery possible. Before they were invented, many people died because of disease or during surgery. Surgery would not have been ~~impossible~~ before then. And many people are alive ~~have~~ today because of them. Besides surgery can now go on for hours. Sometimes the surgery can last as long as 12 hours. The heart lung machine makes things ~~very~~ possible and saves lives.

Heart lung machines circulate blood ~~through~~ through a body. It pumps like a heart. The heart can stop and the heart lung machine will pump instead. Then the blood moves through the body just like the heart ~~is~~ was pumping. So the blood gets to all the viens. It is ~~how~~ unbelievable ~~why~~ how the heart lung machine can work and to keeps people from dying.

The heart lung machine can clean a persons blood. All the bad stuff gets taken out of the blood before it goes back into the body. That way the body wont get poison. I know of someone who had their blood cleaned by the machine while they were operated on. The person was ~~unconscious~~ unconscious. The doctor fixed his heart. ~~Since~~ Because the machine was going the persons heart was stopped. The doctor had to start it up again. It was pretty scary to think about that happening to a person. But the machine took all the bad stuff out of the blood and the person lived.

To conclude, I believe that the heart lung machine is great for people who need open heart surgery. It pumps and cleans their blood too. They are a medical miracle.

PART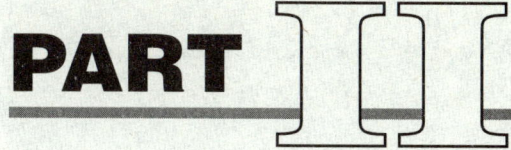

Subject Matter Preparation

# WRITING

USING THIS CHAPTER

This chapter prepares you to take the multiple-choice writing section and the essay section of the PPST and the CBT. You will need to find an English professor, teacher, or tutor to mark the essay portion of the review test. This person may also be able to help you prepare for the essay section of the test. Choose one of these approaches.

- **I want all the writing help I can get.** Skip the review quiz and read the writing review. Then take the English review quiz. Correct the test and reread the indicated parts of the writing review. Take the targeted test at the end of the chapter.

- **I want writing help.** Take the review quiz. Correct the quiz and review the indicated parts of the English review. Take the targeted test at the end of the chapter.

- **I want a quick writing review.** Take the review quiz. Correct the quiz. Then take the targeted test at the end of the chapter.

- **I want to practice a writing test.** Take the targeted test at the end of the chapter.

ENGLISH REVIEW QUIZ

The English Review Quiz assesses your knowledge of the English topics included in the Praxis I tests. The quiz also provides an excellent way to refresh your memory about these topics. The first part of the quiz consists of sentences to mark or correct. Make your marks or corrections right on the sentences. In the second part of the quiz, you are asked to write a brief essay.

This quiz will be more difficult than the questions on the actual certification test. It's not important to answer all these questions correctly and don't be concerned if you miss many of them.

The answers are found immediately after the quiz. It's to your advantage not to look until you have completed the quiz. Once you have completed and marked this review quiz, use the checklist to decide which sections to study.

PART I SENTENCE CORRECTION

> Correct the sentence. Some sentences may not contain errors.

1. Ron and James fathers each sent them to players camp to learn the mysterys of sport.

2. They go to the camp, ridden horses while they were there, and had write letters home.

3. James went to the water and goes skiing.

4. Ron and James called his coach. The operator never answered, and they wondered what happened to her.

5. Bob and Liz went to the store and got some groceries.

6. Dad want me to do my homework. My sisters try their best to help me.

> Underline the subject in each sentence.

7. Chad's project that he showed the teacher improved his final grade.

8. The legs pumped hard, and the racer finished in first place.

9. Through the halls and down the stairs ran the harried student.

10. Where is the dog's leash

> Correct the sentence. Some sentences may not contain errors.

11. Chad was sure correct, the food tastes bad and the singer sang bad but Ryan played really well. Ryan was more happy than Chad who sat closer to the stage than Ryan.

12. The larger table in the restaurant was full.

13. The waiter brought food to the table on a large tray. The waiter wanted a job in the suburbs that paid well.

14. Waiting for the food to come, the complaining began.

15. The food arrived, the eating began. The waiter stood by he was tired.

Correct the sentence. Some sentences may not contain errors.

16. The coach realized that new selection rules to go into effect in May. She also knew what it would take for Ryan to be selected. Ryan winning every game. But the coach and Ryan had a common goal. To see Ryan on the team.

17. Ryan's parents wanted a success rather than see him fail. They knew he stayed in shape by eating right and exercising daily. Ryan was a person who works hard and has talent.

18. Chad was dog tired after soccer practice. He became a coach for the purpose of helping the college to the soccer finals. During the rein of the former coach, the team had miserable seasons. Chad would stay at the job until such time as he could except the first place trophy.

19. Chad was satisfied but the players were grumbling. The players wanted to practice less have more free time. The players didn't like their light blue uniforms! The finals began in May 1996. The first game was scheduled for Tuesday May 9 at 1:00 P.M. The time for the game was here the players were on the field. Chad had the essential materials with him player list score book soccer balls and a cup of hope.

PART II—ESSAY

Time yourself for 30 minutes. Use the lined page to write a brief essay that answers this question.

Should high school students have to pass a standardized test before they graduate?

Write a brief outline here.

STUDY CHECKLIST

PART I—Sentence Correction

The answers are organized by review sections. Check your answers. If you miss any item in a section, check the box and review that section.

❑ *Nouns, page 35*
1. <u>Ron's</u> and <u>James's</u> fathers each sent them to <u>players'</u> camp to learn the <u>mysteries</u> of sport.

❑ *Verbs, page 37*
2. They <u>went</u> to the camp, <u>rode</u> horses while they were there, and <u>wrote</u> letters home.

❑ *Tense Shift, page 38*
3. James <u>went</u> to the water and <u>went</u> skiing. James <u>goes</u> to the water and <u>goes</u> skiing.

❑ *Pronouns, page 40*
4. Ron and James called (<u>Ron's, James's, their</u>) coach. The operator never answered, and they wondered what happened to <u>him or</u> her.

❑ *Subject-Verb Agreement, page 43*
5. No error
6. Dad <u>wants</u> me to do my homework. My sisters try their best to help me.
7. Chad's <u>project</u> that he showed the teacher improved his final grade.
8. The <u>legs</u> pumped hard, and the <u>racer</u> finished in first place.
9. Through the halls and down the stairs ran the harried <u>student.</u>
10. Where is the dog's <u>leash</u>?

❑ *Adjectives and Adverbs, page 45*
11. Chad was <u>surely</u> correct, the food tastes bad and the singer sang <u>badly</u> but Ryan played really well. Ryan was <u>happier</u> than Chad who sat closer to the singer than Ryan <u>did</u>.

❑ *Comparison, page 46*
12. The largest table in the restaurant was full.

❑ *Misplaced Modifiers, page 48*
13. The waiter brought food <u>on a large tray to the table</u>. The waiter wanted <u>a well-paying job in the suburbs</u>.
14. Waiting for the food to come, the (<u>patrons, diners</u>) complained. The (<u>patrons, diners</u>) complained about waiting for the food to come.

❑ *Run-on Sentences and Comma Splices, page 49*
15. The food arrived. The eating began. The food arrived; the eating began. The food arrived and the eating began. The waiter stopped by. He was tired. The waiter stopped by; he was tired. The waiter stopped by and he was tired.

❑ *Sentence Fragments, page 50*
16. The coach realized that new selection rules <u>would</u> go into effect in May. She also knew what it would take for Ryan to be selected. Ryan <u>would have to win</u> every game. But the coach and Ryan had a common goal. <u>They wanted</u> to see Ryan on the team.

❑ *Parallelism, page 52*
17. Ryan's parents wanted a success rather than <u>a failure</u> (wanted success rather than failure). They knew he stayed in shape <u>by</u> eating right and by exercising daily. Ryan was a person who works hard and <u>who</u> has talent. (Ryan is hard-working and talented.)

❑ *Diction, page 53*
18. Chad was [delete "dog"] tired after soccer practice. He became a coach <u>to help</u> the college <u>ascend</u> to the soccer finals. During the <u>reign</u> of the former coach, the team had miserable seasons. Chad would stay at the job until [delete "such time as"] he could <u>accept the first place trophy</u>.

❑ *Punctuation, page 56*

19. Chad was satisfied, but the players were grumbling. The players wanted to practice less <u>and</u> have more free time. The players didn't like their light blue uniforms. The finals began in May 1996. The first game was scheduled for Tuesday, May 9, at 1:00 P.M. The time for the game was here; the players were on the field. Chad had the essential materials with him: player list, score book, soccer balls, (optional) and a cup of hope.

PART II—Essay

Evaluation Guidelines

Find an English professor or a high school English teacher and ask that person to correct your essay and to rate it rigorously 6 through 1 using these criteria.

A rating of 6 or 5 indicates that your writing is acceptable. A rating of 4 or 3 shows you need to work on the errors identified by the raters. A rating of 2 or 1 indicates that you will benefit from English tutoring or additional English coursework.

RATING SCALE

6 This essay is extremely well written. It is the equivalent of an A in-class assignment. The essay addresses the question and provides clear supporting arguments, illustrations, or examples. The paragraphs and sentences are well organized and show a variety of language and syntax. The essay may contain some minor errors.

5 This essay is well written. It is the equivalent of a B+ in-class assignment. The essay addresses the question and provides some supporting arguments, illustrations, or examples. The paragraphs and sentences are fairly well organized and show a variety of language and syntax. The essay may contain some minor mechanical or linguistic errors.

4 This essay is fairly well written. It is the equivalent of a B in-class assignment. The essay adequately addresses the question and provides some supporting arguments, illustrations, or examples for some points. The paragraphs and sentences are acceptably organized and show a variety of language and syntax. The essay may contain mechanical or linguistic errors but is free from an identifiable pattern of errors.

3 This essay may demonstrate some writing ability, but it contains obvious errors. It is the equivalent of a C or C+ in-class assignment. The essay may not clearly address the question and may not give supporting arguments or details. The essay may show problems in diction including inappropriate word choice. The paragraphs and sentences may not be acceptably developed. There will be an identifiable pattern or grouping of errors.

2 This essay shows only the most limited writing ability. It is the equivalent of a D in-class assignment. It contains serious errors and flaws. This essay may not address the question, be poorly organized, or provide no supporting arguments or detail. It usually shows serious errors in diction, usage, and mechanics.

1 This essay does not demonstrate minimal writing ability. It is equivalent of an F in-class assignment. This essay may contain serious and continuing errors, or it may not be coherent.

ENGLISH REVIEW

This review section targets the skills and concepts you need to know in order to pass the English parts of Praxis I tests.

NOUNS AND VERBS

Every sentence has a subject and a predicate. Most sentences are statements. The sentence usually names something (subject). Then the sentence describes the subject or tells what that subject is doing (predicate). Sentences that ask questions also have a subject and a predicate. Here are some examples.

Subject	Predicate
The car	moved.
The tree	grew.
The street	was dark.
The forest	teemed with plants of every type and size.

Many subjects are nouns. Every predicate has a verb. A list of the nouns and verbs from the preceding sentences follows.

Noun	Verb
car	moved
tree	grew
street	was
forest, plants	teemed

NOUNS

Nouns name a person, place, thing, characteristic, or concept. Nouns give a name to everything that is, has been, or will be. Here are some simple examples.

Person	Place	Thing	Characteristic	Concept (Idea)
Abe Lincoln	Lincoln Memorial	beard	mystery	freedom
judge	courthouse	gavel	fairness	justice
professor	college	chalkboard	intelligence	number

Singular and Plural Nouns

Singular nouns refer to only one thing. Plural forms refer to more than one thing. Plurals are usually formed by adding an *s* or dropping a *y* and adding *ies*. Here are some examples.

Singular	Plural
college	colleges
professor	professors
Lincoln Memorial	Lincoln Memorials
mystery	mysteries

Possessive Nouns

Possessive nouns show that the noun possesses a thing or a characteristic. Make a singular noun possessive by adding *'s*. Here are some examples.

The *child's* sled was in the garage ready for use.

The *school's* mascot was loose again.

The rain interfered with *Jane's* vacation.

Ron's and *Doug's* fathers were born in the same year.

Ron and *Doug's* teacher kept them after school.

Make a singular noun ending in *s* possessive by adding *'s* unless the pronunciation is too difficult.

The teacher read *James's* paper several times.

The angler grabbed the *bass'* fin.

Make a plural noun possessive by adding an apostrophe (') only.

The *principals'* meeting was delayed.

The report indicated that *students'* scores had declined.

Practice

Write the plural of each singular noun.

1. sheaf

2. deer

3. fry

4. lunch

5. knee

6. lady

7. octopus

8. echo

9. foot

10. half

Answers on page 60

VERBS

Some verbs are action verbs. Other verbs are linking verbs that link the subject to words that describe it. Here are some examples.

Action Verbs	Linking Verbs
Blaire *runs* down the street.	Blaire *is* tired.
Blaire *told* her story.	The class *was* bored.
The crowd *roared*.	The players *were* inspired.
The old ship *rusted*.	It *had been* a proud ship.

Tense

A verb has three principal tenses: present tense, past tense, and future tense. The present tense shows that the action is happening now. The past tense shows that the action happened in the past. The future tense shows that something will happen. Here are some examples.

Present:	I *enjoy* my time off.
Past:	I *enjoyed* my time off.
Future:	I *will enjoy* my time off.

Present:	I *hate* working late.
Past:	I *hated* working late.
Future:	I *will hate* working late.

Regular and Irregular Verbs

Regular verbs follow the consistent pattern noted previously. However, a number of verbs are irregular. Irregular verbs have their own unique forms for each tense. A partial list of irregular verbs follows. The past participle is usually preceded by *had*, *has*, or *have*.

SOME IRREGULAR VERBS

Present Tense	Past Tense	Past Participle
am, is, are	was, were	been
begin	began	begun
break	broke	broken
bring	brought	brought
catch	caught	caught
choose	chose	chosen
come	came	come
do	did	done
eat	ate	eaten
give	gave	given
go	went	gone
grow	grew	grown
know	knew	known
lie	lay	lain
lay	laid	laid
raise	raised	raised
ride	rode	ridden

see	saw	seen
set	set	set
sit	sat	sat
speak	spoke	spoken
take	took	taken
tear	tore	torn
throw	threw	thrown
write	wrote	written

Tense Shift

Verbs in a sentence should reflect time sequence. If the actions represented by the verbs happened at the same time, the verbs should have the same tense.

Incorrect: Beth sits in the boat while she wore a life jacket.

Correct: Beth sits in the boat while she wears a life jacket.
[Both verbs are present tense.]

Correct: Beth sat in the boat while she wore a life jacket.
[Both verbs are past tense.]

Correct: Beth wears the life jacket she wore last week.
[The verbs show time order.]

Practice

Correct the tense errors. Some sentences may be correct.

1. Ryan driven to Florida.

2. Refereeing soccer games is not work.

3. Chad ride to the game with his team last week.

4. Why did Mary ran her errands now?

5. I have speak to my teacher about the grade.

6. Carl paddled across the river every Saturday.

7. Blaire thrown out the ball for the players to use.

8. Joann will lost her bag if she leaves it in the store.

9. Bob is standing on a stool next to the green table.

10. Liz begun to grasp the depth of her happiness.

Answers on page 38

Practice

Correct the tense shifts. Some sentences may be correct.

1. Lisa already went to the North Pole but she is not going there again.

2. Dennis will take his airline tickets with him because he is leaving for his flight.

3. The runner gasped as she crosses the finish line.

4. I like to hear music so I played the clarinet.

5. Chris wanted to be a producer so he puts in long hours every day.

6. Bertha sews five hours a day because she will need her dress by next month.

7. The car turns over and then bounced down the hill.

8. Lois handed over her money because she wants to buy the computer.

9. The captain wandered out on the deck as she calls to her friends on shore.

10. The sun sets in the west as the moon rose in the east.

Answers on page 60

PRONOUNS

Pronouns take the place of nouns or noun phrases and help avoid constant repetition of the noun or phrase. Here is an example.

> *Blaire* is in law school. *She* studies in *her* room every day.
> [The pronouns *she* and *her* refer to the noun *Blaire*.]

PRONOUN CASES

Pronouns take three case forms: subjective, objective, and possessive. The personal pronouns *I, he, she, it, we, they, you* refer to an individual or individuals. The relative pronoun *who* refers to these personal pronouns as well as to an individual or individuals. These pronouns change their case form depending on their use in the sentence.

Subjective Pronouns: *I, we, he, it, she, they, who, you*

Use the subjective form if the pronoun is, or refers to, the subject of a clause or sentence.

> *He* and *I* studied for the CLAST.

> The proctors for the test were *she* and *I*.
> [*She* and *I* refer to the subject *proctors*.]

> She is the woman *who* answered every question correctly.

> I don't expect to do as well as *she*.
> [*She* is the subject for the understood verb *does*.]

Objective Pronouns: *me, us, him, it, her, them, whom, you*

Use the objective form if the pronoun is the object of a verb or preposition.

> Cathy helps both *him* and *me*.

> She wanted *them* to pass.

> I don't know *whom* she helped most.

Possessive Pronouns: *my, our, his, its, her, their, whose, your*

Use the objective form if the pronoun shows possession.

> I recommended they reduce the time they study with *their* friends.

> He was the person *whose* help they relied on.

CLEAR REFERENCE

The pronoun must clearly refer to a particular noun or noun phrase. Here are some examples.

Unclear

> Chris and Blaire took turns feeding *her* cat.
> [We can't tell which person *her* refers to.]

> Chris gave *it* to Blaire.
> [The pronoun *it* refers to a noun that is not stated.]

Clear

> Chris and Blaire took turns feeding Blaire's cat.
> [A pronoun doesn't work here.]

> Chris got the book and gave it to Blaire.
> [The pronoun works once the noun is stated.]

AGREEMENT

Each pronoun must agree in number (singular or plural) and gender (male or female) with the noun it refers to. Here are some examples.

Nonagreement in Number

> The children played all day, and *she* came in exhausted.
> [*Children* is plural, but *she* is singular.]

> The child picked up the hat and brought *them* into the house.
> [*Hat* is singular, but *them* is plural.]

Agreement

> The children played all day, and *they* came in exhausted.

> The child picked up the hat and brought *it* into the house.

Nonagreement in Gender

> The lioness picked up *his* cub.
> [*Lioness* is female, and *his* is male.]

> A child must bring in a doctor's note before *she* comes to school.
> [The child may be a male or female but *she* is female.]

Agreement

> The lioness picked up *her* cub.

> A child must bring in a doctor's note before *he or she* comes to school.

Practice

> Correct the clear reference and case and number errors in these sentences. Some sentences may not have errors.

1. His was the best table tennis player.

2. Whom was the worst table tennis player?

3. Where are the table tennis balls?

4. Before the game everyone are going to choose teams.

5. The names of the winning team are sent to we.

6. Them are the best table tennis team.

7. Ron and Jeff wanted to use his skates.

8. Jeff went to get them.

9. The couch looked different, depending on how they were arranged.

10. Bob won most of his table tennis games.

11. The student waited for their school bus to come.

12. Either of the buses can arrive on time if they don't break down.

13. The book was most interesting near her beginning.

14. She read the book to find her most interesting parts.

15. I am the winner; victory is ours.

16. His friends got out of the car, and he went over to talk to them.

17. The rain clouds moved toward the pool and the swimmers tried to wish it away.

18. Was Les disappointed that him team did not win?

19. Whom has more experience than Nicky does?

20. You play better after you have experience.

Answers on page 61

SUBJECT-VERB AGREEMENT

SINGULAR AND PLURAL

Singular nouns take singular verbs. Plural nouns take plural verbs. Singular verbs usually end in *s*, and plural verbs usually do not. Here are some examples.

Singular:	My father wants me home early.
Plural:	My parents want me home early.
Singular:	Ryan runs a mile each day.
Plural:	Ryan and Chad run a mile each day.
Singular:	She tries her best to do a good job.
Plural:	Liz and Ann try their best to do a good job.

CORRECTLY IDENTIFY SUBJECT AND VERB

The subject may not be in front of the verb. In fact, the subject may not be anywhere near the verb. Say the subject and the verb to yourself. If it makes sense, you probably have it right.

- Words may come between the subject and the verb.

  Chad's final exam score, which he showed to his mother, improved his final grade.

  The verb is *improved*. The word *mother* appears just before *improved*.

  Is this the subject? Say it to yourself. [Mother improved the grade.]

  That can't be right. *Score* must be the subject. Say it to yourself. [Score improved the grade.] That's right. *Score* is the subject, and *improved* is the verb.

  The racer running with a sore arm finished first.

  Say it to yourself. [Racer finished first.] *Racer* is the noun, and *finished* is the verb.

  It wouldn't make any sense to say the arm finished first.

- The verb may come before the subject.

  Over the river and through the woods romps the merry leprechaun.

  Leprechaun is the subject, and *romps* is the verb. [Think: Leprechaun romps.]

  Where are the car keys?

  Keys is the subject, and *are* is the verb. [Think: The car keys are where?]

Examples of Subject-Verb Agreement

Words such as *each, neither, everyone, nobody, someone,* and *anyone* are singular pronouns. They always take a singular verb.

  Everyone needs a good laugh now and then.

  Nobody knows more about computers than Bob.

Words that refer to number such as *one-half, any, most,* and *some* can be singular or plural.

  One-fifth of the students were absent. [*Students* is plural.]

  One-fifth of the cake was eaten. [There is only one cake.]

Practice

Correct any subject-verb agreement errors. Some sentences may be correct.

1. The chess set are still on the shelf.

2. The shortest route to the college are shown in the catalog.

3. The golf pro drive a gold cart every day.

4. Derek and Ann walks every morning.

5. The tropical birds in the tree adds a festive air to the occasion.

6. No one, not even Rick or Ronnie, walk to school today.

7. Do you know who they is?

8. Ron prepare a paper for submission to the committee.

9. The 15 employees of the coffee house shows up each day at 6:00 A.M.

10. Each person who takes the 12 steps improve his or her view.

Answers on page 62

ADJECTIVES AND ADVERBS

ADJECTIVES

Adjectives modify nouns and pronouns. Adjectives add detail and clarify nouns and pronouns. Frequently, adjectives come immediately before the nouns or pronouns they are modifying. At other times, the nouns or pronouns come first and are connected directly to the adjectives by linking verbs. Here are some examples.

Direct	With a Linking Verb
That is a *large* dog.	That dog is *large*.
He's an *angry* man.	The man seems *angry*.

ADVERBS

Adverbs are often formed by adding *ly* to an adjective. However, many adverbs don't end in *ly* (e.g., *always*). Adverbs modify verbs, adjectives, and adverbs. Adverbs can also modify phrases, clauses, and sentences. Here are some examples.

Modify verb:	Ryan *quickly* sought a solution.
Modify adjective	That is an *exceedingly* large dog.
Modify adverb:	Lisa told her story *quite* truthfully.
Modify sentence:	*Unfortunately*, all good things must end.
Modify phrase:	The instructor arrived *just* in time to start the class.

Avoiding Adjective and Adverb Errors

- Don't use adjectives in place of adverbs.

Correct	Incorrect
Lynne read the book quickly.	Lynne read the book quick.
Stan finished his work easily.	Stan finished his work easy.

- Don't confuse the adjectives *good* and *bad* with the adverbs *well* and *badly*.

Correct	Incorrect
Adverbs	
She wanted to play the piano well.	She wanted to play the piano good.
Bob sang badly.	Bob sang bad.
Adjectives	
The food tastes good.	The food tastes well.
The food tastes bad.	The food tastes badly.

- Don't confuse the adjectives *real* and *sure* with the adverbs *really* and *surely*.

Correct	Incorrect
Chuck played really well.	Chuck played real well.
He was surely correct.	He was sure correct.

Comparison

Adjectives and adverbs can show comparisons. Avoid clumsy modifiers.

Correct	Incorrect
Jim is more clingy than Ray.	Jim is clingier than Ray.
Ray is much taller than Jim.	Ray is more taller than Jim.
Jim is more interesting than Ray	Jim is interesting than Ray.
Ray is happier than Jim.	Ray is more happy than Jim.

Word comparisons carefully to be sure that the comparison is clear.

Unclear:	Chad lives closer to Ryan than Blaire.
Clear:	Chad lives closer to Ryan than Blaire does.
Clear:	Chad lives closer to Ryan than he does to Blaire.

Unclear:	The bus engines are bigger than cars.
Clear:	The bus engines are bigger than cars' engines.

Practice

Correct the adjective and adverb errors. Some sentences may contain no errors.

1. The view of the Grand Canyon was real spectacular.

2. The trainer said the dog behaved very good today.

3. Unfortunate, the tickets for the concert were sold out.

4. Things went smooth.

5. The judge took extremely exception to the defendant's actions.

6. The accident was silly, particularly since driving more careful would have avoided the whole thing.

7. But the reviews said the performance was truly horrible.

8. The manager conveniently forgot that she promised the employee a raise.

9. The bonus was a welcome surprise; it was a real large check.

10. I didn't do good, but didn't do bad either.

Answers on page 62

Practice

> Correct the comparison errors. Some sentences may be correct.

1. Leon was the happier chef in the restaurant.

2. But some of the people eating in the restaurant were happier than Leon.

3. The jet was the faster plane at the airport.

4. John was the fastest of the twins.

5. The taller of the apartment buildings is under repair.

6. The lightest of the two weights is missing.

7. Lonnie was among the most creative students in the school.

8. Ron is the least able of the two drivers.

9. His shoe size is the smallest in his class.

10. She was the more capable of the two referees.

Answers on page 62

MISPLACED AND DANGLING MODIFIERS

Modifiers may be words of groups of words. Modifiers change or qualify the meaning of another word or group of words. Modifiers belong near the words they modify.

Misplaced modifiers appear to modify words in a way that doesn't make sense.

The modifier in the following sentence is *in a large box*. It doesn't make sense for *in a large box* to modify *house*. Move the modifier near *pizza* where it belongs.

> Misplaced: Les delivered pizza to the house in a large box.
> Revised: Les delivered pizza in a large box to the house.

The modifier in the next sentence is *paid well*. *Paid well* can't modify *city*. Move it next to *the job* where it belongs.

> Misplaced: Gail wanted the job in the city that paid well.
> Revised: Gail wanted the well-paying job in the city.

Dangling modifiers modify words not present in the sentence. The modifier in the following sentence is *waiting for the concert to begin*.

This modifier describes the audience, but audience is not mentioned in the sentence. The modifier is left dangling with nothing to attach itself to.

> Dangling: Waiting for the concert to begin, the chanting started.
> Revised: Waiting for the concert to begin, the audience began chanting.
> Revised: The audience began chanting while waiting for the concert to begin.

The modifier in the next sentence is *after three weeks in the country*. The modifier describes the person, not the license. But the person is not mentioned in the sentence. The modifier is dangling.

> Dangling: After three weeks in the country, the license was revoked.
> Revised: After he was in the country for three weeks, his license was revoked.
> Revised: His license was revoked after he was in the country three weeks.

Practice

Correct the misplaced modifiers. Some sentences may be correct.

---

1. Les was reading his book through glasses with dirty lenses.

2. Jim left work early to go to the doctor on the train.

3. The first train car was crowded; which had to go to the next car.

4. Ron's car ran out of gas when on the way to the store.

5. Zena was jogging, when caused her to fall.

6. Derek wrapped the flowers and put them in the delivery van with colorful paper.

7. Which bus stops at the corner where the stop sign is?

8. Fran is going on the plane, which is just pulling up to the gate.

9. Lisa bought a shirt in the store, which was expensive.

10. The car turned around and the headlights shone quickly into the garage.

Answer on page 63

COMMA SPLICES AND RUN-ON SENTENCES

An *independent clause* is a clause that could be a sentence.

Independent clauses should be joined by a semicolon, or by a comma and a conjunction.

A *comma splice* consists of two independent clauses joined by just a comma.

A *run-on* sentence consists of two independent clauses incorrectly joined.

Correct:	The whole family went on vacation; the parents took turns driving. [Two independent clauses are joined by a semicolon.]
	The whole family went on vacation, and the parents took turns driving. [Two independent clauses are joined by a comma and a conjunction.]
Incorrect:	The whole family went on vacation, the parents took turns driving. [Comma splice. Two independent clauses are joined by just a comma.]
	The whole family went on vacation the parents took turns driving. [Run-on sentence. Two independent clauses are incorrectly joined.]

Practice

Correct the run-on sentences and comma splices. Some sentences may be correct.

1. It will be tomorrow before the sea is calm enough to go out.

2. It started to rain unexpectedly the boaters were soaked.

3. But right now my sneakers are soaking wet the towel is too wet to help me.

4. The Marine Police sounded the siren the boat stopped immediately.

5. I put the sneakers next to the fire to dry, although they started to steam after a while.

6. The Coast Guard monitors boats as they enter the river they use the data to monitor water pollution.

7. I like to use my compass when I go out on the boat.

8. When the boat breaks down, Liz calls Sea Tow.

9. The fire went out the sun came up.

10. Splashing through the waves, the water skier was covered with salt spray.

Answers on page 63

SENTENCE FRAGMENTS

English sentences require a subject and a verb. Fragments are parts of sentences written as though they were sentences. Fragments are writing mistakes that lack a subject, a predicate, or both subject and predicate. Here are some examples.

Since when.

To enjoy the summer months.

Because he isn't working hard.

If you can fix old cars.

What the principal wanted to hear.

Include a subject and/or a verb to rewrite a fragment as a sentence.

Fragment	Sentence
Should be coming up the driveway now.	The *car* should be coming up the driveway now.
Both the lawyer and her client.	Both the lawyer and her client *waited* in court.
Which is my favorite subject.	*I took math*, which is my favorite subject.
If you can play.	If you can play, *you'll improve with practice.*

Verbs such as *to be, to go, winning, starring*, etc., need a main verb.

Fragment	Sentence
The new rules to go into effect in April.	The new rules *will* go into effect in April.
The team winning every game.	The team *was* winning every game.

Often, a fragment is related to a complete sentence. Combine the two to make a single sentence.

Fragment: Reni loved vegetables. *Particularly corn, celery, lettuce, squash, and eggplant.*

Revised: Reni loved vegetables, particularly corn, celery, lettuce, squash, and eggplant.

Fragment: *To see people standing on Mars.* This could happen in the 21st century.

Revised: To see people standing on Mars is one of the things that could happen in the 21st century.

Sometimes short fragments can be used for emphasis. However, you should not use fragments in your essay. Here are some examples.

Stop! Don't take one more step toward that apple pie.

I need some time to myself. *That's why.*

Practice

> Correct the sentence fragments. Some items may be correct.

1. A golf bag, golf clubs, and golf balls. That's what she needed to play.

2. As the rocket prepared for blast-off. Mary saw birds flying in the distance.

3. Jim is mowing the lawn. Then, the mower stopped.

4. The lawn looked lush and green. Like a golf course.

5. The polar bears swept across the ice. Like white ghosts in fur jackets.

6. Jim looked across at the igloo. Like an ice fort, it stood a lonely vigil.

7. Astronauts and their equipment went by. These were the people who would go into space.

8. This was what Joe had been waiting for. To graduate from college.

9. To be finished with this test. That's what I'm waiting for.

10. The test finished and done. The papers graded and good.

Answers on page 64

PARALLELISM

When two or more ideas are connected, use a parallel structure. Parallelism helps the reader follow the passage more clearly. Here are some examples.

Not Parallel:	Toni stayed in shape by eating right and exercising daily.
Parallel:	Toni stayed in shape by eating right and *by* exercising daily.
Not Parallel:	Lisa is a student who works hard and has genuine insight.
Parallel:	Lisa is a student who works hard and *who* has genuine insight.
Not Parallel:	Art had a choice either to clean his room or take out the garbage.
Parallel:	Art had a choice either to clean his room or *to* take out the garbage.
Not Parallel:	Derek wanted a success rather than failing.
Parallel:	Derek wanted a success rather than a failure.
Parallel:	Derek wanted success rather than failure.

Practice

Correct any parallel form errors. Some sentences may not have errors.

1. I have to get to work, but first I have to find my way to breakfast.

2. The road was dry; the day was hot and sultry.

3. Jane likes to eat and go shopping when she is at the mall.

4. April chose to be a cameraperson rather than to be a technician who works the sound board.

5. Since I have not heard from you, I decided to write this letter.

6. Although she had driven the road before, Sally proceeded slowly, keeping her eye on the yellow line.

7. The tree withstood the hurricane, but the branches on the tree snapped off.

8. His work on the Board of Education revealed his dedication to the community.

9. Cars, taxis, and buses were my transportation to the airport.

10. The subject matter and the preparation for class created an excellent lesson.

Answers on page 64

DICTION

Diction is choosing and using appropriate words. Good diction conveys a thought clearly without unnecessary words. Good diction develops fully over a number of years; however, there are some rules and tips you can follow.

- Do not use slang, colloquialisms, or other non-standard English. One person's slang is another person's confusion. Slang is often regional, and slang meanings change rapidly. We do not give examples of slang here for that very reason. Do not use slang words in your formal writing.

  Colloquialisms are words used frequently in spoken language. This informal use of terms such as *dog tired*, *kids*, and *hanging around* is not generally accepted in formal writing. Save these informal terms for daily speech and omit or remove them from your writing except as quotations.

  Omit any other non-standard English. Always choose standard English terms that accurately reflect the thought to be conveyed.

- Avoid wordy, redundant, or pretentious writing. Good writing is clear and economical.

  Wordy: I chose my career as a teacher because of its high ideals, the truly self-sacrificing idealism of a career in teaching, and for the purpose of receiving the myriad and cascading recognition that one can receive from the community as a whole and from its constituents.

  Revised: I chose a career in teaching for its high ideals and for community recognition.

Given below is a partial list of wordy phrases and the replacement word.

Wordy Phrases and Replacements

at the present time	now	because of the fact that	because
for the purpose of	for	in the final analysis	finally
in the event that	if	until such time as	until

HOMONYMS

Homonyms are words that sound alike but do not have the same meaning. These words can be confusing and you may use the incorrect spelling of a word. If words are homonyms, be sure you choose the correct spelling for the meaning you intend.

Homonyms

accept (receive)	ascent (rise)
except (other than)	assent (agreement)
board (wood)	fair (average)
bored (uninterested)	fare (a charge)
led (guided)	lessen (make less)
lead (metal)	lesson (learning experience)
past (gone before)	peace (no war)
passed (moved by)	piece (portion)

rain (precipitation)	to (toward)
reign (rule)	too (also)
rein (animal strap)	two (a number)
their (possessive pronoun)	its (shows possession)
there (location)	it's (it is)
they're (they are)	

IDIOMS

Idioms are expressions with special meanings and often break the rules of grammar. Idioms are acceptable in formal writing, but they must be used carefully. Here are some examples.

Idioms

in accordance with	inferior to
angry with	occupied by (someone)
differ from (someone)	occupied with (something)
differ about (an issue)	prior to
independent of	rewarded with (something)

Practice

> Write the word or phrase that fits best in the blank.

1. Many _____ diseases, including pneumonia and swelling in cuts, are caused by bacteria.

innocuous	unfortunate
infectious	ill-fated

2. Sigmund Freud's views of sexuality had become _____, and the country entered the sexual revolution.

well known	all knowing
universal	incolcated

3. After crossing the land bridge near the Bering Strait, groups of Native Americans _____ spread throughout all of North, Central, and South America.

inclusively	eventually
regardless	remotely

4. During the early 1500s Cortez and Pizarro opened up Central America to the Spanish who began _____ slaves from Africa.

importing	exporting
imparting	immigrating

5. The Stamp Act requiring every legal paper to carry a tax stamp was vehemently _____ and eventually repealed by England.

denied	deported
proclaimed	protested

Circle the underlined portion that is unnecessary in the passage.

6. No goal <u>is more noble</u>—<u>no feat more reveal-</u><u>ing</u>—than the <u>strikingly</u> <u>brave exploration of</u> <u>space.</u>

7. <u>As many</u> as a <u>ton of</u> bananas <u>may have</u> spoiled when <u>the ship</u> was stuck <u>and</u> <u>delayed</u> in the Panama Canal.

8. He <u>was concerned</u> about <u>crossing</u> the bridge, <u>but the officer</u> said that it was all right to cross <u>and he need not worry</u>.

9. A <u>professional</u> golfer told the <u>novice</u> begin-ning golfer that <u>professional instruction</u> or more practice <u>improves most golfers'</u> <u>scores</u>.

10. The soccer player's <u>slight</u> strain from the shot on goal <u>that won the game</u> led to a <u>pulled</u> muscle that <u>would</u> keep her from <u>playing</u> the next match.

Circle the word or words used incorrectly in the sentence.

11. He went to the bird's nest near the river, only too realize he missed its assent.

12. The rider pulled back on the horse's reign before the whether turned rainy.

13. The whether turned rainy as he led the hik-ers on there ascent.

14. The lessen was clear; it was fare, but not easy to accept.

15. They're board relatives were not fare too her father.

Correct the idiom errors. Some sentences may not have errors.

16. Her grades had everything to do of her efforts.

17. Joanie expected him to wait to the house until she arrived home?

18. She could spend months absorbed in her studies.

19. The two coaches differ significantly with each other's style.

20. That person is wearing the same coat from you.

Answers on page 65

PUNCTUATION

THE COMMA (,)

The comma may be the most used punctuation mark. This section details a few of these uses.

A clause is part of a sentence that could be a sentence itself. If a clause begins with a conjunction, use a comma before the conjunction.

Incorrect:	I was satisfied with the food but John was grumbling.
Correct:	I was satisfied with the food, but John was grumbling.
Incorrect:	Larry was going fishing or he was going to paint his house.
Correct:	Larry was going fishing, or he was going to paint his house.

A clause or a phrase often introduces a sentence. Introductory phrases or clauses should be set off by a comma. If the introductory element is very short, the comma is optional. Here are some examples.

However, there are other options you may want to consider.

When the de-icer hit the plane's wing, the ice began to melt.

To get a driver's license, go to the motor vehicle bureau.

It doesn't matter what you want, you have to take what you get.

Parenthetical expressions interrupt the flow of a sentence. Set off the parenthetical expression with commas. Do not set off expressions that are essential to understanding the sentence. Here are some examples.

Tom, an old friend, showed up at my house the other day.

I was traveling on a train, in car 8200, on my way to Florida.

John and Ron, who are seniors, went on break to Florida.
[Use a comma. The phrase "who are seniors" is extra information.]

All the students who are seniors take an additional course.
[Don't use a comma. The phrase "who are seniors" is essential information.]

Commas are used to set off items in a list or series. Here are some examples.

Jed is interested in computers, surfing, and fishing.
[Notice the comma before the conjunction *and*. You may omit this comma.]

Mario drives a fast, red car.
[The sentence would make sense with *and* in place of the commas.]

Andy hoped for a bright, sunny, balmy day.
[The sentence would make sense with *and* in place of the commas.]

Lucy had a pale green dress.
[The sentence would not make sense with *and*. The word *pale* modifies *green*. Don't use a comma.]

Randy will go to the movies, pick up some groceries, and then go home.
[Remember, the comma before *and* is optional.]

Practice

> Correct the comma errors. Some sentences may have no comma errors.

1. I had a slow day yesterday, but I worked hard in my junior year.

2. Passing calculus seems a difficult, but achievable, result.

3. After making the sandwich, I looked for some pickles, but the jar was empty.

4. Write an outline first and be sure to leave enough time to write the essay.

5. In the attic I found some old clothes, an old trunk, and a shoe.

6. Chad, Blaire, and Ryan have advanced degrees but they are still children at heart.

7. Using a computer the CBT tests reading, writing, and arithmetic.

8. Either walk the dog or wash the dishes.

9. Every pilot, who has flown over 20 missions, receives an award.

10. Each time I ate lunch at home, my mother made liverwurst sandwiches.

Answers on page 66

SEMICOLON AND COLON

The Semicolon (;)

Use the semicolon to connect main clauses not connected by a conjunction. Include a semicolon with very long clauses connected by a conjunction. Here are some examples.

> The puck was dropped; the hockey game began.

> The puck was dropped, and the hockey game began.

> The general manager of the hockey team was not sure what should be done about the player who was injured during the game; but he did know that the player's contract stipulated that his pay would continue whether he was able to play or not.

The Colon (:)

Use the colon after a main clause to introduce a list. Here are some examples.

> Liz kept these items in her car: spare tire, jack, flares, and a blanket.

> Liz kept a spare tire, jack, flares, and a blanket in her car.

Practice

Correct any semicolon or colon errors. Some sentences may be correct.

---

1. Pack these other things for camp; a bathing suit, some socks and a shirt.

2. In your wallet put: your camp information card and your bus pass.

3. I have one thing left to do; say good-bye.

4. We went to the store; and the parking lot was filled with cars.

5. We fought our way through the crowds, the store was even more crowded than the parking lot.

Answers on page 66

PERIOD, QUESTION MARK, EXCLAMATION POINT
The Period (.)

Use a period to end every sentence, unless the sentence is a direct question, a strong command, or an interjection.

> You will do well on the Praxis I test.

The Question Mark (?)

Use a question mark to end every sentence that is a direct question.

> What is the passing score for the Praxis I test?

The Exclamation Point (!)

Use an exclamation point to end every sentence that is a strong command or interjection. Do not overuse exclamation points.

> Interjection: Pass that test!

> Command: Avalanche, head for cover!

Practice

Correct any punctuation errors.

1. I was so worn out after swimming!

2. Avalanche.

3. Who said that!

4. Warning. The danger signal blared in the background.

5. I can't believe this is the last day of camp?

Answers on page 66

ANSWERS
ENGLISH PRACTICE

Nouns, page 36

1. sheaves

2. deer

3. fries

4. lunches

5. knees

6. ladies

7. octopi

8. echoes

9. feet

10. halves

Verbs, page 38

    drove
1. Ryan ~~driven~~ to Florida.

2. Refereeing soccer games is not work.
   [No tense errors.]

    rode
3. Chad ~~ride~~ to the game with his team last week.
   [The words *last week* indicate that the verb must be past tense.]

    run
4. Why did Mary ~~ran~~ her errands now?

    spoken
5. I have ~~speak~~ to my teacher about the grade.

    paddles
6. Carl ~~paddled~~ across the river every Saturday.
   [Use the present tense because it is a regular event.]

    had thrown
7. Blaire ~~thrown~~ out the ball for the players to use.

    lose
8. Joann will ~~lost~~ her bag if she leaves it in the store.

9. Bob is standing on a stool next to the green table.
   [No tense errors.]

    began
10. Liz ~~begun~~ to grasp the depth of her happiness.

Tense Shift, page 39

1. Lisa already went to the North Pole but she is not going there again.
   [No tense shift errors.]

    took
2. Dennis ~~will take~~ his airline tickets with him because he is leaving for his flight.

3. The runner gasped as she crosses the finish line.

   The runner gasped as she crossed the finish line.
   The runner gasps as she crosses the finish line.

    play
4. I like to hear music so I ~~played~~ the clarinet.

    wants
5. Chris ~~wanted~~ to be a producer so he puts in long hours every day.

6. Bertha sews five hours a day because she will need her dress by next month.
   [No tense shift errors.]

7. The car turns over and then bounced down the hill.

   The car turned over and then bounced down the hill.
   The car turns over and then bounces down the hill.
   The car turned over and then bounces down the hill.

8. Lois handed over her money because she wants to buy the computer.

   Lois hands over her money because she wants to buy the computer.
   Lois handed over her money because she wanted to buy the computer.

9. The captain wandered out on the deck as she calls to her friends on shore.

   The captain wandered out on the deck as she called to her friends on shore.
   The captain wanders out on the deck as she calls to her friends on shore.

10. The sun sets in the west as the moon rose in the east.

    The sun set in the west as the moon rose in the east.
    The sun sets in the west as the moon rises in the east.

Pronouns, page 42

   He
1. ~~His~~ was the best table tennis player.

   Who
2. ~~Whom~~ was the worst table tennis player?

3. Where are the table tennis balls?
   [No errors.]

                                   is
4. Before the game everyone ~~are~~ going to choose teams.

                                        us
5. The names of the winning team are sent to ~~we~~.

   They
6. ~~Them~~ are the best table tennis team.

                        Ron's
7. Ron and Jeff wanted to use ~~his~~ skates.
   [Jeff's, or any other name, could be used in place of Ron's.]

           the skates
8. Jeff went to get ~~them~~.
   [Other nouns that make sense in this context could be used in place of skates.]

9. The couch looked different, depending on **the pillows** how ~~they~~ were arranged.

10. Bob won most of his table tennis games.
    [No errors.]

                        her or his
11. The student waited for ~~their~~ school bus to come.

12. Either of the buses can arrive on time if **it doesn't** ~~they don't~~ break down.

                                    its
13. The book was most interesting near ~~her~~ beginning.

                              the
14. She read the book to find ~~her~~ most interesting parts.

15. I am the winner; victory is ours.

    I am the winner; victory is mine.
    We are the winners; victory is ours.

16. His friends got out of the car, and he went over to talk to them.
    [No errors.]

17. The rain clouds moved toward the pool and the swimmers tried to wish it away.

    The rain cloud moved toward the pool and the swimmers tried to wish it away.
    The rain clouds moved toward the pool and the swimmers tried to wish them away.

                              his
18. Was Les disappointed that ~~him~~ team did not win?

    Who
19. ~~Whom~~ has more experience than Nicky does?

20. You play better after you have experience.
    [No errors.]

Subject Verb Agreement, page 44

          is
1. The chess set ~~are~~ still on the shelf.

                is
2. The shortest route to the college ~~are~~ shown in the catalog.

          drives
3. The golf pro ~~drive~~ a golf cart every day.

       walk
4. Derek and Ann ~~walks~~ every morning.

           add
5. The tropical birds in the tree ~~adds~~ a festive air to the occasion.

            walks
6. No one, not even Rick or Ronnie, ~~walk~~ to school today.

         are
7. Do you know who they ~~is~~?

     prepares
8. Ron ~~prepare~~ a paper for submission to the committee.

9. The 15 employees of the coffee house
show
~~shows~~ up each day at 6:00 A.M.

            improves
10. Each person who takes the 12 steps ~~improve~~ his or her view.

Adjectives and Adverbs, page 46

           really
1. The view of the Grand Canyon was ~~real~~ spectacular.

          well
2. The trainer said the dog behaved very ~~good~~ today.

Unfortunately
3. ~~Unfortunate~~, the tickets for the concert were sold out.

     smoothly
4. Things went ~~smooth~~.

          extreme
5. The judge took ~~extremely~~ exception to the defendant's actions.

6. The accident was silly, particularly since
        carefully
driving more ~~careful~~ would have avoided the whole thing.

7. But the reviews said the performance was truly horrible.
[No adjective or adverb errors.]

8. The manager conveniently forgot that she promised the employee a raise.
[No adjective or adverb errors.]

9. The bonus was a welcome surprise; it was a
really
~~real~~ large check.

       well   **badly**
10. I didn't do ~~good~~, but didn't do ~~bad~~ either.

Comparison, page 47

       happiest
1. Leon was the ~~happier~~ chef in the restaurant.

2. But some of the people eating in the restaurant were happier than Leon.
[No error.]

       fastest
3. The jet was the ~~faster~~ plane at the airport.

       faster
4. John was the ~~fastest~~ of the twins.

      tallest
5. The ~~taller~~ of the apartment buildings is under repair.

      lighter
6. The ~~lightest~~ of the two weights is missing.

7. Lonnie was among the most creative students in the school.
[No error.]

       less
8. Ron is the ~~least~~ able of the two drivers.

9. His shoe size is the smallest in his class.
   [No error.]

10. She was the more capable of the two
    referees.
    [No error.]

Misplaced Modifiers, page 48

1. Les was reading his book through glasses
   with dirty lenses.
   [No modifier errors.]

2. Jim left work early to go to the doctor on
   the train.

   **Jim left work early to go on a train to
   the doctor.**

3. The first train car was crowded; which had
   to go to the next car.

   **The first train car was crowded; some-
   one (he) (she) had to go to the next car.**

4. Ron's car ran out of gas when on the way to
   the store.

   **Ron's car ran out of gas when he was on
   the way to the store.**
   [Many other substitutions are possible for *he was*.]

5. Zena was jogging, when caused her to fall.

   **Zena was jogging, when a hole caused
   her to fall.**
   [Many other substitutions are possible for *a hole*.]

6. Derek wrapped the flowers and put them in
   the delivery van with colorful paper.

   **Derek wrapped the flowers with color-
   ful paper and put them in the delivery
   van.**

7. Which bus stops at the corner where the
   stop sign is?
   [No modifier errors.]

8. Fran is going on the plane, which is just
   pulling up to the gate.
   [No modifier errors.]

9. Lisa bought a shirt in the store, which was
   expensive.

   Lisa bought an expensive shirt in the store.
   Lisa bought a shirt in an expensive store.
   Lisa bought an expensive shirt in an expen-
   sive store.

10. The car turned around and the headlights
    shone quickly into the garage.

    The car turned around quickly and the head-
    lights shone into the garage.

Run-On Sentences and
Comma Splices, page 49

There are three ways to remedy run-on sentence errors and comma splice errors. You
can create two sentences, put a comma and a
conjunction between the clauses, or put a
semicolon between the two clauses. Only one
of these options is shown in the answers.

1. It will be tomorrow before the sea is calm
   enough to go out.
   [No errors.]

2. It started to rain unexpectedly; the boaters
   were soaked.

3. But right now my sneakers are soaking wet;
   the towel is too wet to help me.

4. The Marine Police sounded the siren; the
   boat stopped immediately.

5. I put the sneakers next to the fire to dry,
   although they started to steam after a while.
   [No errors.]

6. The Coast Guard monitors boats as they
   enter the river; they use the data to monitor
   water pollution.

7. I like to use my compass when I go out on
   the boat.
   [No errors.]

8. When the boat breaks down, Liz calls Sea
   Tow.
   [No errors.]

9. The fire went out; the sun came up.

10. Splashing through the waves, the water
skier was covered with salt spray.
[No errors.]

Sentence Fragments, page 51

1. A golf bag, golf clubs, and golf balls. That's
what she needed to play.

   **A golf bag, golf clubs, and golf balls
   were what she needed to play.**

2. As the rocket prepared for blast-off. Mary
saw birds flying in the distance.

   **The rocket prepared for blast-off. Mary
   saw birds flying in the distance.
   As the rocket prepared for blast-off,
   Mary saw birds flying in the distance.**

3. Jim is mowing the lawn. Then, the mower
stopped.
[No sentence fragment errors.]

4. The lawn looked lush and green. Like a golf
course.

   **The lawn looked lush and green, like a
   golf course.**

5. The polar bears swept across the ice. Like
white ghosts in fur jackets.

   **The polar bears swept across the ice,
   like white ghosts in fur jackets.**

6. Jim looked across at the igloo. Like an ice
fort, it stood a lonely vigil.
[No sentence fragment errors.]

7. Astronauts and their equipment went by.
These were the people who would go into
space.
[No sentence fragment errors.]

8. This was what Joe had been waiting for. To
graduate from college.

   **This was what Joe had been waiting for,
   to graduate from college.**

9. To be finished with this test. That's what I'm
waiting for.

   **To be finished with this test is what I'm
   waiting for.**

10. The test finished and done. The papers
graded and good.

   **The tests were finished and done.
   The papers were graded and good.**

Parallelism, page 52

1. I have to get to work, but first I have to ~~find~~ **get**
~~my way~~ to breakfast.

2. The road was dry; the day was hot and
sultry.
[No parallel form errors.]

3. Jane likes to eat and go shopping when she
is at the mall.
[No parallel form errors.]

4. April chose to be a cameraperson rather
than to be a ~~technician who works the~~ **sound technician**
~~sound board~~.

5. Since I have not heard from you, I decided
to write this letter.
[No parallel form errors. The conjunction *since* shows
subordination.]

6. Although she had driven the road before,
Sally proceeded slowly, keeping her eye
on the yellow line.
[No parallel form errors. The conjunction *although*
shows subordination.]

7. The tree withstood the hurricane, but
~~the branches on the tree~~ **tree branches** snapped off.

8. His work on the Board of Education
revealed his dedication to the community.
[No parallel form errors.]

9. Cars, taxis, and buses were my transportation to the airport.
   [No parallel form errors.]

class preparation

10. The subject matter and the ~~preparation for class~~ created an excellent lesson.

Diction, page 54

1. Many <u>infectious</u> diseases, including pneumonia and swelling in cuts, are caused by bacteria.

   Infectious means a disease caused by bacteria. While the disease may be unfortunate, the context of the sentence calls for a word that means *caused by bacteria*.

2. Sigmund Freud's views of sexuality had become <u>well known</u>, and the country entered the sexual revolution.

   Well known means known by many people. *Universal* means known everywhere, which does not fit the context of this sentence.

3. After crossing the land bridge near the Bering Strait, groups of Native Americans <u>eventually</u> spread throughout all of North, Central, and South America.

   Eventually means over a period of time. The other words do not make sense in this context.

4. During the early 1500s Cortez and Pizarro opened up Central America to the Spanish who began <u>importing</u> slaves from Africa.

   Importing means to bring in. Exporting means to send out, which does not fit the context of the sentence.

5. The Stamp Act requiring every legal paper to carry a tax stamp was vehemently <u>protested</u> and eventually repealed by England.

   The act could only be *protested* in this context. It was not *denied*, and it does not make sense to say it was *vehemently* denied.

Circle the underlined portion that is unnecessary in the passage.

6. <u>No goal</u> <u>is more noble</u>—<u>no feat more revealing</u>—than the (strikingly) <u>brave exploration of space</u>.

7. <u>As many</u> as a <u>ton of</u> bananas <u>may have spoiled</u> when <u>the ship</u> was stuck (and delayed) in the Panama Canal.

8. He <u>was concerned</u> about <u>crossing</u> the bridge, <u>but the officer</u> said that it was all right to cross (and he need not worry).

9. A <u>professional</u> golfer told the (novice) beginning golfer that <u>professional instruction</u> or more practice <u>improves most golfers' scores</u>.

10. The soccer player's <u>slight</u> strain from the shot on goal (that won the game) led to a <u>pulled</u> muscle that <u>would</u> keep her from <u>playing</u> the next match.

Circle the word or words used incorrectly in the sentence.

11. He went to the bird's nest near the river, only (too) realize he missed its (assent).

12. The rider pulled back on the horse's (reign) before the (whether) turned rainy.

13. The (whether) turned rainy as he led the hikers on (there) ascent.

14. The (lessen) was clear; it was (fare), but not easy to accept.

15. (They're) (board) relatives were not (fare,) (too) her father.

Correct the idiom errors.

with

16. Her grades had everything to do ~~of~~ her efforts.

at

17. Joanie expected him to wait ~~to~~ the house until she arrived home?

18. She could spend months absorbed in her studies.
    [No idiom error.]

from

19. The two coaches differ significantly ~~with~~ each other's style.

as

20. That person is wearing the same coat ~~from~~ you.

Commas, page 57

1. I had a slow day yesterday, but I worked hard in my junior year.
   [No comma errors.]

2. Passing calculus seems a difficult, but achievable, result.
   [No comma errors.]

3. After making the sandwich, I looked for some pickles, but the jar was empty.
   [No comma errors.]

4. Write an outline first, and be sure to leave enough time to write the essay.
   [Add a comma before the conjunction to separate the two clauses.]

5. In the attic I found some old clothes, an old trunk, and a shoe.
   [No comma errors.]

6. Chad, Blaire, and Ryan have advanced degrees, but they are still children at heart.
   [Add a comma to separate the clauses.]

7. Using a computer, the CBT tests reading, writing, and arithmetic.
   [Add a comma to set off the introductory phrase.]

8. Either walk the dog or wash the dishes.
   [No comma errors.]

9. Every pilot who has flown over 20 missions receives an award.
   [Remove the commas.]

10. Each time I ate lunch at home my mother made liverwurst sandwiches.
    [Remove the comma.]

Semicolons and Colons, page 58

1. Pack these other things for camp: a bathing suit, some socks, and a shirt.
   [Replace the semicolon with a colon.]

2. In your wallet put your camp information card and your bus pass.
   [Remove the colon.]

3. I have one thing left to do: say good-bye.
   [Replace the semicolon with a colon.]

4. We went to the store, and the parking lot was filled with cars.
   [Replace the semicolon with a comma.]

5. We fought our way through the crowds; the store was even more crowded than the parking lot.
   [Replace the comma with a semicolon.]

Period, Question Mark, and Exclamation Point, page 59

1. I was so worn out after swimming.
   [Change the exclamation point to a period.]

2. Avalanche!
   [Change the period to an exclamation point.]

3. Who said that?
   [Change the exclamation point to a question mark.]

4. Warning! The danger signal blared in the background.
   [Change the period to an exclamation point.]

5. I can't believe this is the last day of camp.
   [Change the question mark to a period.]

STRATEGIES FOR TAKING THE MULTIPLE-CHOICE WRITING TEST

This section shows you how to pass the multiple-choice writing portion of the PPST and CBT writing test.

TYPES OF QUESTIONS

The multiple-choice writing test is very similar to the old Test of Standard Written English (TSWE). You may have taken the TSWE along with the old Scholastic Aptitude Test. Educational Testing Service did away with the TSWE in 1994, but they kept this test.

This test gives you a chance to show what you know about grammar, sentence structure, and word usage. You should be familiar with the subjects covered in the English Review section.

The following topics may be particularly important:

- subject-verb and noun-pronoun agreement
- correct verb tense
- the best word or phrase for a sentence
- parallel verb forms and parallel sentence structure
- sentence fragments and wordy sentences
- distinguishing clear and exact sentences from awkward or ambiguous ones

You may be able to get the correct answer from your sense or feel about the sentence. If you are someone who has an intuitive grasp of English usage, you should rely on your intuition as you complete this section of the tests.

There are two types of questions on the PPST and the CBT.

Usage

You are shown a sentence with four parts underlined and lettered (A), (B), (C), and (D). There is a fifth choice: (E) No error. You choose the letter of the flawed part or E if there is no error. You do not have to explain what the error is or what makes the other parts correct. No sentence contains more than one error. You just have to recognize the error or realize that there is no error.

> Example: <u>Every week</u>, Doug took <u>a child from</u> the
>   (A)   (B)
>   class on <u>a visit to the</u> art room <u>until he</u>
>   (C)   (D)
>   got tired. <u>No error</u>.
>   (E)

Sentence Correction

You are shown a sentence with one part underlined. Choice (A) repeats the underlined selection exactly. Choices (B) through (E) give suggested changes for the underlined part. You choose the letter of the best choice that does not change the meaning of the original sentence. If the original is best, choose (A). Otherwise, select one of the suggested changes.

> Example: Many times a shopper will prefer value <u>to price</u>.
> (A) to price
> (B) instead of price
> (C) rather than price
> (D) more than price
> (E) than price

STRATEGIES FOR PASSING THE MULTIPLE-CHOICE TEST

Read Carefully

In this section it is often small details that count. Read each sentence or passage carefully. Read the whole sentence, not just the underlined sections. Remember that an underlined section by itself can look fine but be incorrect in the whole sentence or passage. Read each sentence or passage a few times until you get a sense for its rhythm and flow.

This Is a Test of Written English

Evaluate each sentence and passage as written English. Do not apply the more informal rules of spoken English.

Don't Focus on Punctuation

Use the English rules discussed in the English Review section. However, don't be overly concerned about punctuation. Punctuation rules are seldom tested.

Write in the PPST Test Booklet or the CBT Scrap Paper

The test booklet is yours. You can write on the passage as well as on the question and answers.

> Example: (1) Space exploration is an expensive undertaking. (2) However, many believe that this investment has been returned to the public manyfold. (3) These people often point out the number of jobs created by the space industry. (4) Still others believe that space should be explored at any cost independent of the return to mankind. (5) A number of people think that the cost of space exploration should be _____ . (6) These people believe that much of the money for space exploration should be spent on social programs.

Eliminate and Guess

Eliminate the answers you know are incorrect. If you can't pick out the correct answer, guess from among the remaining choices.

1. Which of these words would best fit the empty space in Sentence (5)?
    (A) completed
    (B) increased
    (C) omitted
    (D) reduced
    (E) allocated

REVIEW QUESTIONS

Usage

Choose the letter that indicates an error, or choose (E) for no error.

1. <u>Every week</u>, Doug took <u>a child from</u>
      (A)   (B)
   the class on <u>a visit to the</u> art room
                        (C)
   <u>until he</u> got tired. <u>No error</u>.
      (D)   (E)

2. Doug <u>walks</u> two miles <u>every day</u> and
         (A)   (B)
   he rubbed off <u>the dirt</u> on <u>his shoes</u> as
                      (C)   (D)
   he went. <u>No error</u>.
                (E)

3. Jim and Tom, <u>a salesman</u>, <u>was doing</u> a
                      (A)   (B)
   good job <u>directing</u> the <u>under twelve</u>
                 (C)   (D)
   soccer league. <u>No error</u>.
                       (E)

4. The <u>students</u> were <u>greatly</u> <u>effected</u> by
            (A)   (B)   (C)
   the retirement of a <u>very popular</u>
                              (D)
   teacher. <u>No error</u>.
                (E)

5. The Rathburn is a <u>high rated</u> and
                           (A)
   <u>singularly successful</u>
            (B)
   <u>Italian restaurant</u> near <u>the beach</u> in
            (C)   (D)
   Avalon. <u>No error</u>.
                (E)

Sentence Correction

Choose the letter of the best choice for the underlined section, without changing the meaning of the sentence. If the original is best, choose (A). Otherwise, select one of the suggested changes.

6. Many times a shopper will prefer value <u>to price</u>.
   (A) to price
   (B) instead of price
   (C) rather than price
   (D) more than price
   (E) than price

7. The tug boat strained against the ship, revved up its engines <u>and was able to maneuver the ship into the middle of the channel</u>.
   (A) and was able to maneuver the ship into the middle of the channel.
   (B) and moves the ship into the middle of the channel.
   (C) moving the ship into the middle of the channel.
   (D) and moved the ship into the middle of the channel.
   (E) with the ship moved into the middle of the channel.

8. After it had snowed steadily for days, the snow plows and snow blowers <u>most important priorities</u>.
   (A) most important priorities.
   (B) were ready for action.
   (C) concentrated on the most important priorities.
   (D) most significant priorities.
   (E) most frequent difficulties.

9. The zoo opened for <u>the day, the children ran</u> to the exhibits.
   (A) the day, the children ran
   (B) the day. the children ran
   (C) the day; the children ran
   (D) the day: the children ran
   (E) the day the children ran

EXPLANATION OF ANSWERS

Usage

1. **D** Pronoun error—it is not clear which noun the pronoun *he* refers to.
2. **A** Verb tense error—the verb *walks* should be *walked* to agree with the verb *rubbed*.
3. **B** Number error—the subject, *Jim and Tom*, is plural. The verb *was* should be the plural verb *were*.
4. **C** Diction error—the word *effected* should be replaced by the word *affected*.
5. **A** Adjective-adverb error—the adjective *high* should be changed to the adverb *highly*.

Sentence Correction

6. **A** No error—Always choose (A) if there is no error.
7. **D** Parallelism error—Choice (D) maintains the parallel development of the sentence.
8. **C** Sentence fragment error—The original choice is a sentence fragment. There is no verb for the subject *snow plows and snow blowers*. Choice (B) is grammatically correct but changes the meaning of the sentence.
9. **C** Run-on sentence error—Use a semicolon to separate two independent clauses.

STRATEGIES FOR TAKING THE ESSAY WRITING TEST

FORM OF THE TEST

You will be given one essay topic. You will have 30 minutes to write the essay. Your essay is graded holistically by two raters using the six-point scale described on page 34. Holistic grading means that the raters grade you based on their informed sense about your writing and not on a detailed analysis of the essay.

Pages 17–20 in Chapter 2 contain a detailed step-by-step approach for writing essays.

STRATEGIES FOR PASSING THE ESSAY TEST

Read the Topic

Take a few minutes to read and understand the topic. Part of your rating will depend on how well you address the topic.

Make Notes and Sketch a Brief Outline

On the PPST, the page listing the topic has room for notes. On the CBT, use the scrap paper. Think for a few minutes and take up to five more minutes to write a brief outline showing how you will structure each of the three or four paragraphs in the essay.

Use the time writing the outline to plan your essay. Use the time working on the essay to write well.

Follow These Rules as You Write

You should have a little more than 15 minutes to write your essay. Plan to write three or four paragraphs. Essays scored 6 are usually longer than those scored 5 or less. Your essay should be a maximum of 350 words.

This does not mean that longer is necessarily better. It does mean that you will need at least four well-written paragraphs to receive a 6 and three or four well-written paragraphs to receive a 5.

Compose and write the topic sentence for your first paragraph. Write two more sentences that develop the topic sentence. These sentences may contain examples, illustrations, and other supporting facts or arguments. You can close your paragraph with a summary sentence.

If you follow this plan for the remaining paragraphs, you should be able to get a 4 or higher.

Use the rules of grammar as you write. Punctuate as carefully as you can but do not spend an inordinate amount of time on punctuation. Raters will often ignore minor grammatical or spelling errors if the essay is well developed.

Refer to your outline as you write.

TARGETED WRITING TEST

This targeted test is designed to help you practice the strategies presented in this chapter. For that reason, questions may have a different emphasis than the actual test, and the actual test will certainly be more complete.

Mark your choice, then check your answers.

Use the strategies on pages 67–69.

PART A

Choose the letter that indicates an error, or choose (E) for no error.

1. Kitty and Harry's anniversary will fall on
       (A)   (B)
   Father's Day this year. No error.
       (C)   (D)   (E)

2. The trees leaves provide a fall festival
       (A)   (B)
   called "Fall Foliage"
              (C)
   in most New England states. No error.
              (D)   (E)

3. Most colleges require
       (A)   (B)
   a specific number
          (C)
   of academic credits for admission.
                  (D)
   No error.
     (E)

4. My brother Robert
       (A)
   loves to read novels but would enjoy
          (B)   (C)
   good mystery's more. No error.
       (D)   (E)

5. Louise had lay her mitt on the bench
       (A)   (B)   (C)
   when she got a glass of water.
               (D)
   No error.
     (E)

6. It seems to me that I had spoke to my
       (A)   (B)
   landlord about the crack in the ceiling
                 (C)
   about two months ago. No error.
          (D)   (E)

7. The committee on fund-raising
       (A)   (B)
   gathers in the hall,
          (C)
   but Joe went to the room. No error.
          (D)   (E)

8. The administrator wanted
        (A)   (B)
   all lesson plan books
          (C)
   handed in by Friday. No error.
          (D)   (E)

9. Behind the tree, she was reading a book,
       (A)   (B)
   eating a banana, and she waited for the
          (C)   (D)
   sunset. No error.
           (E)

10. Is Washington, D. C. closer to Arlington
    (A)   (B)   (C)
    Cemetery than Charleston? No error.
              (D)   (E)

11. The <u>student</u> <u>would not do nothing</u>
       (A)   (B)
<u>to redeem</u> himself
   (C)
<u>in the eyes of the principal.</u> <u>No error.</u>
         (D)   (E)

12. <u>Good teachers</u> <u>are distinguished</u> by
     (A)   (B)
their <u>enthusiasm</u> and <u>organization.</u>
        (C)   (D)
<u>No error.</u>
  (E)

13. <u>The principle</u> <u>of the middle</u> school
     (A)   (B)
<u>wanted</u> to reorganize
  (C)
the lunch schedule. <u>No error.</u>
    (D)   (E)

14. <u>Grandmother's</u> shopping list <u>consisted of</u>
    (A)   (B)
mustard, green beans, <u>buttermilk,</u> and
                (C)
<u>included some eggs.</u> <u>No error.</u>
    (D)   (E)

15. Unless <u>you arm yourself</u> with
        (A)
<u>insect repellent,</u> you <u>will get</u> <u>a bight.</u>
    (B)   (C)   (D)
<u>No error.</u>
  (E)

16. Graduation <u>exercises</u> will be held on __
          (A)   (B)
Friday __ June 19th, at <u>7:00</u> P.M. <u>No error.</u>
  (C)   (D)   (E)

17. <u>With a quick</u> <u>glance</u> <u>the noisy room</u>
   (A)   (B)   (C)
<u>was silenced.</u> <u>No error.</u>
   (D)   (E)

18. <u>Without even trying,</u> <u>the sprinter</u>
    (A)   (B)
<u>passed the world record</u>
    (C)
<u>by five tenths</u> of a second. <u>No error.</u>
   (D)   (E)

19. <u>Prior to</u> <u>the passage of PL 94-142,</u>
  (A)   (B)
<u>special-education students</u>
     (C)
<u>were not unrepresented legally.</u>
       (D)
<u>No error.</u>
  (E)

20. <u>Combine</u> the <u>sugar,</u> <u>waters,</u> cornstarch,
   (A)   (B)   (C)
and <u>eggs.</u> <u>No error.</u>
   (D)   (E)

PART B

Choose the letter of the best choice for the underlined section, without changing the meaning of the sentence. If the original is best, choose (A). Otherwise, select one of the suggested changes.

21. Postman's talents were missed <u>not any more</u> as a student but also in his extracurricular activities on campus.
    (A) not any more
    (B) not
    (C) not only
    (D) never any
    (E) any

22. <u>Piled on the table, the students started sorting through their projects.</u>
    (A) Piled on the table, the students started sorting through their projects.
    (B) The students started sorting through their projects, which were piled on the table.
    (C) Piled on the table, the students sorted through their projects.
    (D) The students sorted through their projects as they piled on the table.
    (E) Students started sorting through the table piled with projects.

23. All the soccer players, <u>who are injured</u>, must not play the game.
    (A) ,who are injured,
    (B) ,who are injured
    (C) who are injured,
    (D) who are injured
    (E) (who are injured)

24. The plumber kept these tools in his <u>truck; plunger, snake, washers and faucets.</u>
    (A) truck; plunger, snake, washers and faucets
    (B) truck (plunger, snake, washers and faucets
    (C) truck: plunger; snake; washers and faucets
    (D) truck; plunger, snake, washers, and faucets
    (E) truck: plunger, snake, washers, and faucets.

25. The two <u>attorneys meet</u> and agreed on an out-of-court settlement.
    (A) attorneys meet
    (B) attorney's meet
    (C) attorney's met
    (D) attorneys met
    (E) attorney meets

PART C

Use the lined pages to write a brief essay based on this topic.

Which of your elementary teachers do you think of most often? What was there about that teacher's style or classroom that you would either use the most or avoid the most in your own classroom?

Write a brief outline here.

ANSWERS

Part A

1. **E**	5. **A**	9. **D**	13. **A**	17. **E**
2. **A**	6. **B**	10. **D**	14. **D**	18. **D**
3. **E**	7. **C**	11. **B**	15. **D**	19. **D**
4. **D**	8. **E**	12. **E**	16. **C**	20. **C**

Part B

21. **C**   22. **B**   23. **D**   24. **E**   25. **D**

Part C

Show your essay to an English teacher or an English professor for evaluation. Use the rating scale shown on page 34, and the sample essays starting on page 20.

Example of an Essay That Would Be Rated in the Upper Half

It's been a long time since I was in elementary school. The school that I attended isn't even there anymore. But I remember most of my elementary school teachers.

Who would I choose as my favorite teacher. When I was in fifth grade, my teacher was Miss Stendel. Even though it was a long time ago, I can almost see her now.

Miss Stendel is probably the teacher I think about the most. She liked Indians, and she used to spend a lot of time in the western states.

Miss Stendel was very nice to me while I was in her classroom. She seemed to understand boys, which many teachers did not. I would say that she is the teacher I think about the most, but of course there are lots of other teachers whom I liked and still like.

Even though I liked her the most, she had an approach to teaching that I will probably avoid when I am a teacher. She used to have piles of mathematics worksheets all around the window sill in the classroom. You had to work your way around the window sill to do the math program. The sheets were boring and I hated them.

I don't know where Miss Stendel is today, but I would like to be able to thank her for being so nice.

Example of an Essay That Would Be Rated in the Lower Half

Miss Willis was my second grade teacher who I respected very much.

I remember her the most of all of my teachers. Good teachers are very important if we expect to have good students.

Miss Willis would have come to school every day with a very sunny attitude even when there was some other problem at home or in the school. She never got mad at us or yeled when we did stuff that was not good.

That was the style which Miss Willis had that I would use if I was a teacher. She never made me feel bad and she was always trying to be helpful and nice. I would try my very best to be as nice as she was and to follow her examples to. If I could be as good a teacher as she was that when I was a teacher my superviser would have to say that she thought that I was doing all the things that she had done to make her a good teacher.

So Miss Willis is the most favorite teacher I can remember.

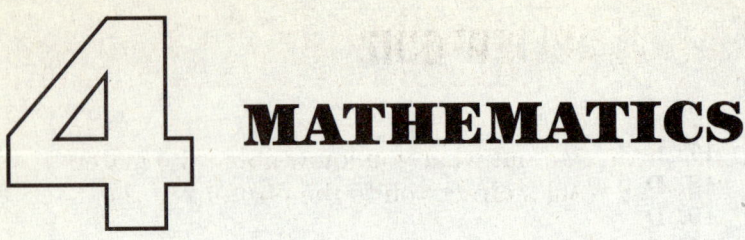

MATHEMATICS

TEST INFO BOX		
PPST	40 Multiple-Choice Items	50 minutes
CBT	29 Multiple-Choice Items	65 minutes

USING THIS CHAPTER

This chapter prepares you to take the mathematics part of the PPST and CBT tests. Choose one of these approaches to the information in this chapter.

- **I want all the math help I can get.** Skip the review quiz and read the mathematics review section. Then take the mathematics review quiz. Correct the quiz and reread the indicated parts of the mathematics review. Take the targeted test at the end of the chapter.

- **I want math help.** Take the mathematics review quiz. Correct the quiz and review the indicated parts of the mathematics review. Take the targeted test at the end of the chapter.

- **I want a quick math review.** Take the mathematics review quiz. Correct the quiz. Take the targeted test at the end of the chapter.

- **I want to practice math items.** Take the targeted test at the end of the chapter.

MATHEMATICS REVIEW QUIZ

This quiz uses a short answer format to help you find out what you know about the mathematics topics reviewed in this chapter. The quiz results direct you to the portions of the chapter you should review.

This quiz will also help focus your thinking about Mathematics, and these questions and answers are a good review in themselves. It's not important to answer all these questions correctly, and don't be concerned if you miss many of them.

The answers are found immediately after the quiz. It's to your advantage not to look at them until you have completed the quiz. Once you have completed and corrected this review quiz, use the answer checklist to decide which sections of the review to study.

Write the answers in the space provided or on a separate sheet of paper.

---

1. Which number is missing from this sequence?

   3 6 _____ 12

Questions 2–4: *Use symbols for less than, greater than, and equal to, and compare these numbers:*

2. 23 _____ 32

3. 18 _____ 4 + 14

4. 9 _____ 10 _____ 11

5. Write the place value of the digit 7 in the numeral 476,891,202,593.

   _____

6. Write this number in words:

   6,000,000,000,000.

   _____

7. 2,826 + 13,874 =

8. 9,030 − 6,231 =

9. 23 × 689 =

10. 14,832 ÷ 72 =

11. 4^3 = _____

12. $2^2 \times 2^3$ = _____

13. $6^9 \div 6^7$ = _____

14. $3^2 \times 2^3$ = _____

15. Simplify this square root $\sqrt{98}$ = _____

16. $5 + 7 \times 3^2$ _____

17. $5 \times 8 - (15 - 7 \times 2)$ _____

18. Write the place value of the digit 4 in the numeral 529.354.

    _____

Questions 19–20: *Use symbols for less than, greater than, and equal to, and compare these numbers:*

19. 9.879 _____ 12.021

20. 98.1589 _____ 98.162

Questions 21–24

   Round 234,489.0754 to the:

21. thousands place _____

22. hundredths place _____

23. tenths place _____

24. hundreds place _____

25. 203.61 + 9.402 + 0.78 = _____

26. $30.916 - 8.72$ _____

27. 3.4×0.0021 _____

28. $0.576 \div 0.32$ _____

29. Write these fractions from least to greatest.

$$\frac{7}{8}, \quad \frac{11}{12}, \quad \frac{17}{20}$$

_____, _____, _____

30. $1\frac{2}{3} \times 3\frac{3}{4} =$ _____

31. $1\frac{2}{3} \div \frac{3}{8} =$ _____

32. $1\frac{4}{9} + \frac{5}{6} =$ _____

33. $4\frac{5}{6} - 2\frac{3}{5} =$ _____

34. Write a seven-digit number divisible by 4.

_____

35. Write the GCF and LCM of 6 and 14.

_____

36. Complete the following ratio so that it is equivalent to 4 : 5

28 : _____

37. Use a proportion and solve this problem. Bob uses jelly and peanut butter in a ratio of 5 : 2. He uses 10 teaspoons of jelly. How much peanut butter will he use?

_____

Questions 38–43: *Change among decimals, percents, and fractions to complete the table.*

Decimal	Percent	Fraction
0.56	38. _____	39. _____
40. _____	15.2%	41. _____
42. _____	43. _____	$\frac{3}{8}$

44. What is 35 percent of 50? _____

45. What percent of 120 is 40? _____

46. 15 percent of what number is 6? _____

47. A $68 sweater is on sale for 15% off. What is the sale price? _____

48. A store marks up their prices 45% over the wholesale cost and adds a 6% sales tax. What is the final cost of an item with a $30 wholesale price? _____

49. What is the probability of rolling one die and getting a 7? _____

50. You flip a fair coin five times in a row and it comes up heads each time. What is the probability that it will come up tails on the next flip?

_____

51. You pick one card from a deck. Then you pick another one without replacing the first. Are these dependent or independent events? Explain.

_____

Questions 52–54: *Find the mean, median, and mode of this set of data.*

10, 5, 2, 1, 8, 5, 3, 0

52. Mean _____

53. Median _____

54. Mode _____

55. A librarian picks two books out of three books. How many different groups of two books are there? _____

56. There are four seats next to one another at the movies. In how many ways could four students arrange themselves in the seats? _____

57. $^-8 + {}^+4 =$ _____

58. $^+85 + ^-103 =$ _____

59. $^-12 - ^+7 =$ _____

60. $^-72 - ^-28 =$ _____

61. $^-9 \times ^+8 =$ _____

62. $^-12 \times ^-6 =$ _____

63. $^-28 \div ^+7 =$ _____

64. $^-72 \div ^-9 =$ _____

65. Write 3,982 in scientific notation.

   _____

66. Write 0.976 in scientific notation.

   _____

Write the value of the variable.

67. $x - 35 = 26$ _____

68. $x + 81 = 7$ _____

69. $y \div 8 = 3$ _____

70. $3z = 54$ _____

71. $4y - 9 = 19$ _____

72. $k \div 6 + 5 = 17$ _____

Questions 73–79: *Draw a model of:*

73. a point

74. a line

75. a ray

76. an acute angle

77. complementary angles

78. an isosceles triangle

79. a rectangle

80. Use this coordinate grid and plot these points: A (3,2) B (−4,−2).

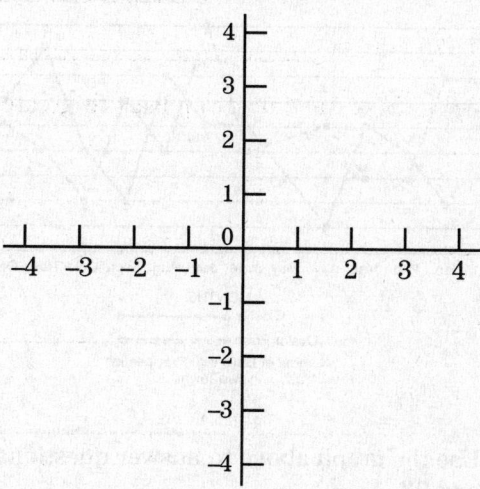

81. What is the difference between the mass of an object on earth and the mass of the same object on the moon?

   _____

82. How many inches would it take to make 5 yards? _____

83. How many cups would it take to make 3 quarts? _____

84. A kilogram is how many grams? _____

85. A centimeter is how many meters? _____

86. Find the area of a triangle with a base of 3 and a height of 2.

   _____

87. Find the area of a square with a side of 5.

   _____

88. Find the area of a circle with a radius of 6.

   _____

89. Find the volume of a cube with a side of 5.

   _____

90. It's 1:00 P.M. in Los Angeles. What time is it in New York? _____

91. It's 32° Celsius. How would you describe a day with that temperature? _____

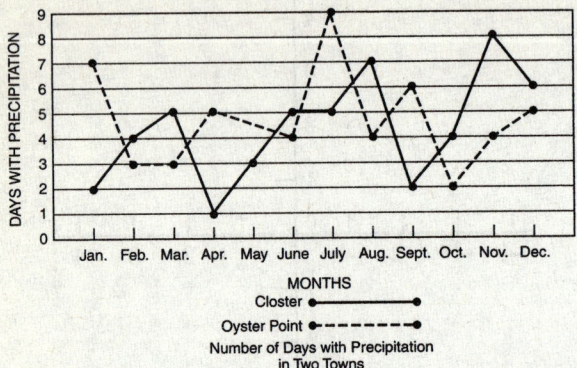

MONTHS

Closter •———————•

Oyster Point •– – – – – –•

Number of Days with Precipitation
in Two Towns

Use the graph above to answer questions 92 and 93.

92. In which month was the Closter precipitation days twice the Oyster Point precipitation days? _____

93. What is the sum of the precipitation days in September? _____

94. Draw a stem and leaf plot that shows these data: 12, 12, 23, 25, 36, 38.

_____

95. Draw a flow chart that "prints" even whole numbers but does not "print" odd whole numbers.

_____

96. Draw a diagram to show that all vowels (*a, e, i, o, u*) are letters and that all consonants are letters, but that no vowels are consonants.

_____

STUDY CHECK LIST

The answers are organized by review sections. Check your answers. If you miss any questions in a section, check the box and review that section. Always review the CBT Calculator section on pages 88–91 and the Problem Solving section on pages 153–155.

❏ *Understanding and Ordering Whole Numbers, page 90*
1. 9
2. <
3. =
4. <, <
5. 10 billion
6. six trillion

❏ *Whole Number Computation, page 92*
7. 16,700
8. 2,799
9. 15,874
10. 206

❏ *Positive Exponents, page 94*
11. 64
12. 32
13. 36
14. 72

❏ *Square Roots, page 95*
15. $7\sqrt{2}$

❏ *Order of Operations, page 96*
16. 68
17. 39

❏ *Understanding and Ordering Decimals, page 97*
18. thousandths
19. <
20. <

❏ *Rounding Whole Numbers and Decimals, page 99*
21. 234,000
22. 234,489.08
23. 234,489.1
24. 234,500

❏ *Add, Subtract, Multiply, and Divide Decimals, page 100*
25. 213.792
26. 22.196
27. 0.00714
28. 1.8

❏ *Understanding and Ordering Fractions, page 101*
29. $\dfrac{17}{20}, \dfrac{7}{8}, \dfrac{11}{12}$

❏ *Multiply, Divide, Add, and Subtract Fractions, page 104*
30. $6\dfrac{1}{4}$
31. $4\dfrac{4}{9}$
32. $2\dfrac{5}{18}$
33. $2\dfrac{7}{30}$

❏ *Number Theory, page 106*
34. The last 2 digits have to be divisible by 4.
35. GCF is 2. LCM is 42.

❏ *Ratio and Proportion, page 109*
36. 35
37. 4

❏ *Percent, page 111*

Decimal	Percent	Fraction
0.56	**38.** 56%	**39.** 14/25
40. 0.152	15.2%	**41.** 19/125
42. 0.375	**43.** 37.5%	3/8

❏ *Three Types of Percent Problems, page 113*
44. 17.5
45. $33\dfrac{1}{3}\%$
46. 40

❏ *Percent of Increase and Decrease,*
  page 115
  47. $57.80
  48. $46.11

❏ *Probability, page 117*
  49. Zero

  50. $\frac{1}{2}$

  51. Dependent. The outcome of one event
    affects the probability of the other
    event.

❏ *Statistics, page 119*
  52. 4.25
  53. 4
  54. 5

❏ *Permutations and Combinations, page 121*
  55. 3
  56. 24

❏ *Integers, page 122*
  57. −4
  58. −18
  59. −19
  60. −44
  61. −72
  62. +72
  63. −4
  64. +8

❏ *Scientific Notation, page 124*
  65. 3.982×10^3
  66. 9.76×10^{-1}

❏ *Equations, page 125*
  67. 61
  68. −74
  69. 24
  70. 18
  71. 7
  72. 72
  73. ·
  74. ↔
  75. ↦

❏ *Geometry, page 127*

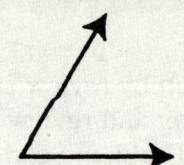

76. Acute angle

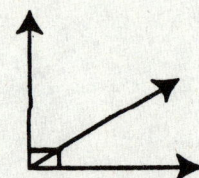

77. Complementary □ angles

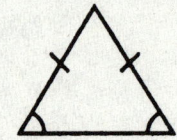

78. Isosceles triangle

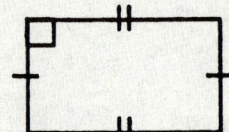

79. Rectangle

❏ *Coordinate Grid, page 131*
  80.

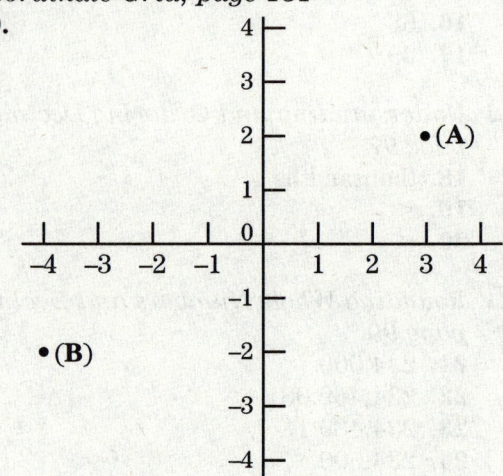

❏ *Measurement, page 134*
81. None. Mass remains constant.

❏ *Customary (English) Units, page 135*
82. 180 inches
83. 12

❏ *Metric System, page 135*
84. 1,000
85. 0.01

❏ *Formulas, page 138*
86. 3
87. 25
88. about 113 (113.097...)
89. 125

❏ *Time and Temperature, page 142*
90. 4:00 P.M.
91. Hot—about 90°F.

❏ *Graphs, page 145*
92. November
93. 8

❏ *Stem-and-Leaf and Box-and-Whisker Plots, page 148*
94.

1	2,2
2	3,5
3	6,8

❏ *Flow Charts, page 150*
95.

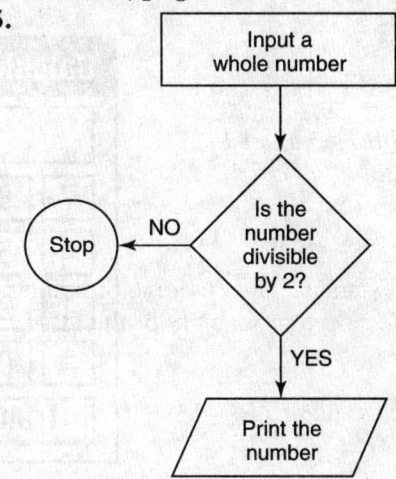

❏ *Logic, page 152*
96.

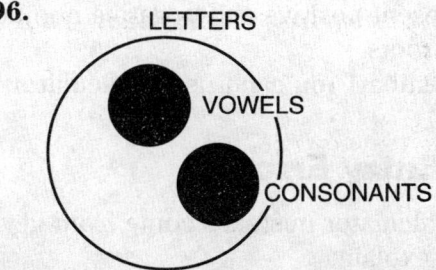

☑ *Problem Solving, page 153*
Everyone should review this section.

USING THE CBT MATHEMATICS CALCULATOR

The calculator above is available on screen as you take the Mathematics CBT. You can use it to represent positive and negative numbers and to add, subtract, multiply, divide, and find square roots.

Remember! You can't use a calculator on the paper and pencil PPST.

Key Entry Errors

Many calculator mistakes come from key entry errors. I would want to avoid that at all costs. Let me explain.

When you work with paper and pencil, you see all your work. On most calculators, you see only the last entry or the last answer. So it is possible to make a key entry error and, in a flurry of entries, never catch your mistake. We all put an enormous amount of trust in the calculator answer, and we don't usually question the answer it produces. This makes us particularly vulnerable to the results of these key entry errors.

How Should I Use a Calculator?

Use your calculator to calculate. Remember that the calculator is best at helping you find answers quickly. Use it to calculate the answers to numerical problems. Use it to try out answers quickly to find which is correct. Whenever you come across a problem involving calculation, you can use the calculator to do or check your work.

Estimate before you calculate. Earlier in this section we mentioned that many calculator errors are caused by key entry mistakes. You think you put in one number, but you really put in another. One way to avoid this type of error is to estimate before you calculate. Then compare the estimate to your answer. If they aren't close, then either your estimate or your calculation is off.

Recognize when your calculator will be helpful. Let's think of problems in three categories. The calculator can be a big help, some help, or no help. The idea is to use your calculator on the first two types of problems and not to use it when it won't help.

Big Help

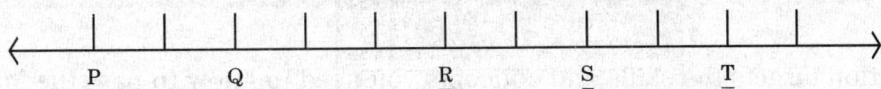

The segment $\overline{PT}$ has a length of 31.5. What is the length of segment $\overline{QS}$?

A calculator is a big help here. There are 9 units from P to T. So divide 31.5 by 9 = 3.5 to find the length of each unit. Multiply 3.5 by 5 = 17.5 to find the length of QS.

Some Help

A rectangle has a length 3 and width 5. What is the area?

You can do this computation in your head. A calculator could help you check the answer, but you don't absolutely need it.

No Help

Calculators are no help with problems involving equations or nonnumerical solutions. Using a calculator when it won't help can cause trouble and waste time.

How Are Calculator Keys Used?

Press the numeral keys and the decimal point to represent numbers.

Press the ⊞, ⊟, ⊠, and ⊡ keys to add, subtract, multiply, and divide.

Press the equal ⊟ key when you are through to get the final answer.

$$4 \boxtimes 7 \boxplus 9 \boxminus \mathbf{13.7} \qquad\qquad 12 \boxminus 18 \boxminus \mathbf{-6}$$

$$6 \boxtimes 4 \boxtimes 3 \boxminus \mathbf{25.8} \qquad\qquad 10 \boxdiv 3 \boxminus \mathbf{3.3333333}$$

Square Root. The calculator has a √ key. To find the square root of 38.44 enter 38.44 √ . Note also that the square root key will not simplify a square root. So the square root shows up as 2.8284, not $2\sqrt{2}$.

Integers. The subtraction key on the calculator cannot be used to represent negative integers. Use the +/− key on the calculator after a number to change the sign. For example, to subtract ⁻62 − ⁺25, enter 62 +/− ⊟ 25 ⊟ . To multiply ⁻8 × ⁻6, enter 8 +/− ⊠ 6 +/− ⊟ .

The CE key clears the current display.

The C key clears the entry and all the work you have done.

MATHEMATICS REVIEW

This review section targets the skills and concepts you need to know to pass the Mathematics part of the PPST and the CBT.

UNDERSTANDING AND ORDERING WHOLE NUMBERS

Whole numbers are the numbers you use to tell how many. They include 0, 1, 2, 3, 4, 5, 6 . . . The dots tell us that these numbers keep going on forever. There are an infinite number of whole numbers, which means you will never reach the last one.

Cardinal numbers such as 1, 9, and 18 tell how many. There are 9 players on the field in a baseball game. Ordinal numbers such as 1st, 2nd, 9th, and 18th tell about order. For example, Lynne batted 1st this inning.

You can visualize whole numbers evenly spaced on a number line.

You can use the number line to compare numbers. Numbers get smaller as we go to the left and larger as we go to the right. We use the terms *equal to* (=), *less than* (<), *greater than* (>), and *between* to compare numbers.

12 equals 10 + 2	2 is less than 5	9 is greater than 4	6 is between 5 and 7
12 = 10 + 2	2 < 5	9 > 4	5 < 6 < 7

PLACE VALUE

We use ten digits, 0–9, to write out numerals. We also use a place value system of numeration. The value of a digit depends on the place it occupies. Look at the following place value chart.

millions	hundred thousands	ten thousands	thousands	hundreds	tens	ones
3	5	7	9	4	1	0

The value of the 9 is 9,000. The 9 is in the thousands place. The value of the 5 is 500,000. The 5 is in the hundred thousands place. Read the number three million, five hundred seventy-nine thousand, four hundred ten.

Some whole numbers are very large. The distance from Earth to the planet Pluto is about six trillion (6,000,000,000,000) yards. The distance from Earth to the nearest star is about 40 quadrillion (40,000,000,000,000,000) yards.

Completed Examples

A. What is the value of 8 in the numeral 47,829?

The value of the 8 is 800; this is because the 8 is in the hundreds place.

B. Use >, <, or = to compare 2 and 7.

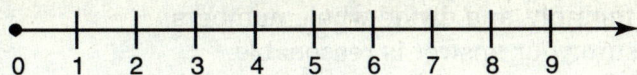

Use the number line to see that 2 < 7 (2 is less than 7).

Practice

Fill in the space with = , <, or > to make each statement true.

1. 2 ____ 3

2. 4 ____ 1

3. 8 ____ 9

4. 1 ____ 1

5. 7 ____ 6

6. Write a numeral in which the value of 7 is seven, the value of 9 is nine thousand, the value of 3 is thirty, and the 0 is in the hundreds place.

7. Write a numeral in which the value of 5 is fifty, the value of 2 is two thousand, the value of 1 is one, and the value of 8 is eight hundred.

8. What place values in the numeral 65,747 contain the same digit?

9. Write the whole numbers between 0 and 15.

10. How many whole numbers are there between 0 and 50?

Answers on page 174

WHOLE NUMBER COMPUTATION

Follow these steps to add, subtract, multiply, and divide whole numbers.
Estimate first and then check to be sure your answer is reasonable.

Add: 24,262 + 8,921.

Estimate first.

24,262 rounded to the nearest ten thousand is 24,000.
8,921 rounded to the nearest thousand is 9,000.
24,000 + 9,000 = 33,000. The answer should be close to 33,000.

Add.

```
                          1 1
    2 4 2 6 2           2 4 2 6 2
  +   8 9 2 1         +   8 9 2 1
                       3 3 1 8 3
```

            Align digits.   Add.

33,183 is close to 33,000 so the answer is reasonable.

Subtract: 20,274 − 17,235.

Estimate first.

20,274 rounded to the nearest thousand is 20,000.
17,235 rounded to the nearest thousand is 17,000.
20,000 − 17,000 = 3,000.
The answer should be close to 3,000.

Subtract.

```
                       1 10  6 14
    2 0 2 7 4          2̸ 0̸ 2 7̸ 4
  - 1 7 2 3 5        - 1 7 2 3 5
                       3 0 3 9
```

            Align digits.   Subtract.

3,039 is close to 3000, so the answer seems reasonable.

Multiply: 32 × 181.

Estimate first.

Multiplication answers may look correct but may be wrong by a multiple of 10.

32 rounded to the nearest ten is 30.
181 rounded to the nearest hundred is 200.

30 × 200 = 6,000

The answer should be near 6,000.

Multiply.

$$\begin{array}{r} 181 \\ \times\ 32 \\ \hline 362 \\ 543 \end{array}\qquad\begin{array}{r} 181 \\ \times\ 32 \\ \hline 362 \\ 543 \\ \hline 5792 \end{array}$$

       Find the partial products.   Add the partial products.

The answer is close to 6,000.
The answer seems reasonable.

Divide: $927 \div 43$

Estimate first.

You may make a division error if you misalign digits.

927 rounded to the nearest hundred is 900.
43 rounded to the nearest ten is 40.

$900 \div 45 = 20$

The answer should be somewhere near 20.

Divide.

$$43\overline{)927}\qquad\begin{array}{r} 21\ \mathbf{R24} \\ 43\overline{)927} \\ 86 \\ \hline 67 \\ 43 \\ \hline 24 \end{array}$$

       Divide.   Find the quotient and the remainder.

The answer is close to 20.
The answer seems reasonable.

Practice

Find the answer.

1. $\begin{array}{r} 97,218 \\ +\ 1,187 \end{array}$ **2.** $\begin{array}{r} 23,045 \\ +\ 4,034 \end{array}$ **3.** $\begin{array}{r} 67,914 \\ +27,895 \end{array}$ **4.** $\begin{array}{r} 48,549 \\ +17,635 \end{array}$

5. $\begin{array}{r} 20,591 \\ -\ 4,578 \end{array}$ **6.** $\begin{array}{r} 34,504 \\ -\ \ \ 405 \end{array}$ **7.** $\begin{array}{r} 57,895 \\ -23,207 \end{array}$ **8.** $\begin{array}{r} 84,403 \\ -42,194 \end{array}$

9. $\begin{array}{r} 240 \\ \times\ 57 \end{array}$ **10.** $\begin{array}{r} 302 \\ \times\ 91 \end{array}$ **11.** $\begin{array}{r} 725 \\ \times\ 41 \end{array}$ **12.** $\begin{array}{r} 146 \\ \times\ 36 \end{array}$

13. $328 \div 41 =$ **14.** $240 \div 59 =$ **15.** $754 \div 26 =$ **16.** $2,370 \div 74 =$

Answers on page 174

POSITIVE EXPONENTS

You can show repeated multiplication as an exponent. The exponent shows how many times the factor appears.

$$\text{Base} \rightarrow 3^5 = 3 \times 3 \times 3 \times 3 \times 3 = 243$$

[Exponent]

[Factors]

RULES FOR EXPONENTS

$$a^0 = 1 \qquad a^1 = a$$

Use these rules to multiply and divide exponents with the *same base*.

$$7^8 \times 7^5 = 7^{13} \qquad a^n \times a^m = a^{m+n} \qquad\qquad 7^8 \div 7^5 = 7^3 \qquad a^n \div a^m = a^{n-m}$$

Completed Examples

A. $4^3 + 6^2 \quad = 4 \times 4 \times 4 + 6 \times 6 \quad = 64 + 36 \ = 100$

B. $(2^3)\,(4^2) \ = (2 \times 2 \times 2) \times (4 \times 4) = 8 \times 16 \quad = 128$

C. $(3^2)^2 \qquad = 3^4 \ = 3 \times 3 \times 3 \times 3 \ = 81$

D. $(10 - 9)^2 = 1^2 \quad = 1$

Practice

1. $5^2 + 6^3 =$

2. $(3^2)^2 =$

3. $(8 - 6)^3 =$

4. $(5^2)\,(6^2) =$

5. $3^3 + 2^3 =$

6. $10^2 - 7^2 =$

7. $(4^3)^2 =$

8. $(2^1)^5 =$

9. $6^2 + 2^3 =$

10. $(25 - 15)^3 =$

11. $(4^2)^2 =$

12. $(2^3)\,(3^2) =$

Answers on page 174

SQUARE ROOTS

The square root of a given number, when multiplied by itself, equals the given number. This symbol ($\sqrt{25}$) means the square root of 25. The square root of 25 is 5. $5 \times 5 = 25$.

SOME SQUARE ROOTS ARE WHOLE NUMBERS

The numbers with whole-number square roots are called perfect squares.

$$\sqrt{1} = 1 \quad \sqrt{4} = 2 \quad \sqrt{9} = 3 \quad \sqrt{16} = 4 \quad \sqrt{25} = 5 \quad \sqrt{36} = 6$$
$$\sqrt{49} = 7 \quad \sqrt{64} = 8 \quad \sqrt{81} = 9 \quad \sqrt{100} = 10 \quad \sqrt{121} = 11 \quad \sqrt{144} = 12$$

USE THIS RULE TO WRITE A SQUARE ROOT IN ITS SIMPLEST FORM

$$\sqrt{a \times b} = \sqrt{a} \times \sqrt{b} \qquad \sqrt{5 \times 3} = \sqrt{5} \times \sqrt{3}$$
$$\sqrt{72} = \sqrt{36 \times 2} = \sqrt{36} \times \sqrt{2} = 6 \times \sqrt{2}$$

Completed Examples

A. Write the square root of 162 in simplest form.

$$\sqrt{162} = \sqrt{81 \times 2} = \sqrt{81} \times \sqrt{2} = 9\sqrt{2}$$

B. Write the square root of 112 in simplest form.

$$\sqrt{112} = \sqrt{16 \times 7} = \sqrt{16} \times \sqrt{7} = 4\sqrt{7}$$

Practice

Simplify.

1. $\sqrt{256}$ 6. $\sqrt{48}$

2. $\sqrt{400}$ 7. $\sqrt{245}$

3. $\sqrt{576}$ 8. $\sqrt{396}$

4. $\sqrt{900}$ 9. $\sqrt{567}$

5. $\sqrt{1225}$ 10. $\sqrt{832}$

Answers on page 174

ORDER OF OPERATIONS

Use this phrase to remember the order in which we do operations:

Please Excuse My Dear Aunt Sally

(1) Parentheses **(2) E**xponents **(3) M**ultiplication or **D**ivision **(4) A**ddition or **S**ubtraction
For example,

$$4 + 3 \times 7^2 \quad = 4 + 3 \times 49 = 4 + 147 \quad = 151$$
$$(4 + 3) \times 7^2 = 7 \times 7^2 \quad = 7 \times 49 \quad = 343$$
$$(6 - 10 \div 5) + 6 \times 3 = (6 - 2) + 6 \times 3 = 4 + 6 \times 3 = 4 + 18 = 22$$

Completed Example

$$7 + 3 \times 6 + 4^2 - (8 + 4) = 7 + 3 \times 6 + 4^2 - \underline{12} =$$
$$7 + 3 \times 6 + \underline{16} - 12 \quad = 7 + \underline{18} + 16 - 12 \quad = 29$$

Practice

Find the answer.

---

1. $4 \times 5 + 4 \div 2 =$

2. $(5 + 7 - 9) \times 8^2 + 2 =$

3. $((7 + 4) - (1 + 4)) \times 6 =$

4. $6^2 + 3(9 - 5 + 7)^2 =$

5. $(12 + 5) \times 3 - 6^2 =$

6. $8 \times 5 + 4 - 8 \div 2 =$

7. $100 - 30 \times 5 + 7 =$

8. $((5 + 2)^2 + 16) \times 8 =$

Answers on page 174

UNDERSTANDING AND ORDERING DECIMALS

Decimals are used to represent numbers between 0 and 1. Decimals can also be shown on a number line.

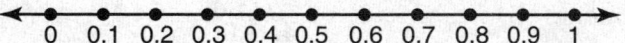

We also use ten digits, 0–9, and a place value system of numeration to write decimals. The value of a digit depends on the place it occupies. Look at the following place value chart.

ones	tenths	hundredths	thousandths	ten thousandths	hundred thousandths	millionths	ten millionths	hundred millionths	billionths
0 .	3	6	8	7					

The value of 3 is three tenths. The 3 is in the tenths place. The value of 8 is eight thousandths. The 8 is in the thousandths place.

COMPARING WHOLE NUMBERS AND DECIMALS

To compare two numbers, compare the value of the digits in each place.

Compare 9,879 and 16,459   23,801 and 23,798   58.1289 and 58.132

9,879	23,**8**01	58.1**2**89
16,459	23,**7**98	58.1**3**2
9,879 < 16,459	23,801 > 23,798	58.1289 < 58.132
Less than	Greater than	Less than

Completed Examples

A. What is the value of the digit 2 in the decimal 35.6829?

The 2 is in the thousandths place. $2 \times 0.001 = 0.002$.
The value of the 2 is 0.002 or 2 thousandths.

B. Use $<$, $>$, or $=$ to compare 1248.9234 and 1248.9229

1248.9234   1248.9229 The digits in the numerals are the same until you reach the thousandths place where $3 > 2$. Since $3 > 2$, then $1248.9234 > 1248.9229$.

Practice

Use <, >, or = to compare.

---

1. 0.02 ____ 0.003

2. 4.6 ____ 1.98

3. 0.0008 ____ 0.00009

4. 1.0 ____ 1

5. 7.6274 ____ 7.6269

Write the answer.

---

6. Write a numeral in which the value of 5 is five tenths, the value of 2 is two, the value of 6 is six thousandths, and the value of 8 is eight hundredths.

7. Write a numeral in which the value of 4 is in the ten thousandths place, the value of 3 is three hundred, the 7 is in the hundredths place, the 1 is in the tens place, the 9 is in the ten thousands place, and the rest of the digits are zeros.

8. In the numeral 6.238935, which place values contain the same digit?

9. Using only the tenths place, write all the decimals from 0 to 1.

10. If you used only the tenths and hundredths places, how many decimals are between 0 and 1?

Answers on page 174

ROUNDING WHOLE NUMBERS AND DECIMALS

Follow these steps to round a number to a place.

- Look at the digit to the right of a specific place.

- If the digit to the right is 5 or more, round up. If the digit is less than 5, round down.

Completed Examples

A. *Round 859,465 to the nearest hundred thousand.*
Underline the hundred thousands place.
Look at the digit to the right of 8. The digit is 5 or more, so round up.
859,465 rounded to the *nearest hundred thousand* is 900,000.

B. *Round 8.647 to the nearest hundredth.*
Underline the hundredths place.
Look at the digit to the right of 4. The digit 7 is 5 or more, so you round up.
8.647 rounded to the *hundredths* place is 8.65.
8.647 rounded to the *tenths* place is 8.6.

Practice

1. Round 23,465 to the hundreds place.

2. Round 74.1508 to the thousandths place.

3. Round 975,540 to the ten thousands place.

4. Round 302.787 to the tenths place.

5. Round 495,244 to the tens place.

6. Round 1508.75 to the hundreds place.

7. Round 13.097 to the hundredths place.

8. Round 198,704 to the hundred thousands place.

9. Round 51.8985 to the ones place.

10. Round 23,457 to the hundreds place.

Answers on page 175

ADD, SUBTRACT, MULTIPLY, AND DIVIDE DECIMALS

Estimate first. Then add, subtract, multiply, or divide.

ADD AND SUBTRACT DECIMALS

Line up the decimal points

Add: $14.9 + 3.108 + 0.16$

```
  14.9
  3.108
+ 0.16
  18.168
```

Subtract: $14.234 - 7.14$

```
  14.234
-  7.14
   7.094
```

MULTIPLY DECIMALS

Multiply decimals as you would whole numbers. Count the total number of decimal places in the factors. Put that many decimal places in the product. You may have to write leading zeros.

Multiply: 17.4×1.3

```
    17.4
×    1.3
     522
    174
   22.62
```

Multiply: 0.016×1.7

```
   0.016
×    1.7
     112
     16
   .0272
```

DIVIDE DECIMALS

Move the decimal point to make the divisor a whole number. Move the decimal point in the dividend the same number of places. Then divide.

```
0.16)1.328
```

```
016.)132.8
```

```
        8.3
  16)132.8
      128
       48
       48
        0
```

Practice

1.
```
  12.79
   8.1
+  5.2
```

2.
```
  40.267
  23.2
+  9.15
```

3.
```
  940.17
   36.15
+  12.07
```

4.
```
  5290.3
   167.8
+   15.09
```

5.
```
  37.9
- 29.7
```

6.
```
  136.804
-  65.7944
```

7.
```
  513.72
-  59.75
```

8.
```
  2451.06
-  683.19
```

9.
```
  0.249
×   2.5
```

10.
```
  46.7
×  3.5
```

11.
```
  56.2
× 65.49
```

12.
```
  93.57
× 40.2
```

13. $10.08 \div 2.1 =$

14. $16.32 \div 1.7 =$

15. $248.64 \div 7.4 =$

16. $653.276 \div 5.2 =$

Answers on page 175

UNDERSTANDING AND ORDERING FRACTIONS

A fraction names a part of a whole or of a group. A fraction has two parts, a numerator and a denominator. The denominator tells how many parts in all. The numerator tells how many parts you identified.

$$\frac{3}{4} \quad \text{Numerator} \atop \text{Denominator}$$

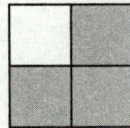

MIXED NUMBERS AND IMPROPER FRACTIONS

Change an improper fraction to a mixed number:

$$\frac{23}{8} = 8\overline{)23} \begin{array}{c} 2\frac{7}{8} \\ \underline{16} \\ 7 \end{array}$$

Change a mixed number to an improper fraction:

$$3\frac{2}{5} = \frac{17}{5}$$

Multiply denominator and whole number. Then add the numerator.

$$\frac{(3 \times 5) + 2}{5} = \frac{15 + 2}{5} = \frac{17}{5}$$

EQUIVALENT FRACTIONS

Two fractions that stand for the same number are called equivalent fractions. Multiply or divide the numerator and denominator by the same number to find an equivalent fraction.

$$\frac{2 \times 3}{5 \times 3} = \frac{6}{15} \qquad \frac{6 \div 3}{9 \div 3} = \frac{2}{3} \qquad \frac{6 \times 4}{8 \times 4} = \frac{24}{32} \qquad \frac{8 \div 2}{10 \div 2} = \frac{4}{5}$$

Fractions can also be written and ordered on a number line. You can use the number line to compare fractions. Fractions get smaller as we go to the left and larger as we go to the right. We use the terms equivalent to (=), less than (<), greater than (>), and between to compare fractions.

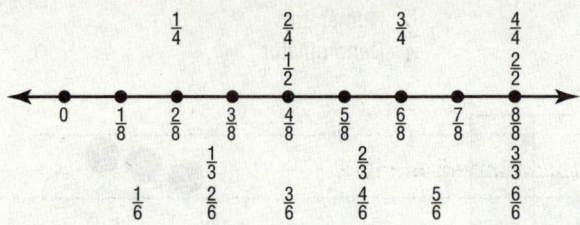

$\frac{1}{2}$ is equivalent to $\frac{2}{4}$

$$\frac{1}{2} = \frac{2}{4}$$

$\frac{2}{3}$ is less than $\frac{3}{4}$

$$\frac{2}{3} < \frac{3}{4}$$

$\frac{5}{8}$ is greater than $\frac{1}{2}$

$$\frac{5}{8} > \frac{1}{2}$$

$\frac{1}{3}$ is between $\frac{1}{4}$ and $\frac{3}{8}$

$$\frac{1}{4} < \frac{1}{3} < \frac{3}{8}$$

COMPARE TWO FRACTIONS

Use this method to compare two fractions. For example, compare $\frac{13}{18}$ and $\frac{5}{7}$. First, write the two fractions and cross multiply as shown. The larger cross product appears next to the larger fraction. If cross products are equal, then the fractions are equivalent.

$$91 = \qquad = 90$$

$$\frac{13}{18} \times \frac{5}{7}$$

$$91 > 90 \text{ so } \frac{13}{18} > \frac{5}{7}$$

Completed Examples

A. Compare $\frac{5}{7}$ and $\frac{18}{19}$,

Use cross multiplication.

$\frac{5}{7} \times \frac{18}{19}$, $5 \times 19 = 95$ and $7 \times 18 = 126$, therefore $\frac{5}{7} < \frac{18}{19}$.

B. Write $\frac{27}{7}$ as a mixed number.

$$\begin{array}{r} 3 \text{ R6} \\ 7\overline{)27} \\ 21 \\ \hline 6 \end{array}$$

$$\frac{27}{7} = 3\frac{6}{7}$$

C. Write $6\frac{5}{8}$ as a fraction.

$6 \times 8 = 48$. Multiply the denominator and the whole number.
$48 + 5 = 53$. Add the numerator to the product.

$$6\frac{5}{8} = \frac{53}{8}$$

Practice

Write the improper fraction as a mixed number.

1. $\frac{5}{3}$

3. $\frac{24}{9}$

2. $\frac{15}{7}$

Write the mixed number as an improper fraction.

4. $8\frac{1}{5}$

6. $9\frac{5}{7}$

5. $6\frac{7}{8}$

Use $>$, $<$, $=$ to compare the fractions.

7. $\frac{3}{7}, \frac{4}{9}$

9. $\frac{4}{5}, \frac{7}{8}$

8. $\frac{5}{6}, \frac{25}{30}$

Answers on page 175

MULTIPLY, DIVIDE, ADD, AND SUBTRACT FRACTIONS AND MIXED NUMBERS

MULTIPLY FRACTIONS AND MIXED NUMBERS

To write any mixed number as an improper fraction, multiply the numerator and the denominator. Write the product in simplest form. For example, multiply $\frac{3}{4}$ and $\frac{1}{6}$.

$$\frac{3}{4} \times \frac{1}{6} = \frac{3}{24} = \frac{1}{8}$$

Now, multiply $3\frac{1}{3}$ by $\frac{3}{5}$.

$$3\frac{1}{3} \times \frac{3}{5} = \frac{10}{3} \times \frac{3}{5} = \frac{30}{15} = 2$$

DIVIDE FRACTIONS AND MIXED NUMBERS

To divide $1\frac{4}{5}$ by $\frac{3}{8}$:

$$1\frac{4}{5} \div \frac{3}{8} = \frac{9}{5} \div \frac{3}{8} = \frac{9}{5} \times \frac{8}{3} = \frac{72}{15} = 4\frac{12}{15} = 4\frac{4}{5}$$

Write mixed numbers as improper fractions.   Invert the divisor and multiply.   Write the product.   Write the quotient in simplest form.

ADD FRACTIONS AND MIXED NUMBERS

To add, write fractions with common denominators. Then write in simplest form.

Add: $\frac{3}{8} + \frac{1}{4}$ Add: $\frac{7}{8} + \frac{5}{12}$ Add: $2\frac{1}{3} + \frac{5}{7}$

$$\frac{3}{8} = \frac{3}{8}$$
$$+\frac{1}{4} = \frac{2}{8}$$
$$\overline{\quad\frac{5}{8}\quad}$$

$$\frac{7}{8} = \frac{21}{24}$$
$$+\frac{5}{12} = \frac{10}{24}$$
$$\overline{\quad\frac{31}{24} = 1\frac{7}{24}\quad}$$

$$2\frac{1}{3} = 2\frac{7}{21}$$
$$+\frac{5}{7} = \frac{15}{21}$$
$$\overline{\quad 2\frac{22}{21} = 3\frac{1}{21}\quad}$$

SUBTRACT FRACTIONS AND MIXED NUMBERS

Write fractions with common denominators. Subtract and then write in simplest form.

Subtract: $\dfrac{5}{6} - \dfrac{1}{3}$ Subtract: $\dfrac{3}{8} - \dfrac{1}{5}$ Subtract: $3\dfrac{1}{6} - 1\dfrac{1}{3}$

$$\dfrac{5}{6} = \dfrac{5}{6}$$ $$\dfrac{3}{8} = \dfrac{15}{40}$$ $$\dfrac{1}{6} = 3\dfrac{1}{6} = 2\dfrac{7}{6}$$

$$\dfrac{1}{3} = \dfrac{2}{6}$$ $$\dfrac{1}{5} = \dfrac{8}{40}$$ $$1\dfrac{1}{3} = 1\dfrac{2}{6} = 1\dfrac{2}{6}$$

$$\dfrac{3}{6} = \dfrac{1}{2}$$ $$\dfrac{7}{40}$$ $$1\dfrac{5}{6}$$

Practice

1. $\dfrac{1}{3} \times \dfrac{5}{9} =$

2. $\dfrac{2}{3} \times \dfrac{1}{4} =$

3. $3\dfrac{3}{8} \times 4\dfrac{1}{8} =$

4. $3\dfrac{1}{5} \times 2\dfrac{4}{7} =$

5. $\dfrac{3}{4} \div \dfrac{7}{8} =$

6. $\dfrac{2}{5} \div \dfrac{7}{9} =$

7. $9\dfrac{5}{7} \div 4\dfrac{1}{3} =$

8. $2\dfrac{4}{5} \div 7\dfrac{3}{5} =$

9. $\dfrac{5}{9} + \dfrac{2}{3} =$

10. $\dfrac{7}{10} + \dfrac{2}{4} =$

11. $1\dfrac{6}{7} + 2\dfrac{3}{14} =$

12. $5\dfrac{2}{3} + 6\dfrac{5}{6} =$

13. $\dfrac{2}{7} - \dfrac{5}{21} =$

14. $\dfrac{2}{5} - \dfrac{3}{8} =$

15. $3\dfrac{4}{5} - 3\dfrac{2}{15} =$

16. $8\dfrac{1}{7} - 4\dfrac{2}{9} =$

Answers on page 175

NUMBER THEORY

Number theory explores the natural numbers [1, 2, 3, 4,...]. We'll review just a few important number theory concepts.

FACTORS

The factors of a number evenly divide the number with no remainder. For example, 2 is a factor of 6, but 2 is not a factor of 5.

The number 1 is a factor of every number. Each number is a factor of itself.

1	The only factor is 1
2	Factors 1, 2
3	1, 3
4	1, 2, 4
5	1, 5
6	1, 2, 3, 6
7	1, 7
8	1, 2, 4, 8
9	1, 3, 9
10	1, 2, 5, 10

PRIME NUMBERS AND COMPOSITE NUMBERS

A prime number has exactly two factors, itself and 1.

2 is prime. The only factors are 1 and 2.
3 is prime. Factors: 1, 3
5 is prime. Factors: 1, 5
7 is prime. Factors: 1, 7

A composite number has more than two factors.

4 is composite. The factors are 1, 2, 4.
6 is composite. Factors: 1, 2, 3, 6
8 is composite. Factors: 1, 2, 4, 8
9 is composite. Factors: 1, 3, 9
10 is composite. Factors: 1, 2, 5, 10

The number 1 has only one factor, itself. The number 1 is neither prime nor composite.

LEAST COMMON MULTIPLE (LCM), GREATEST COMMON FACTOR (GCF)

Multiples. The multiples of a number are all the numbers you get when you count by that number. Here are some examples.

Multiples of 1: 1, 2, 3, 4, 5,...
Multiples of 2: 2, 4, 6, 8, 10,...
Multiples of 3: 3, 6, 9, 12, 15,...
Multiples of 4: 4, 8, 12, 16, 20,...
Multiples of 5: 5, 10, 15, 20, 25,...

Least common multiple is the smallest multiple shared by two numbers.

The least common multiple of 6 and 8 is 24.

List the multiples of 6 and 8. Notice that 24 is the smallest multiple common to both numbers.

Multiples of 6: 6, 12, 18, **24**, 30, 36
Multiples of 8: 8, 16, **24**, 32, 40

Greatest common factor is the largest factor shared by two numbers.

The greatest common factor of 28 and 36 is 4.

List the factors of 28 and 36.

Factors of 28: 1, 2, **4**, 7, 28
Factors of 36: 1, 2, 3, **4**, 6, 9, 12, 18, 36

DIVISIBILITY RULES

Use these rules to find out if a number is divisible by the given number. Divisible means the given number divides evenly with no remainder.

2 Every even number is divisible by 2.

3 If the sum of the digits is divisible by 3, the number is divisible by 3.

347   3 + 4 + 7 = 14   14 is not divisible by 3, so 347 is not divisible by 3.

738   7 + 3 + 8 = 18   18 is divisible by 3, so 738 is divisible by 3.

4 If the last two digits are divisible by 4, the number is divisible by 4.

484,8<u>42</u>   42 is not divisible by 4, so 484,842 is not divisible by 4.

371,9<u>56</u>   56 is divisible by 4, so 372,956 is divisible by 4.

5 If the last digit is 0 or 5, then the number is divisible by 5.

6 If the number meets the divisibility rules for both 2 *and* 3, then it is divisible by 6.

8 If the last three digits are divisible by 8, then the number is divisible by 8.

208,513,<u>114</u>   114 is not divisible by 8, so 208,513,114 is not divisible by 8.

703,628,<u>920</u>   920 is divisible by 8, so 703,628,920 is divisible by 8.

9 If the sum of the digits is divisible by 9, then the number is divisible by 9.

93,163   9 + 3 + 1 + 6 + 3 = 22   22 is not divisible by 9, so 93,163 is not divisible by 9.

86,715   8 + 6 + 7 + 1 + 5 = 27   27 is divisible by 9, so 86,715 is divisible by 9.

10 If a number ends in 0, the number is divisible by 10.

Completed Examples

A. Find the factors of 24.

The factors are 1, 2, 3, 4, 6, 8, 12, and 24.
These are the only numbers that divide 24 with no remainder.

B. Find the GCF of 14 and 22.

Write out the factors of each number.
14: 1, 2, 7, 14
22: 1, 2, 11, 22

The greatest common factor is 2.

C. Find the LCM of 6 and 9.

List some of the multiples of each number.
6: 6, 12, 18, 24, ...
9: 9, 18, 27, ...

The least common multiple is 18.

Practice

Write the factors of each number.

---

1. 13   **2.** 26

3. 40   **4.** 23

Find the LCM of the two numbers.

---

5. 6 and 8   **6.** 5 and 12

7. 7 and 35   **8.** 4 and 14

Find the GCF of the two numbers.

---

9. 24 and 30   **10.** 15 and 40

11. 32 and 64   **12.** 56 and 84

Answers on page 175

RATIO AND PROPORTION

RATIO

A ratio is a way of comparing two numbers with division. It conveys the same meaning as a fraction. There are three ways to write a ratio.

Using words 3 to 4   As a fraction $\frac{3}{4}$ Using a colon 3:4

PROPORTION

A proportion shows two ratios that have the same value; that is, the fractions representing the ratios are equivalent. Use cross multiplication. If the cross products are equal, then the two ratios form a proportion.

$\frac{3}{8}$ and $\frac{27}{72}$ form a proportion. The cross products are equal. ($3 \times 72 = 8 \times 27$)

$\frac{3}{8}$ and $\frac{24}{56}$ do not form a proportion. The cross products are not equal.

Writing a Proportion: You may have to write a proportion to solve a problem. For example, the mason mixes cement and sand using a ratio of 2:5. Twelve bags of cement will be used. How much sand is needed? To solve, use the numerator to stand for cement. The denominator will stand for sand.

$$\frac{2}{5} = \frac{12}{S}$$

$$2 \times S = 5 \times 12$$
$$2S = 60$$
$$S = 30$$

Cross multiply to solve.

Thirty bags of sand are needed.

Completed Example

The problem compares loaves of whole wheat bread with loaves of rye bread. Let the numerators stand for loaves of whole wheat bread. The denominators stand for loaves of rye bread.

Ratio of whole wheat to rye. $-\frac{3}{7}$ Ratio of whole wheat to rye for $\frac{51}{R}$
51 loaves of whole wheat.

Write a proportion. $-\frac{3}{7} = \frac{51}{R}$

Solution: $3R = 357$ $R = 119$

There are 119 loaves of bread.

Practice

1. A salesperson sells 7 vacuum cleaners for every 140 potential buyers. If there are 280 potential buyers, how many vacuums are sold?

2. There is one teacher for every 8 preschool students. How many teachers are needed if there are 32 preschool students?

3. There are 3 rest stops for every 20 miles of highway. How many rest stops would there be on 140 miles of highway?

4. Does $\frac{7}{9}$ and $\frac{28}{36}$ form a proportion? Explain.

Answers on page 176

PERCENT

Percent comes from *per centum*, which means per hundred. Whenever you see a number followed by a percent sign it means that number out of 100.

DECIMALS AND PERCENTS

To write a decimal as a percent, move the decimal point two places to the right and write the percent sign.

$$0.34 = 34\% \qquad 0.297 = 29.7\% \qquad 0.6 = 60\% \qquad 0.001 = 0.1\%$$

To write a percent as a decimal, move the decimal point two places to the left and delete the percent sign.

$$51\% = 0.51 \qquad 34.18\% = 0.3418 \qquad 0.9\% = 0.009$$

FRACTIONS AND PERCENTS

Writing Fractions as Percents

- Divide the numerator by the denominator. Write the answer as a percent.

  Write $\dfrac{3}{5}$ as a percent.   Write $\dfrac{5}{8}$ as a percent.

  $$\begin{array}{r} 0.6 \\ 5\overline{)3.0} \end{array} \quad 0.6 = 60\% \qquad\qquad \begin{array}{r} 0.625 \\ 8\overline{)5.00} \end{array} \quad 0.625 = 62.5\%$$

- Write an equivalent fraction with 100 in the denominator. Write the numerator followed by a percent sign.

  Write $\dfrac{13}{25}$ as a percent.

  $$\frac{13}{25} = \frac{52}{100} = 52\%$$

- Use these equivalencies.

  $$\frac{1}{4} = 25\% \qquad \frac{1}{2} = 50\% \qquad \frac{3}{4} = 75\% \qquad \frac{4}{4} = 100\%$$

  $$\frac{1}{5} = 20\% \qquad \frac{2}{5} = 40\% \qquad \frac{3}{5} = 60\% \qquad \frac{4}{5} = 80\%$$

  $$\frac{1}{6} = 16\tfrac{2}{3}\% \qquad \frac{1}{3} = 33\tfrac{1}{3}\% \qquad \frac{2}{3} = 66\tfrac{2}{3}\% \qquad \frac{5}{6} = 83\tfrac{1}{3}\%$$

  $$\frac{1}{8} = 12\tfrac{1}{2}\% \qquad \frac{3}{8} = 37\tfrac{1}{2}\% \qquad \frac{5}{8} = 62\tfrac{1}{2}\% \qquad \frac{7}{8} = 87\tfrac{1}{2}\%$$

Writing Percents as Fractions

Write a fraction with 100 in the denominator and the percent in the numerator. Simplify.

$$18\% = \frac{18}{100} = \frac{9}{50} \qquad 7.5\% = \frac{7.5}{100} = \frac{75}{1000} = \frac{3}{40}$$

Completed Examples

A. Write 0.567 as a percent.

Move the decimal two places to the right and write a percent sign, therefore, 0.567 = 56.7%.

B. Write $\frac{1}{4}$ as a percent.

Write $\frac{1}{4}$ as a decimal $(1 \div 4) = 0.25$

Write 0.25 as a decimal 0.25 = 25%

C. Write 26% as a fraction.

Place the percent number in the numerator and 100 in the denominator.

$$26\% = \frac{26}{100} = \frac{13}{50}.$$

Simplify: $\frac{26}{100} = \frac{13}{50}$

Practice

Write the decimal as a percent.

1. 0.359

2. 0.78

3. 0.215

4. 0.041

Write the fraction as a percent.

5. $\frac{1}{9}$

6. $\frac{5}{8}$

7. $\frac{3}{10}$

8. $\frac{4}{9}$

Write the percents as fractions in simplest form.

9. 58%

10. 79%

11. 85.2%

12. 97.4%

Answers on page 176

THREE TYPES OF PERCENT PROBLEMS

FINDING A PERCENT OF A NUMBER

To find a percent of a number, write a number sentence with a decimal for the percent and solve.

$$\text{Find 40\% of 90.}$$
$$0.4 \times 90 = 36$$

It may be easier to write a fraction for the percent.

$$\text{Find } 62\frac{1}{2}\% \text{ of 64.}$$

$$\frac{5}{8} \times 64 = 5 \times 8 = 40$$

FINDING WHAT PERCENT ONE NUMBER IS OF ANOTHER

To find what percent one number is of another, write a number sentence and solve to find the percent.

$$\text{What percent of 5 is 3?}$$
$$n \times 5 = 3$$

$$n = \frac{3}{5} = 0.6 = 60\%$$

FINDING A NUMBER WHEN A PERCENT OF IT IS KNOWN

To find a number when a percent of it is known, write a number sentence with a decimal or a fraction for the percent and solve to find the number.

$$\text{5\% of what number is 2?}$$

$$0.05 \times n = 2$$

$$n = 2 \div 0.05$$

$$n = 40$$

Completed Examples

A. What percent of 70 is 28?

$$\square \times 70 = 28$$

$$\square = \frac{28}{70} = \frac{4}{10}$$

$$\square = 40\%$$

B. 30% of 60 is what number?

$$30\% \times 60 = \square$$

$$0.3 \times 60 = \square$$

$$\square = 18$$

C. 40% of what number is 16?

$$0.40 \times \square = 16$$

$$\square = \frac{16}{0.4}$$

$$\square = 40$$

Practice

1. 120 is what percent of 240?

2. 15% of 70 is what number?

3. 60% of 300 is what number?

4. What percent of 60 is 42?

5. What percent of 25 is 2.5?

6. 40% of what number is 22?

7. 70% of what number is 85?

8. 25% of 38 is what number?

9. 35% of what number is 24?

10. 24 is what percent of 80?

Answers on page 176

PERCENT OF INCREASE AND DECREASE

PERCENT OF INCREASE

A price increases from $50 to $65. What is the percent of increase?

Subtract to find the amount of increase.

$65 − $50 = $15
$15 is the amount of increase

Write a fraction. The amount of increase is the numerator. The original amount is the denominator.

$\dfrac{\$15}{\$50}$ Amount of increase
       Original amount

Write the fraction as a percent.
The percent of increase is 30%.

$$50\overline{)15.00}^{\;0.3} \qquad 0.3 = 30\%$$

PERCENT OF DECREASE

A price decreases from $35 to $28. What is the percent of decrease?

Subtract to find the amount of decrease.

$35 − $28 = $7
$7 is the amount of decrease

Write a fraction. The amount of decrease is the numerator. The original amount is the denominator.

$\dfrac{\$7}{\$35}$ Amount of decrease
     Original amount

Write the fraction as a percent.
The percent of decrease is 20%.

$$\frac{7}{35} = \frac{1}{5} = 20\%$$

Completed Examples

A. The price increased from $30 to $36. What is the percent increase?
$36 − $30 = $6
$$\frac{6}{30} = \frac{1}{5} = 20\%$$

B. An $80 item goes on sale for 25% off. What is the sale price?
$80 × 25% = $80 × 0.25 = $20
$80 − $20 = $60. $60 is the sale price.

Practice

1. The price increased from $25 to $35. What is the percent of increase?

2. A sale marks down a $100 item 25%. What is the sale price?

3. The price decreases from $80 by 15%. What is the new price?

4. The price increased from $120 to $150. What is the percent of increase?

5. A sale marks down a $75 item 10%. What is the sale price?

6. The price decreases from $18 to $6. What is the percent of decrease?

7. A sale marks down a $225 item to $180. What is the percent of decrease?

8. A sale price of $150 was 25% off the original price. What was the original price?

Answers on page 176

PROBABILITY

The probability of an occurrence is the likelihood that it will happen. Most often, we write probability as a fraction.

Flip a fair coin and the probability that it will come up heads is $\frac{1}{2}$. The same is true for tails. Write the probability this way.

$$P\,(H) = \frac{1}{2} \qquad P\,(T) = \frac{1}{2}$$

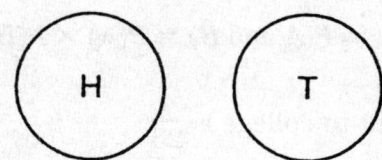

If something will never occur the probability is 0. If something will always occur, the probability is 1. Therefore, if you flip a fair coin,

$$P\,(7) = 0 \qquad P\,(H \text{ or } T) = 1$$

Write the letters A, B, C, D, and E on pieces of paper. Pick them randomly without looking. The probability of picking any letter is $\frac{1}{5}$.

$$\boxed{A} \quad \boxed{B} \quad \boxed{C} \quad \boxed{D} \quad \boxed{E}$$

$$P\,(\text{vowel}) = \frac{2}{5} \qquad P\,(\text{consonant}) = \frac{3}{5}$$

RULES FOR COMPUTING PROBABILITY

$$P(A \text{ or } B) = P(A) + P(B) = \frac{1}{5} + \frac{1}{5} = \frac{2}{5}$$

when A and B have no common elements

$$P(A \text{ and } B) = P(A) \times P(B) = \frac{1}{5} \times \frac{1}{5} = \frac{1}{25}$$

$$P(\text{not } C) = 1 - P(C) = 1 - \frac{1}{5} = \frac{4}{5}$$

Completed Example

In one high school, 40% of the students go on to college. Two graduates of the high school are chosen at random. What is the probability that they both went to college?

Write the probabilities you know.

$$P(\text{college}) = \frac{40}{100} = \frac{2}{5}$$

Solve the problem.

$P(A \text{ and } B)$ probability the two students went to college.

$$P(A \text{ and } B) = P(A) \times P(B) = \frac{2}{5} \times \frac{2}{5} = \frac{4}{25}$$

The probability that they both went to college is $\frac{4}{25}$.

Practice

1. There are 3 black, 2 white, 2 gray, and 3 blue socks in a drawer. What is the probability of drawing a sock that is not black?

2. Six goldfish are in a tank; 4 are female and 2 are male. What is the probability of scooping out a male?

3. A standard deck of 52 playing cards is spread facedown on a table. What is the probability of choosing a card that is a king or a queen?

4. Six names are written on pieces of paper. The names are Aaron, Ben, Carl, Edith, Elizabeth, and Phyllis. One name is picked and replaced. Then another name is picked. What is the probability that the names were Carl and Phyllis?

5. A fair die having six sides is rolled. What is the probability that the side facing up is a prime number?

6. A fair coin is tossed in the air 5 times. What is the probability of getting five tails?

Answers on page 177

STATISTICS

Descriptive statistics are used to explain or describe a set of numbers. Most often we use the mean, median, or mode to describe these numbers.

MEAN (AVERAGE)

The mean is a position midway between two extremes. To find the mean:

1. Add the items or scores.
2. Divide by the number of items.

For example, find the mean of 23, 17, 42, 51, 36.

$$23 + 17 + 42 + 51 + 36 = 170 \quad 170 \div 5 = 34$$

The mean or average is 34.

MEDIAN

The median is the middle number. To find the median:

1. Arrange the numbers from least to greatest.
2. If there are an odd number of scores, then find the middle score.
3. If there is an even number of scores, average the two middle scores.

For example, find the median of these numbers.

6, 9, 11, 17, 21, 33, 45, 71

There are an even number of scores.

$$17 + 21 = 38 \quad 38 \div 2 = 19$$

The median is 19.

Don't forget to arrange the scores in order before finding the middle score!

MODE

The mode is the number that occurs most often. For example, find the mode of these numbers.

6, 3, 7, 6, 9, 3, 6, 1, 2, 6, 7, 3

The number 6 occurs most often, so 6 is the mode.

Not all sets of numbers have a mode. Some sets of numbers may have more than one mode.

Completed Example

What is the mean, median, and mode of 7, 13, 18, 4, 14, 22?

Mean	Add the scores and divide by the number of scores.	
	$7 + 13 + 18 + 4 + 14 + 22 = 78 \div 6 = 13$	The mean is 13.
Median	Arrange the scores in order. Find the middle score.	
	4, 7, 13, 14, 18, 22 $13 + 14 = 27 \div 2 = 13.5$	The median is 13.5.
Mode	Find the score that occurs most often.	
	Each score occurs only once.	There is no mode.

Practice

1. A group of fourth graders received the following scores on a science test.

   80, 87, 94, 100, 75, 80, 98, 85, 80, 95, 92

   Which score represents the mode?

2. What is the mean of the following set of data?

   44, 13, 84, 42, 12, 18

3. What is the median of the following set of data?

   8, 9, 10, 10, 8, 10, 7, 6, 9

4. What measure of central tendency does the number 16 represent in the following data?

   14, 15, 17, 16, 19, 20, 16, 14, 16

5. What is the mean of the following set of scores?

   100, 98, 95, 70, 85, 90, 94, 78, 80, 100

6. What is the mode of the following data?

   25, 30, 25, 15, 40, 45, 30, 20, 30

Answers on page 177

PERMUTATIONS, COMBINATIONS, AND THE FUNDAMENTAL COUNTING PRINCIPLE

PERMUTATIONS

A permutation is the way a set of things can be arranged in order. There are 6 permutations of the letters A, B, and C.

ABC   **ACB**   **BAC**   **BCA**   **CAB**   **CBA**

Permutation Formula

The formula for the number of permutations of n things is **n! (n factorial)**.

$$6! = 6 \times 5 \times 4 \times 3 \times 2 \times 1 \qquad 4! = 4 \times 3 \times 2 \times 1 \qquad 2! = 2 \times 1$$

There are 120 permutations of 5 things.

$$n! = 5! = 5 \times 4 \times 3 \times 2 \times 1 = 120$$

COMBINATIONS

A combination is the number of ways of choosing a given number of elements from a set. The order of the elements does not matter. There are 3 ways of choosing 2 letters from the letters A, B, and C.

AB AC BC

FUNDAMENTAL COUNTING PRINCIPLE

The fundamental counting principle is used to find the total number of possibilities. Multiply the number of possibilities from each category.

Completed Example

An ice cream stand has a sundae with choices of 28 flavors of ice cream, 8 types of syrups, and 5 types of toppings. How many different sundae combinations are available?

28	$\times$	8	$\times$	5	$=$	1,120
flavors		syrups		toppings		sundaes

There are 1,120 possible sundaes.

Practice

1. There are 2 chairs left in the auditorium, but 4 people are without seats. In how many ways could 2 people be chosen to sit in the chairs?

2. The books *Little Women, Crime & Punishment, Trinity, The Great Santini, Pygmalion, The Scarlet Letter*, and *War and Peace* are on a shelf. In how many different ways can they be arranged?

3. A license plate consists of 2 letters and 2 digits. How many different license plates can be formed?

4. There are four students on line for the bus, but there is only room for three students on this bus. How many different ways can 3 of the 4 students get on the bus?

Answer on page 177

INTEGERS

The number line can also show negative numbers. There is a negative whole number for every positive whole number. Zero is neither positive nor negative. The negative whole numbers, the positive whole numbers, and zero, together, are called integers.

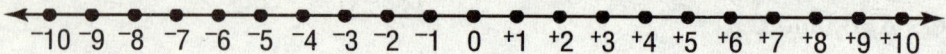

$$^-10 \ ^-9 \ ^-8 \ ^-7 \ ^-6 \ ^-5 \ ^-4 \ ^-3 \ ^-2 \ ^-1 \ 0 \ ^+1 \ ^+2 \ ^+3 \ ^+4 \ ^+5 \ ^+6 \ ^+7 \ ^+8 \ ^+9 \ ^+10$$

ADD AND SUBTRACT INTEGERS

Add

When the signs are the same, keep the sign and add.

$$
\begin{array}{r}
^+7 \\
+ \ ^+8 \\
\hline
^+15
\end{array}
\qquad
\begin{array}{r}
^-3 \\
+ \ ^-11 \\
\hline
^-14
\end{array}
$$

When the signs are different, disregard the signs, subtract the numbers, and keep the sign of the larger number.

$$
\begin{array}{r}
^+28 \\
+ \ ^-49 \\
\hline
^-21
\end{array}
\qquad
\begin{array}{r}
^-86 \\
+ \ ^+135 \\
\hline
^+49
\end{array}
$$

Subtract

Change the sign of the number being subtracted. Then add using the preceding rules.

$$
\begin{array}{r}
^+13 \\
- \ ^-18 \\
\Downarrow
\end{array}
\qquad
\begin{array}{r}
^-43 \\
- \ ^-17 \\
\Downarrow
\end{array}
\qquad
\begin{array}{r}
^+29 \\
- \ ^-49 \\
\Downarrow
\end{array}
\qquad
\begin{array}{r}
^-92 \\
- \ ^+135 \\
\Downarrow
\end{array}
$$

$$
\begin{array}{r}
^+13 \\
+ \ ^+18 \\
\hline
31
\end{array}
\qquad
\begin{array}{r}
^-43 \\
+ \ ^+17 \\
\hline
^-26
\end{array}
\qquad
\begin{array}{r}
^+29 \\
+ \ ^+49 \\
\hline
^+78
\end{array}
\qquad
\begin{array}{r}
^-92 \\
+ \ ^-135 \\
\hline
^-227
\end{array}
$$

MULTIPLY AND DIVIDE INTEGERS

Multiply

Multiply as you would whole numbers. The product is *positive* if there are an even number of negative factors. The product is *negative* if there are an odd number of negative factors.

$$^-2 \times \ ^+14 \times \ ^-6 \times \ ^+3 = \ ^+144 \qquad ^-2 \times \ ^-4 \times \ ^+6 \times \ ^-3 = \ ^-144$$

Divide

Forget the signs and divide. The quotient is *positive* if both integers have the same sign. The quotient is *negative* if the integers have different signs.

$$^+24 \div \ ^+4 = \ ^+6 \qquad ^-24 \div \ ^-4 = \ ^+6 \qquad ^+24 \div \ ^-4 = \ ^-6 \qquad ^-24 \div \ ^+4 = \ ^-6$$

Practice

1. $6 + 9 =$

2. $18 + {}^-17 =$

3. ${}^-24 + {}^-45 =$

4. ${}^-38 + 29 =$

5. $7 - 6 =$

6. $15 - {}^-39 =$

7. ${}^-36 - {}^-58 =$

8. ${}^-27 - 53 =$

9. $9 \times 11 =$

10. $26 \times {}^-25 =$

11. ${}^-31 \times {}^-59 =$

12. ${}^-42 \times 35 =$

13. $120 \div 8 =$

14. $68 \div {}^-4 =$

15. ${}^-352 \div {}^-8 =$

16. ${}^-66 \div 3 =$

Answers on page 177

SCIENTIFIC NOTATION

Scientific notation uses powers of 10. The power shows how many zeros to use.

$$10^0 = 1 \quad 10^1 = 10 \quad 10^2 = 100 \quad 10^3 = 1{,}000 \quad 10^4 = 10{,}000 \quad 10^5 = 100{,}000$$
$$10^{-1} = 0.1 \quad 10^{-2} = 0.01 \quad 10^{-3} = 0.001 \quad 10^{-4} = 0.0001 \quad 10^{-5} = 0.00001$$

Write whole numbers and decimals in scientific notation. Use a decimal with one numeral to the left of the decimal point.

2,345	=	2.345×10^3	The decimal point moved three places to the left. Use 10^3.
176.8	=	1.768×10^2	The decimal point moved two places to the left. Use 10^2.
0.0034	=	3.4×10^{-3}	The decimal point moved three places to the right. Use 10^{-3}.
2.0735	=	2.0735×10^0	The decimal is in the correct form. Use 10^0 to stand for 1.

Completed Examples

A. Write 7,952 in scientific notation.

Move the decimal point three places to the left and write $7{,}952 = 7.952 \times 10^3$.

B. Write 0.03254 in scientific notation.

Move the decimal point two places to the right and write 3.254×10^{-2}.

Practice

Rewrite using scientific notation.

1. 0.0564

2. 0.00897

3. 0.06501

4. 0.000354

5. 545

6. 7,790

7. 289,705

8. 1,801,319

Answers on page 177

EQUATIONS

The whole idea of solving equations is to isolate the variable on one side of the equal sign. The value of the variable is what's on the other side of the equal sign. Substitute your answer in the original equation to check your solution.

SOLVING EQUATIONS BY ADDING OR SUBTRACTING

Solve: $y + 19 = 23$

Subtract 19 $\qquad y + 19 - 19 = 23 - 19$

$$y = 4$$

Check: Does $4 + 19 = 23$? Yes. It checks.

Solve: $x - 23 = 51$

Add 23 $\qquad x - 23 + 23 = 51 + 23$

$$x = 74$$

Check: Does $74 - 23 = 51$? Yes. It checks.

SOLVING EQUATIONS BY MULTIPLYING OR DIVIDING

Solve: $\frac{z}{7} = 6$

Multiply by 7 $\qquad \frac{z}{7} \times 7 = 6 \times 7$

$$z = 42$$

Check: Does $\frac{42}{7} = 6$? Yes. It checks.

Solve: $21 = -3x$

Divide by -3 $\qquad \frac{21}{-3} = \frac{-3x}{-3}$

$$-7 = x$$

Check: Does $21 = (-3)(-7)$? Yes. It checks.

SOLVING TWO-STEP EQUATIONS

Add or subtract before you multiply or divide.

Solve: $3x - 6 = 24$

$$3x - 6 + 6 = 24 + 6$$
$$3x = 30$$

Divide by 3 $\qquad \frac{3x}{3} = \frac{30}{3}$

$$x = 10$$

Check: Does $3 \times 10 - 6 = 24$? Yes. Its checks.

Solve: $\dfrac{y}{7} + 4 = 32$

Subtract 4 $\qquad\qquad \dfrac{y}{7} + 4 - 4 = 32 - 4$

$$\dfrac{y}{7} = 28$$

Multiply by 7 $\qquad\qquad \dfrac{y}{7} \times 7 = (28)(7)$

$$y = 196$$

Check: Does $\dfrac{196}{7} + 4 = 32$? Yes. It checks.

Check: Does $28 + 4 = 32$? Yes. It checks.

Practice

Solve.
---

1. $w - 3 = 5$

2. $x + 9 = 24$

3. $y - 10 = 60$

4. $z + 50 = 46$

5. $3w = 12$

6. $\dfrac{x}{18} = 7$

7. $^{-}9y = 45$

8. $\dfrac{z}{6} = {}^{-}11$

9. $5w + 6 = 41$

10. $^{-}3 - 2x = 23$

11. $\dfrac{y}{19} + 11 = 35$

12. $26z - 13 = 65$

Answers on page 177

GEOMETRY

We can think of geometry in two or three dimensions. A two-dimensional model is this page. A three-dimensional model is the room you'll take the test in.

Definition	Model	Symbol
Point—a location	· A	A
Plane—a flat surface that extends infinitely in all directions		plane ABC
Space—occupies three dimensions and extends infinitely in all directions		space xyz
Line—a set of points in a straight path that extends infinitely in two directions		$\overleftrightarrow{AB}$
Line segment—part of a line with two endpoints		$\overline{AB}$
Ray—part of a line with one endpoint		$\overrightarrow{AB}$
Parallel lines—lines that stay the same distance apart and never touch		
Perpendicular lines—lines that meet at right angles		
Angle—two rays with a common endpoint, which is called the vertex.		∠ABC
Acute angle—angle that measures between 0° and 90°		
Right angle—angle that measures 90°		
Obtuse angle—angle that measures between 90° and 180°		

Complementary angles—angles that have a total measure of 90°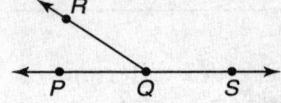

Supplementary angles—angles that have a total measure of 180°

Polygon—a closed figure made up of line segments; if all sides are the same length, the figure is a regular polygon

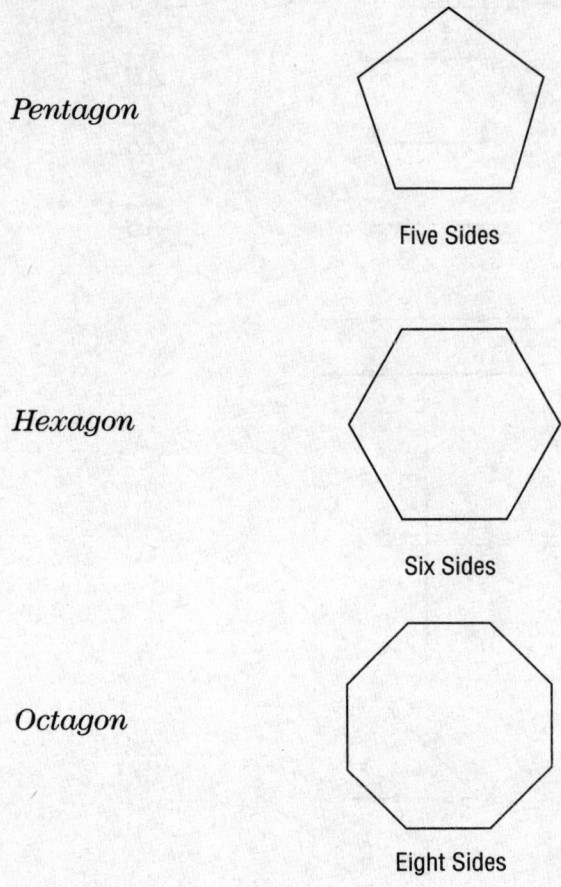

Pentagon

Five Sides

Hexagon

Six Sides

Octagon

Eight Sides

Triangle—polygon with three sides and three angles; the sum of the angles is always 180°

Equilateral triangle—all the sides are the same length; all the angles are the same size, 60°

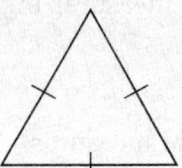

Isosceles triangle—two sides the same length; two angles the same size

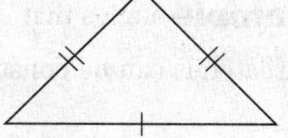

Scalene triangle—all sides different lengths; all angles different sizes

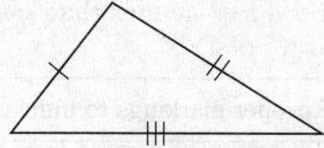

Quadrilateral—polygon with four sides

Square

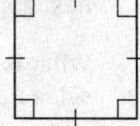

Rhombus

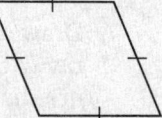

Rectangle

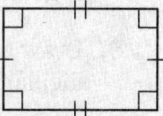

Parallelogram

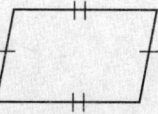

Trapezoid

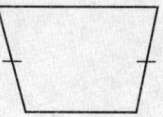

Completed Example

Which types of quadrilaterals can be constructed using four congruent line segments *AB*, *BC*, *CD*, and *DA*?

You can create a square and a rhombus.

Practice

> Be certain to use proper markings to indicate congruent segments and congruent angles.

1. What is the name of a quadrilateral that has exactly one pair of parallel sides?

2. Use the figure below. The m∠1 = 45°. What is m∠2?

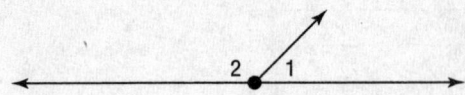

3. In the triangle below, *AB* = *AC* and m∠*BAC* = 80°.

What are the measures of ∠*ABC* and ∠*ACB*?

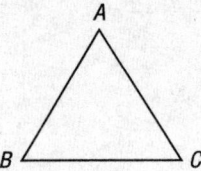

4. Draw a diagram of an equilateral triangle.

5. Which has more sides, an octagon or a hexagon?

What is the difference in the number of sides for these figures?

6. What type of angle with a measure less than 180° is neither obtuse nor acute?

7. Draw a diagram in which ray (*AB*) intersects ray (*AC*) at point *A*, and name the new figure that is formed.

8. Draw a diagram of line *AB* intersecting line segment *CD* at point *E*.

9. Draw a diagram of two parallel lines perpendicular to a third line.

10. Given a triangle *ABC*, describe the relationship among the measures of the three angles.

Answers on page 178

COORDINATE GRID

You can plot ordered pairs of numbers on a coordinate grid.

The *x*-axis goes horizontally from left to right. The first number in the pair tells how far to move left or right from the origin. A minus sign means move left. A plus sign means move right.

The *y*-axis goes vertically up and down. The second number in the pair tells how far to move up or down from the origin. A minus sign means move down. A plus sign means move up.

Pairs of numbers show the *x*-coordinate first and the *y*-coordinate second (*x*, *y*). The origin is point (0, 0) where the *x*-axis and the *y*-axis meet.

Plot these pairs of numbers on the grid.

A (⁺3, ⁻7)   **B** (⁺5, ⁺3)   **C** (⁻6, ⁺2)   **D** (⁻3, ⁻6)

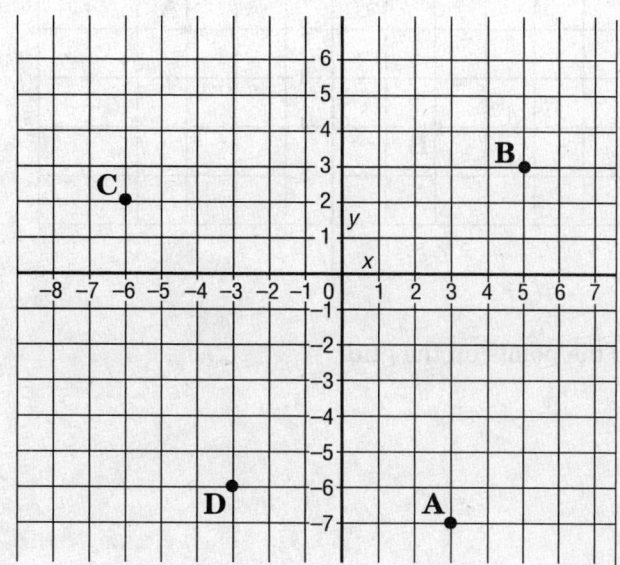

Practice

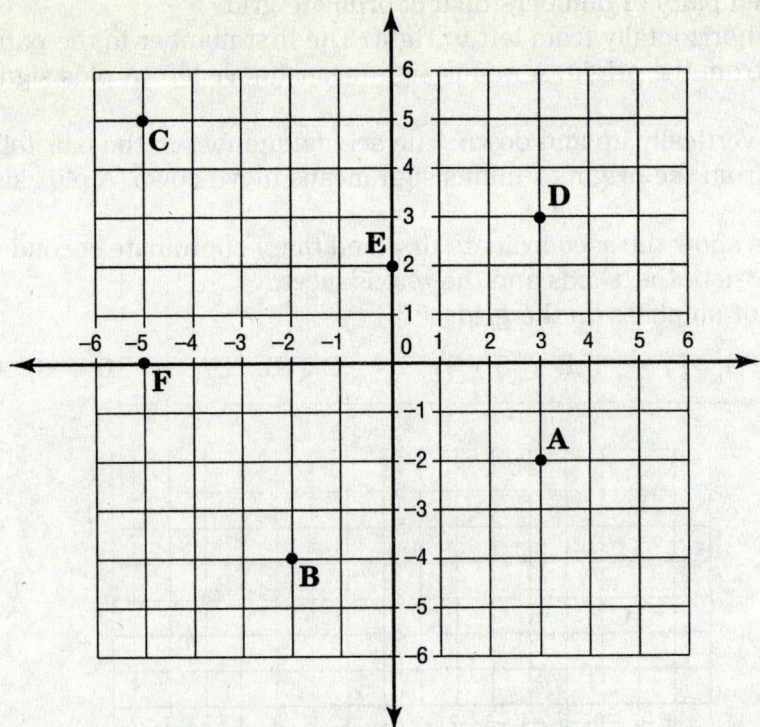

1. Write the coordinates of the points on the grid.

A _____

B _____

C _____

D _____

E _____

F _____

2. Plot these points on the grid below.

$G\,(3, -1)$ $H\,(2, -3)$ $I\,(5, 6)$ $J\,(-4, 0)$ $K\,(-5, -2)$ $L\,(-1, 6)$ $M\,(0, 3)$ $N\,(-5, 2)$

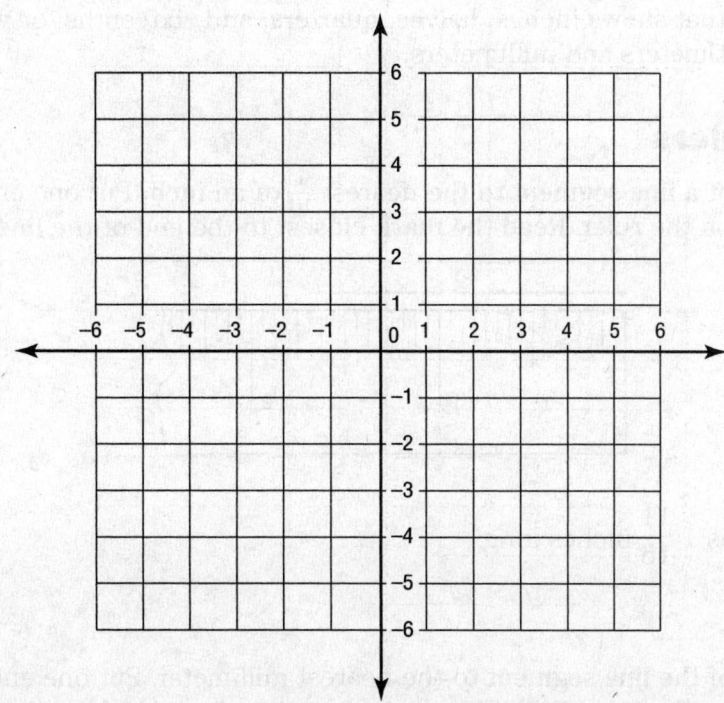

3. Plot these points on the grid below and connect them in the order shown.

$Z\,(-5, 5)$ $Y\,(-2, 0)$ $X\,(2, -6)$ $W\,(3, 5)$ $V\,(-6, -2)$ $U\,(2, 0)$ $T\,(6, 1)$ $S\,(-5, 5)$

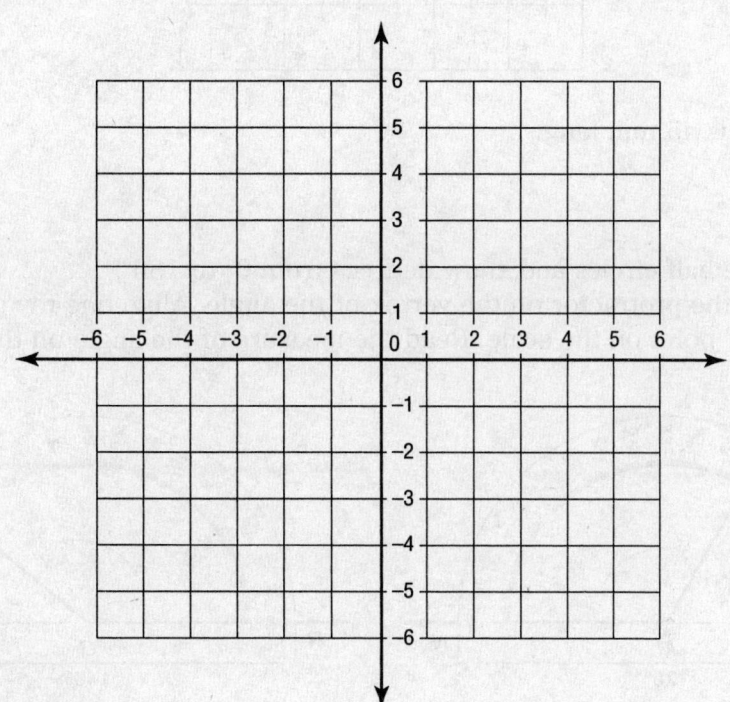

Answers on page 178

MEASUREMENT

MEASURING WITH A RULER AND A PROTRACTOR

You may use a ruler that shows inches, halves, quarters, and sixteenths, or you may use a ruler that shows centimeters and millimeters.

Customary Rulers

Measure the length of a line segment to the nearest $\frac{1}{16}$ of an inch. Put one end of the line segment at the 0 point on the ruler. Read the mark closest to the end of the line.

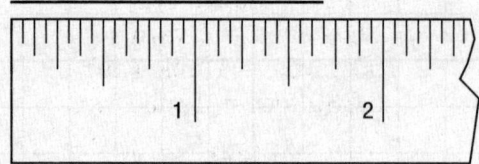

The line segment is $1 \frac{11}{16}$ inches long.

Metric Rulers

Measure the length of the line segment to the nearest millimeter. Put one end of the line segment at the 0 point on the ruler. Read the mark closest to the end of the line.

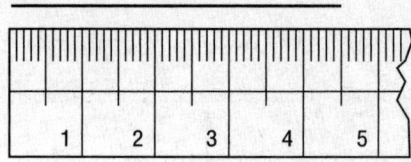

The line segment is 45 mm long.

Protractors

Most protractors are half circles and show degrees from 0° to 180°.

Put the center of the protractor on the vertex of the angle. Align one ray of the angle on the inner or outer 0° point on the scale. Read the measure of the angle on that scale.

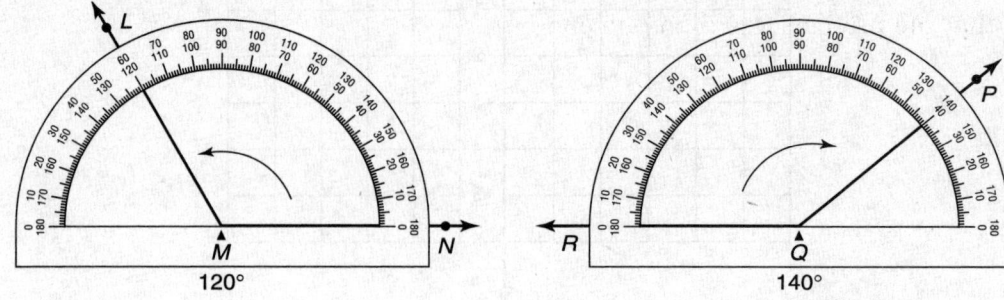

WEIGHT AND MASS

Mass is the amount of matter in a body. Weight is a measure of the force of gravity on a body. Mass is the same everywhere, but weight depends on its location in a gravitational field. That is, an object has the same mass whether on the moon or on earth. However, the object weighs less on the moon than on earth.

CUSTOMARY (ENGLISH) UNITS

Length

12 inches (in.) = 1 foot
3 feet = 1 yard (yd)
36 inches = 1 yard
1,760 yards = 1 mile (mi)
5,280 feet = 1 mile

Weight

16 ounces (oz) = 1 pound (lb)
2,000 pounds = 1 ton (T)

Capacity

2 cups = 1 pint (pt)
2 pints = 1 quart (qt)
4 quarts = 1 gallon (gal)

METRIC SYSTEM

The metric system uses common units of measure. The system uses prefixes that are powers of 10 or 0.1.

The common units used in the metric system follow:

Length—meter

Mass—gram

Capacity—liter

The prefixes used in the metric system follow:

1000	100	10	Unit	0.1	0.01	0.001
Kilo	Hecto	Deka		Deci	Centi	Milli

Notice that the prefixes less than one end in *i*.

References for commonly used metric measurements

Unit	Description
Length	
Meter	A little more than a yard
Centimeter (0.01 meter)	The width of a paper clip (About 2.5 per inch)
Millimeter (0.001 meter)	The thickness of the wire on a paper clip
Kilometer (1,000 meters)	About 0.6 of a mile
Mass	
Gram	The weight of a paper clip
Kilogram (1,000 grams)	About 2.2 pounds
Capacity	
Liter	A little more than a quart
Milliliter	The amount of water in a cubic centimeter

Completed Example

Use your protractor and a ruler to construct an angle measuring 45°.

First construct a ray *AB*. Next place the center of the protractor at point *A*. Find the 45° measure and place a mark there. Call it point *C*. Now use the straight edge of the protractor and create ray *AC*.

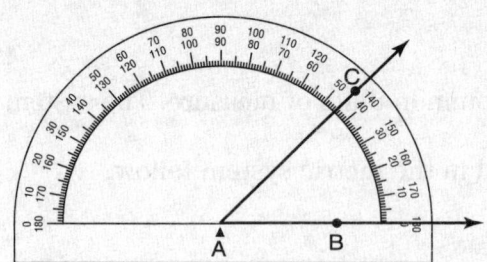

Practice

1. 220 centimeters is equal to how many decameters?

2. How many feet equal 5.5 miles?

3. What is the length of the segment below to the nearest $\frac{1}{4}$ of an inch?

•———————————————————•

4. How many pounds equal 8 ounces?

5. How many ounces equal 2 tons?

6. What is the length of the segment below to the nearest centimeter?

•————————————•

7. How many inches in 3 miles?

8. 2.367 hectoliters is how many milliliters?

9. How many quarts are in $\frac{1}{2}$ gallon?

10. What is the measure of $\angle ABC$ below?

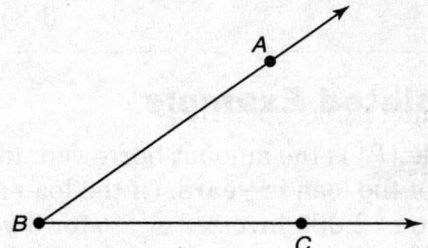

Answers on page 178

FORMULAS

EVALUATING AN EXPRESSION OR FORMULA

Evaluate an expression by replacing the variables with values. Remember to use the correct order of operations. For example, evaluate

$$3x - \frac{y}{z} \text{ for } x = 3, y = 8, \text{ and } z = 4$$

$$3(3) - \frac{8}{4} = 9 - 2 = 7$$

Completed Example

Principle (P) is the amount borrowed. Interest (I) is the simple interest rate. Time (T) is the length of the loan in **years**. (If the loan is for 6 months, $T = \frac{1}{2}$.) Find the simple interest earned on \$2,000 invested at 9% for 3 years.

$I = PRT$
$I = (2000)\,(0.09)\,(3)$
$I = 180 \times 3 \; I = 540$

The investment earns \$540 in interest.

DISTANCE AND AREA

Perimeter   The distance around a figure. The perimeter of a circle is called the circumference.

Area   The amount of space occupied by a two-dimensional figure.

FORMULAS FOR PERIMETER AND AREA

Figure	Formula	Description
Triangle	Area $= \frac{1}{2}bh$ Perimeter $= s_1 + s_2 + s_3$	
Square	Area $= s^2$ Perimeter $= 4s$	
Rectangle	Area $= lw$ Perimeter $= 2l + 2w$	
Parallelogram	Area $= bh$ Perimeter $= 2b + 2s$	

Trapezoid

$$\text{Area} = \frac{1}{2}h\,(b_1 + b_2)$$
$$\text{Perimeter} = b_1 + b_2 + s_1 + s_2$$

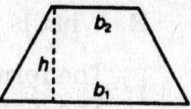

Circle

$$\text{Area} = \pi r^2$$
$$\text{Circumference} = 2\pi r \text{ or}$$
$$= \pi d$$

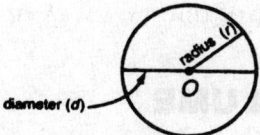

Pythagorean Theorem

The Pythagorean Theorem for right triangles states that the sum of the square of the legs equals the square of the hypotenuse.

$$a^2 + b^2 = c^2$$

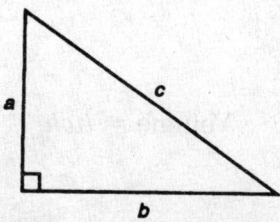

Other Polygons

Pentagon	5 sides	Octagon	8 sides
Hexagon	6 sides	Nonagon	9 sides
Heptagon	7 sides	Decagon	10 sides

Regular Polygon—All sides are the same length.

Completed Examples—Distance and Area

Let's solve the distance and area problems.

A. How many meters is it around a regular hexagon with a side of 87 centimeters?
A hexagon has 6 sides. It's a regular hexagon, so all the sides are the same length.
$6 \times 87 = 522$. The perimeter is 522 centimeters, which equals 5.22 meters.

B. What is the area of this figure?

The formula for the area of a circle is πr^2.
The diameter is 18, so the radius is 9. Use 3.14 for π.
$A = 3.14 \times (9)^2 = 3.14 \times 81 = 254.34$ or about 254.

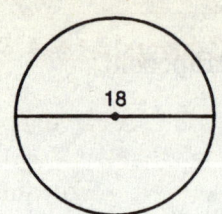

VOLUME

Volume—The amount of space occupied by a three-dimensional figure.

Formulas for Volume

Figure	Formula	Description
Cube	Volume $= s^3$	
Rectangular Prism	Volume $= lwh$	
Sphere	Volume $= \dfrac{4}{3}\pi r^3$	
Cone	Volume $= \dfrac{1}{3}\pi r^2 h$	
Cylinder	Volume $= \pi r^2 h$ Surface Area $= 2\pi r(h+r)$	

Completed Example—Volume

A circular cone has a radius of 8 cm and a height of 10 cm. What is the volume?

Formula for the volume of a cone = $\frac{1}{3} \pi r^2 h$.

$$V = \left(\frac{1}{3}\right)(3.14)(8^2)(10) = \left(\frac{1}{3}\right)(3.14)(64)(10) = \left(\frac{1}{3}\right)(3.14)(640) = 669.87$$

The volume of the cone is 669.87 cubic centimeters or about 670 cubic centimeters.

Practice

1. A circle has a radius of 9 meters. What is the area?

2. The faces of a pyramid are equilateral triangles. What is the surface area of the pyramid if the sides of the triangles equal 3 inches and the height is 2.6 inches?

3. A regular hexagon has one side 5 feet long. What is the distance around its edge?

4. What is the surface area of the side of a cylinder (not top and bottom) with a height of 10 cm and a diameter of 2.5 cm?

5. A rectangle has a width x and a length $(x + 5)$. If the perimeter is 90 feet, what is the length?

6. The perimeter of one face of a cube is 20 cm. What is the surface area?

7. What is the length of the third side in the right triangle below?

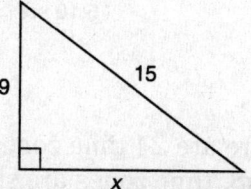

8. What is the area of a trapezoid whose height is 5 inches, the length of one base is 5 inches, and the length of the other base is 8 inches?

9. What is the volume of a sphere that has a diameter of length 20 cm?

10. What is the volume of a cube having a side length of 15 inches.

Answers on page 179

TIME AND TEMPERATURE

TIME

Each of the 24 hours in a day is partitioned into 60 minutes. Each minute is partitioned into 60 seconds. In the United States we use a 12-hour clock. The time between midnight and noon is called A.M., while the time between noon and midnight is called P.M. In other countries and in the scientific and military communities, a 24-hour clock is used. Both analog and digital clocks are used to keep track of time.

Digital 12-hour clock
5:15 P.M.

Analog 24-hour clock
1715 hours (5:15 P.M.)

There are 24 time zones in the world and four time zones in the continental United States. The U.S. time zones are shown in the following map. As you travel west, the sun rises later and the time gets earlier—10 A.M. in New York is 7 A.M. in Los Angeles.

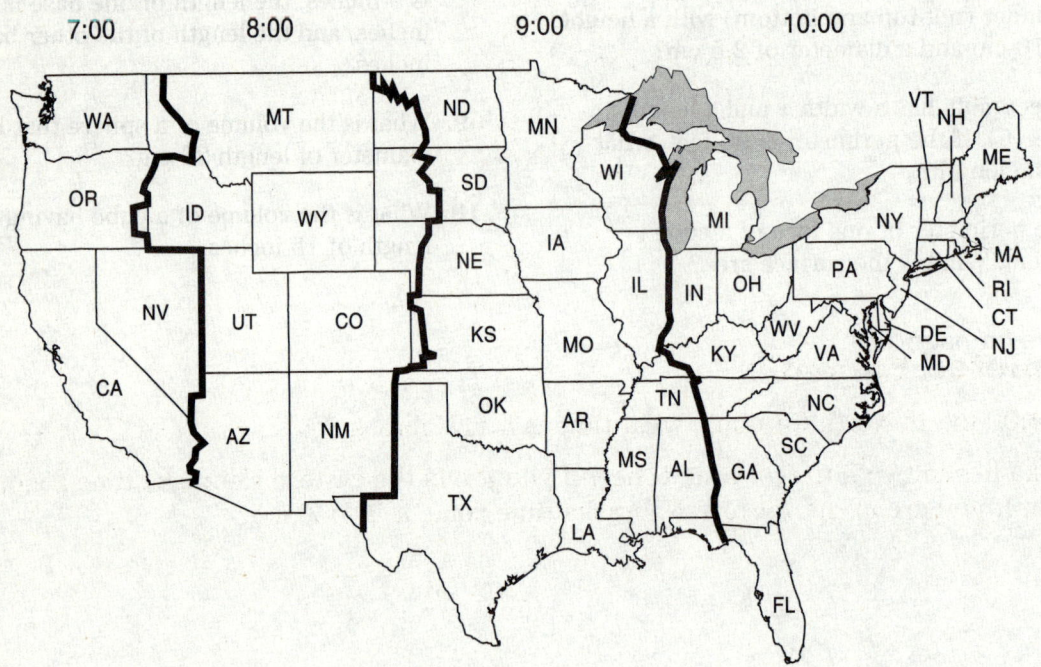

TEMPERATURE

Temperature is the degree of warmth or cold. We use Fahrenheit and Celsius thermometers to measure warmth. On a Fahrenheit thermometer water freezes at 32° and boils at 212°. A temperature of 98.6° Fahrenheit is normal body temperature and 90° Fahrenheit is a hot day. On the Celsius thermometer water freezes at 0° and boils at 100°. A temperature of 37° is normal body temperature and about 32° is a hot day.

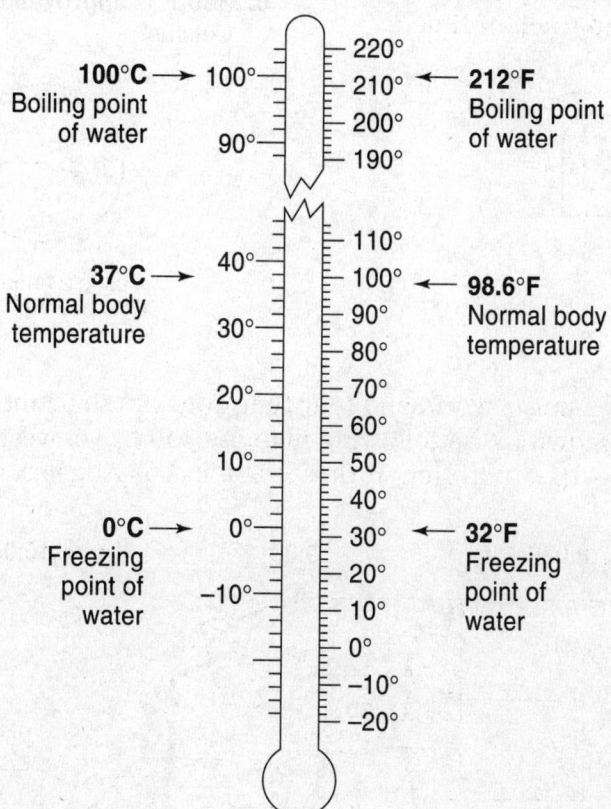

Completed Example

If it is 4:00 P.M. in North Carolina, what time is it in Nebraska?

Nebraska lies in two different time zones. If you are in the eastern Nebraska time zone, it is 3:00 P.M. If you are in the western Nebraska time zone, it is 2:00 P.M.

Practice

1. What is colder, 0°C or 0°F?

2. If it is 10:00 A.M. in Washington State, what time is it in Maine?

3. Draw a picture of an analog 24-hour clock displaying 6:30 P.M.

4. If it is 9:00 A.M. in Minnesota, what time is it in Georgia?

5. 10°C is approximately how many degrees Fahrenheit?

6. 220°F is approximately how many degrees Celsius?

Answers on page 179

GRAPHS

You will encounter four main types of graphs on the test.

THE PICTOGRAPH

The pictograph uses symbols to stand for numbers. In the following graph, each picture represents 1,000 phones.

Number of Phones in Five Towns

Find the number of phones in Emerson.

Count the number of phones on the pictograph for Emerson. There are $7\frac{1}{2}$. That means there are $7.5 \times 1,000 = 7,500$ phones in Emerson.

THE BAR GRAPH

The bar graph represents information by the length of a bar.

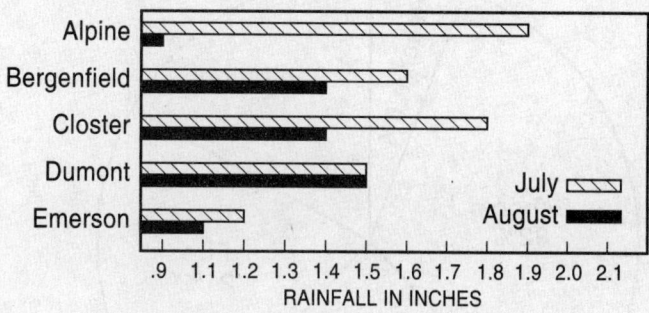

Rainfall in July and August for Five Towns

Find the August rainfall for Emerson and the July rainfall for Closter.

Follow the bar across and then read down to find that 1.1 inches of rain fell in Emerson during August.

Read down from the striped bar for Closter to find that 1.8 inches of rain fell in Closter during July.

THE LINE GRAPH

The line graph plots information against two axes.

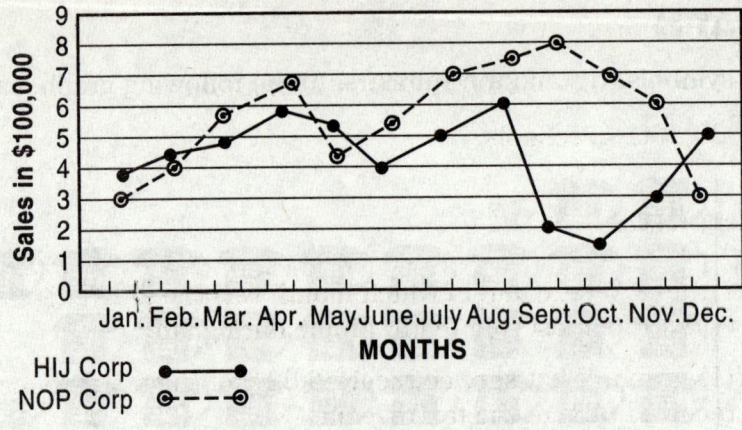

Sales for Two Companies During the Year

Find the June sales for HIJ Corp.

Read up from June and across from Sales to find that the HIJ Corp. had $400,000 in sales during June.

THE CIRCLE GRAPH

The circle represents an entire amount. Each wedge-shaped piece of the graph represents some percent of that whole.

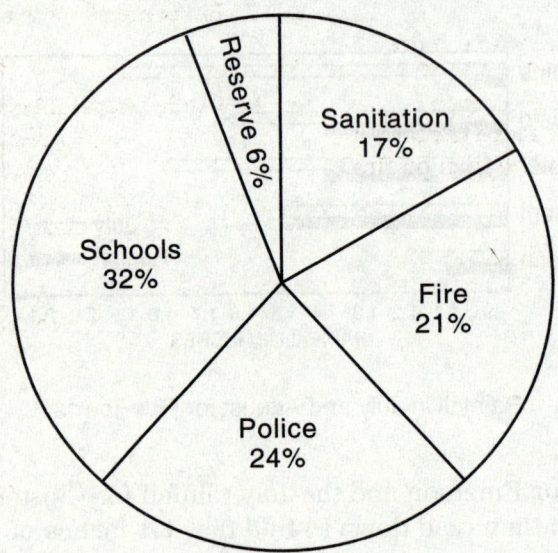

Percent of Tax Money Spent for Town Services

Multiply the percent and the entre budget amount to find the amount spent in a budget area.

For example, the town spends $4,000,000 on services. How much does the town spend on schools?

Multiply 32% and $4,000,000.

$$0.32 \times \$4,000,000 = \$1,280,000$$

The town spends $1,280,000 on schools.

Completed Examples

A. Use the bar graph. Where and in which month was the most monthly rainfall? The graph shows that the most rain fell in Alpine during July.

B. Use the circle graph. What service received 32% of the tax revenue? Education received 32% of the tax revenue.

Practice

Use the graphs shown earlier in this section to answer these practice items.

1. Pictograph How many more phones are there in Bergenfield than in Closter?

2. Bar Graph Which town has the greatest rainfall difference between July and August?

3. Line Graph Which company sold more items in May?

4. Circle Graph What percent more tax money is spent on police than on fire?

5. Pictograph Which town has the smallest number of phones?

6. Bar Graph Which town has the most consistent amount of rainfall between July and August?

7. Line Graph What were the sales for the NOP Corp. in September?

8. Circle Graph The town collects $1,400,000 in taxes. How much money will be placed in reserve?

Answers on page 179

STEM-AND-LEAF AND BOX-AND-WHISKER PLOTS

STEM-AND-LEAF PLOTS

Stem-and-leaf plots represent data in place value–oriented plots. Each piece of data is shown in the plot. The following stem-and-leaf plot shows test scores. The stem represents 10, and the leaves represent 1. You can read each score. In the 50s the scores are 55, 55, and 58. There are no scores in the 60s. You can find the lowest score, 40, and the highest score, 128.

Stem	Leaves
4	0, 7
5	5, 5, 8
6	
7	1, 4, 4, 6
8	2, 3, 4, 5
9	9, 9
10	
11	
12	3, 4, 8

Example: 7 | 4   means 74

BOX-AND-WHISKER PLOTS

Box-and-whisker plots show the range and quartiles of scores. The plot is a box divided into two parts with a whisker at each end. The ends of the left and right whiskers show the lowest and highest scores. Quartiles partition scores into quarters. The left and right parts of the box show the upper and lower quartiles; the dividing line shows the median.

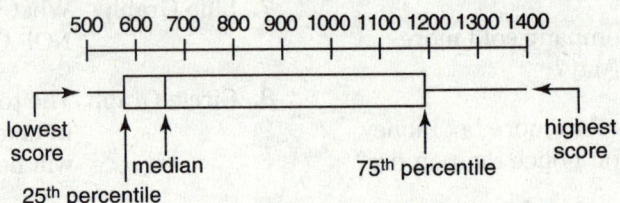

The median of these scores is about 660, while the highest score is about 1,390.

Completed Example

Use the stem-and-leaf plot above. How many people scored in the 100s on the test?

No one scored 100 on the test. Look at the stem and find 10, and see that there are no leaves attached to that stem.

Practice

1. Create a stem-and-leaf plot using the following test scores.

   15, 19, 94, 10, 56, 23, 106, 28, 36, 38, 42, 48, 45, 26, 42, 105, 55, 53, 76, 47, 77, 29, 79, 49, 92, 96, 17, 13, 101, 75, 33

   Check the answer before continuing.

Use the stem-and-leaf graph from exercise 1.

2. Which score is between 56 and 75?

3. What is the median of these test scores?

4. What is the mode of these test scores?

Answers on page 179

FLOW CHARTS

A flow chart shows the steps for completing a task.
The flow chart uses these special symbols.

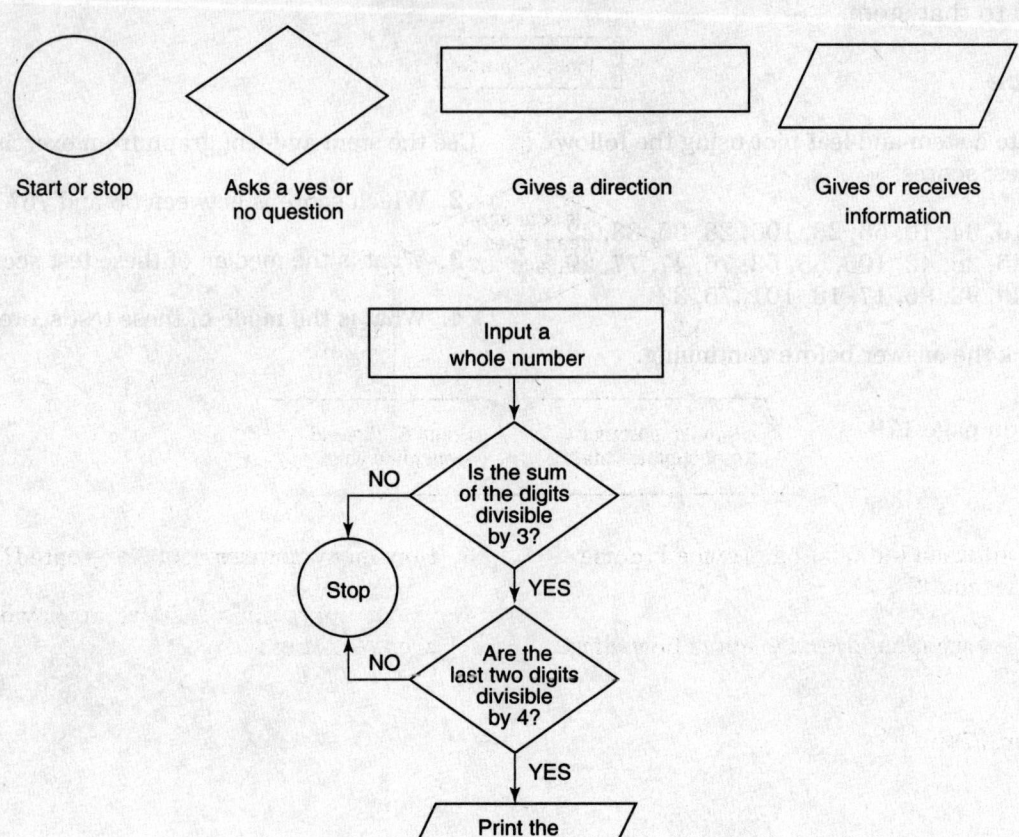

According to the steps in the flow chart, the number printed will always be any number that gets a yes answer from both decision boxes and is divisible by both 3 and 4. These numbers are divisible by 12.

Practice

Use the flowchart below for exercises 1–3.

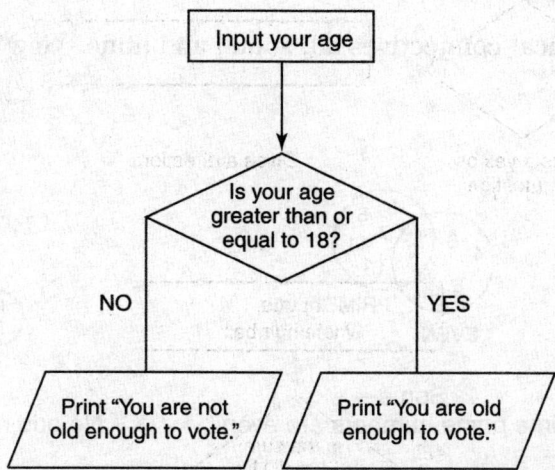

1. What information must be provided to use the flow chart?

2. What information does the above flow chart output?

Answers on 179

3. How many phrases could be printed?

4. Create a flow chart that will display only prime numbers.

LOGIC

USING DIAGRAMS

All, Some, and None

Diagrams can show the logical connectives all, some, and none. View the following diagrams for an explanation.

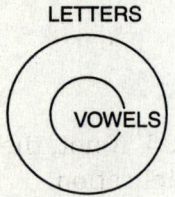

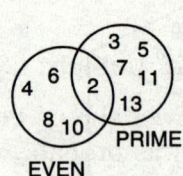

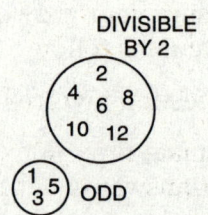

All—
All vowels are letters.

Some—
Some prime numbers are even.

None—
No odd numbers are divisible by two.

Deductive Reasoning

Deductive reasoning draws conclusions from statements or assumptions. Diagrams may help you draw a conclusion. Consider this simple example.

Assume that all even numbers are divisible by two and that all multiples of ten are even. Draw a diagram:

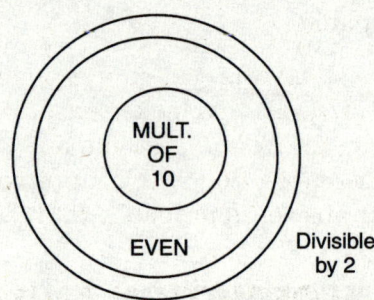

The multiple of ten circle is entirely within the divisible by two circle. Conclusion: All multiples of ten are divisible by two.

Practice

Write whether the statement is true or false. Explain your answer.

1. A ball is used in all sports.

2. Some numbers divisible by 5 are also divisible by 7.

3. There are no even numbers divisible by 3.

4. Some prime numbers are divisible by 2.

Answers on page 180

PROBLEM SOLVING

Use these problem-solving strategies.

ESTIMATE TO BE SURE YOUR ANSWER IS REASONABLE

You can use estimation and common sense to be sure that the answer is reasonable. You may make a multiplication error or misalign decimal points. You may be so engrossed in a problem that you miss the big picture because of the details. These difficulties can be headed off by making sure your answer is reasonable.

A few examples follow.

A question involves dividing or multiplying. Multiply: 28×72.

Estimate first: $30 \times 70 = 2,100$. Your answer should be close to 2,100. If not, then your answer is not reasonable. A mistake was probably made in multiplication.

A question involves subtracting or adding. Add: $12.9 + 0.63 + 10.29 + 4.3$.

Estimate first: $13 + 1 + 10 + 4 = 28$. Your answer should be close to 28. If not, then your answer is not reasonable. The decimal points may not have been aligned.

A question asks you to compare fractions to $\frac{11}{10}$.

Think: $\frac{11}{10}$ is more than 1. Any number 1 or less will be less than $\frac{11}{10}$. Any number $1\frac{1}{8}$ or larger will be more than $\frac{11}{10}$. You have to look closely only at numbers between 1 and $1\frac{1}{8}$.

A question asks you to multiply two fractions or decimals.

The fractions or decimals are less than 1. The product of two fractions or decimals less than one is less than either of the two fractions or decimals. If not, you know that your answer is not reasonable.

Stand back for a second after you answer each question and ask, "Is this reasonable? Is this at least approximately correct? Does this make sense?"

Check answers to computation, particularly division and subtraction. When you have completed a division or subtraction example, do a quick, approximate check. Your check should confirm your answer. If not, your answer is probably not reasonable.

CIRCLE IMPORTANT INFORMATION AND KEY WORDS
ELIMINATE EXTRA INFORMATION

This approach will draw your attention to the information needed to answer the question. A common mistake is to use from the question information that has nothing to do with the solution.

Example:

In the morning, a train travels at a constant speed over an 800 kilometer distance. In the afternoon the train travels back over this same route. There is less traffic and the train travels four times as fast as it did that morning. However, there are more people on the train during the afternoon. Which of the following do you know about the train's afternoon trip?

(A) The time is divided by four
(B) The time is multiplied by four
(C) The rate and time are divided by four
(D) The rate is divided by four
(E) The distance is the same, so the rate is the same

To solve the problem you just need to know that the speed is constant, four times as fast, and the same route was covered. Circle this information you need to solve the problem.

The distance traveled or that there were more people in the afternoon is extra information. Cross off this extra information, which may interfere with your ability to solve the problem.

> In the morning, a train travels at a ⟨constant speed⟩ over an 800 kilometer distance. In the afternoon the train travels back over this ⟨same route⟩. There is less traffic and the train travels ⟨four times as fast⟩ as it did that morning. However, there are more people on the train during the afternoon. Which of the following do you know about the train's afternoon trip?

The correct answer is (A), the time is divided by four. The route is the same, but the train travels four times as fast. Therefore, the time to make the trip is divided by four. Rate means the same thing as speed, and we know that the speed has been multiplied by four.

WORDS TO SYMBOLS PROBLEMS

Before you solve a problem, you may have to decide which operation to use. You can use key words to help you decide which operation to use.

Key Words

Addition	sum, and, more, increased by
Subtraction	less, difference, decreased by
Multiplication	of, product, times
Division	per, quotient, shared, ratio
Equals	is, equals

You can't just use these key words without thinking. You must be sure that the operation makes sense when it replaces the key word. For example,

19 and 23 is 42	16 is 4 more than 12	30% of 19 is 57?
$19 + 23 = 42$	$16 = 4 + 12$	$0.3 \times 19 = 57$

three more than y	$y + 3$	The product of 3 and y		$3y$
y increased by 3	$y + 3$	3 times y		$3y$
y more than 3	$3 + y$	3% of y		$0.03y$
3 less than y	$y - 3$	3 divided by y		$\dfrac{3}{y}$
y decreased by 3	$y - 3$	y divided by 3		$\dfrac{y}{3}$
3 decreased y	$3 - y$	ratio of 3 to y		$\dfrac{3}{y}$
The opposite of y	$-y$	The reciprocal of y		$\dfrac{1}{y}$

Completed Examples

    A. 18 divided by what number is 3?

        $18 \div y = 3$ $18 = 3y$ $y = 6$

    B. 25 less 6 is what number?

        $25 - 6 = y$ $y = 19$

    C. A student correctly answered 80% of 120 mathematics problems. How many mathematics problems did he answer correctly?

        $0.8 \times 120 = y$ $y = 96$

    The student correctly answered 96 problems.

    D. The product of a number and its opposite is -25. What is the number?

        $(y) \times (-y) = 25$ $y = 5$

    The number is 5.

Practice

Solve the problem.

---

1. What number decreased by 9 is 25?

2. What is 60% of 90?

3. Bob lives $\frac{2}{3}$ mile from Gina and $\frac{1}{2}$ mile from Sam. Bob's walk to the school is three times the sum of these distances. How far is Bob's walk to school?

4. The ratio of two gears is 20 to y. If the ratio equals 2.5, what is the value of y?

5. The sum of 5 and the reciprocal of another number is $5\frac{1}{8}$. What is the other number?

6. Car A travels at a constant speed of 60 mph for 2.5 hours. Car B travels at a constant speed of 70 mph for 2 hours. What is the total distance traveled by both cars?

Answers on page 180

FINDING AND INTERPRETING PATTERNS

Sequences

Arithmetic Sequence

A sequence of numbers formed by adding the same nonzero number.

3, 11, 19, 27, 35, 42, 50	Add 8 to get each successive term
53, 48, 44, 40, 36, 32	Add (-4) to get each successive term

Geometric Sequence

A sequence of numbers formed by multiplying the same nonzero number.

3, 15, 75, 375	Multiply by 5 to get each successive term.
160, 40, 10, $2\frac{1}{2}$	Multiply by $\frac{1}{4}$ to get each successive term.

Harmonic Sequence

A sequence of fractions with a numerator of 1 in which the denominators form an arithmetic sequence.

$$\frac{1}{2} \quad \frac{1}{9} \quad \frac{1}{16} \quad \frac{1}{23} \quad \frac{1}{30}$$

Each numerator is 1. The denominators form an arithmetic sequence.

Relationships

Linear Relationships

Linear relationships are pairs of numbers formed by adding or multiplying the same number to the first term in a pair. Here are some examples.

(3, 12), (5, 14), (11, 20), (15, 24)	Add 9 to the first term to get the second.
(1, 6), (2, 12), (3, 18), (4, 24), (5, 30)	Multiply the first term by 6 to get the second.
(96, 12), (72, 9), (56, 7), (24, 3), (16, 2)	Multiply the first term by $\frac{1}{8}$ to get the second.

Completed Examples

A. What term is missing in this number pattern?

$$2 \quad 5 \quad 10 \quad 17 \quad \underline{\quad}$$
$$+3 \quad +5 \quad +7 \quad +9$$

26 is the missing term.

B. These points are all on the same line.
Find the missing term.

$$(-7, -15) \left(\frac{2}{3}, \frac{1}{3}\right) (2, 3) (4, 7) (8, \underline{\quad})$$

Multiply the first term by 2 and subtract 1.
The missing term is (8, 15).

Practice

Find the missing term in each pattern below.

1. 4, 2, 0, −2, −4, ____ −8, −10

2. 4, 6.5, 9, 11.5, ____

3. 120, 60, 30, 15, ____

4. 1, 2, 6, 24, 120, ____

5. 5 9 13 17 ____

The points in each sequence below are on the same line. Find the missing term.

6. (4, 12), (2, 10), (10, 18), (18, 26), (22, ____)

7. (100, 11), (70, 8), (90, 10), (40, 5), (30, ____)

8. (3, 9), (7, 49), (2, 4), (100, 10000), (5, ____)

9. A meteorologist placed remote thermometers at sea level and up the side of the mountain at 1,000, 2,000, 5,000, and 6,000 feet. Readings were taken simultaneously and entered in the following table. What temperatures would you predict for the missing readings?

Temperature

0	1,000	2,000	3,000	4,000	5,000	6,000	7,000	8,000	9,000	10,000
52°	49°	46°			37°	34°				

10. Consider another example. A space capsule is moving in a straight line and is being tracked on a grid. The first four positions on the grid are recorded in the following table. Where will the capsule be on the grid when the x position is 13?

x-value	1	2	3	4
y-value	1	4	7	10

Answers on page 180

ESTIMATION PROBLEMS

Follow these steps.

1. Round the numbers.

2. Use the rounded numbers to estimate the answer.

Completed Example

It takes a person about $7\frac{1}{2}$ minutes to run a mile. The person runs 174 miles in a month. What is a reasonable estimate of the time it takes for the person to run that distance?

Round $7\frac{1}{2}$ to 8.

Round 174 to 180.

$180 \times 8 = 1440$ minutes or 24 hours.
24 hours is a reasonable estimate of the answer.

Practice

1. A class took a spelling quiz and the grades were 93, 97, 87, 88, 98, 91. What is a reasonable estimate of the average of these grades?

2. To build a sandbox, you need lumber in the following lengths: 12 ft, 16 ft, 18 ft, and 23 ft. What is a reasonable estimate of the total length of the lumber?

3. Each batch of cookies yields 11 dozen. You need 165 dozen. What is a reasonable estimate for the number of batches you will need?

4. It takes 48 minutes for a commuter to travel back and forth from work each day. If the commuter drives back and forth 26 days a month, what is a reasonable estimate of the number of hours that are spent driving?

Answers on page 180

CHART PROBLEMS

Follow these steps:

1. Identify the data in the chart.
2. Add when necessary to find the total probability.

Completed Example

Table 1

	Air Express	Rail	Truck
5 pounds and over	0.07	0.34	0.18
Under 5 pounds	0.23	0.02	0.16

The table shows the percent of packages shipped by the method used and the weight classes.

What is the probability that a package picked at random was sent Air Express?

Add the two proportions for Air Express.
0.07 + 0.23 = 0.30
The probability that a randomly picked package was sent Air Express is 0.3.

What is the probability that a package picked at random weighed under five pounds?

Add the three proportions for under five pounds.
0.23 + 0.02 + 0.16 = 0.42.
The probability that a randomly chosen package weighed under five pounds is 0.42.

What is the probability that a package picked at random weighing under five pounds was sent by rail?

Look at the cell in the table where *under five pounds* and *rail* intersect.
That proportion is 0.02.
The probability that a randomly chosen package under five pounds was sent by rail is 0.02.

Practice

Use Table 1 above.

1. What is the probability that a package was sent by truck?

2. What is the probability of a package five pounds and over being randomly chosen?

3. What is the probability that a package five pounds and over picked at random was sent by Air Express?

4 What is the probability of randomly choosing a package under 5 pounds that was sent other than by rail?

Answers on page 181

FREQUENCY TABLE PROBLEMS

Percent

Percent tables show the percent or proportion of a particular score or characteristic. We can see from Table 1 that 13% of the students got a score from 90 through 100.

Completed Example

Table 1

Scores	Percent of Students
0−59	2
60−69	8
70−79	39
80−89	38
90−100	13

Which score interval contains the mode?

> The largest percentage is 39% for 70−79. The interval 70−79 contains the mode.

Which score interval contains the median?

> The cumulative percentage of 0−79 is 49%.
> The median is in the interval in which the cumulative percentage of 50% occurs. The score interval 80−89 contains the median.

What percent of the students scored above 79?

> Add the percentiles of the intervals above 79.   38 + 13 = 51
> 51% of the students scored above 79.

Percentile Rank

The percentile rank shows the percent of scores below a given value. We can see from Table 2 that 68% of the scores fell below 60.

Completed Example

Table 2

Standardized Score	Percentile Rank
80	99
70	93
60	68
50	39
40	22
30	13
20	2

What percent of the scores are below 50?

The percentile rank next to 50 is 39. That means 39% of the scores are below 50.

What percent of the scores are between 30 and 70?

Subtract the percentile rank for 30 from the percentile rank for 70.
93% − 13% = 80%. 80% of the scores are between 30 and 70.

What percent of the scores are at or above 60?

Subtract the percentile rank for 60 from 100%.
100% − 68% = 32%. 32% of the scores are at or above 60.

Practice

Use Table 1 and Table 2 on pages 160 and 161.

Table 1

1. What percent of the scores are below 70?

2. In which score interval is the median?

3. What percent of the scores are from 80 to 100?

Answers on page 181

Table 2

4. The lowest passing score is 50. What percent of the scores are passing?

5. What percent of the scores are from 20 to 50?

FORMULA PROBLEMS

Concentrate on substituting values for variables. If you see a problem to be solved with a proportion, set up the proportion and solve.

Completed Examples

A. A mechanic uses this formula to estimate the displacement (P) of an engine. $P = 0.8 (d^2)(s)(n)$ where d is the diameter, s is the stroke length of each cylinder, and n is the number of cylinders. Estimate the displacement of a 6-cylinder car whose cylinders have a diameter of 2 inches and a stroke length of 4 inches.

1. Write the formula. $P = 0.8(d^2)(s)(n)$

2. Write the values of the variables. $d = 2, s = 4, n = 6$

3. Substitute the values for the variables. $P = 0.8(2^2)(4)(6)$

4. Solve. $P = 0.8(4)(24) = (3.2)(24)$

       $P = 76.8$

The displacement of the engine is about 76.8 cubic inches.

B. The accountant calculates that it takes $3 in sales to generate $0.42 in profit. How much cost does it take to generate a profit of $5.46?

1. Write a proportion
   Use s for sales. $\dfrac{3}{0.42} = \dfrac{s}{5.46}$

2. Cross multiply. $0.42s = 16.38$

3. Solve. $s = \dfrac{16.38}{0.42}$

       $s = 39$

It will take $39 in sales to generate $5.46 in profits.

Practice

1. A retail store makes a profit of $3.75 for each $10 of goods sold. How much profit would the store make on a $45 purchase?

2. The formula for calculating average speed is $d/(T_2 - T_1)$. If T_1 (start time) is 5:00 P.M. and T_2 (end time) is midnight the same day, and 287 miles were traveled, what was the average speed?

3. A car purchased for $12,000 ($O$) depreciates 10% ($P$) a year ($Y$). If the car is sold in 3 years, what is its depreciated value if $V = O - POY$?

4. There is a square grid of dots. A figure is made of line segments that connect the dots. The formula for the area of a figure on the grid is $\dfrac{T-2}{2} + I$.

   T is the number of dots touching the figure, and I is the number of dots inside. What is the area of a figure with 14 dots touching and 5 dots inside?

Answers on page 181

PYTHAGOREAN THEOREM PROBLEMS

Follow these steps to solve this type of problem.

1. Sketch and label the right triangle.

2. Use the Pythagorean formula.

3. Solve the problem.

Completed Example

A radio tower sticks 40 feet straight up into the air. Engineers attached a wire with no slack from the top of the tower to the ground 30 feet away from the tower. If it costs $90 a foot to attach the wire, how much did the wire cost?

    1. Sketch and label the right triangle.

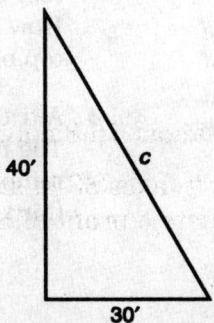

    2. Use the Pythagorean formula.
$$a^2 + b^2 = c^2$$
$$(40)^2 + (30)^2 = c^2$$
$$1{,}600 + 900 = c^2$$
$$2{,}500 = c^2$$
$$50 = c$$
The wire is 50 feet long.

    3. Solve the problem.
50 feet at $95 a foot.
$50 \times 95 = 4{,}740$. The wire costs $4,740 to install.

Practice

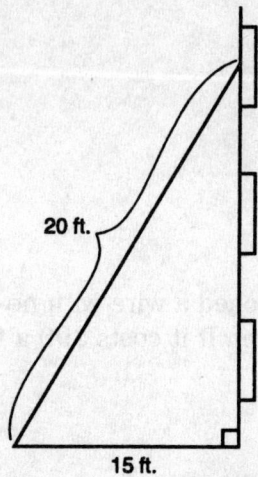

20 ft.

15 ft.

1. A 20-foot ladder is leaning against the side of a tall apartment building. The bottom of the ladder is 15 feet from the wall. At what height on the wall does the top of the ladder touch the building?

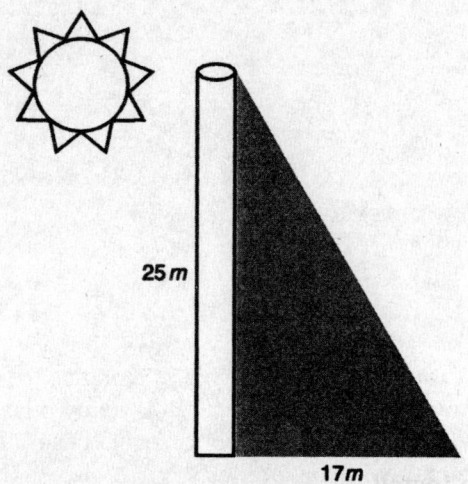

25 m

17m

2. A 25-meter telephone pole casts a shadow. The shadow ends 17 meters from the base of the pole. How long is it straight from the top of the pole to the end of the shadow?

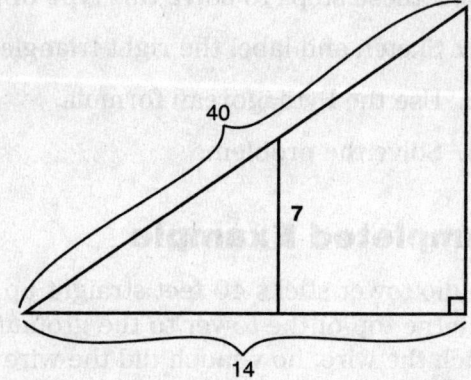

40

7

14

3. You are building a staircase. The wall is 14 feet wide and the stairs are 40 feet long. How high is the wall where it touches the top of the stairs?

4. A truck ramp is shaped like a right triangle. The base of the ramp is 300 feet long. The ramp itself is 340 feet long. How high is the third side of the ramp?

Answers on page 181

GEOMETRIC FIGURE PROBLEMS

Follow these steps to solve this type of problem.

1. Identify the figure or figures involved.

2. Use the formulas for these figures.

3. Use the results of the formulas to solve the problem.

Completed Example

A circular pool with a radius of 10 feet is inscribed inside a square wall. What is the area of the region outside the pool but inside the fence?

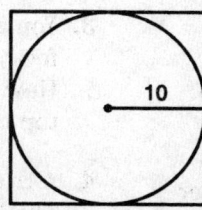

1. There is a square with $s = 20$ and a circle with $r = 10$. The side of the square is twice the radius of the circle.

2. Find the areas.
   Square: $(A = s^2)$ $(20) \times (20) = 400$
   Circle: $(A = \pi r^2)$ $3.14 \times 10^2 = 3.14 \times 100 = 314$

3. Subtract to find the area inside the square but outside the circle.
   $400 - 314 = 86$

Practice

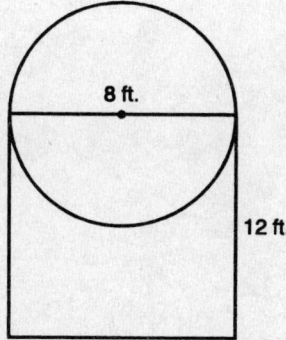

8 ft.

12 ft.

2. A roofer uses one bushel of shingles to cover 1200 square feet. How many bushels of shingles are needed to cover these three rectangular roofs?

   Roof 1: 115 ft by 65 ft
   Roof 2: 112 ft by 65 ft
   Roof 3: 72 ft by 52 ft

1. The dimensions of part of a basketball court are shown in the diagram above. One pint of paint covers 35 square feet. How much paint would it take to paint the inside region of this part of the court?

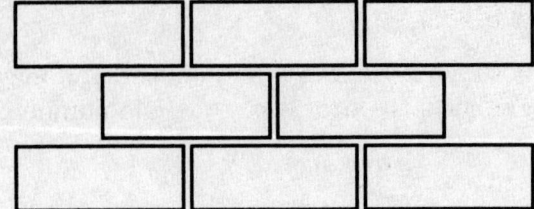

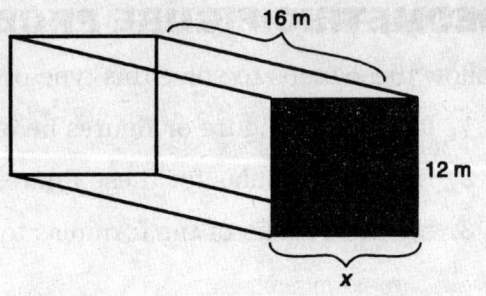

16 m

12 m

x

3. The bricks in the wall pictured here measure 2 inches by 4 inches by 8 inches. What is the volume of the bricks in this section of the wall?

4. A circular cone has a radius of 4 cm. If the volume is 134 cm^2, what is the height?

5. The official basketball has a radius of 6.5 inches. What is the volume?

6. The rectangular solid shown here has a volume of 1,920 m^3. What is the area of the shaded side?

Answers on page 182

INTERPRETING REMAINDER PROBLEMS

When you divide to solve a problem there may be both a quotient and a remainder. You may need to (1) use only the quotient, (2) round the quotient to the next greater whole number, or (3) use only the remainder.

Completed Example

Stereo speakers are packed 4 to a box. There are 315 stereo speakers to be packed.

Questions:

1. How many boxes can be filled?

2. How many boxes would be needed to hold all the stereo speakers?

3. How many stereo speakers will be in the box that is not completely full?

Divide 315 by 4.

$$
\begin{array}{r}
78 \text{ R}3 \\
4\overline{)315} \\
\underline{28} \\
35 \\
\underline{32} \\
3
\end{array}
$$

Answers:

1. Use only the quotient—78 of the boxes can be filled.

2. Round the quotient to the next higher number. It would take 79 boxes to hold all the stereo speakers.

3. Use only the remainder. Three stereo speakers would be in the partially filled box.

Practice

At the quarry, workers are putting 830 pounds of sand into bags that hold 25 pounds.

1. How much sand is left over after the bags are filled?

2. How many bags are needed to hold all the sand?

3. How many bags can be filled with sand?

Answers on page 182

STRATEGIES FOR TAKING THE MATHEMATICS TEST

The mathematics tested is the kind you probably had in high school and in college. It is the kind of mathematics you will use as you teach and go about your everyday life. Computational ability, alone, is expected but is held to a minimum. Remember to use the general test strategies discussed in the Introduction.

WRITE IN THE TEST BOOKLET

It is particularly important to write in the test booklet while taking the mathematics portion of the test. Use these hints for writing in the test booklet.

Do Your Calculations in the Test Booklet

Do all your calculations in the PPST test booklet to the right of the question or on the CBT scrap paper. This makes it easy to refer to the calculations as you choose the correct answer.
   This example should make you feel comfortable about writing in the test booklet.

   What number times 0.00708 is equal to 70.8

   (A) $\cancel{100,000 \times \mathit{0.00708} = \mathit{700.8}}$
   (B) $10,000 \times \mathit{0.00708} = \mathit{70.8}$
   (C) 1,000
   (D) 0.01
   (E) 0.0001

   The correct answer is (B) 10,000.

Draw Diagrams and Figures in the Test Booklet or on Scrap Paper

When you come across a geometry problem or related problem, draw a diagram in the PPST test booklet or on the CBT scrap paper to help.

   All sides of a rectangle are shrunk in half. What happens to the area?

   (A) Divided by two
   (B) Divided by four
   (C) Multiplied by two
   (D) Multiplied by six
   (E) Does not change

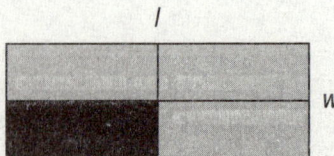

Answer (B), divided by 4, is the correct answer. The original area is evenly divided into four parts.

Work from the Answers

If you don't know how to solve a formula or relation, try out each answer choice until you get the correct answer. Look at this example.

What percent times $\frac{1}{4}$ is $\frac{1}{5}$?

(A) 25%
(B) 40%
(C) 80%
(D) 120%
(E) None of the above

Just take each answer in turn and try it out.

$$0.25 \times \frac{1}{4} = \frac{1}{4} \times \frac{1}{4} = \frac{1}{16}$$ That's not it.

$$0.40 \times \frac{1}{4} = \frac{4}{10} \times \frac{1}{4} = \frac{4}{40} = \frac{1}{10}$$ That's not it either.

$$0.8 \times \frac{1}{4} = \frac{4}{5} \times \frac{1}{4} = \frac{4}{20} = \frac{1}{5}$$

You know that 0.8 is the correct answer, and so choice (C) is correct.

Try Out Numbers

Look at the preceding question.

Work with fractions at first. Ask: What number times $\frac{1}{4}$ equals $\frac{1}{5}$?

Through trial and error you find out that $\frac{4}{5} \times \frac{1}{4} = \frac{1}{5}$.

The answer in fractions is $\frac{4}{5}$.

$$\frac{4}{5} = 0.8 = 80\%$$

The correct choice is (C).

In this example, we found the answer without ever solving an equation. We just tried out numbers until we found the one that works.

Eliminate and Guess

Use this approach when all else has failed. Begin by eliminating the answers you know are wrong. Sometimes you know with certainty that an answer is incorrect. Other times, an answer looks so unreasonable that you can be fairly sure that it is not correct.

Once you have eliminated incorrect answers, a few will probably be left. Just guess among these choices. There is no method that will increase your chances of guessing correctly.

TARGETED MATHEMATICS TEST

This targeted test is designed to help you practice the problem-solving and test-taking strategies presented in this chapter. For that reason, questions may have a different emphasis than the actual test, and the actual test will certainly be more complete.

Mark your choice, then check your answers.

Use the strategies on pages 15–16.

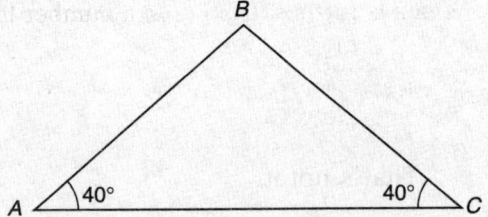

1. What is the measure of angle B?
   (A) 10
   (B) 40
   (C) 80
   (D) 100
   (E) 180

2. After a discount of 25%, the savings on a pair of roller blades was $12.00. What was the sale price?
   (A) $48.00
   (B) $36.00
   (C) $24.00
   (D) $25.00
   (E) $60.00

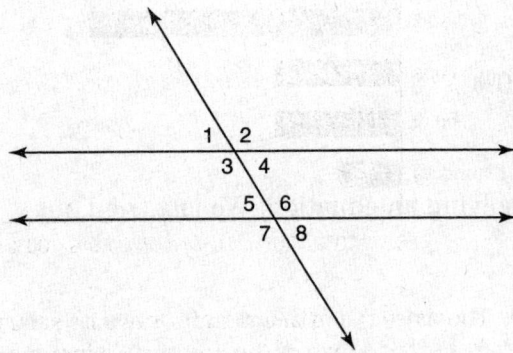

3. Which two angles are supplementary?
   (A) 6 & 7
   (B) 1 & 4
   (C) 3 & 6
   (D) 2 & 4
   (E) 4 & 8

4. Chad rolls a fair die. The sides of the die are numbered from 1 to 6. Ten times in a row he rolls a 5. What is the probability that he will roll a 5 on his next roll?
   (A) $\frac{1}{5}$

   (B) $\frac{1}{6}$

   (C) $\frac{1}{50}$

   (D) $\frac{1}{11}$

   (E) $\frac{1}{10}$

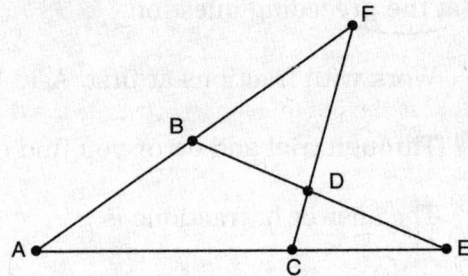

5. Which of the following set of points do not form an angle in the diagram?
   (A) ABF
   (B) ABE
   (C) AFC
   (D) ABC
   (E) CDE

6. An apple costs (*C*). You have (*D*) dollars. What equation would represent the amount of apples you could buy for the money you have?
   (A) C/D
   (B) CD
   (C) $C + D$
   (D) D/C
   (E) $C + 2D$

7. If a worker gets $144.00 for 18 hours' work, how much would that worker get for 32 hours' work?
   (A) $200.00
   (B) $288.00
   (C) $400.00
   (D) $432.00
   (E) $256.00

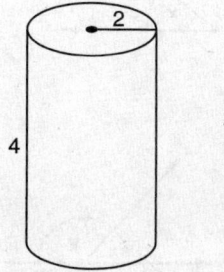 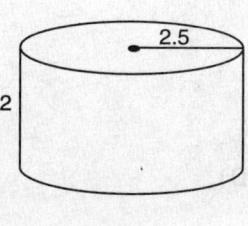

$V = \pi r^2 h$

8. What is the combined volume of these two cylinders?
   (A) $12.5\ \pi$
   (B) $16\ \pi$
   (C) $26.5\ \pi$
   (D) $28.5\ \pi$
   (E) $24\ \pi$

9. r = regular price
   d = discount
   s = sale price

   What equation would represent the calculations for finding the discount?
   (A) $d = r - s$
   (B) $d = s - r$
   (C) $d = sr$
   (D) $d = s + r$
   (E) $d = \dfrac{1}{2} r$

10. A printing company makes pamphlets that cost $.75 per copy plus $5.00 as a setter's fee. If $80 were spent printing a pamphlet, how many pamphlets were ordered?
    (A) 50
    (B) 75
    (C) 100
    (D) 150
    (E) 225

11. Which is furthest from $\dfrac{1}{2}$ on a number line?
    (A) $\dfrac{1}{12}$
    (B) $\dfrac{7}{8}$
    (C) $\dfrac{3}{4}$
    (D) $\dfrac{2}{3}$
    (E) $\dfrac{5}{6}$

12. Which of the following could be about 25 centimeters long?
    (A) a human thumb
    (B) a doorway
    (C) a car
    (D) a house
    (E) a notebook

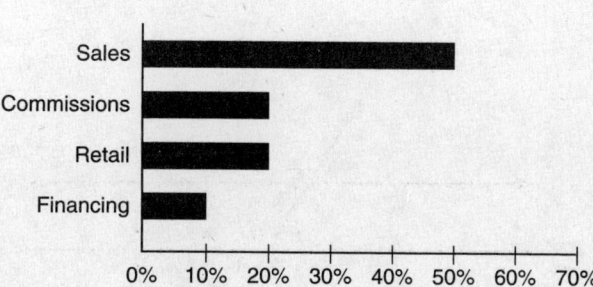

13. The sales department staff draws its salary from four areas of the company's income. Using the above graph, determine what percentage is drawn from the retail fund.
    (A) 10%
    (B) 20%
    (C) 25%
    (D) 30%
    (E) 15%

14. What percentage of 250 is 25?
    (A) 5%
    (B) 10%
    (C) 20%
    (D) 25%
    (E) 50%

15. For a fund raiser the Science and Technology Club is selling raffles at the cost of six raffles for $5.00. It cost the club $250.00 for the prizes and tickets that will be given away. How many raffles will the club have to sell in order to make $1,000.00?
    (A) 300
    (B) 600
    (C) 750
    (D) 1200
    (E) 1500

16. $5.3 \times 10^4 =$
    (A) 0.0053
    (B) 0.00053
    (C) 5,300
    (D) 53,000
    (E) 530,000

17. Which of the following represents supplementary angles?

(A)

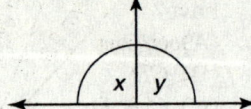

(B)

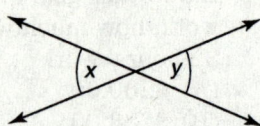

(C)

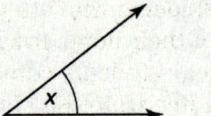

(D)

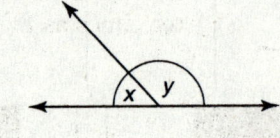

(E)

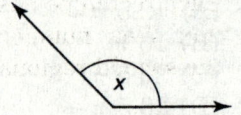

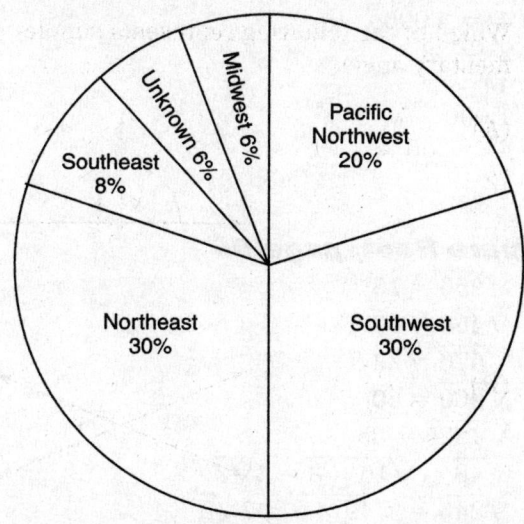

18. The above graph shows the percentage of students who attend college by the location of their home towns. How many more college students come from the Northeast than come from the Midwest?
    (A) twice as many
    (B) three times as many
    (C) half as many
    (D) five times as many
    (E) ten times as many

19. Each rectangle has a total area of 1 square unit. What number represents the area of the shaded regions?

    (A) $\dfrac{5}{6}$ square units

    (B) $\dfrac{7}{8}$ square units

    (C) $1\dfrac{3}{4}$ square units

    (D) $1\dfrac{1}{3}$ square units

    (E) $1\dfrac{5}{24}$ square units

20. Which diagram shows both the set of whole numbers between 1 and 20 and multiples of 5?

    (A)

    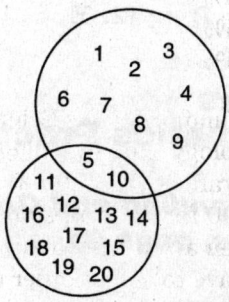

    (B)

    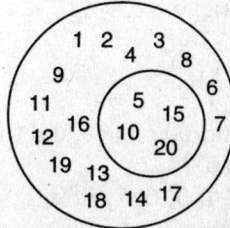

    (C)

    (D)

    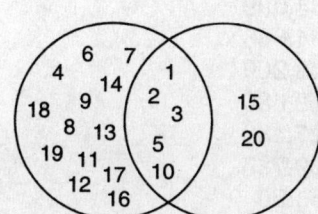

    (E)

    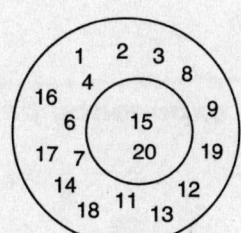

Answers

1. D	5. D	9. A	13. B	17. A, D
2. B	6. D	10. C	14. B	18. D
3. D	7. E	11. A	15. E	19. E
4. B	8. D	12. E	16. D	20. B

Answers
Mathematics Practice

Understanding and Ordering Whole Numbers, page 91

1. $2 < 3$
2. $4 > 1$
3. $8 < 9$
4. $1 = 1$
5. $7 > 6$
6. 9,037
7. 2,851
8. The hundreds place and the ones place each contain a 7.
9. 1, 2, 3, 4, 5, 6, 7, 8, 9, 10, 11, 12, 13, 14
   The problem asks for the numbers between 0 and 15, so 0 and 15 are not included.
10. There are 49. (1, 2, 3, . . . , 47, 48, 49)

Whole Number Computation, page 92

1. 98,405
2. 27,079
3. 95,809
4. 66,184
5. 16,013
6. 34,099
7. 34,688
8. 42,209
9. 13,680
10. 27,482
11. 29,725
12. 5,256
13. 8
14. 4 R4
15. 29
16. 32 R2

Positive exponents, page 94

1. 241
2. 81
3. 8
4. 900
5. 35
6. 51

7. $4^6 = 4,096$
8. $2^5 = 32$
9. 44
10. 1,000
11. $4^4 = 256$
12. 72

Square Root, page 95

1. $\sqrt{256} = 16$
2. $\sqrt{400} = 20$
3. $\sqrt{576} = 24$
4. $\sqrt{900} = 30$
5. $\sqrt{1225} = 35$
6. $\sqrt{48} = \sqrt{16 \times 3} = 4\sqrt{3}$
7. $\sqrt{245} = \sqrt{49 \times 5} = 7\sqrt{5}$
8. $\sqrt{396} = \sqrt{36 \times 11} = 6\sqrt{11}$
9. $\sqrt{567} = \sqrt{81 \times 7} = 9\sqrt{7}$
10. $\sqrt{832} = \sqrt{64 \times 13} = 8\sqrt{13}$

Order of Operations, page 96

1. $4 \times 5 + 4 \div 2 = 20 + 2 = 22$
2. $(5 + 7 - 9) \times 8^2 + 2 = 3 \times 8^2 + 2 = 194$
3. $((7 + 4) - (1 + 4)) \times 6 = (11 - 5) \times 6 = 36$
4. $6^2 + 3(9 - 5 + 7)^2 = 36 + 3 \times 11^2 = 399$
5. $51 - 36 = 15$
6. $40 + 4 - 4 = 40$
7. $^-50 + 7 = {}^-43$
8. $(49 + 16) \times 8 = 520$

Understanding and Ordering Decimals, page 98

1. $0.02 > 0.003$
2. $4.6 > 1.98$
3. $0.0008 > 0.00009$
4. $1.0 = 1$
5. $7.6274 > 7.6269$
6. 2.586
7. 90310.0704
8. The hundredths place and the hundred thousandths place each contain a 3.
9. 0, 0.1, 0.2, 0.3, 0.4, 0.5, 0.6, 0.7, 0.8, 0.9, 1.0
10. There are 99—0.01, 0.02, 0.03, . . . , 0.50, 0.51, 0.52, . . . , 0.97, 0.98, 0.99

Rounding Whole Numbers and Decimals, page 99

1. 23,500
2. 74.151
3. 980,000

4. 302.8
5. 495,240
6. 1500
7. 13.1
8. 200,000
9. 52
10. 23,500

Add, Subtract, Multiply, and Divide Decimals, page 100

1. 26.09
2. 72.617
3. 988.39
4. 5473.19
5. 8.2
6. 71.0096
7. 453.97
8. 1767.87
9. .6225
10. 163.45
11. 3680.538
12. 3761.514
13. 4.8
14. 9.6
15. 33.6
16. 125.63

Understanding and Ordering Fractions, page 103

1. $1\frac{2}{3}$

2. $2\frac{1}{7}$

3. $2\frac{2}{3}$

4. $\frac{41}{5}$

5. $\frac{55}{8}$

6. $\frac{68}{7}$

7. $\frac{3}{7} < \frac{4}{9}$

8. $\frac{5}{6} = \frac{25}{30}$

9. $\frac{4}{5} < \frac{7}{8}$

Multiply, Divide, Add, and Subtract Fractions and Mixed Numbers, page 105

1. $\frac{5}{27}$

2. $\frac{1}{6}$

3. $13\frac{59}{64}$

4. $8\frac{8}{35}$

5. $\frac{6}{7}$

6. $\frac{18}{35}$

7. $2\frac{22}{91}$

8. $\frac{7}{19}$

9. $1\frac{2}{9}$

10. $1\frac{1}{5}$

11. $4\frac{1}{14}$

12. $12\frac{1}{2}$

13. $\frac{1}{21}$

14. $\frac{1}{40}$

15. $\frac{2}{3}$

16. $3\frac{58}{63}$

Number Theory, page 108

1. 13: 1 and 13
2. 26: 1, 2, 13, and 26
3. 40: 1, 2, 4, 5, 8, 10, 20, 40
4. 23: 1 and 23
5. 24
6. 60
7. 35
8. 28
9. 6

10. 5
11. 32
12. 28

Ratio and Proportion, Page 110
1. 14 vacuum cleaners for 280 houses
2. 4 teachers for 32 children
3. 21 rest stops for 140 miles
4. Yes. $\frac{7}{9} = \frac{28}{36}$ because $7 \times 36 = 252 = 9 \times 28$

Percent, page 112
1. 35.9%
2. 78%
3. 21.5%
4. 4.1%
5. $11\frac{1}{9}$%
6. 62.5%
7. 30%
8. $44\frac{4}{9}$%
9. $\frac{29}{50}$
10. $\frac{79}{100}$
11. $\frac{213}{250}$
12. $\frac{487}{500}$

Three Types of Percent Problems, page 114
1. $\square \times 240 = 120$
   $\square = \frac{120}{240}$
   $\square = .5 = 50\%$

2. $.15 \times 70 = \square$
   $.15 \times 70 = 10.5$
   $\square = 10.5$

3. $.6 \times 300 = \square$
   $.6 \times 300 = 180$
   $\square = 180$

4. $\square \times 60 = 42$
   $\square = \frac{42}{60}$
   $\square = 70\%$

5. $\square \% \times 25 = 2.5$
   $\square \% = \frac{2.5}{25}$
   $\square = 10\%$

6. $40\% \times \square = 22$
   $\square = \frac{22}{.4}$
   $\square = 55$

7. $.7 \times \square = 85$
   $\square = \frac{85}{.7}$
   $\square = 121\frac{3}{7}$

8. $25\% \times 38 = \square$
   $.25 \times 38 = 9.5$
   $\square = 9.5$

9. $.35 \times \square = 24$
   $\square = \frac{24}{.35}$
   $\square = 68\frac{4}{7}$

10. $24 = \square \times 80$
    $\frac{24}{80} = \square$
    $\square = 30\%$

Percent of Increase, page 116
1. Amount of increase $35 - 25 = \$10$
   $\frac{10}{25} = 0.4 = 40\%$
   Percent of increase = 40%

2. Discount: $100 \times .25 = \$25$
   $100 - \$25 = \$75$
   Sale price = $75

3. Discount $80 \times 15\% = \$12$
   $80 - \$12 = \$68$
   New price = $68

4. Amount of increase $150 - \$120 = \$30$
   $\frac{30}{120} = \frac{1}{4} = 25\%$
   Percent of increase = 25%

5. Discount $75 \times 10\% = \$7.50$
   $75 - \$7.50 = \$67.50$
   Sale price = $67.50

6. Amount of decrease $18 − $6 = $12

$$\frac{12}{18} = \frac{2}{3} = 66\frac{2}{3}\%$$

Percent of decrease $= 66\frac{2}{3}\%$

7. Amount of decrease $225 − $180 = $45

$$\frac{45}{225} = 0.2 = 20\%$$

Percent of decrease $= 20\%$

8. Discount $150 = x − 0.25x
   $150 = 0.75x$
   $x = 200
   Original price: $200

Probability, page 118

1. There are 10 socks in the drawer. 7 of the 10 are not black.

$$P\ (\text{not black}) = \frac{7}{10}$$

2. There are 6 goldfish; 2 of the 6 are male

$$P\ (\text{male}) = \frac{2}{6} = \frac{1}{3}$$

3. There are 52 cards in a deck. There are 4 kings and 4 queens.

$P\ (\text{king or queen}) = P\ (\text{king}) + P\ (\text{queen}) =$

$$\frac{4}{52} + \frac{4}{52} = \frac{8}{52} = \frac{2}{13}$$

4. There are 6 different names.
   $P\ (\text{Carl and Phyllis}) =$
   $P\ (\text{Carl}) \times P\ (\text{Phyllis}) =$

$$\frac{1}{6} \times \frac{1}{6} = \frac{1}{36}$$

5. $\frac{1}{2}$

6. This is an "and" problem. Multiply the probability.

$$\left(\frac{1}{2}\right)\left(\frac{1}{2}\right)\left(\frac{1}{2}\right)\left(\frac{1}{2}\right)\left(\frac{1}{2}\right) = \frac{1}{32}$$

Statistics, page 120

1. mode 80
2. mean (average) 35.5
3. median 9 (Remember to arrange the numbers in order.)
4. 16 is the median, the mode, and very close to the mean.
5. mean 89
6. mode 30

Permutations and Combinations, page 121

1. There are 6 combinations of 2 people to sit in the chairs.
2. There are 5,040 possible arrangements of the 7 books on the shelf.
3. 67,600 ($26 \times 26 \times 10 \times 10$)
4. The positions on the bus are not specified. Order does not matter. This is a combination problem.

Four students   A   B   C   D

ABC   ABD   ACD   BCD

There are four ways for three of four students to board the bus.

Integers, page 123

1. 15
2. 1
3. −69
4. −9
5. 1
6. 54
7. 22
8. −80
9. 99
10. −650
11. 1829
12. −1470
13. 15
14. −17
15. 44
16. −22

Scientific Notation, page 124

1. $0.0564 = 5.64 \times 10^{-2}$
2. $0.00897 = 8.97 \times 10^{-3}$
3. $0.06501 = 6.501 \times 10^{-2}$
4. $0.000354 = 3.54 \times 10^{-4}$
5. $545 = 5.45 \times 10^{2}$
6. $7{,}790 = 7.79 \times 10^{3}$
7. $289{,}705 = 2.89705 \times 10^{5}$
8. $1{,}801{,}319 = 1.801319 \times 10^{6}$

Equations, page 126

1. $w = 8$
2. $x = 15$
3. $y = 70$
4. $z = -4$
5. $w = 4$
6. $x = 126$
7. $y = -5$
8. $z = -66$

9. $w = 7$
10. $x = -13$
11. $y = 456$
12. $z = 3$

Geometry, page 130

1. trapezoid
2. $m\angle 2 = 135°$
3. $m\angle ABC = 50° = m\angle ACB$

4.

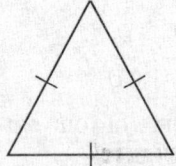

5. An octagon (8 sides) has two more sides than a hexagon (6 sides).
6. A right angle, which has a measure of 90°.

7. (Picture may vary)

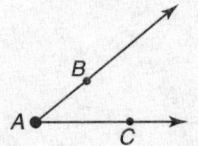

The new figure is $\angle BAC$.

8. (Picture may vary)

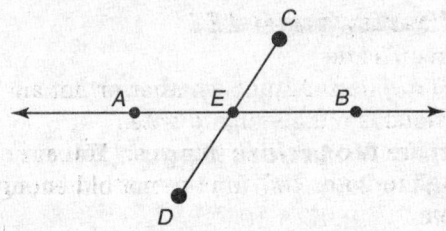

9. (Picture may vary)

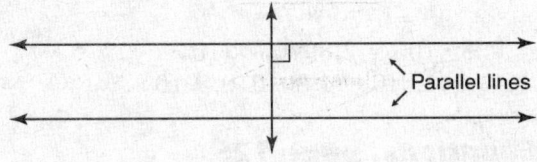

Parallel lines

10. The sum of the measures is 180° ($m\angle A + m\angle B + m\angle C = 180°$).

Coordinate Grid, page 132

1. $A(3, -2)$
   $B(-2, -4)$
   $C(-5, 5)$
   $D(3, 3)$
   $E(0, 2)$
   $F(-5, 0)$

2.

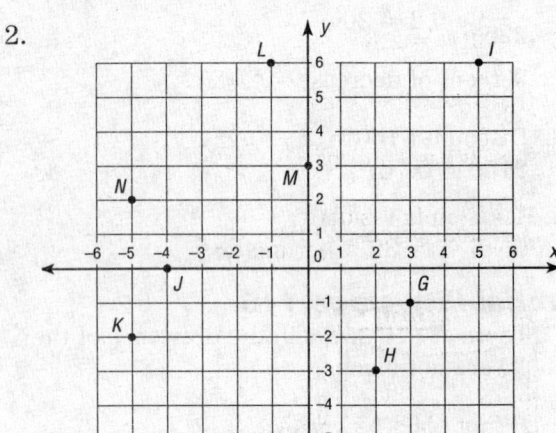

3.

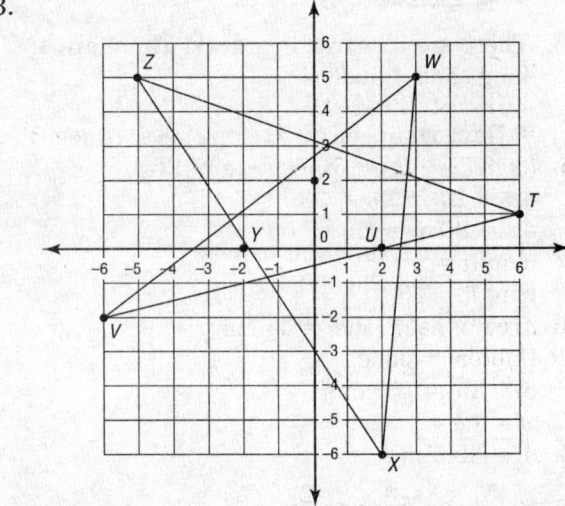

Measurement, page 137

1. 0.22 decameters
2. 29,040 feet
3. $2\frac{3}{4}$ inches
4. $\frac{1}{2}$ pound
5. 64,000 ounces
6. 4 centimeters
7. 190,080 inches
8. 236,700 milliliters

9. 2 quarts
10. 35°

Formulas, page 141

1. πr^2
   $3.14 \times (9)^2 =$
   $3.14 \times 81 = 254.34 \text{ m}^2$

2. $b = 3, h = 2.6$
   $(\frac{1}{2})(3)(2.6) = 3.9$
   $4 \times 3.9 = 15.6 \text{ in}^2$

3. Hexagon is 6-sided
   6×5 ft = 30 ft perimeter

4.
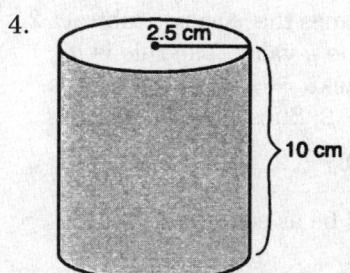

   $2 \quad \pi \quad r \quad h$
   $2 \ (3.14)(1.25)(10)$
   $= 78.5 \text{ cm}^2$
5. $(x + 5) + (x + 5) + x + x = 90$
   $4x + 10 = 90$
   $4x = 80 \ x = 20$
   length $= x + 5$
   length $= 25$ ft
6. Area of each side $= 25 \text{ cm}^2$
   Cube is 6-sided.
   $6 \times 25 = 150 \text{ cm}^2$
7. $x = 12$
8. $A = 32.5 \text{ in.}^2$

9. $V = 4186.\overline{6} \ (4186\frac{2}{3}) \text{ cm}^3$

10. $V = 3375 \text{ in}^3$

Time and Temperature, page 144

1. 0°F (0°C is 32°F)
2. 1:00 P.M.

3.
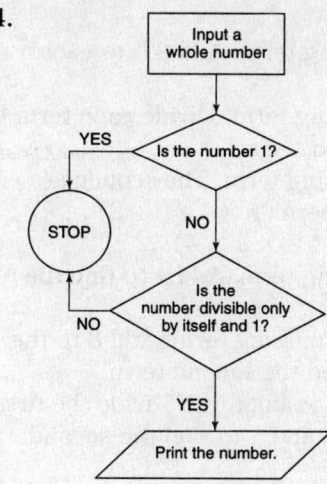

4. 10:00 A.M.
5. 50°F
6. 104°C

Graphs, page 147

1. 1,000 phones
2. Alpine
3. HIJ Corp.
4. 3%
5. Alpine
6. Dumont
7. $800,000
8. $84,000

Stem-and-Leaf and Box-and-Whisker Plots, page 149

1.
1	0, 3, 5, 7, 9
2	3, 6, 8, 9
3	3, 6, 8,
4	2, 2, 5, 7, 8, 9
5	3, 5, 6,
6	
7	5, 6, 7, 9
8	
9	2, 4, 6,
10	1, 5, 6

2. There is no score between 56 and 75.
3. 47
4. 42

Flow Charts, page 151

1. A person's age
2. The flow chart outputs whether or not an individual is old enough to vote.
3. There are two possible phrases: "You are old enough to vote. "*or*" You are not old enough to vote."

4.

```
            ┌──────────────────┐
            │  Input a          │
            │  whole number     │
            └──────────────────┘
                    │
         YES        ▼
        ┌─────< Is the number 1? >
        │              │ NO
        ▼              ▼
    ┌───────┐    < Is the
    │ STOP  │      number divisible only
    └───────┘      by itself and 1? >
        ▲  NO          │
        │           YES│
        │              ▼
        └────< Print the number. >
```

Logic, page 152

1. False—Some sports, such as hockey, do not use a ball.
2. True—For example, 35 is divisible by both 5 and 7.
3. False—For example, 12 is divisible by 3.
4. True—For example, 2 is both prime and divisible by 2.

Words to Symbols Problems, page 155

1. 34; $34 - 9 = 25$

2. $0.6 \times 90 = 54$

3. Add: $\dfrac{2}{3} + \dfrac{1}{2} = \dfrac{7}{6}$

   Multiply: $\dfrac{7}{6} \times 3 = \dfrac{21}{6}$

   Divide: $\dfrac{21}{6} \div 3\dfrac{3}{6} = 3\dfrac{1}{2}$.

   Bob's walk to school is $3\dfrac{1}{2}$ miles.

4. $\dfrac{20}{y} = 2.5 \quad 20 = 2.5y \quad y = 8$

5. $5\dfrac{1}{x} = 5\dfrac{1}{8} \qquad x = 8$

   The number is 8.

6. Multiply: $60 \times 2.5 = 150$
   $70 \times 2 = 140$
   Add: $150 + 140 = 290$
   The cars traveled a total distance of 290 miles.

Findings and Interpreting Patterns, page 157

1. **−6** is the missing term. Subtract 2 from each term.
2. **14** is the missing term. Add 2.5 to each term.
3. **7.5** is the missing term. Divide each term by 2 to get the next term.
4. **720** is the missing term. The sequence follows the pattern $(1 \times 1)(1 \times 2)$ $(1 \times 2 \times 3)(1 \times 2 \times 3 \times 4)$. . .
5. **21** is the missing term. Add 4 to find the next term.
6. (22, **30**) is the missing term. Add 8 to the first term to find the second term.
7. (30, **4**) is the missing term. Divide the first term by 10 and add 1 to find the second term.

8. (5, **25**) is the missing term. Square the first term to get the second term.
9. The temperatures drops 3° from 52° to 49° and from 49° to 46°. If it drops at the same rate, the temperature drop at 3,000 feet would be 43° and 4,000 feet would be 40° (followed by 37° and 34°). Continue to fill in the table accordingly, as follows.

Temperature

0	1,000	2,000	3,000	4,000	5,000
52°	49°	46°	*43°*	*40°*	37°

6,000	7,000	8,000	9,000	10,000
34°	*31°*	*28°*	*25°*	*22°*

10. Multiply three times the x value, subtract 2, and that gives the y value. The rule is y equals three times $x - 2$ so that the equation is $y = 3x - 2$. Substitute 13 for x:

$$y = 3(13) - 2 = 39 - 2 = 37$$

The capsule will be at position (13, 37).

Estimation Problems, page 158

1. Round all the scores and add the rounded scores.

   $90 + 100 + 90 + 90 + 100 + 90 = 560$

   Divide by the number of scores.
   $560 \div 6 = 93.3$
   93 is a reasonable estimate of the average.

2. Round the lengths and add the rounded lengths.

   $10 + 20 + 20 + 20 = 70$

   70 is a reasonable estimate of the amount of wood needed.

3. Round the number of dozens to the nearest 10.

   Divide the rounded numbers.
   $\dfrac{170}{10} = 17$

   17 is a reasonable estimate of the number of batches needed.

4. Round the number of minutes and number of days to the nearest 10.

   Multiply the rounded numbers.

   $50 \times 30 = 1,500$
   Divide to find hours.

   $1,500 \div 60 = 25$
   25 is a reasonable estimate of the number of hours.

Chart Problems, page 159

1. Add two proportions for truck.

   $0.18 + 0.16 = 0.34$

   The probability that a package picked at random was sent by truck is 34%.

2. Add the three proportions for 5 pounds and over.

   $0.07 + 0.34 + 0.18 = 0.59$

3. The proportion for Air Express over 5 pounds is .07.

4. Add proportions for under 5 pounds by Air Express and under 5 pounds by truck.

   $0.23 + 0.16 = 0.39$

Frequency Table Problems, page 161

1. Add the percentiles of the intervals below 70.

   $2 + 8 = 10$ 10% of the students scored below 70.

2. The median score is in the interval $80-89$.

3. The percent of scores from 80 to 100 is $38 + 13 = 51$

   51% of the students scored from 80 to 100.

4. The question is asking for the number of scores that are above 50. The percentile rank next to 50 is 39. So 39% of the scores are below 50, 39% failed. $100 - 39 = 61$. 61% passed.

5. The percent of the scores from 20 to 50 is the percentile rank for 50, less the percentile rank for 20.

   $39 - 2 = 37$

   37% of the scores are from 20 to 50.

Formula Problems, page 162
1. $P =$ about \$16.88
2. $s = 41$ mph
3. $Y = \$8,400$
4. $A = 11$

Pythagorean Theorem Problems, page 164

1.

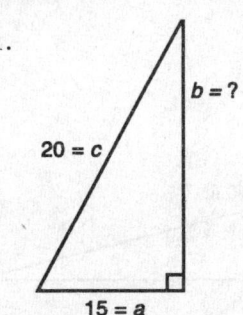

$a^2 + b^2 = c^2$
$(15)^2 + b^2 = (20)^2$
$225 + b^2 = 400$
$b^2 = 400 - 225 = 175$
$b =$ approximately 13.2 ft.

2.

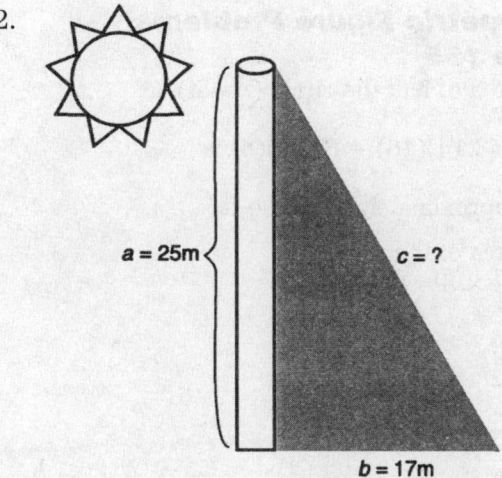

$a^2 + b^2 = c^2$
$(25)^2 + (17)^2 = c^2$
$625 + 289 = c^2$
$c^2 = 914$, $c =$ approximately 30.2 m.

3.

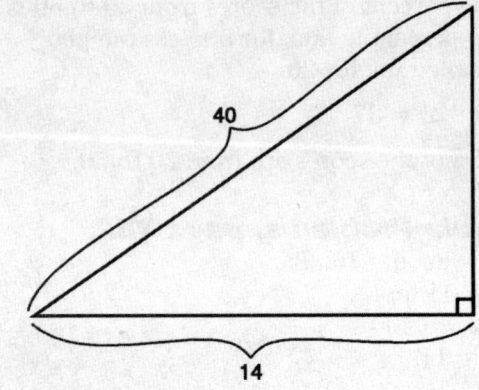

$a^2 + b^2 = c^2$
$(14)^2 + b^2 = (40)^2$
$196 + b^2 = 1,600$
$b^2 = 1,404$
$b = $ approximately 37.5
The height is about 37.5 feet.

4.

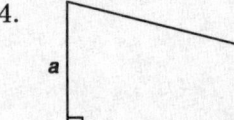

$a^2 + b^2 = c^2$
$a^2 + (300)^2 = (340)^2$
$a^2 = 115,600 - 90,000 = 25,600$
$a = 160$ ft
The ramp is 160 feet high.

Geometric Figure Problems, page 165

1. Area of half the circle ($r = 4$)

   $\frac{1}{2}(3.14)(16) = (3.14)(8)$ is

   approximately 25.12 sq ft

   Area of the rectangle
   $12 \times 8 = 96$ sq ft

Area of the entire figure
$25.12 + 96 = 121.12$ sq ft

$121.12 \div 35$ is approximately 3.5 pints
Round up. You need 4 pints of paint.

2. Find the area of the roofs.
   Roof 1: $115 \times 65 = 7,475$ sq ft
   Roof 2: $112 \times 65 = 7,280$ sq ft
   Roof 3: $72 \times 52 = \underline{2,744 \text{ sq ft}}$
   TOTAL   18,499 sq ft
   $18,499 \div 1,200 = 15.4$
   Round up. You need 16 bushels.

3. Volume of a brick $= lwh$

   $V = 2 \times 4 \times 8 = 64$ in^3

   8×64 in$^3 = 512$ in^3

4. Volume of a cone $= \frac{1}{3}\pi r^2 h$

   $134 = \frac{1}{3}(3.14)(4)^2 h$

   $134 = 16.7\,h$
   $h = 8$ cm

5. Volume of a sphere $= \frac{4}{3}\pi r^3$

   $V = \frac{4}{3}(3.14)(274.6)$

   $V = 1149.76$ in^3

6. Volume of a rectangular solid $= lwh$
   $1920 = (16)(12)\,w$
   $1920 = 192\,w \quad w = 10$

   Shaded area $= 12 \times 10 = 120\,m^2$

Interpret the Remainder Problems, page 167

1. 5 pounds
2. 34 bags
3. 33 bags

READING

TEST INFO BOX		
PPST	40 Multiple-Choice Items	50 minutes
CBT	36 Multiple-Choice Items	95 minutes

USING THIS CHAPTER

This chapter prepares you to take the PPST and CBT reading comprehension tests. Choose one of these approaches.

- **I want vocabulary and reading help.** Review the entire chapter and take the targeted test at the end.

- **I just want reading help.** Read Strategies for Taking the Reading Test beginning on page 192. Take the targeted test at the end of the chapter.

- **I want to practice reading items.** Take the targeted test at the end of the chapter.

VOCABULARY REVIEW

You can't read if you don't know the vocabulary. But you don't have to know every word in the dictionary. Follow this reasonable approach to developing a good vocabulary for these tests.

CONTEXT CLUES

Many times you can figure out a word from its context. Look at these examples. Synonyms, antonyms, examples, or descriptions may help you figure out the word.

1. The woman's mind wandered as her two friends **prated** on. It really did not bother her though. In all the years she had known them, they had always <u>babbled</u> about their lives. It was almost comforting.

2. The wind **abated** in the late afternoon. Things were different yesterday when the wind had <u>picked up</u> toward the end of the day.

3. The argument with her boss had been her **Waterloo**. She wondered if the <u>defeat</u> suffered by Napoleon <u>at this famous place</u> had felt the same.

4. The events swept the politician into a **vortex** of controversy. The politician knew what it meant to be spun around like a toy boat in the <u>swirl of water</u> that swept down the bathtub drain.

   Passage 1 gives a synonym for the unknown word. We can tell that *prated* means babbled. *Babbled* is used as a synonym of *prated* in the passage.

   Passage 2 gives an antonym for the unknown word. We can tell that *abated* means slowed down or diminished because *picked up* is used as an antonym of *abated*.

   Passage 3 gives a description of the unknown word. The description of *Waterloo* tells us that the word means *defeat*.

   Passage 4 gives an example of the unknown word. The example of a *swirl of water* going down the bathtub drain gives us a good idea of what a *vortex* is.

ROOTS

A root is the basic element of a word. The root is usually related to the word's origin. Roots can often help you figure out the word's meaning. Here are some roots that may help you.

Root	Meaning	Examples
bio	life	biography, biology
circu	around	circumference, circulate
frac	break	fraction, refract
geo	earth	geology, geography
mal	bad	malicious, malcontent
matr, mater	mother	maternal, matron
neo	new	neonate, neoclassic
patr, pater	father	paternal, patron
spec	look	spectacles, specimen
tele	distant	telephone, television

PREFIXES

Prefixes are syllables that come at the beginning of a word. Prefixes usually have a standard meaning. They can often help you figure out the word's meaning. Here is a list of prefixes that may help you figure out a word.

Prefix	Meaning	Examples
a-	not	amoral, apolitical
il-, im-, ir-	not	illegitimate, immoral, incorrect
un-	not	unbearable, unknown
non-	not	nonbeliever, nonsense
ant-, anti-	against	antiwar, antidote
de-	opposite	defoliate, declaw
mis-	wrong	misstep, misdeed
ante-	before	antedate, antecedent
fore-	before	foretell, forecast
post-	after	postfight, postoperative
re-	again	refurbish, redo
super-	above	superior, superstar
sub-	below	subsonic, subpar

THE VOCABULARY LIST

Here is a list of a few hundred vocabulary words. The list includes everyday words and a few specialized education terms. Read through the list and visualize the words and their definitions. After a while you will become very familiar with them.

Of course, this is not anywhere near all the words you need to know for the exams. But they will give you a start. These words also will give you some idea of the kinds of words you may encounter on the examinations.

Another great way to develop a vocabulary is to read a paper every day and a news magazine every week, in addition to the other reading you are doing. There are also several inexpensive books, including *1100 Words You Need to Know* and *Pocket Guide to Vocabulary* from Barron's, which may help you develop your vocabulary further.

abhor To regard with horror
I abhor violence.

abstain To refrain by choice
Ray decided to abstain from fattening foods.

abstract Not related to any object, theoretical
Mathematics can be very abstract.

acquisition An addition to an established group or collection
The museum's most recent acquisition was an early Roman vase.

admonish To correct firmly but kindly
The teacher admonished the student not to chew gum in class.

adroit Skillful or nimble in difficult circumstances
The nine year old was already an adroit gymnast.

adversary A foe or enemy
The wildebeest was ever-alert for its ancient adversary, the lion.

advocate To speak for an idea; a person who speaks for an idea
Lou was an advocate of gun control.

aesthetic Pertaining to beauty
Ron found the painting a moving aesthetic experience.

affective To do with the emotional or feeling aspect of learning
Len read the Taxonomy of Educational Objectives: Affective Domain.

alias An assumed name
The check forger had used an alias.

alleviate To reduce or make more bearable
The hot shower helped alleviate the pain in her back.

allude To make an indirect reference to, hint at
Elaine only alluded to her previous trips through the state.

ambiguous Open to many interpretations
That is an ambiguous statement.

apathy Absence of passion or emotion
The teacher tried to overcome their apathy toward the subject.

apprehensive Fear or unease about possible outcomes
Bob was apprehensive about visiting the dentist.

aptitude The ability to gain from a particular type of instruction
The professor pointed out that aptitude, alone, was not enough for success in school.

articulate To speak clearly and distinctly, present a point of view
Chris was chosen to articulate the group's point of view.

assess To measure or determine an outcome or value
There are many informal ways to assess learning.

attest To affirm or certify
I can attest to Cathy's ability as a softball pitcher.

augment To increase or add to
The new coins augmented the already large collection.

belated Past time or tardy
George sent a belated birthday card.

benevolent Expresses goodwill or kindly feelings
The club was devoted to performing benevolent acts.

biased A prejudiced view or action
The judge ruled that the decision was biased.

bolster To shore up, support
The explorer sang to bolster her courage.

candid Direct and outspoken
Lee was well known for her candid comments.

caricature Exaggerated, ludicrous picture, in words or a cartoon
The satirist presented world leaders as caricatures.

carnivorous Flesh eating or predatory
The lion is a carnivorous animal.

censor A person who judges the morality of others; act on that judgment
Please don't censor my views!

censure Expression of disapproval, reprimand
The senate acted to censure the congressman.

cessation The act of ceasing or halting
The eleventh hour marked the cessation of hostilities.

chronic Continuing and constant
Asthma can be a chronic condition.

clandestine Concealed or secret
The spy engaged in clandestine activities.

cogent Intellectually convincing
He presented a cogent argument.

cognitive Relates to the intellectual area of learning
Lou read the Taxonomy of Educational Objectives: Cognitive Domain.

competency Demonstrated ability
Bert demonstrated the specified mathematics competency.

complacent Unaware self-satisfaction
The tennis player realized she had become complacent.

concept A generalization
The professor lectured on concept development.

congenital Existing at birth but non-hereditary
The baby had a small congenital defect.

contemporaries Belonging in the same time period, about the same age
Piaget and Bruner were contemporaries.

contempt Feeling or showing disdain or scorn
She felt nothing but contempt for their actions.

contentious Argumentative
Tim was in a contentious mood.

corroborate To make certain with other information, to confirm
The reporter would always corroborate a story before publication.

credence Claim to acceptance or trustworthiness
They did not want to lend credence to his views.

cursory Surface, not in depth
Ron gave his car a cursory inspection.

daunt To intimidate with fear
Harry did not let the difficulty of the task daunt him.

debacle Disastrous collapse or rout
The whole trip had been a debacle.

debilitate To make feeble
He was concerned that the flu would debilitate him.

decadent Condition of decline/decay
Joan said in frustration, "We live in a decadent society."

deductive Learning that proceeds from general to specific
He proved his premise using deductive logic.

demographic Population data
The census gathers demographic information.

denounce To condemn a person or idea
The diplomat rose in the United Nations to denounce the plan.

deter To prevent or stop an action, usually by some threat
The president felt that the peace conference would help deter aggression.

diligent A persistent effort; a person who makes such an effort
The investigator was diligent in her pursuit of the truth.

discern To perceive or recognize, often by insight
The principal attempted to discern which student was telling the truth.

discord Disagreement or disharmony
Gail's early promotion led to discord in the office.

discriminate To distinguish among people or groups based on their characteristics
It is not appropriate to discriminate based on race or ethnicity.

disdain To show or act with contempt
The professional showed disdain for her amateurish efforts.

disseminate To send around, scatter
The health organization will disseminate any new information on the flu.

divergent Thinking that extends in many directions, is not focused
Les was an intelligent but divergent thinker.

diverse Not uniform, varied
Alan came from a diverse neighborhood.

duress Coercion
He claimed that he confessed under duress.

eccentric Behaves unusually, different from the norm
His long hair and midnight walks made Albert appear eccentric.

eclectic Drawing from several ideas or practices
Joe preferred an eclectic approach to the practice of psychology.

eloquent Vivid, articulate expression
The congregation was held spellbound by the eloquent sermon.

emanate To flow out, come forth
How could such wisdom emanate from one so young?

embellish To make things seem more than they are
Art loved to embellish the facts.

empirical From observation or experiment
The scientist's conclusions were based on empirical evidence.

employment A job or professional position (paid)
You seek employment so you can make the big bucks.

enduring Lasting over the long term
Their friendship grew into an enduring relationship.

enhance To improve or build up
The mechanic used a fuel additive to enhance the car's performance.

enigma A mystery or puzzle
The communist bloc was an "enigma wrapped inside a mystery." (Churchill)

equity Equal attention or treatment
The workers were seeking pay equity with others in their industry.

equivocal Uncertain, capable of multiple interpretations
In an attempt to avoid conflict the negotiator took an equivocal stand.

expedite To speed up, facilitate
Hal's job at the shipping company was to expedite deliveries.

exploit Take maximum advantage of, perhaps unethically
Her adversary tried to exploit her grief to gain an advantage.

extrinsic Coming from outside
The teacher turned to extrinsic motivation.

farce A mockery
The attorney objected, saying that the testimony made the trial a farce.

feign To pretend, make a false appearance of
Some people feign illness to get out of work.

fervent Marked by intense feeling
The spokesman presented a fervent defense of the company's actions.

fiasco Total failure
They had not prepared for the presentation, and it turned into a fiasco.

formidable Difficult to surmount
State certification requirements can present a formidable obstacle.

fracas A noisy quarrel or a scrap
The debate turned into a full-fledged fracas.

gamut Complete range or extent
Waiting to take the test, her mind ran the gamut of emotions.

glib Quickness suggesting insincerity
The glib response made Rita wonder about the speaker's sincerity.

grave Very serious or weighty
The supervisor had grave concerns about the worker's ability.

guile Cunning, craftiness, duplicity
When the truth failed, he tried to win his point with guile.

handicapped Having one or more disabilities
The child study team classified Loren as handicapped.

harass Bother persistently
Some fans came to harass the players on the opposing team.

heterogeneous A group with normal variation in ability or performance
Students from many backgrounds formed a heterogeneous population.

homogeneous A group with little variation in ability or performance
The school used test scores to place students in homogeneous groups.

hypocrite One who feigns a virtuous character or belief
Speaking against drinking and then driving drunk made him a hypocrite!

immune Protected or exempt from disease or harm
The vaccination made Ray immune to measles.

impartial Fair and objective
The contestants agreed on an objective, impartial referee.

impasse Situation with no workable solution
The talks had not stopped, but they had reached an impasse.

impede To retard or obstruct
Mason did not let adversity impede his progress.

implicit Understood but not directly stated
They never spoke about the matter, but they had an implicit understanding.

indifferent Uncaring or apathetic
The teacher was indifferent to the student's pleas for an extension.

indigenous Native to an area
The botanist recognized it as an indigenous plant.

inductive Learning that proceeds from specific to general
Science uses an inductive process, from examples to a generalization.

inevitable Certain and unavoidable
After the rains, the collapse of the dam was inevitable.

infer To reach a conclusion not explicitly stated
The viewer could infer that this product is superior to all others.

inhibit To hold back or restrain
The hormone was used to inhibit growth.

innovate To introduce something new or change established procedure
Mere change was not enough, they had to innovate the procedure.

inquiry Question-based Socratic learning
Much of science teaching uses inquiry-based learning.

intrinsic Inherent, the essential nature
The teacher drew on the meaning of the topic for an intrinsic motivation.

inundate To overwhelm, flood
It was December, and mail began to inundate the Post Office.

jocular Characterized by joking or good nature
The smiling man seemed to be a jocular fellow.

judicial Relating to the administration of justice
His goal was to have no dealings with the judicial system.

knack A talent for doing something
Ron had a real knack for mechanical work.

languid Weak, lacking energy
The sunbather enjoyed a languid afternoon at the shore.

liaison An illicit relationship or a means of communication
The governor appointed his chief aid liaison to the senate.

lucid Clear and easily understood
The teacher answered the question in a direct and lucid way.

magnanimous Generous in forgiving
Loretta is magnanimous to a fault.

malignant Very injurious, evil
Crime is a malignant sore on our society.

malleable Open to being shaped or influenced
He had a malleable position on gun control.

meticulous Very careful and precise
Gina took meticulous care of the fine china.

miser A money hoarder
The old miser had more money than he could ever use.

monotonous Repetitive and boring
Circling the airport, waiting to land, became dull and monotonous.

mores Understood rules of society
Linda made following social mores her goal in life.

motivation Something that creates interest or action
Most good lessons begin with a good motivation.

myriad Large indefinite number
Look skyward and be amazed by the myriad of stars.

naive Lacking sophistication
Laura is unaware, and a little naive, about the impact she has on others.

nemesis A formidable rival
Lex Luthor is Superman's nemesis.

novice A beginner
Her unsteady legs revealed that Sue was a novice skater.

nullified Removed the importance of
The penalty nullified the 20-yard gain made by the running back.

objective A goal
The teacher wrote an objective for each lesson.

oblivious Unaware and unmindful
Les was half asleep and oblivious to the racket around him.

obscure Vague, unclear, uncertain
The lawyer quoted an obscure reference.

ominous Threatening or menacing
There were ominous black storm clouds on the horizon.

palatable Agreeable, acceptable
Sandy's friends tried to make her punishment more palatable.

panorama A comprehensive view or picture
The visitors' center offered a panorama of the canyon below.

pedagogy The science of teaching
Parts of certification tests focus on pedagogy.

perpetuate To continue or cause to be remembered
A plaque was put up to perpetuate the memory of the retiring teacher.

pompous Exaggerated self-importance
Rona acted pompous, but Lynne suspected she was very empty inside.

precarious Uncertain, beyond one's control
A diver sat on a precarious perch on a cliff above the water.

precedent An act or instance that sets the standard
The judge's ruling set a precedent for later cases.

preclude To act to make impossible or impracticable
Beau did not want to preclude any options.

precocious Very early development
Chad was very precocious and ran at six months.

prolific Abundant producer
Isaac Asimov was a prolific science fiction writer.

prognosis A forecast or prediction
The stockbroker gave a guarded prognosis for continued growth.

provoke To stir up or anger
Children banging on the cage would provoke the circus lion to growl.

psychomotor Relates to the motor skill area of learning
I read the Taxonomy of Behavioral Objectives: Psychomotor Domain.

quagmire Predicament or difficult situation
The regulations were a quagmire of conflicting rules and vague terms.

qualm Feeling of doubt or misgiving
The teacher had not a single qualm about giving the student a low grade.

quandary A dilemma
The absence of the teacher aide left the teacher in a quandary.

quench To put out, satisfy
The glass of water was not enough to quench his thirst.

rancor Bitter continuing resentment
A deep rancor had existed between the two friends since the accident.

rationale The basis or reason for something
The speeder tried to present a rationale to the officer who stopped her.

reciprocal Mutual interchange
Each person got something out of their reciprocal arrangement.

refute To prove false
The lawyer used new evidence to refute claims made by the prosecution.

remedial Designed to compensate for learning deficits
Jim spent one period a day in remedial instruction.

reprove Criticize gently
The teacher would reprove students for chewing gum in class.

repudiate To reject or disown
The senator repudiated membership in an all male club.

resolve To reach a definite conclusion
A mediator was called in to resolve the situation.

retrospect Contemplation of the past
Ryan noted, in retrospect, that leaving home was his best decision.

revere To hold in the highest regard
Citizens of the town revere their longtime mayor.

sanction To issue authoritative approval or a penalty
The boxing commissioner had to sanction the match.

scrutinize To inspect with great care
You should scrutinize any document before signing it.

siblings Brothers or sisters
The holidays give me the chance to spend time with my siblings.

skeptical Doubting, questioning the validity
The principal was skeptical about the students' reason for being late.

solace Comfort in misfortune
Her friends provided solace in her time of grief.

solitude Being alone
Pat enjoyed her Sunday afternoon moments of solitude.

stagnant Inert, contaminated
In dry weather the lake shrank to a stagnant pool.

stereotype An oversimplified generalized view or belief
We are all guilty of fitting people into stereotypes.

subsidy Financial assistance
Chris received a subsidy from her company so she could attend school.

subtle Faint, not easy to find or understand
Subtle changes in the teller's actions alerted the police to the robbery.

subterfuge A deceptive strategy
The spy used a subterfuge to gain access to the secret materials.

superficial Surface, not profound
The inspector gave the car a quick, superficial inspection.

tacit Not spoken, inferred
They had a tacit agreement.

taxonomy Classification of levels of thinking or organisms
I read each Taxonomy of Educational Objectives.

tenacious Persistent and determined
The police officer was tenacious in pursuit of a criminal.

tentative Unsure, uncertain
The athletic director set up a tentative basketball schedule.

terminate To end, conclude
He wanted to terminate the relationship.

transition Passage from one activity to another
The transition from college student to teacher was not easy.

trepidation Apprehension, state of dread
Erin felt some trepidation about beginning her new job.

trivial Unimportant, ordinary
The seemingly trivial occurrence had taken on added importance.

ubiquitous Everywhere, omnipresent
A walk through the forest invited attacks from the ubiquitous mosquitoes.

ultimatum A final demand
After a trying day, the teacher issued an ultimatum to the class.

usurp To wrongfully and forcefully seize and hold, particularly power
The association vice president tried to usurp the president's power.

vacillate To swing indecisively
He had a tendency to vacillate in his stance on discipline.

valid Logically correct
The math teacher was explaining a valid mathematical proof.

vehement Forceful, passionate
The child had a vehement reaction to the teacher's criticism.

vestige A sign of something no longer there or existing
Old John was the last vestige of the first teachers to work at the school.

vicarious Experience through the activities or feelings of others
He had to experience sports in a vicarious way through his students.

virulent Very poisonous or noxious
The coral snake has a particularly virulent venom.

vital Important and essential
The school secretary was a vital part of the school.

waffle To write or speak in a misleading way
The spokesperson waffled as she tried to explain away the mistake.

wary Watchful, on guard
The soldiers were very wary of any movements across the DMZ.

Xanadu An idyllic, perfect place
All wished for some time in Xanadu.

yearned Longed or hoped for
Liz yearned for a small class.

zeal Diligent devotion to a cause
Ron approached his job with considerable zeal.

STRATEGIES FOR TAKING THE READING TEST

This chapter gives an integrated approach to answering literal and critical reading items on the PPST and the CBT.

The reading test consists of passages followed by multiple-choice questions. You do not have to know what an entire reading passage is about. You just have to know enough to get the answer correct. Less than half, often less than 25%, of the information in any passage is needed to answer all the questions.

You do not have to read the passage in detail. In fact, careful slow reading will almost certainly get you in trouble. Strange as it seems, follow this advice—avoid careful, detailed reading at all costs.

Buried among all the false gold in the passage are a few valuable nuggets. Follow these steps to hit pay dirt and avoid the fool's gold.

READING ABOUT READING

Reading seems to be a natural process. Reading about reading and about steps to taking reading tests can seem contrived and confusing. However, we know that these steps and techniques work. Once you apply the steps to the practice exercises, your reading ability and scores will improve.

FIVE STEPS TO TAKING A READING TEST

Reading seems to be a natural process. Reading about reading and about steps to taking reading tests can seem contrived and confusing. However, we know that these steps and techniques work. Once you apply the steps to the practice exercises, your reading ability and scores will improve.

During a reading test follow these steps.

1. Skim to find the topic of each paragraph.

2. Read the questions and answers.

3. Eliminate incorrect answers.

4. Scan the details to find the answer.

5. Choose the answer that is absolutely correct.

1. Skim to Find the Topic of Each Paragraph

Your first job is to find the topic of each paragraph. The topic is what a paragraph or passage is about.

The topic of a paragraph is usually found in the first and last sentences. Read the first and last sentences just enough to find the topic. You can write the topic in the margin next to the passage on the PPST; for the CBT, use scrap paper. Remember, the PPST test booklet is yours. You can mark it up as much as you like.

Reading Sentences

Every sentence has a subject that tells what the sentence is about. The sentence also has a verb that tells what the subject is doing or links the subject to the complement. The sentence may also contain a complement that receives the action or describes what is being said about the subject. The words underlined in the following examples are the ones you would focus on as you preview.

1. The famous educator <u>John Dewey founded</u> an educational movement called <u>progressive education</u>.

2. Sad to say, we have learned <u>American school children</u> of all ages <u>are poorly nourished</u>.

You may occasionally encounter a paragraph or passage in which the topic can't be summarized from the first and last sentences. This type of paragraph usually contains factual information. If this happens, you will have to read the entire paragraph.

Fact, Opinion, or Fiction

If it is a factual passage, the author will present the fact and support it with details and examples. If the passage presents an opinion, the author will give the opinion and support it with arguments, examples, and other details. Many passages combine fact and opinion. If it is a fiction passage, the author will tell a story with details, descriptions, and examples about people, places, or things.

Once you find the topic, you will probably need more information to answer the questions. But don't worry about this other information and details now. You can go back and find it after you have read the questions.

2. Read the Questions and the Answers

Now read the questions—one at a time. Read the answers for the question you are working on. Be sure that you understand what each question and its answers mean.

Before you answer a question, be sure you know whether it is asking for a fact or an inference. If the question asks for a fact, the correct answer will identify a main idea or supporting detail. We'll discuss more about main ideas and details later. The correct answer may also identify a cause and effect relationship among ideas or be a paraphrase or summary of parts of the passage. Look for these.

If the question asks for an inference, the correct answer will identify the author's purpose, assumptions, or attitude and the difference between fact and the author's opinion. Look for these elements.

3. Eliminate Incorrect Answers

Read the answers and eliminate the ones that you absolutely know are incorrect. Read the answers literally. Look for words such as *always*, *never*, *must*, *all*. If you can find a single exception to this type of sweeping statement, then the answer can't be correct. Eliminate it.

4. Scan the Details to Find the Answer

Once you have eliminated answers, compare the other answers to the passage. When you find the answer that is confirmed by the passage—stop. That is your answer choice. Follow these other suggestions for finding the correct answer.

You will often need to read details to find the main idea of a paragraph. The main idea of a paragraph is what the writer has to say about the topic. Most questions are about the main idea of a paragraph. Scan the details about the main idea until you find the answer. Scanning means skipping over information that does not answer the question.

Look at this paragraph.

> There are many types of boats. Some are very fast while others could sleep a whole platoon of soldiers. I prefer the old putt-putt fishing boat with a ten horsepower motor. That was a boat with a purpose. You didn't scare many people, but the fish were sure worried.

The topic of this paragraph is boats. The main idea is that the writer prefers small fishing boats to other boats.

Unstated Topic and Main Idea

Sometimes the topic and main idea are not stated. Consider this passage.

> The Chinese were the first to use sails thousands of years ago, hundreds of years before sails were used in Europe. The Chinese also used the wheel and the kite long before they were used on the European continent. Experts believe that many other Chinese inventions were used from three hundred to one thousand three hundred years before they were used in Europe.

The topic of this paragraph is inventions. The main idea of the paragraph is that the Chinese invented and used many things hundreds and thousands of years before they appeared in Europe.

Some Answers Are Not Related to the Main Idea

Some answers are not related to the main idea of a paragraph. These questions may be the most difficult to answer. You just have to keep scanning the details until you find the correct answer.

Who Wrote This Answer?

People who write tests go to great lengths to choose a correct answer that cannot be questioned. That is what they get paid for. They are not paid to write answers that have a higher meaning or include great truths.

Test writers want to be asked to write questions and answers again. They want to avoid valid complaints from test takers like you who raise legitimate concerns about their answers.

They usually accomplish this difficult task in one of two ways. They may write answers that are very specific and based directly on the reading. They may also write correct answers that seem very vague.

A Vague Answer Can Be Correct

How can a person write a vague answer that is correct? Think of it this way. If I wrote that a person is 6 feet 5 inches tall, you could get out a tape measure to check my facts. Since I was very specific, you are more likely to be able to prove me wrong.

On the other hand, if I write that the same person is over 6 feet tall you would be hard pressed to find fault with my statement. So my vague statement was hard to argue with. If the person in question is near 6 feet 5 inches tall, then my vague answer is most likely to be the correct one.

Don't choose an answer just because it seems more detailed or specific. A vague answer may just as likely be correct.

5. Choose the Answer That Is Absolutely Correct

Be sure that your choice answers the question. Be sure that your choice is based on the information contained in the paragraph. Don't choose an answer to another question. Don't choose an answer just because it sounds right. Don't choose an answer just because you agree with it.

There is no room on tests like these for answers that are partially wrong. It is not enough for an answer to be 99.9% correct. It must be absolutely, incontrovertibly, unquestionably, indisputably, and unarguably correct.

AUTHOR'S PURPOSE

The author's primary purpose explains why the author wrote the passage. The purpose is closely related to the main idea. You might think, "Fine, I know the main idea. But why did the author take the time to write about that main idea? What is the author trying to make me know or feel?"

The author's purpose will be in one of five categories. The categories and their descriptions are given below.

Describe	Present an image of physical reality or a mental image.
Entertain	Amuse, Perform
Inform	Clarify, Explain, State
Narrate	Relate, Tell a story
Persuade	Argue, Convince, Prove

There is no hard and fast rule for identifying the author's purpose. Rely on your informed impression of the passage.

Bias

A statement or passage reveals bias if the author has prejudged or has a predisposition to a doctrine, idea, or practice. Bias means the author is trying to convince or influence the reader through some emotional appeal or slanted writing.

Bias can be positive or negative.

Positive Bias: She is so lovely, she deserves the very best.
Negative Bias: She is so horrible, I hope she gets what's coming to her.

Forms of Bias

Biased writing can often be identified by the presence of one or more of the following forms of bias.

Emotional Language	Language that appeals to the reader's emotions, and not to common sense or logic.
	Positive: If I am elected, I will help your family get jobs. Negative: If my opponent is elected, your family will lose their jobs.
Inaccurate Information	Language that presents false, inaccurate, or unproved information as though it were factual.
	Positive: My polls indicate that I am very popular. Negative: My polls indicate that a lot of people disagree with my opponent.

Name Calling	Language that uses negative, disapproving terms without any factual basis. Negative: I'll tell you, my opponent is a real jerk.
Slanted Language	Language that slants the facts or evidence toward the writer's point of view. Positive: I am a positive person, looking for the good side of people. Negative: My opponent finds fault with everyone and everything.
Stereotyping	Language that indicates that a person is like all the members of a particular group. Positive: I belong to the Krepenkle party, the party known for its honesty. Negative: My opponent belongs to the Lerplenkle party, the party of increased taxes.

Author's Tone

The author's tone is the author's attitude as reflected in the passage. How do you think the author would sound while speaking? What impression would you form about the speaker's attitude or feeling? The answer to the latter question will usually lead you to the author's tone. A partial list of tone words is given below.

absurd	excited	outraged
amused	formal	outspoken
angry	gentle	pathetic
apathetic	hard	pessimistic
arrogant	imnpassioned	playful
bitter	indignant	prayerful
cheerful	intense	reverent
comic	intimate	righteous
compassionate	joyous	satirical
complex	loving	sentimental
concerned	malicious	serious
cruel	mocking	solemn
depressed	nostalgic	tragic
distressed	objective	uneasy
evasive	optimistic	vindictive

APPLYING THE STEPS

Let's apply the five steps to this passage and questions.

Many vocational high schools in the United States give off-site work experience to their students. Students usually work in local businesses part of the school day and attend high school the other part. These programs have made American vocational schools world leaders in making job experience available to teenage students.

According to this paragraph, American vocational high schools are world leaders in making job experience available to teenage students because they
(A) have students attend school only part of the day.
(B) were quick to move their students to schools off-site.
(C) require students to work before they can attend the school.
(D) involve their students in cooperative education programs.
(E) involve their students in after-school part time work.

Step 1: Skim to find the topic of each paragraph. Both the first and last sentences tell us that the topic is vocational schools and work experience.

Step 2: Read the questions and answers. Why are American vocational education high schools the world leaders in offering job experience?

Step 3: Eliminate incorrect answers. Answer (C) is obviously wrong. It has to do with work before high school. Answer (B) is also incorrect. This has to do with attending school off-site. This leaves answers (A), (D), and (E).

Step 4: Scan the details to find the answer. Scan the details and find that parts of answer (A) are found in the passage. In answer (D) you have to know that cooperative education is another name for off-site work during school. There is no reference to the after-school work found in answer (E).

Step 5: Choose the answer that is absolutely correct. It is down to answer (A) or answer (D). But answer (A) contains only part of the reason that vocational education high schools have gained such acclaim. Answer (D) is the absolutely correct answer.

Here's how to apply the steps to the following passage.

Problem Solving

Problem solving has become the main focus of mathematics learning. Students learn problem-solving strategies and then apply them to problems. Many tests now focus on problem solving and limit the number of computational problems. The problem-solving movement is traced to George Polya who wrote several problem-solving books for high school teachers.

Problem Solving Strategies

Problem-solving strategies include guess and check, draw a diagram, and make a list. Many of the strategies are taught as skills, which inhibits flexible and creative thinking. Problems in textbooks can also limit the power of the strategies. However, the problem-solving movement will be with us for some time, and a number of the strategies are useful.

Step 1: Skim to find the topic of each paragraph. The topic of the first paragraph is problem solving. You find the topic in both the first and last sentences. Write the topic next to the paragraph. The topic for the second paragraph is problem-solving strategies. Write the topic next to the paragraph.

Now we are ready to look at the questions. If the question is about problem solving "in general" we start looking in the first paragraph for the answer. If the question is about strategies, we start looking in the second paragraph for the answer.

Step 2: Read the questions and answers.

According to this passage, a difficulty with teaching problem-solving strategies is:
(A) The strategies are too difficult for children.
(B) The strategies are taught as skills.
(C) The strategies are in textbooks.
(D) The strategies are part of a movement.
(E) Problem solving is for high school teachers.

Step 3: Eliminate incorrect answers. Answer (A) can't be right because difficulty is not mentioned in the passage. Choice (E) can't be correct because it does not mention strategies at all. That leaves (B), (C), and (D) for us to consider.

Step 4: Scan the details to find the answer. The question asks about strategies so we look immediately to the second paragraph for the answer. The correct answer is (B). Choice (C) is not correct because the passage does not mention strategies in textbooks. There is no indication that (D) is correct.

Step 5: Choose the answer that is absolutely correct. The correct choice is (B).

PRACTICE PASSAGE

Apply the five steps to this practice passage. Mark the letter of the correct answer. Follow the directions given below. The answers to these questions are found on page 200. Do not look at the answers until you complete your work.

Read the following passage. After reading the passage, choose the best answer to each question from among the five choices. Answer all the questions following the passage on the basis of what is stated or implied in the passage.

Today's students have hand-held calculators that can graph one or even many equations. Students can even type in several equations and the calculator will "solve" them. This is the best way just to see a plotted graph quickly.

This is the worst way to learn about graphing and equations. The calculator can't tell the students anything about the process of graphing and does not teach them how to plot a graph.

Left to this electronic graphing process, students will not have the hands-on experience needed to see the patterns and symmetry that characterize graphing and equations. They may become too dependent on the calculator and be unable to reason effectively about equations and the process of graphing.

It may be true that graphing and solving equations is taught mechanically in some classrooms. There is also something to be said for these electronic devices, which give students the opportunity to try out several graphs and solutions quickly before deciding on a final solution.

For all their electronic accuracy and patience, these graphing calculators cannot replace the process of graphing and solving equations on your own. For mastery of equations and graphing comes not just from seeing the graph automatically displayed on a screen, but also comes from a hands-on involvement with graphing.

1. The main idea of the passage is that:
    (A) a child can be good at graphing equations only through hands-on experience.
    (B) teaching approaches for graphing equations should be improved.
    (C) accuracy and patience are the keys to effective graphing instruction.
    (D) the new graphing calculators have limited ability to teach students about graphing.
    (E) graphing calculators provide one of the best possible ways to practice graphing equations.

2. According to this passage, what negative impact will graphing calculators have on students who use them?
    (A) They will not have experience with four-function calculators.
    (B) They will become too dependent on the calculator.
    (C) They can quickly try out several graphs before coming up with a final answer.
    (D) They will get too much hands-on experience with calculators.
    (E) The teachers will not know how to use the electronic calculator because they use mechanical aids.

3. According to the passage, which of the following is a major drawback of the graphing calculator?
    (A) It graphs many equations with their solutions.
    (B) It does not give students hands-on experience with graphing.
    (C) It does not give students hands-on experience with calculators.
    (D) This electronic method interferes with the mechanical method.
    (E) It does not replace the patient teacher.

4. The passage includes information that would answer which of the following questions?
    (A) What are the shortcomings of graphing and solving equations as it sometimes takes place?
    (B) How many equations can you type into a graphing calculator?
    (C) What hands-on experience should students have as they learn about graphing equations?
    (D) What is the degree of accuracy and speed that can be attained by a graphing calculator?
    (E) What level of ability is needed to show mastery of equations and graphing?

5. The description of a graphing calculator found in this passage tells about which of the following?
    I. The equations that can be graphed
    II. The approximate size of the calculator
    III. The advantages of the graphing calculator
    (A) I only
    (B) II only
    (C) I and II only
    (D) II and III only
    (E) I, II, and III

Practice Passage Explained Answers

Don't read this section until you have completed the practice passage. Here's how to apply the steps.

Step 1: Skim to find the topic of each paragraph. You should have written a topic next to each paragraph. Suggested topics are shown next to the following selection. Your topics don't have to be identical, but they should accurately reflect the paragraph's content.

Graphing Calculators

Today's students have hand-held calculators that can graph one or even many equations. Students can even type in several equations and the calculator will "solve" them. This is the best way to just see a plotted graph quickly.

Problem with Graphing Calculators

This is the worst way to learn about graphing and equations. The calculator can't tell the students anything about the process of graphing and does not teach them how to plot a graph.

Why it's a Problem

Left to this electronic graphing process, students will not have the hands-on experience needed to see the patterns and symmetry that characterize graphing and equations. They may become too dependent on the calculator and be unable to reason effectively about equations and the process of graphing.

Good Points

It may be true that graphing and solving equations is taught mechanically in some classrooms. There is also something to be said for these electronic devices, which give students the opportunity to try out several graphs and solutions quickly before deciding on a final solution.

For all their electronic accuracy and patience, these graphing calculators cannot replace the process of graphing and solving equations on your own. Mastery of equations and graphing comes not just from seeing the graph automatically displayed on a screen, but also from a hands-on involvement with graphing.

Apply Steps 2 through 5 to each of the questions.

1. The main idea of the passage is that
   (A) a student can be good at graphing equations only through hands-on experience.
   (B) teaching approaches for graphing equations should be improved.
   (C) accuracy and patience are the keys to effective graphing instruction.
   (D) the new graphing calculators have limited ability to teach students about graphing.
   (E) graphing calculators provide one of the best possible ways to practice graphing equations.

Step 2: Read the question and answers. You have to identify the main idea of the passage. This is a very common question on reading tests. Remember that the main idea is what the writer is trying to say or communicate in the passage.

Step 3: Eliminate incorrect answers. Answers (B) and (C) are not correct. Answer (C) is not at all correct based on the passage. Even though (B) may be true, it does not reflect what the writer is trying to say in this passage. Answer (E) is also not the correct answer. You might be able to imply this answer from the paragraph, but it is not the main idea.

Step 4: Scan the details to find the answer. As we review the details we see that both answer (A) and answer (D) are stated or implied in the passage. A scan of the details, alone, does not reveal which is the main idea. We must determine that on our own.

Step 5: Choose the answer that is absolutely correct. Which answer is absolutely correct? The whole passage is about graphing calculators, and they must be an important part of the main idea. The correct answer is (D). The author certainly believes that (A) is true, but uses this point to support the main idea.

2. According to this passage, what negative impact will graphing calculators have on students who use them?
   (A) They will not have experience with four-function calculators.
   (B) They will become too dependent on the calculator.
   (C) They can quickly try out several graphs before coming up with a final answer.
   (D) They will get too much hands-on experience with calculators.
   (E) The teachers will not know how to use the electronic calculator because they use mechanical aids.

Step 2: Read the question and answers. This is a straightforward comprehension question. What negative impact will calculators have on students who use them? The second and third paragraphs have topics related to problems with calculators. We'll probably find the answer there.

Step 3: Eliminate incorrect answers. Answer (E) is obviously incorrect. The question asks about students. This answer is about teachers. Answer (C) is not a negative impact of graphing calculators. Scan the details to find the correct answer from (A), (B), and (D).

Step 4: Scan the details to find the answer. The only detail that matches the question is in paragraph 3. The author says that students may become too dependent on the calculators. That's our answer.

Step 5: Choose the answer that is absolutely correct. Answer (B) is the only correct choice.

3. According to the passage, which of the following is a major drawback of the graphing calculator?
   (A) It graphs many equations with their solutions.
   (B) It does not give students hands-on experience with graphing.
   (C) It does not give students hands-on experience with calculators.
   (D) This electronic method interferes with the mechanical method.
   (E) It does not replace the patient teacher.

Step 2: Read the question and answers. This is another straightforward comprehension question. This question is somewhat different from Question 2. Notice that the question asks for a drawback of the calculator. It does not ask for something that is wrong with the calculator itself. The topics indicate that we will probably find the answer in paragraph 1 or paragraph 2.

Step 3: Eliminate incorrect answers. Answer (C) is obviously wrong. Graphing calculators do give students hands-on experience with calculators. Be careful! It is easy to mix up (C) with (B). Answer (A) is a strength of the calculator and is also incorrect. Let's move on to the details.

Step 4: Scan the details to find the answer. Choices (B), (D), and (E) remain. The details in paragraph 2 reveal that the correct answer is (B).

Step 5: Choose the answer that is absolutely correct. Answer (B) is the only absolutely correct answer. Notice that answers (B) and (C) are similar. The absolutely correct answer for this question was a possible correct answer for the previous question. Just because an answer seems correct doesn't mean that it is the absolutely correct answer.

4. The passage includes information that would answer which of the following questions?
   (A) What are the shortcomings of teaching about graphing equations as it sometimes takes place?
   (B) How many equations can you type into a graphing calculator?
   (C) What hands-on experience should students have as they learn about graphing equations?
   (D) What is the degree of accuracy and speed that can be attained by a graphing calculator?
   (E) What level of ability is needed to show mastery of equations and graphing?

Step 2: Read the question and answers. This is yet another type of reading comprehension question. You are asked to identify the questions that could be answered from the passage.

Step 3: Eliminate incorrect answers. Choices (B), (D), and (E) are not correct. None of this information is included in the passage. This is not to say that these questions, particularly (E), are not important. Rather it means that the answers to these questions are not found in this passage.

Step 4: Scan the details to find the answer. Both (A) and (C) are discussed in the passage. However, a scan of the details reveals that the answer to (C) is not found in the passage. The passage mentions hands-on experience, but it does not mention what types of hands-on experience students should have. There is an answer for (A). Graphing is taught mechanically in some classrooms.

Step 5: Choose the answer that is absolutely correct. Answer (A) is the absolutely correct answer. This is the only question that can be answered from the passage. The answer is not related to the writer's main idea and this may make it more difficult to answer.

5. The description of a graphing calculator found in this passage tells about which of the following?
   I.   The equations that can be graphed
   II. The approximate size of the calculator
   III. The advantages of the graphing calculator
   (A) I only
   (B) II only
   (C) I and II only
   (D) II and III only
   (E) I, II, and III

Step 2: Read the question and answers. This is another classic type of reading comprehension question. You are given several choices. You must decide which combination of these choices is the absolutely correct answer.

Step 3: Eliminate incorrect answers. If you can determine that Statement I, for example, is not addressed in the passage, you can eliminate ALL answer choices that include Statement I.

Step 4: Scan the details to find which of the original three statements is (are) true.
   I. No, there is no description of which equations can be graphed.
   II. Yes, paragraph 1 mentions that the calculators are hand-held.
   III. Yes, paragraph 4 mentions the advantages.
   Both II and III are correct.

Step 5: Choose the answer that is absolutely correct. Choice (D) is absolutely correct. It lists both II and III.

TARGETED READING TEST

This targeted test is designed to help you practice the strategies presented in this chapter. For that reason, questions may have a different emphasis than the actual test, and the actual test will certainly be more complete.

Mark your choice, then check your answers. Use the strategies on pages 192–196.

While becoming a teacher, I spent most of my time with books. I read books about the subjects I would teach in school and books that explained how to teach the subjects. As a new teacher, I relied on books to help my students learn. But I learned, and now the basis for my teaching is to help students apply what they have learned to the real world.

1. Which of the following would most likely be the next line of this passage?
   (A) The world is a dangerous and intimidating place; be wary of it.
   (B) Children should be taught to seek whatever the world has to offer.
   (C) A teacher has to be in the world, not just study about the world.
   (D) But you can't forget about books.
   (E) Teaching is like learning.

2. Which of the following is the underlying moral of this passage?
   (A) Teaching art is very rewarding.
   (B) Children learn a lot from field trips.
   (C) There is much to be said for teachers who think of their students' experiences first.
   (D) Firsthand experiences are important for children's learning and development.
   (E) You never know what you will end up teaching.

The American alligator is found in Florida and Georgia, and has also been reported in other states, including North and South Carolina. Weighing in at more than 400 pounds, the length of an adult alligator is twice that of its tail. Adult alligators eat fish and small mammals while young alligators prefer insects, shrimp, and frogs.

An untrained person may mistake a crocodile for an alligator. Crocodiles are found in the same areas as alligators and both have prominent snouts with many teeth. The crocodile has a long thin snout with teeth in both jaws. The alligator's snout is wider with teeth only in the upper jaw.

3. Which of the following would be a good title for this passage?
   (A) Large Reptiles
   (B) Eating Habits of Alligators
   (C) The American Alligator
   (D) How Alligators and Crocodiles Differ
   (E) American Alligator: Endangered Species

4. Which of the following would be a way to distinguish an alligator from a crocodile?
   (A) number of teeth
   (B) shape of snout
   (C) habitat
   (D) diet
   (E) mating rituals

5. Which of the following best describes the purpose of the passage?
   (A) All animals are noteworthy.
   (B) Reptiles are interesting animals.
   (C) To educate readers about differences in similar animals.
   (D) To describe the life cycle of wetland creatures.
   (E) To provide information about the American alligator.

Remove the jack from the trunk. Set the jack under the car. Use the jack to raise the car. Remove the lug nuts. Remove the tire and replace it with the doughnut. Reset the lug nuts loosely and use the jack to lower the chassis to the ground. Tighten the lug nuts once the tire is touching the ground.

6. Which of the following is the main idea of this passage?
   (A) using a jack
   (B) changing a tire on a car
   (C) maintaining a car
   (D) following directions
   (E) caring for a car

Farmers and animals are fighting over rain forests. The farmers are clearing the forests and driving out the animals to make room for crops. If this battle continues, the rain forest will disappear. Both the farmers and the animals will lose, and the soil in the cleared forest will form a hard crust.

Of course, there are global implications as well. Clearing the forests increases the amount of carbon dioxide in the atmosphere. The most promising solution to the problems caused by clearing the rain forests is the education of the local farmers.

7. Which information below is not provided in the passage?
   (A) reasons the animals are being run out
   (B) reasons the farmers need more land
   (C) effects of lost rain forests
   (D) ways that people can help globally
   (E) ways that people can help locally

8. What most likely would the opinion of the author be about wildlife conservation?
   (A) All animals must fend for themselves.
   (B) Damage to the earth affects both people and animals.
   (C) Our greatest resource on earth is the human intellect.
   (D) Testing products on animals is a practice that should be outlawed.
   (E) Animals and people should have equal rights.

I love gingerbread cookies, which are flavored with ginger and molasses. I can remember cold winter days when my brother and I huddled around the fire eating gingerbread cookies and sipping warm apple cider. In those days, gingerbread cookies came in many shapes and sizes. When you eat a gingerbread cookie today, you have to bite a "person's" head off.

9. Why did the author of the passage above put quotes around the word *person*?
   (A) to emphasize the difference between gingerbread cookies that appear as people rather than windmills
   (B) because gingerbread cookies often don't look like people
   (C) to emphasize the most popular current shape of gingerbread cookies
   (D) to emphasize the choice of this word rather than the word *man*
   (E) to emphasize how our culture now puts more importance on people than on things

Use this fable attributed to Aesop to answer questions 10 and 11.

The Frogs Who Wanted a King

The frogs lived a happy life in the pond. They jumped from lily pad to lily pad and sunned themselves without a care. But a few of the frogs were not satisfied with this relaxed and enjoyable life. These frogs thought that they needed a king to rule them. So they sent a note to the god Jupiter requesting that he appoint a king.

Jupiter was amused by this request. In a good-natured response, Jupiter threw a log into the pond, which landed with a big splash. All the frogs jumped to safety. Some time passed and one frog started to approach the log, which lay still in the pond. When nothing happened, the other frogs jumped on the floating giant, treating it with disdain.

The frogs were not satisfied with such a docile king. They sent another note to Jupiter asking for a strong king to rule over them. Jupiter was not amused by this second request and he was tired of the frogs' complaints.

So Jupiter sent a stork. The stork immediately devoured every frog in sight. The few surviving frogs gave Mercury a message to carry to Jupiter pleading for Jupiter to show them mercy.

Jupiter was very cold. He told Mercury to tell the frogs that they were responsible for their own problems. They had asked for a king to rule them and they would have to make the best of it.

10. Which of the following morals fits the passage?
    (A) Let well enough alone.
    (B) Familiarity breeds contempt.
    (C) Slow and steady wins the race.
    (D) Liberty is too high a price to pay for revenge.
    (E) Misery loves company.

11. Why did the frogs treat the log with contempt?
    (A) The log was sent by Jupiter.
    (B) The log floated in the pond.
    (C) The log was not alive.
    (D) The log could not speak.
    (E) The log was not assertive.

You may want to go to a park on a virgin prairie in Minnesota. The park borders Canada and is just west of the Mississippi River. The thousands of acres of park land are home to hundreds of species of birds and mammals. In the evening, a sotto wind sweeps across the prairie, creating wave-like ripples in the tall grasses. This prairie park is just one of the wonders you can see when you visit marvelous Minnesota.

12. Where might you find this excerpt?
    (A) cook book
    (B) travel brochure
    (C) hunting magazine
    (D) national parks guide
    (E) conservation organization mailing

13. In which part of the United States is this park located?
    (A) Midwest
    (B) Northeast
    (C) Southeast
    (D) Northwest
    (E) Southwest

14. What does the author mean by "virgin prairie"?
    (A) desolate taiga
    (B) untouched grasslands
    (C) wooded plains
    (D) Indian reservation
    (E) untainted meadows

There was a time in the United States when a married woman was expected to take her husband's last name. Most women still follow this practice, but things are changing. In fact, Hawaii is the only state with a law requiring a woman to take her husband's last name when she marries.

Many women look forward to taking their husband's surname. They may enjoy the bond it establishes with their husband, or want to be identified with their husband's professional status. Other women want to keep their own last name. They may prefer their original last name, or want to maintain their professional identity.

Some women resolve this problem by choosing a last name that hyphenates their surname and their husband's surname. This practice of adopting elements of both surnames is common in other cultures.

15. What would be the best title for this passage?
    (A) Women Have Rights
    (B) Determining a Woman's Name After Marriage
    (C) Determining a Woman's Name After Divorce
    (D) Legal Aspects of Surname Changing
    (E) Hawaii's Domestic Laws

16. What position is the author taking on women's rights?
    (A) for women but against men
    (B) for women and against equality
    (C) for women and for men
    (D) against women but for men
    (E) against women and against men

17. The passage would LEAST likely be found in a
    (A) fashion magazine.
    (B) woman's corporate magazine.
    (C) teen magazine aimed at girls.
    (D) fitness magazine.
    (E) bridal magazine.

18. What is the main idea of this passage?
    (A) Women are at the mercy of the law.
    (B) Women in Hawaii have no options.
    (C) Women today have many options related to surnames.
    (D) Children should have the same name as their mother.
    (E) Men have stopped demanding that women change their names.

In recent years, cooperative learning, which involves students in small group activities, has gained popularity as an instructional approach. Cooperative learning provides students with an opportunity to work on projects presented by the teacher. This type of learning emphasizes group goals, cooperative learning, and shared responsibility. All students must contribute in order for the group to be successful.

19. What is the main idea of this passage?
    (A) to show different learning styles
    (B) to examine the best way to teach
    (C) to explain why cooperative learning is the best method for eliminating classrooms
    (D) to illustrate the method of cooperative learning
    (E) to show the role of the teacher in a cooperative learning environment

20. According to this passage what would be a good definition of cooperative learning?
    (A) An instructional arrangement in which children work in small groups in a manner that promotes student responsibility.
    (B) An instructional arrangement in which the teacher pairs two students in a tutor–tutee relationship to promote learning of academic skills or subject content.
    (C) An instructional arrangement consisting of three to seven students that represents a major format for teaching academic skills.
    (D) An instructional arrangement that is appropriate for numerous classroom activities such as show and tell, discussing interesting events, taking a field trip, or watching a movie.
    (E) An instructional arrangement in which the teaching responsibilities are shared.

Answers

1. **C**	5. **C**	9. **D**	13. **A**	17. **D**
2. **D**	6. **B**	10. **A**	14. **B**	18. **C**
3. **D**	7. **D**	11. **E**	15. **D**	19. **D**
4. **B**	8. **C**	12. **B**	16. **B**	20. **A**

PART III

Practice Tests

6 PRACTICE PPST 1

READING	40 items	50 minutes
WRITING MULTIPLE CHOICE	45 items	50 minutes
WRITING ESSAY	1 essay	30 minutes
MATHEMATICS	40 items	50 minutes

Take this test in a realistic, timed setting. You should not take this practice test until you have completed your review.

The setting will be most realistic if another person times the test and ensures that the test rules are followed exactly. If another person is acting as test supervisor, he or she should review these instructions with you and say "Start" when you should begin a section and "Stop" when time has expired.

Use the multiple-choice answer sheet on page 213. Use a pencil to mark the answer sheet. The actual test will be machine scored, so completely darken in the answer space.

Once the test is complete, review the answers and explanations for each item as you correct the test.

ANSWER SHEET FOR PRACTICE PPST 1

Reading—50 minutes

1 Ⓐ Ⓑ Ⓒ Ⓓ	9 Ⓐ Ⓑ Ⓒ Ⓓ	17 Ⓐ Ⓑ Ⓒ Ⓓ	25 Ⓐ Ⓑ Ⓒ Ⓓ	33 Ⓐ Ⓑ Ⓒ Ⓓ
2 Ⓐ Ⓑ Ⓒ Ⓓ	10 Ⓐ Ⓑ Ⓒ Ⓓ	18 Ⓐ Ⓑ Ⓒ Ⓓ	26 Ⓐ Ⓑ Ⓒ Ⓓ	34 Ⓐ Ⓑ Ⓒ Ⓓ
3 Ⓐ Ⓑ Ⓒ Ⓓ	11 Ⓐ Ⓑ Ⓒ Ⓓ	19 Ⓐ Ⓑ Ⓒ Ⓓ	27 Ⓐ Ⓑ Ⓒ Ⓓ	35 Ⓐ Ⓑ Ⓒ Ⓓ
4 Ⓐ Ⓑ Ⓒ Ⓓ	12 Ⓐ Ⓑ Ⓒ Ⓓ	20 Ⓐ Ⓑ Ⓒ Ⓓ	28 Ⓐ Ⓑ Ⓒ Ⓓ	36 Ⓐ Ⓑ Ⓒ Ⓓ
5 Ⓐ Ⓑ Ⓒ Ⓓ	13 Ⓐ Ⓑ Ⓒ Ⓓ	21 Ⓐ Ⓑ Ⓒ Ⓓ	29 Ⓐ Ⓑ Ⓒ Ⓓ	37 Ⓐ Ⓑ Ⓒ Ⓓ
6 Ⓐ Ⓑ Ⓒ Ⓓ	14 Ⓐ Ⓑ Ⓒ Ⓓ	22 Ⓐ Ⓑ Ⓒ Ⓓ	30 Ⓐ Ⓑ Ⓒ Ⓓ	38 Ⓐ Ⓑ Ⓒ Ⓓ
7 Ⓐ Ⓑ Ⓒ Ⓓ	15 Ⓐ Ⓑ Ⓒ Ⓓ	23 Ⓐ Ⓑ Ⓒ Ⓓ	31 Ⓐ Ⓑ Ⓒ Ⓓ	39 Ⓐ Ⓑ Ⓒ Ⓓ
8 Ⓐ Ⓑ Ⓒ Ⓓ	16 Ⓐ Ⓑ Ⓒ Ⓓ	24 Ⓐ Ⓑ Ⓒ Ⓓ	32 Ⓐ Ⓑ Ⓒ Ⓓ	40 Ⓐ Ⓑ Ⓒ Ⓓ

Writing—50 minutes

1 Ⓐ Ⓑ Ⓒ Ⓓ Ⓔ	10 Ⓐ Ⓑ Ⓒ Ⓓ Ⓔ	19 Ⓐ Ⓑ Ⓒ Ⓓ Ⓔ	28 Ⓐ Ⓑ Ⓒ Ⓓ Ⓔ	37 Ⓐ Ⓑ Ⓒ Ⓓ Ⓔ
2 Ⓐ Ⓑ Ⓒ Ⓓ Ⓔ	11 Ⓐ Ⓑ Ⓒ Ⓓ Ⓔ	20 Ⓐ Ⓑ Ⓒ Ⓓ Ⓔ	29 Ⓐ Ⓑ Ⓒ Ⓓ Ⓔ	38 Ⓐ Ⓑ Ⓒ Ⓓ Ⓔ
3 Ⓐ Ⓑ Ⓒ Ⓓ Ⓔ	12 Ⓐ Ⓑ Ⓒ Ⓓ Ⓔ	21 Ⓐ Ⓑ Ⓒ Ⓓ Ⓔ	30 Ⓐ Ⓑ Ⓒ Ⓓ Ⓔ	39 Ⓐ Ⓑ Ⓒ Ⓓ Ⓔ
4 Ⓐ Ⓑ Ⓒ Ⓓ Ⓔ	13 Ⓐ Ⓑ Ⓒ Ⓓ Ⓔ	22 Ⓐ Ⓑ Ⓒ Ⓓ Ⓔ	31 Ⓐ Ⓑ Ⓒ Ⓓ Ⓔ	40 Ⓐ Ⓑ Ⓒ Ⓓ Ⓔ
5 Ⓐ Ⓑ Ⓒ Ⓓ Ⓔ	14 Ⓐ Ⓑ Ⓒ Ⓓ Ⓔ	23 Ⓐ Ⓑ Ⓒ Ⓓ Ⓔ	32 Ⓐ Ⓑ Ⓒ Ⓓ Ⓔ	41 Ⓐ Ⓑ Ⓒ Ⓓ Ⓔ
6 Ⓐ Ⓑ Ⓒ Ⓓ Ⓔ	15 Ⓐ Ⓑ Ⓒ Ⓓ Ⓔ	24 Ⓐ Ⓑ Ⓒ Ⓓ Ⓔ	33 Ⓐ Ⓑ Ⓒ Ⓓ Ⓔ	42 Ⓐ Ⓑ Ⓒ Ⓓ Ⓔ
7 Ⓐ Ⓑ Ⓒ Ⓓ Ⓔ	16 Ⓐ Ⓑ Ⓒ Ⓓ Ⓔ	25 Ⓐ Ⓑ Ⓒ Ⓓ Ⓔ	34 Ⓐ Ⓑ Ⓒ Ⓓ Ⓔ	43 Ⓐ Ⓑ Ⓒ Ⓓ Ⓔ
8 Ⓐ Ⓑ Ⓒ Ⓓ Ⓔ	17 Ⓐ Ⓑ Ⓒ Ⓓ Ⓔ	26 Ⓐ Ⓑ Ⓒ Ⓓ Ⓔ	35 Ⓐ Ⓑ Ⓒ Ⓓ Ⓔ	44 Ⓐ Ⓑ Ⓒ Ⓓ Ⓔ
9 Ⓐ Ⓑ Ⓒ Ⓓ Ⓔ	18 Ⓐ Ⓑ Ⓒ Ⓓ Ⓔ	27 Ⓐ Ⓑ Ⓒ Ⓓ Ⓔ	36 Ⓐ Ⓑ Ⓒ Ⓓ Ⓔ	45 Ⓐ Ⓑ Ⓒ Ⓓ Ⓔ

Mathematics—50 minutes

1 Ⓐ Ⓑ Ⓒ Ⓓ	9 Ⓐ Ⓑ Ⓒ Ⓓ	17 Ⓐ Ⓑ Ⓒ Ⓓ	25 Ⓐ Ⓑ Ⓒ Ⓓ	33 Ⓐ Ⓑ Ⓒ Ⓓ
2 Ⓐ Ⓑ Ⓒ Ⓓ	10 Ⓐ Ⓑ Ⓒ Ⓓ	18 Ⓐ Ⓑ Ⓒ Ⓓ	26 Ⓐ Ⓑ Ⓒ Ⓓ	34 Ⓐ Ⓑ Ⓒ Ⓓ
3 Ⓐ Ⓑ Ⓒ Ⓓ	11 Ⓐ Ⓑ Ⓒ Ⓓ	19 Ⓐ Ⓑ Ⓒ Ⓓ	27 Ⓐ Ⓑ Ⓒ Ⓓ	35 Ⓐ Ⓑ Ⓒ Ⓓ
4 Ⓐ Ⓑ Ⓒ Ⓓ	12 Ⓐ Ⓑ Ⓒ Ⓓ	20 Ⓐ Ⓑ Ⓒ Ⓓ	28 Ⓐ Ⓑ Ⓒ Ⓓ	36 Ⓐ Ⓑ Ⓒ Ⓓ
5 Ⓐ Ⓑ Ⓒ Ⓓ	13 Ⓐ Ⓑ Ⓒ Ⓓ	21 Ⓐ Ⓑ Ⓒ Ⓓ	29 Ⓐ Ⓑ Ⓒ Ⓓ	37 Ⓐ Ⓑ Ⓒ Ⓓ
6 Ⓐ Ⓑ Ⓒ Ⓓ	14 Ⓐ Ⓑ Ⓒ Ⓓ	22 Ⓐ Ⓑ Ⓒ Ⓓ	30 Ⓐ Ⓑ Ⓒ Ⓓ	38 Ⓐ Ⓑ Ⓒ Ⓓ
7 Ⓐ Ⓑ Ⓒ Ⓓ	15 Ⓐ Ⓑ Ⓒ Ⓓ	23 Ⓐ Ⓑ Ⓒ Ⓓ	31 Ⓐ Ⓑ Ⓒ Ⓓ	39 Ⓐ Ⓑ Ⓒ Ⓓ
8 Ⓐ Ⓑ Ⓒ Ⓓ	16 Ⓐ Ⓑ Ⓒ Ⓓ	24 Ⓐ Ⓑ Ⓒ Ⓓ	32 Ⓐ Ⓑ Ⓒ Ⓓ	40 Ⓐ Ⓑ Ⓒ Ⓓ

Answers on pages 250–256

PRACTICE PPST READING TEST

You should not take this practice test until you have completed Chapter 5 and the targeted test at the end of that chapter.

The test rules allow you exactly 50 minutes for this test.

Keep the time limit in mind as you work. Answer the easier questions first. Be sure you answer all the questions. There is no penalty for guessing. You may write on the test booklet and mark up the questions.

Each question or statement on the multiple-choice portions of the test has five answer choices. Exactly one of these choices is correct. Mark your choice on the answer sheet provided for this test.

Your score is based on the spaces you fill in on the answer sheet. Make sure that you mark your answer on the answer sheet in the correct space next to the correct question number.

Once the test is complete, review the answers and explanations for each item as you correct the test.

When instructed, turn the page and begin.

READING

40 items   50 minutes

You will read selections followed by one or more questions with five answer choices. Select the best answer choice based on what the selection states or implies and mark that letter on the answer sheet.

1. The computers in the college dormitories are actually more sophisticated than the computers in the college computer labs, and they cost less. It seems that the person who bought the dormitory computers looked around until she found powerful computers at a low price. The person who runs the labs just got the computers offered by the regular supplier.

   The best statement of the main idea of this paragraph is
   (A) it is better to use the computers in the dorms.
   (B) it is better to avoid the computers in the labs.
   (C) the computers in the dorms are always in use so, for most purposes, it is better to use the computers in the labs.
   (D) it is better to shop around before you buy.
   (E) wholesale prices are usually better than retail prices.

Questions 2–4 are based on this passage.

   Researchers were not sure at first what caused AIDS or how it was transmitted. They did know early on that everyone who developed AIDS died. Then researchers began to understand that the disease is caused by the HIV virus, which could be transmitted through blood and blood products. Even after knowing this, some blood companies resisted testing blood for the HIV virus. Today we know that the HIV virus is transmitted through blood and other bodily fluids. Women may be more susceptible than men, and the prognosis hasn't changed.

2. The main intent of this passage is to
   (A) show that blood companies can't be trusted.
   (B) detail the history of AIDS research.
   (C) detail the causes and consequences of AIDS.
   (D) warn women that they are susceptible to AIDS.
   (E) raise awareness about AIDS.

3. Which of the following questions could be answered from this passage?
   (A) How do intravenous drug users acquire AIDS?
   (B) Is AIDS caused by a germ or a virus?
   (C) Through what mediums is AIDS transmitted?
   (D) How do blood companies test for AIDS?
   (E) What does AIDS mean?

4. Which of the following would be the best concluding summary sentence for this passage?
   (A) AIDS research continues to be underfunded in the United States.
   (B) Sexual activity and intravenous drug use continue to be the two primary ways that AIDS is transmitted.
   (C) People develop AIDS after being HIV positive.
   (D) Our understanding of AIDS has increased significantly over the past several years, but we are no closer to a cure.
   (E) It is better to be transfused with your own blood, if possible.

5. The retired basketball player said that, while modern players were better athletes because there was so much emphasis on youth basketball and increased focus on training, he still believed that the players of his day were better because they were more committed to the game, better understood its nuances, and were more dedicated to team play.

In this passage, the retired basketball player believed that which of the following factors led to today's basketball players being better athletes?
(A) more dedication
(B) increased salaries
(C) better nutrition
(D) youth basketball
(E) more commitment

6. The way I look at it, Robert E. Lee was the worst general in the Civil War—he was the South's commanding general, and the South lost the war.

What assumption does the writer of this statement make?
(A) War is horrible and should not be glorified.
(B) Picket's charge at Gettysburg was a terrible mistake.
(C) A general should be judged by whether he wins or loses.
(D) The South should have won the Civil War.
(E) Slavery is wrong.

7. Advances in astronomy and space exploration during the past twenty-five years have been significant, and we now know more answers to questions about the universe than ever before, but we still cannot answer the ultimate question, "How did our universe originate?"

Which of the following best characterizes the author's view of how the advances in astronomy and space exploration affect our eventual ability to answer the ultimate question?
(A) We now know more answers than ever before.
(B) All the questions have not been answered.
(C) Eventually we will probably find out.
(D) The question can't be answered.
(E) We will have the answer very soon.

Questions 8–12 are based on this passage.

The Board of Adjustment can exempt a person from the requirements of a particular land use ordinance. Several cases have come before the Board concerning three ordinances. One ordinance states that religious and other organizations cannot build places of worship or meeting halls in residential zones. A second ordinance states that any garage must be less than 25 percent of the size of a house on the same lot, while a third ordinance restricts a person's right to convert a one-family house to a two-family house.

It is interesting to note how a person can be in favor of an exemption in one case but opposed to exemption in another. For example, one homeowner applied to build a garage 45 percent of the size of her house but was opposed to a neighbor converting his house from a one-family to a two-family house. This second homeowner was opposed to a church being built in his neighborhood. The woman opposed to his proposal was all for the church construction project.

The pressure on Board of Adjustment members who also live in the community is tremendous. It must sometimes seem to them that any decision is the wrong one. But that is what Board of Adjustments are for, and we can only hope that this example of America in action will best serve the community and those who live there.

8. Which of the following sentences is the author of the passage most likely to DISAGREE with?
   (A) These Boards serve a useful purpose.
   (B) No exemptions should be granted to any zoning ordinance.
   (C) People can be very fickle when it comes to the exemptions they favor.
   (D) Some people may try to influence Board of Adjustment members.
   (E) The garage the woman wanted to build was about twice the allowable size.

9. The author finds people's reactions to exemption requests interesting because
   (A) so many different types of exemptions are applied for.
   (B) a person's reaction is often based on religious principles and beliefs.
   (C) a person can both support and not support requested exemptions.
   (D) people put so much pressure on Board members.
   (E) men usually oppose exemptions sought by women.

10. In which of the following publications would you expect this passage to appear?
   (A) A government textbook
   (B) A local newspaper
   (C) A national newspaper
   (D) A civics textbook
   (E) A newsmagazine

11. According to the author, the actions of a Board of Adjustment
   (A) oppress religious and community groups.
   (B) favor men over women.
   (C) enforce town ordinances.
   (D) are examples of America in action.
   (E) exempt people from property taxes.

12. Which of the following does the passage convey?
   (A) A person should be consistently for or against Board exemptions.
   (B) The Board of Adjustments should act only when all agree.
   (C) People are interested in their own needs when it comes to zoning.
   (D) Board of Adjustments members should not be from town.
   (E) The Board of Adjustments should not approve any of the requests.

13. The college sororities are "interviewed" by students during rush week. Rush week is a time when students get to know about the different sororities and decide which ones they want to join. Each student can pledge only one sorority. Once students have chosen the three they are most interested in, the intrigue begins. The sororities then choose from among the students who have chosen them.

Which of the following strategies will help assure a student that she will be chosen for at least one sorority and preferably get into a sorority she likes?

   I   Choose at least one sorority she is sure will choose her

  II Choose one sorority she wants to get into

 III Choose her three favorite sororities

 IV Choose three sororities she knows will choose her

(A) I and II

(B) I and III

(C) I only

(D) III only

(E) IV only

14. During a Stage 4 alert, workers in an energy plant must wear protective pants, a protective shirt, and a helmet, except that protective coveralls can be worn in place of protective pants and shirt. When there is a Stage 5 alert, workers must also wear filter masks in addition to the requirements for the Stage 4 alert.

During a Stage 5 alert, which of the following could be worn?

   I   masks, pants, shirt, helmet

  II coveralls, helmet, mask

 III coveralls, mask

(A) I only

(B) II only

(C) III only

(D) I and II only

(E) I, II, and III

Questions 15 and 16 are based on this passage.

Using percentages to report growth patterns can be deceptive. If there are 100 new users for a cereal currently used by 100 other people, the growth rate is 100 percent. However if there are 50,000 new users for a cereal currently used by 5,000,000 people, the growth rate is 1 percent. It seems obvious that the growth rate of 1 percent is preferable to the growth rate of 100 percent. So while percentages do provide a useful way to report growth patterns, we must know the initial number the growth percentage is based on before we make any conclusions.

15. According to this passage,

(A) lower growth rates mean higher actual growth.

(B) higher growth rates mean higher actual growth.

(C) the growth rate depends on the starting point.

(D) the growth rate does not depend on the starting point.

(E) a lower starting point means a higher growth rate.

16. Which of the following can be implied from this passage?

(A) Don't believe any advertisements.

(B) Question any percentage growth rate.

(C) Percentages should never be used.

(D) Any growth rate over 50 percent is invalid.

(E) Percentages are deceptive advertising.

17. (1) The science fiction story started with a description of the characters.
    (2) Some of the descriptions were hard for me to understand.
    (3) The book was about time travel in the 22nd century, an interesting subject.
    (4) The authors believed time travel would be possible by then.

    In these four sentences, a person describes a science fiction book. Which of the following choices most accurately characterizes these statements made by the person describing the book?
    (A) (2) alone states an opinion
    (B) (1) and (4) alone state facts
    (C) (3) states both facts and opinion
    (D) (1), (3), and (4) state facts only
    (E) (4) states an opinion

18. The public schools in Hinman have devoted extra resources to mathematics instruction for years. Their programs always reflect the most current thinking about the way mathematics should be taught, and the schools are always equipped with the most recent teaching aids. These extra resources have created a mathematics program that is now copied by other schools throughout America.

    The mathematics program at the Hinman schools is copied by other schools because
    (A) their programs always reflect the most current thinking about the way mathematics should be taught.
    (B) the schools are always equipped with the most recent teaching aids.
    (C) the schools use the NCTM standards.
    (D) extra resources were devoted to mathematics instruction.
    (E) their successful programs were publicized to other schools.

Questions 19–24 apply to this passage.

Computer graphing programs are capable of graphing almost any equations, including advanced equations from calculus. The student just types in the equation and the graph appears on the computer screen. The graphing program can also show the numerical solution for any entered equation. I like having a computer program that performs the mechanical aspects of these difficult calculations. However, these programs do not teach about graphing or mathematics because the computer does not "explain" what is going on. A person could type in an equation, get an answer, and have not the slightest idea what either meant.

Relying on this mindless kind of graphing and calculation, students will be completely unfamiliar with the meaning of the equations they write or the results they get. They will not be able to understand how to create a graph from an equation or to understand the basis for the more complicated calculations.

It may be true that a strictly mechanical approach is used by some teachers. There certainly is a place for students who already understand equations and graphing to have a computer program that relieves the drudgery. But these computer programs should never and can never replace the teacher. Mathematical competence assumes that understanding precedes rote calculation.

19. What is the main idea of this passage?
    (A) Mechanical calculation is one part of learning about mathematics.
    (B) Teachers should use graphing programs as one part of instruction.
    (C) Graphing programs are not effective for initially teaching mathematics.
    (D) Students who use these programs won't learn mathematics.
    (E) The programs rely too heavily on a student's typing ability.

20. Which of the following questions could be answered from the information in the passage?
    (A) How does the program do integration and differentiation?
    (B) What type of mathematics learning experiences should students have?
    (C) When is it appropriate to use graphing programs?
    (D) Why do schools buy these graphing programs?
    (E) Which graphing program does the author recommend?

21. Which of the following information can be found in the passage?
    I   The type of computer that graphs the equation
    II The graphing program's two main outputs
    III How to use the program to teach about mathematics
    (A) I only
    (B) II only
    (C) I and II only
    (D) II and III only
    (E) I, II, and III

22. Which aspect of graphing programs does the author of the passage like?
    (A) That you just have to type in the equation
    (B) That the difficult mechanical operations are performed
    (C) That the calculations and graphing are done very quickly
    (D) That you don't have to know math to use them
    (E) That they can't replace teachers

23. Which of the following could be used in place of the first sentence of the last paragraph?
    (A) It may be true that some strict teachers use a mechanical approach.
    (B) It may be true that some teachers use only a mechanical approach.
    (C) It may be true that a stringently mechanical approach is used by some teachers.
    (D) It may be true that inflexible mechanical approaches are used by some teachers.
    (E) It may be true that the mechanical approach used by some teachers is too rigorous.

24. According to this passage, what could result in students' unfamiliarity with the meaning of equations or results?
    (A) Using a graphing program to display the graph of an equation
    (B) Relying on mindless graphing and calculation
    (C) Strictly mechanical approaches
    (D) Using microcomputers to graph equations and find solutions
    (E) Being able to just type in equations

25. An analysis of models of potential space vehicles prepared by engineers revealed that the parts of the hull of the vehicles that were strongest were the ones that had the most potential for being weak.

    What conclusion can be drawn from the analysis mentioned here?
    (A) The parts of the hull that are potentially strongest do not receive as much attention from engineers as those that are potentially weakest.
    (B) The potentially weaker parts of the hull appear stronger in models than the potentially stronger parts of the hull.
    (C) Being potentially weaker, these parts of the hull appear relatively stronger in a model.
    (D) Potentially weaker parts of the hull have the most potential for being stronger.
    (E) The parts of the hull that are potentially weakest receive less attention from engineers than those parts that are potentially stronger.

Questions 26 and 27 are based on this passage.

The growth of the town led to a huge increase in the number of students applying for kindergarten admission. Before this time, students had been admitted to kindergarten even if they were "technically" too young. At first the school administrators considered a testing plan for those applicants too young for regular admission, admitting only those who passed the test. Luckily the administrators submitted a plan that just enforced the official, but previously ignored, birth cut-off date for kindergarten admission. This decision set the stage for fairness throughout the town.

26. What main idea is the author trying to convey?
    (A) Testing of young children doesn't work.
    (B) All children should be treated equally.
    (C) Tests are biased against minority children.
    (D) The testing program would be too expensive.
    (E) Age predicts a child's performance level.

27. Which of the following is the primary problem with this plan for the schools?
    (A) Parents will sue.
    (B) Parents will falsify birth certificates to get their children in school.
    (C) Next year the schools will have to admit a much larger kindergarten group.
    (D) Missing kindergarten because a child is born one day too late doesn't seem fair.
    (E) Parents would not be able to dispute the results of an objective testing plan.

28. A person who is not treated with respect cannot be expected to be a good worker.

    Which of the following can be concluded from this statement?
    (A) A person treated with respect can be expected to be a good worker.
    (B) A person who is expected to be a good worker should be treated with respect.
    (C) A person who cannot be expected to be a good worker is not treated with respect.
    (D) A person not treated with respect can still be expected to be a good worker.
    (E) A person who is not a good worker can't expect to be treated with respect.

Questions 29 and 30 are based on these circumstances.

The state highway department has sets of regulations for the number of lanes a highway can have and how these lanes are to be used. A summary of these regulations follows.

- All highways must be five lanes wide and either three or four of these lanes must be set aside for passenger cars only.

- If four lanes are set aside for passenger cars, then one of these lanes must be set aside for cars with three or more passengers, with a second lane of the four passenger lanes also usable by school vehicles such as buses, vans, and cars.

- If three lanes are set aside for passenger cars, then one of these lanes must be set aside for cars with two or more passengers, except that school buses, vans, and cars may also use this lane.

29. Officials in one county submit a plan for a five-lane highway, with three lanes set aside for passenger cars, and school buses able to use the lane set aside for cars with two or more passengers. Based on their regulations, which of the following is most likely to be the state highway department's response to this plan?
    (A) Your plan is approved because you have five lanes with three set aside for passenger cars and one set aside for passenger cars with two or more passengers.
    (B) Your plan is approved because you permitted school buses to use the passenger lanes.
    (C) Your plan is disapproved because you don't include school vans and school cars among the vehicles that can use the lane for cars with two or more passengers.
    (D) Your plan is disapproved because you include school buses in the lane for passenger cars with two or more passengers.
    (E) Your plan is disapproved because you set aside only three lanes for passenger cars when it should have been four.

30. County officials send a list of three possible highway plans to the state highway department. Using their regulations, which of the following plans would the state highway department approve?

   I 5 lanes—3 for passenger cars, 1 passenger lane for cars with 3 or more passengers, school buses and vans can also use the passenger lane for 3 or more people

   II 5 lanes—4 for passenger cars, 1 passenger lane for cars with 3 or more passengers, 1 of the 4 passenger lanes can be used by school buses, vans, and cars

   III 5 lanes—3 for passenger cars, 1 passenger lane for cars with 2 or more passengers, school vehicles can also use the passenger lane for 2 or more passengers

  (A) I only
  (B) II only
  (C) III only
  (D) I and II only
  (E) II and III only

Questions 31–34 are based on this passage.

The choice of educational practices sometimes seems like choosing fashions. Fashion is driven by the whims, tastes, and zeitgeist of the current day. The education system should not be driven by these same forces. But consider, for example, the way mathematics is taught. Three decades ago, teachers were told to use manipulative materials to teach mathematics. In the intervening years, the emphasis was on drill and practice. Now teachers are being told again to use manipulative materials. This cycle is more akin to random acts than to sound professional practice.

31. What does the author most likely mean by the word *zeitgeist* in the second sentence?
  (A) Tenor
  (B) Emotional feeling
  (C) Fabric availability
  (D) Teaching methods
  (E) Intelligence

32. Which of the following sentences contains an opinion?
  (A) "But consider for example . . ."
  (B) "Three decades ago . . . "
  (C) "In the intervening years . . . "
  (D) "Now teachers are being told . . . "
  (E) "This cycle is more akin . . . "

33. For what reason did the author most likely use the phrase *three decades* in the fifth sentence?
  (A) To represent 30 years
  (B) For emphasis
  (C) To represent 10-year intervals
  (D) To represent the passage of years
  (E) To bring the reader to the current year

34. Which of the following could be substituted for the phrase "random acts" in the last sentence?
  (A) Unsound practice
  (B) A fashion designer's dream
  (C) The movement of hemlines
  (D) A fashion show
  (E) Pressure from mathematics manipulative manufacturers

35. Empty halls and silent walls greeted me. A summer day seemed like a good day for me to take a look at the school in which I would student teach. I tiptoed from door to door looking. Suddenly the custodian appeared behind me and said, "Help you?" "No sir," I said. At that moment, he could have been Aristotle or Plato for all I knew. Things worked out.

Which of the following best describes the main character in the passage?
  (A) Timid and afraid
  (B) Confident and optimistic
  (C) Pessimistic and unsure
  (D) Curious and respectful
  (E) Careful and quiet

Questions 36–38 are based on the following reading.

I remember my childhood vacations at a bungalow colony near a lake. Always barefoot, my friend and I spent endless hours playing and enjoying our fantasies. We were pirates, rocket pilots, and detectives. Everyday objects were transformed into swords, ray guns, and two-way wrist radios. With a lake at hand, we swam, floated on our crude rafts made of old lumber, fished, and fell in. The adult world seemed so meaningless while our world seemed so full. Returning years later I saw the colony for what it was—tattered and torn. The lake was shallow and muddy. But the tree that had been our lookout was still there. And there was the house where the feared master spy hid from the FBI. There was the site of the launching pad for our imaginary rocket trips. The posts of the dock we had sailed from many times were still visible. But my fantasy play did not depend on this place. My child-mind would have been a buccaneer wherever it was.

Line
5

10

15

20

36. Which of the following choices best characterizes this passage?
    (A) An adult describes disappointment at growing up.
    (B) A child describes the adult world through the child's eyes.
    (C) An adult discusses childhood viewed as a child and as an adult.
    (D) An adult discusses the meaning of fantasy play.
    (E) An adult describes a wish to return to childhood.

37. The sentence "The adult world seemed so meaningless while our world seemed so full." on lines (9) and (10) is used primarily to
    (A) emphasize the emptiness of most adult lives.
    (B) provide a transition from describing childhood to describing adulthood.
    (C) show how narcissistic children are.
    (D) describe the difficulty this child had relating to adults.
    (E) emphasize the limited world of the child compared to the more comprehensive world of the adult.

38. Which of the following best characterizes the last sentence in the passage?
    (A) The child would have been rebellious, no matter what.
    (B) Childhood is not a place but a state of mind.
    (C) We conform more as we grow older.
    (D) The writer will always feel rebellious.
    (E) A part of us all stays in childhood.

Questions 39–40 apply to this passage.

Sometimes parents are more involved in little league games than their children. I remember seeing a game in which a player's parent came on the field to argue with the umpire. The umpire was not that much older than the player.

Before long, the umpire's mother was on the field. There the two parents stood, toe to toe. The players and the other umpires formed a ring around them and looked on in awe.

Of course, I have never gotten too involved in my children's sports. I have never yelled at an umpire at any of my kid's games. I have never even—well, I didn't mean it.

39. What other "sporting" event is the author trying to recreate in the second paragraph?
    (A) Bull fight
    (B) Wrestling match
    (C) Boxing match
    (D) Football game
    (E) Baseball game

40. The author portrays herself as "innocent" of being too involved in her children's sports. How would you characterize this portrayal?
    (A) False
    (B) A lie
    (C) Tongue in cheek
    (D) Noble
    (E) Self-effacing

PRACTICE PPST WRITING TEST

Take this test in a realistic, timed setting. You should not take this practice test until you have completed Chapter 3 and the targeted test at the end of that chapter.

The test rules allow exactly 50 minutes for this section.

Keep the time limit in mind as you work. Answer the easier questions first. Be sure you answer all the questions. There is no penalty for guessing. You may write on the test booklet and mark up the questions.

Each question or statement has five answer choices. Exactly one of these choices is correct. Mark your choice on the answer sheet provided for this test.

Your score is based on the spaces you fill in on the answer sheet. Make sure that you mark your answer on the answer sheet in the correct space next to the correct question number.

When instructed, turn the page and begin.

WRITING

45 items   30 minutes

USAGE

(Use about 30 minutes)

> You will read sentences with four parts underlined and lettered. Determine whether one of the underlined parts contains grammatical, word use, or punctuation errors. If so, mark the letter of that part on your answer sheet. If there are no errors, mark E.

1. <u>Disgusted by</u> the trash <u>left behind</u> by
      (A)   (B)
   picnickers, the <u>town</u> council passed a
             (C)
   law <u>requiring convicted litterers</u> to
         (D)
   spend five hours cleaning up the town park.

   <u>No error</u>.
     (E)

2. The teacher <u>was sure</u> that the child's
         (A)
   <u>difficult home</u> life <u>effected</u> her
      (B)   (C)
   <u>school work</u>. <u>No error</u>.
     (D)   (E)

3. It <u>took</u> Ron a long time <u>to realize</u> that
     (A)   (B)
   the <u>townspeople</u> <u>were completely</u>
      (C)   (D)
   opposed to his proposal. <u>No error</u>.
                 (E)

4. A newspaper <u>columnist</u> promised to
         (A)
   print the <u>people who</u> were <u>involved in</u>
       (B)   (C)
   the secret negotiations concerning the

   <u>sports stadium</u> in the next column.
     (D)
   <u>No error</u>.
     (E)

5. The silent <u>halo</u> of a <u>solar eclipse</u>
         (A)   (B)
   <u>could be seen</u> by astronomers across
     (C)
   <u>asia</u>. <u>No error</u>.
    (D)   (E)

6. <u>Also found</u> during the archaeological
     (A)
   dig <u>was</u> a <u>series</u> of animal bone
     (B)   (C)
   fragments, fire signs, and <u>arrow points</u>.
                       (D)
   <u>No error</u>.
     (E)

7. The <u>teacher</u> asked all of <u>her</u> students to
       (A)   (B)
   bring in <u>they're</u> permission slips
         (C)
   <u>to go on</u> the Washington trip. <u>No error</u>.
     (D)   (E)

8. The <u>plumber</u> <u>did not go to</u> the dripping
       (A)   (B)
   water <u>than to</u> the place the water
        (C)
   <u>seemed to be</u> coming from. <u>No error</u>.
     (D)   (E)

9. The driver realized that she

   <u>would either</u> have to <u>go completely out of</u>
     (A)   (B)
   the <u>way</u> or have to wait for the
     (C)
   <u>swollen creek</u> to subside. <u>No error</u>.
     (D)   (E)

10. The <u>tracker</u> was so <u>good that</u> he could
      (A)   (B)
 tell the <u>difference between</u> a hoofprint
          (C)
 made by a horse with a saddle <u>or a</u>
                        (D)
 hoofprint made by a horse without a

 saddle. <u>No error.</u>
      (E)

11. The mayor <u>estimated</u> that it <u>would cost</u>
         (A)   (B)
 $1,200 for each <u>citizen individually</u> to
              (C)
 repair the storm damage <u>to the town.</u>
                   (D)
 <u>No error.</u>
   (E)

12. <u>Sustaining</u> a <u>month-long</u> winning streak
   (A)   (B)
 in the town baseball A B league, the

 young team <u>pressed on</u> with
         (C)
 <u>unwavering determination.</u> <u>No error.</u>
       (D)   (E)

13. The fire chief, <u>like the police chief,</u>
             (A)
 <u>has so much</u> responsibility, that
   (B)
 <u>they often have</u> a personal <u>driver.</u>
    (C)   (D)
 <u>No error.</u>
   (E)

14. A talented chef <u>making customers</u>
           (A)
 smack their lips at her great

 <u>gustatorial delights,</u> the likes of which
      (B)
 <u>are not available</u> in any
     (C)
 <u>ordinary restaurant.</u> <u>No error.</u>
    (D)   (E)

15. The fate of small towns in America,

 which were <u>popularized</u> in movies
        (A)
 when it seemed that everyone came

 from a small town <u>and now</u> face
         (B)
 <u>anonymity</u> as cars on highways speed
   (C)
 by, <u>is perilous</u>. <u>No error.</u>
    (D)   (E)

16. The coach <u>not only</u> <u>works with</u> each
        (A)   (B)
 pitcher and each catcher, but he

 <u>also has to</u> change <u>him.</u> <u>No error.</u>
   (C)   (D)   (E)

17. When I <u>was a child</u>, a wet washcloth
       (A)
 was the <u>main method</u> of first <u>aid; it</u>
       (B)   (C)
 reduced swelling, eliminated pain,

 <u>and inflammation was</u> reduced. <u>No error.</u>
      (D)   (E)

18. I am going to a <u>World Cup game</u> next
          (A)
 week, and I <u>would be surprised</u> if
         (B)
 <u>there is even</u> one empty seat
   (C)
 <u>in the stadium.</u> <u>No error.</u>
    (D)   (E)

19. It is <u>not uncommon</u> for the claims of
     (A)
 land developers to <u>go too</u> far, <u>like</u> the
         (B)   (C)
 one reported several years ago in which

 <u>the land was</u> on the side of a sheer cliff.
   (D)
 <u>No error.</u>
   (E)

20. During <u>the fall</u>, some fruits are in
    (A)   (B)
<u>so short supply</u> that the prices <u>triple.</u>
      (C)   (D)
<u>No error.</u>
   (E)

21. The <u>volleyball team</u> won their
        (A)
<u>third consecutive</u> scholastic title,
    (B)
<u>both because</u> of their dedication and
   (C)
because <u>they are talented. No error.</u>
        (D)   (E)

22. A horse trainer was surprised <u>to</u> find out
                       (A)
<u>how</u> her horse was able <u>to have</u> such a
 (B)   (C)
fast time because the horse <u>wore</u>
              (D)
blinders. <u>No error.</u>
       (E)

23. <u>It is essential</u> that school children have
    (A)
an opportunity to write creatively,

<u>without concern</u> for spelling or
    (B)
punctuation; <u>therefore</u>, teachers should
        (C)
not <u>hesitate</u> to correct the spelling in
    (D)
everything that students write. <u>No error.</u>
                     (E)

24. On a <u>day like today</u> you can see the
      (A)
<u>distant mountains</u> <u>as clear as</u> though
    (B)   (C)
they <u>were only</u> a mile away. <u>No error.</u>
   (D)   (E)

25. If the caravan <u>would have</u> taken the
       (A)
<u>northern</u> route, the <u>travelers</u> would not
   (B)   (C)
now be <u>suffering</u> in the desert heat.
      (D)
<u>No error.</u>
 (E)

SENTENCE CORRECTION

> You will read sentences with some or all of the sentence underlined, followed by five answer choices. The first answer choice repeats the underlined portion and the other four present possible replacements. Select the answer choice that best represents standard English without altering the meaning of the original sentence. Mark that letter on the answer sheet.

26. The quality of the parts received in the most recent shipment <u>was inferior to parts in the previous shipments, but still in accordance with</u> manufacturers' specifications.
    (A) was inferior to parts in the previous shipments, but still in accordance with
    (B) were inferior to the previous shipments' parts but still in accordance with
    (C) was the inferior of the previous shipments' parts but still in accordance with
    (D) was inferior to the previous parts' shipments but still not on par with
    (E) was inferior to the previous parts' shipments and the manufacturers' specifications

27. <u>The painful rabies treatment first developed by Pasteur</u> saved the boy's life.
    (A) The painful rabies treatment first developed by Pasteur
    (B) The painful rabies treatment which was first discovered by Pasteur
    (C) Pasteur developed the painful rabies treatment
    (D) First developed by Pasteur the treatment for painful rabies
    (E) The fact that Pasteur developed a rabies treatment

28. By 10:00 A.M. every morning, <u>the delivery service brought important papers to the house in sealed envelopes</u>.
    (A) the delivery service brought important papers to the house in sealed envelopes
    (B) important papers were brought to the house by the delivery service in sealed envelopes
    (C) sealed envelopes were brought to the house by the delivery service with important papers
    (D) the delivery service brought important papers in sealed envelopes to the house
    (E) the deliver service brought sealed envelopes to the house containing important papers

29. The shadows shortened as the sun <u>begun the</u> ascent into the morning sky.
    (A) begun the
    (B) begin the
    (C) began the
    (D) begun that
    (E) begun an

30. Liz and Ann spent all day climbing the mountain, and <u>she was almost</u> too exhausted for the descent.
    (A) she was almost
    (B) they were almost
    (C) they were
    (D) she almost was
    (E) was

31. The embassy announced that at the present time, they could neither confirm <u>nor deny that the ambassador would return home in the event that</u> hostilities broke out.
    (A) nor deny that the ambassador would return home in the event that
    (B) or deny that the ambassador would return home in the event that
    (C) nor deny that the ambassador would return home if
    (D) nor deny that the ambassador would leave
    (E) nor deny that ambassador will return home in the event that

32. Every person <u>has the ultimate capacity to</u> control his or her own destiny.
    (A) has the ultimate capacity to
    (B) ultimately has the capacity to
    (C) has the capacity ultimately to
    (D) can
    (E) could

33. In all likelihood, her mother's absence would be devastating, <u>were it not</u> for the presence of her sister.
    (A) were it not
    (B) it was not
    (C) it were not
    (D) were they not
    (E) was it not

34. She had listened very carefully to all the candidates, and the Independent candidate was the only <u>one who had not said something that did not make sense</u>.
    (A) one who had not said something that did not make sense
    (B) one who did not make sense when he said something
    (C) one who had only said things that made sense
    (D) one to not say something that made sense
    (E) one who never said anything that made no sense

35. The author knew that the book would be finished <u>only by working every day and getting</u> lots of sleep at night.
    (A) only by working every day and getting
    (B) only working every day and getting
    (C) only by working every day and by getting
    (D) only through work and sleep
    (E) only by daily work and by sleepless nights

36. The teacher was sure that Tom's difficult home life affected <u>his school work</u>.
    (A) his school work
    (B) his school's work
    (C) him school work
    (D) his school works
    (E) him school works

37. Small town sheriffs in America, <u>whom were popularized in movies when it seemed that everyone came from a small town</u>, now face anonymity.
    (A) whom were popularized in movies when it seemed that everyone came from a small town
    (B) who were popularized in movies when it seemed that everyone came from a small town
    (C) whom were popularized in movies when it seemed that anyone came from a small town
    (D) whom were popularized in movies when they seemed that everyone came from a small town
    (E) whom were popularized in movies when it seemed that everyone comes from a small town

38. The professor asked the class to consider the development of the human race. She pointed out that, throughout the ages, <u>human beings has learned to communicate by nonverbal means</u>.
    (A) human beings has learned to communicate by nonverbal means
    (B) human beings had learned to communicate by nonverbal means
    (C) human beings has learn to communicate by nonverbal means
    (D) human beings have learn to communicate by nonverbal means
    (E) human beings have learned to communicate by nonverbal means

39. There are a number of specialty business stores. Office World, the office supply store, <u>claimed to be the quintessential supplier of office machines in the United States</u>.
    (A) claimed to be the quintessential supplier of office machines in the United States
    (B) claiming to be the quintessential supplier of office machines in the United States
    (C) claimed to be the quardassential supplier of office machines in the United States
    (D) claims to be the quintessential supplier of office machines in the United States
    (E) has claim to be the quintessential supplier of office machines in the United States

40. The *Hardy Boys* was a book series. <u>As a child he read the *Hardy Boys* series of books and was in awe of the author Franklin Dixon.</u>
    (A) As a child he read the *Hardy Boys* series of books and was in awe of the author Franklin Dixon.
    (B) As a child he read the *Hardy Boys* series of books, but was in awe of the author Franklin Dixon.
    (C) As a child he read the *Hardy Boys* series of books; however he was in awe of the author Franklin Dixon.
    (D) As a child he read the *Hardy Boys* series of books but was also in awe of the author Franklin Dixon.
    (E) As a child he read the *Hardy Boys* series of books; however he was also in awe of the author Franklin Dixon.

41. Bob is deciding which event to compete in. <u>He is a strong swimmer but he is best known for his diving.</u>
    (A) He is a strong swimmer but he is best known for his diving.
    (B) He is a strong swimmer; but, he is best known for his diving.
    (C) He is a strong swimmer, but he is best known for his diving.
    (D) He is a strong swimmer: but he is best known for his diving.
    (E) He is a strong swimmer, but, he is best known for his diving.

42. It was almost time for the test. Vincent and Laura said to <u>their friends "I wonder if we're through studying for the PPST"</u>?
    (A) their friends "I wonder if we're through studying for the PPST"?
    (B) their friends ",I wonder if we're through studying for the PPST"?
    (C) their friends, "I wonder if we're through studying for the PPST"?
    (D) their friends, "I wonder if we're through studying for the PPST?"
    (E) their friends ",I wonder if we're through studying for the PPST?"

43. The bulldozer continued to operate because <u>of it's metal treads</u>.
    (A) of it's metal treads
    (B) of it's treads being metal
    (C) of its metal treads
    (D) of its treads being metal
    (E) of it's treads, which were metal

44. The dog loved to be out on the water, but the salt spray <u>would sometimes lead him to sneeze</u>.
    (A) would sometimes lead him to sneeze
    (B) would sometimes led him to sneeze
    (C) would sometimes leads him to sneeze
    (D) will sometimes led him to sneeze
    (E) will sometimes leads him to sneeze

45. <u>Besides the opinion held in the future</u>, there is no basis for time travel.
    (A) Besides the opinion held in the future
    (B) Besides the opinion that is held in the future
    (C) Besides the opinion being held in the future
    (D) Besides the opinion that might be held in the future
    (E) Besides the opinion holding in the distant future

PRACTICE PPST ESSAY

Take this test in a realistic, timed setting. You should not take this practice test until you have completed Chapter 3 and the targeted test at the end of that chapter.

Write an essay on the topic found on the next page. Write on this topic only. An essay written on another topic, no matter how well done, will receive a 0. You have 30 minutes to complete the essay.

Use the space provided to briefly outline your essay and to organize your thoughts before you begin to write. Use this opportunity to demonstrate how well you can write but be sure to cover the topic.

Write your essay on the lined paper provided. Write legibly and do not skip any lines. Your entire essay must fit on these pages.

Once the test is complete, ask an English professor or English teacher to evaluate your essay holistically using the rating scale on page 34.

When instructed, turn the page and begin.

ESSAY

You have 30 minutes to complete this essay question. Use the lined pages to write a brief essay based on this topic.

Describe your most uplifting or most devastating experience in elementary school. Explain how this experience shaped you as a person and how this experience will affect your own teaching.

Write a brief outline here.

PRACTICE PPST MATHEMATICS TEST

Take this test in a realistic, timed setting. You should not take this practice test until you have completed Chapter 4 and the targeted test at the end of that chapter.

The test rules allow you exactly 50 minutes for this test.

Keep this time limit in mind as you work. Answer the easier items first. Be sure you answer all the items. There is no penalty for guessing. You may write in the test booklet and mark up the items.

Each item has five answer choices. Exactly one of these choices is correct. Mark your choice on the answer sheet provided for the test.

Your score is based on the spaces you fill in on the answer sheet. Make sure you mark your answer in the correct space next to the correct item number.

When instructed, turn the page and begin.

MATHEMATICS

40 items   50 minutes

> Each item below includes five answer choices. Select the best choice for each item and mark that letter on the answer sheet.

1. **Percent of Freshmen, Sophomores, Juniors, and Seniors at a College**

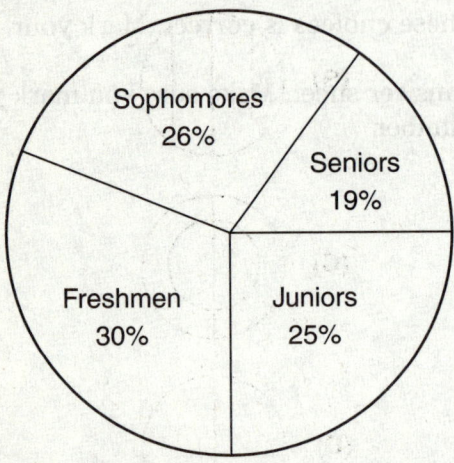

There are a total of 12,000 students. How many more freshmen are there than seniors?
(A) 1,320 students
(B) 2,280 students
(C) 3,000 students
(D) 3,120 students
(E) 3,600 students

2. Steve pays $520 a month for rent, and his monthly paycheck after taxes is $1,300. Which computation shows the percent of Steve's paycheck that is used to pay rent?
(A) $(1300 \div 520) \cdot 100$
(B) $(520 \div 1300) \cdot 100$
(C) $(5.2 \cdot 1300) \cdot 100$
(D) $(13 \cdot 520) \cdot 100$
(E) $(5.2 \cdot 13) \cdot 100$

3. All of the windows in the house are rectangles. None of the windows in the house are squares.

Which of the following conclusions in the statements above are true?
(A) Some of the windows have four sides of equal length.
(B) None of the windows contain right angles.
(C) None of the windows are parallelograms.
(D) None of the windows have four sides of equal length.
(E) All of the windows contain an acute angle.

4. The area of a square is 4 in². There is a larger square made up of 49 of these squares. What is the length of one side of the larger square?
(A) 7 in
(B) 14 in
(C) 28 in
(D) 56 in
(E) 112 in

5. Which of the following is written in scientific notation?
(A) 53794×10
(B) 5379.4×10
(C) 537.94×10
(D) 53.794×10
(E) 5.3794×10

6. **NUMBER OF AWARDS**

Person 1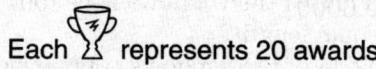

Person 2

Person 3

Person 4

Person 5

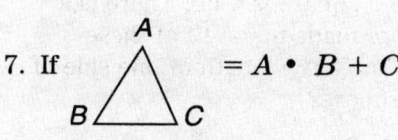

Each 🏆 represents 20 awards

How many more awards did person 5 have than person 3?
(A) 20
(B) 40
(C) 60
(D) 80
(E) 100

7. If $\triangle\begin{smallmatrix}A\\B\quad C\end{smallmatrix} = A \bullet B + C$

then $\triangle\begin{smallmatrix}-4\\2\quad 11\end{smallmatrix}$

(A) −88
(B) −19
(C) −3
(D) 3
(E) 19

8. The following is a list of the ages of ten different people: 53, 27, 65, 21, 7, 16, 70, 41, 57, and 37.

What is the mean age of these people?
(A) 39.4
(B) 40
(C) 65.7
(D) 69
(E) 70.2

9. A pizza has crust all around the edge. Which of the following figures shows a way to cut the pizza into four equal pieces where only two have crust?

(A)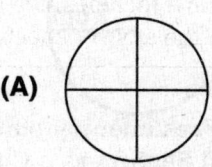

(B)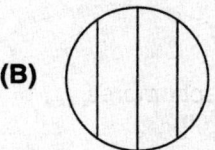

(C)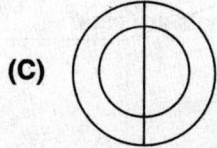

(D)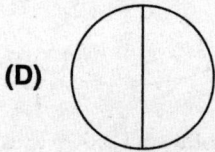

(E)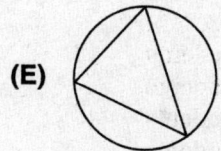

10. What is the area of the circle seen below?

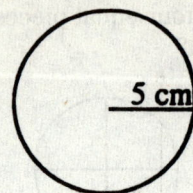

5 cm

(A) 25 cm^2
(B) 10π cm^2
(C) 25π cm^2
(D) 20 cm^2
(E) 166 $\frac{2}{3}$ π cm^2

11. Frank has 2 dogs and 5 cats. What fraction of these animals are cats?

(A) $\frac{2}{5}$

(B) $\frac{2}{7}$

(C) $\frac{5}{2}$

(D) $\frac{5}{7}$

(E) $\frac{7}{2}$

12. $\frac{4}{9}$ is less than which of the following?

(A) 44%
(B) 0.45
(C) 0.4444
(D) $\frac{4}{10}$
(E) 44.4%

13. 0.45 is how many times 45,000?

(A) 0.1
(B) 0.01
(C) 0.001
(D) 0.0001
(E) 0.00001

14. Which of the following shows a line with x- and y-intercepts equal to 1?

(A)

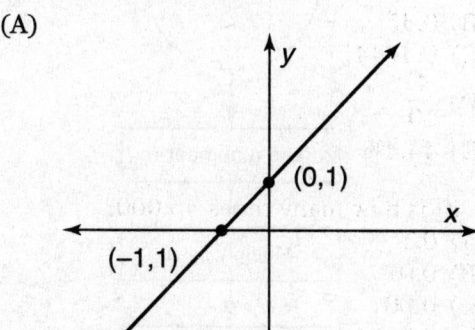

(B)

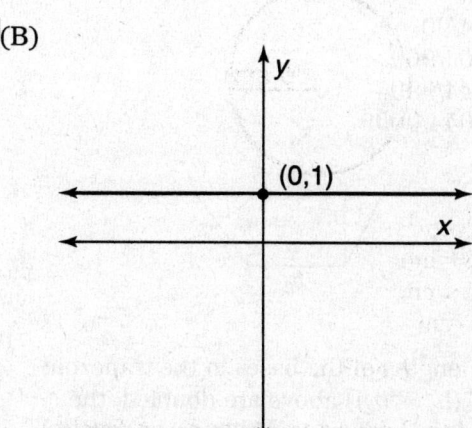

(C)

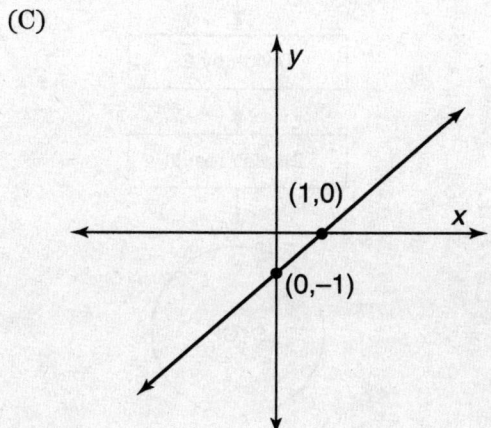

(D)

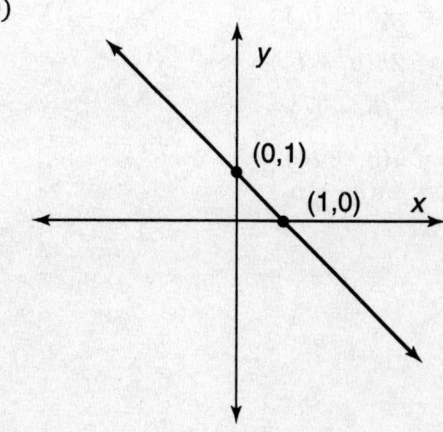

(E)

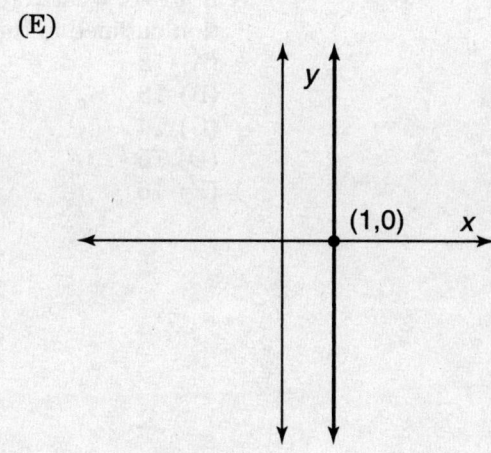

15. All of the following numbers are equal except for:
    (A) 4/9
    (B) 44/90
    (C) 404/909
    (D) 444/999
    (E) 4044/9099

16.

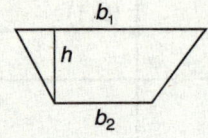

If the lengths of the bases in the trapezoid $(A = \frac{h}{2}(b_1 + b_2))$ above are doubled, the area of the new trapezoid is given by the formula:

(A) $A = \frac{h}{2}(b_1 + b_2)$

(B) $A = 2h(b_1 + b_2)$

(C) $A = \frac{h}{4}(b_1 + b_2)$

(D) $A = h(b_1 + b_2)$

(E) $A = 4h(b_1 + b_2)$

17.

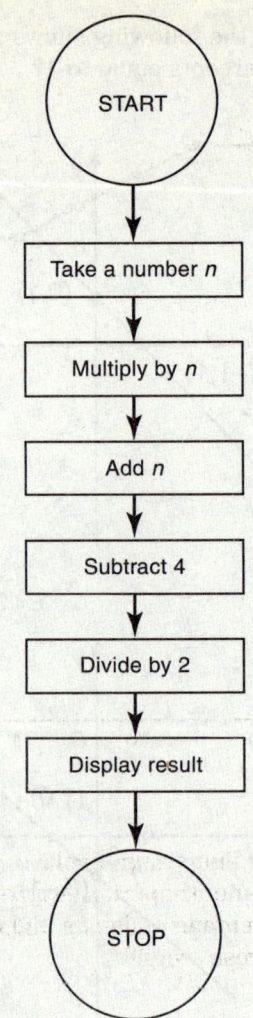

If $n = 5$, what is the result of the computation outlined in the flowchart?
(A) 12
(B) 13
(C) 14
(D) 15
(E) 16

18.

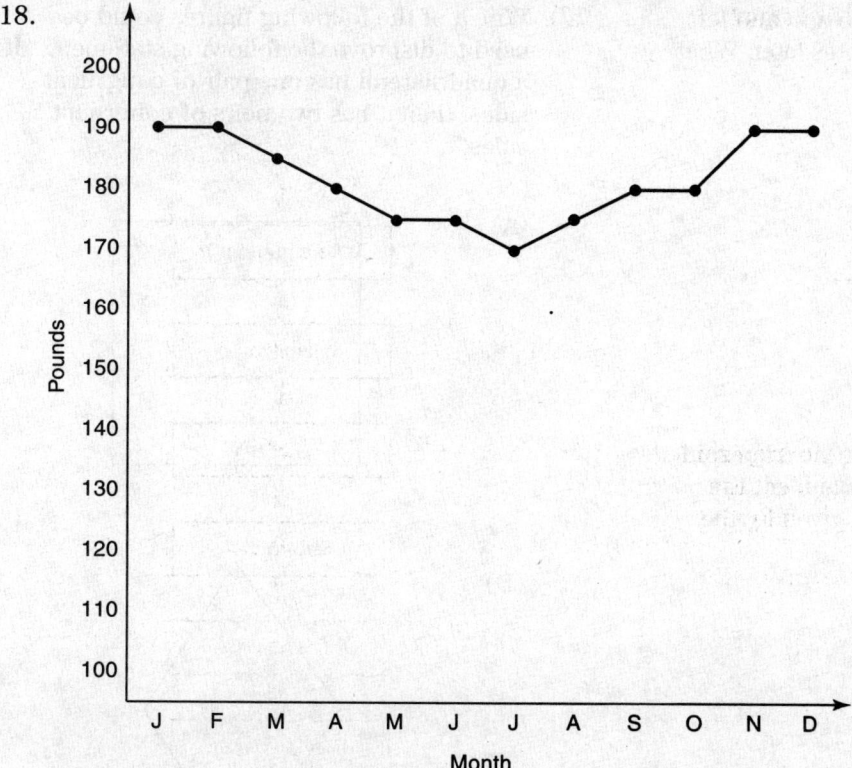

The above line graph displays Jack's weight
over a 12-month period. Approximately
what percentage of Jack's highest weight is
Jack's lowest weight?
(A) 97%
(B) 94%
(C) 91%
(D) 89%
(E) 85%

19. Alice arrived at work at 7:45 A.M. and left work 11 hours and 15 minutes later. What time did Alice leave work?
    (A) 8:00 P.M.
    (B) 7:15 P.M.
    (C) 7:00 P.M.
    (D) 6:45 P.M.
    (E) 6:15 P.M.

20. Which of the following figures could be used to disprove the following statement: "If a quadrilateral has one pair of congruent sides, then it has two pairs of congruent sides."

(A)

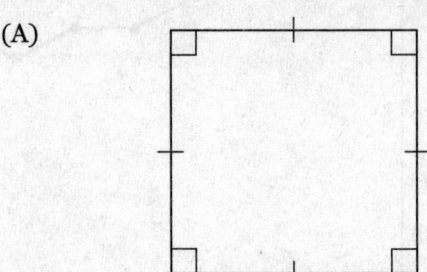

(B)

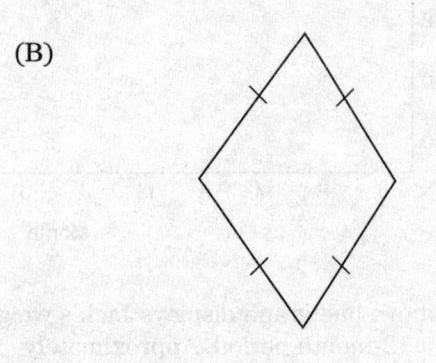

(C)

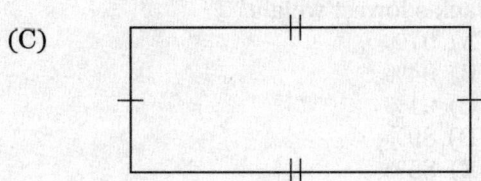

(D)

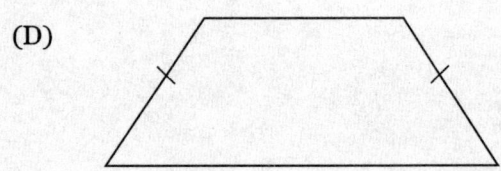

(E)

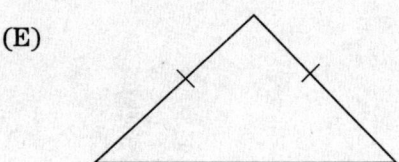

21. The five shapes seen below are made up of identical semi-circles and identical quarter-circles. Which of the five shapes has the greatest perimeter?

(A)

(B)

(C)

(D)

(E)

22. Which of the following choices is not equivalent to the others?
(A) $3^4 \times 9 \times 12$
(B) $3^3 \times 27 \times 12$
(C) $3^5 \times 36$
(D) $3^3 \times 9^3 \times 4$
(E) $3^5 \times 4 \times 9$

23. The salaries of 4 individuals in a company are:

　　Person 1: $45,250
　　Person 2: $78,375
　　Person 3: $52,540
　　Person 4: $62,325

The total salary of these individuals, in thousands of dollars, is closest to:
(A) $237 thousand
(B) $238 thousand
(C) $239 thousand
(D) $240 thousand
(E) $241 thousand

24. Which of the following is true about the graph seen below?

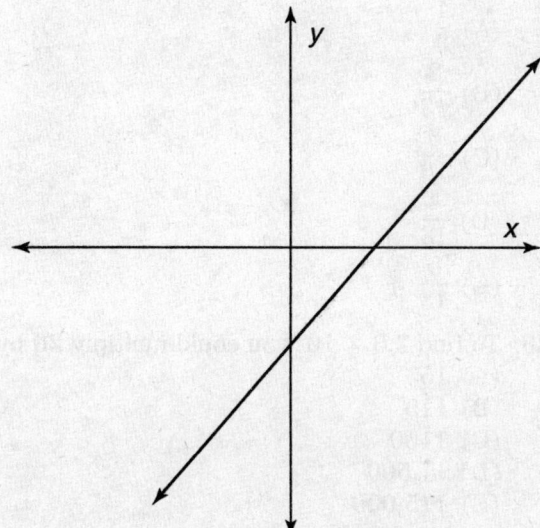

(A) As x increases, y decreases
(B) As x decreases, y does not change
(C) As x decreases, y increases
(D) As x increases, y increases
(E) As x decreases, y decreases

25. If x is 65% of 400, then what is the value of x?
    (A) 660
    (B) 540
    (C) 260
    (D) 200
    (E) 140

26. What is the average of $\frac{1}{2}$, $\frac{2}{3}$, and $\frac{5}{12}$?

    (A) $\frac{19}{12}$

    (B) $\frac{19}{24}$

    (C) $\frac{19}{36}$

    (D) $\frac{19}{44}$

    (E) $\frac{19}{52}$

27. In a standard deck of 52 cards, what is the probability of being dealt a king, a queen, or a jack?

    (A) $\frac{1}{3}$

    (B) $\frac{2}{13}$

    (C) $\frac{3}{13}$

    (D) $\frac{4}{13}$

    (E) $\frac{5}{13}$

28. To find 2.3×10^5 you could multiply 20 by
    (A) 15
    (B) 115
    (C) 1150
    (D) 11,500
    (E) 115,000

29. A circle can be a part of any of the following except a
    (A) circle
    (B) sphere
    (C) cylinder
    (D) cone
    (E) cube

30. According to the thermometer, what is the temperature?

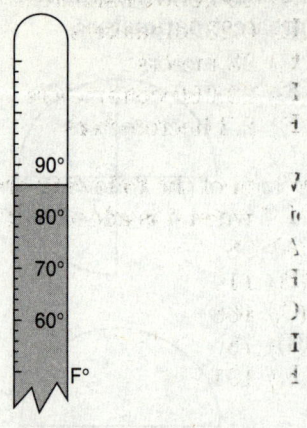

    (A) 80.3°F
    (B) 86°F
    (C) 80.4°F
    (D) 83°F
    (E) 80.6°F

31. If $6x + 2y = 10$, which of the following choices are possible values for x and y?
    (A) $x = 2$, $y = -1$
    (B) $x = 2$, $y = 11$
    (C) $x = 3$, $y = 4$
    (D) $x = 3$, $y = 14$
    (E) $x = 4$, $y = -8$

32. Tickets for a baseball game are $8 each, or 4 tickets for $30. What is the lowest cost for 18 tickets?
    (A) $144
    (B) $136
    (C) $132
    (D) $130
    (E) $126

33. If $4A + 6 = 2(B - 1)$, then $B = $?
    (A) $2A + 4$
    (B) $8A + 13$
    (C) $2A + 2$
    (D) $4A + 7$
    (E) $4A + 5$

34. Which of the following measurements is not equal to the others?
   (A) 230,000 millimeters
   (B) 0.23 kilometers
   (C) 23 meters
   (D) 23,000 centimeters
   (E) 2.3 hectometers

35. Which of the following choices is a multiple of 7 when 4 is added to it?
   (A) 58
   (B) 114
   (C) 168
   (D) 78
   (E) 101

36. Ryan has gone $3\frac{1}{5}$ miles of his 5-mile run. How many more miles has he left to run?
   (A) A little less than 2 miles
   (B) A little more than 2 miles
   (C) A little less than 3 miles
   (D) A little more than 3 miles
   (E) A little less than 4 miles

37. For every 2 hours that Barbara works she earns $17. How much money will she earn if she works 45 hours?
   (A) $391
   (B) $382.50
   (C) $374
   (D) $365.50
   (E) $357

38. Use the data presented in the pictograph. About how many times greater is the number of computers sold in December than the number of computers sold in January?

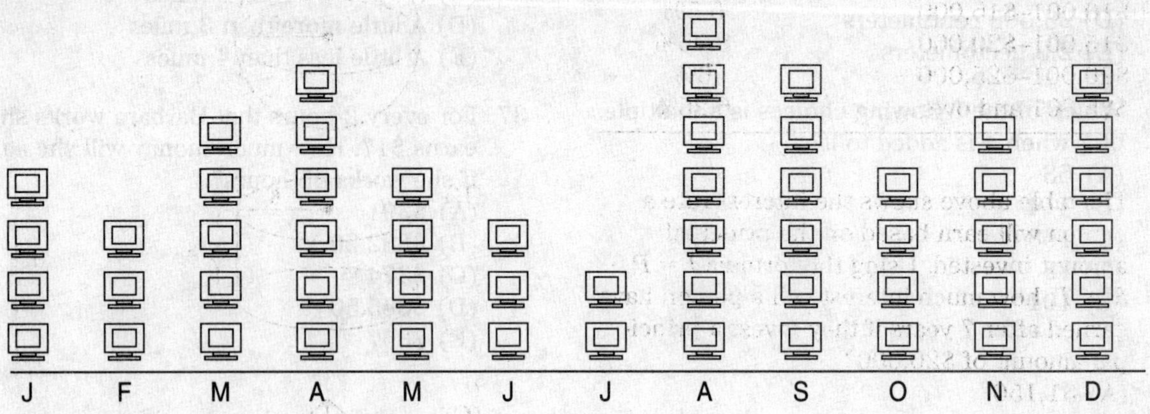

(A) 1.5
(B) 2
(C) 2.5
(D) 3
(E) 3.5

39.

Principal Amount	Simple Interest Rate
$1–$5,000	5%
$5,001–$10,000	5.25%
$10,001–$15,000	5.5%
$15,001–$20,000	5.75%
$20,001–$25,000	6%
$25,001 and over	6.25%

The table above shows the interest rate a person will earn based on the principal amount invested. Using the formula $I = P \cdot R \cdot T$, how much interest will a person have earned after 7 years if they invest a principal amount of $20,000?
(A) $1,150
(B) $8,400
(C) $1,200
(D) $8,050
(E) $9,800

40. Which of the following figures has a volume of 72π?

(A)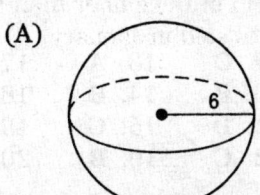

(B)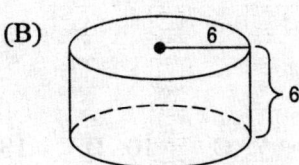

(C)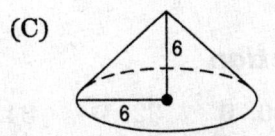

(D)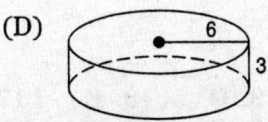

(E)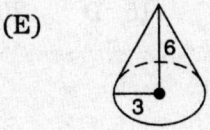

PPST 1 ANSWER KEYS

Reading

1. D	5. D	9. C	13. A	17. C	21. B	25. A	29. C	33. B	37. B
2. E	6. C	10. B	14. B	18. D	22. B	26. B	30. B	34. C	38. B
3. C	7. C	11. D	15. C	19. C	23. B	27. C	31. B	35. D	39. C
4. D	8. B	12. C	16. B	20. C	24. B	28. B	32. E	36. C	40. C

Writing

Usage

1. E	4. B	7. C	10. D	13. C	16. E	19. C	22. B	25. A
2. C	5. D	8. C	11. C	14. A	17. D	20. C	23. C	
3. E	6. B	9. E	12. E	15. B	18. B	21. D	24. C	

Sentence Correction

26. A	28. D	30. B	32. D	34. C	36. A	38. B	40. A	42. D	44. A
27. A	29. C	31. C	33. A	35. C	37. B	39. D	41. C	43. C	45. D

Mathematics

1. A	5. E	9. C	13. E	17. B	21. B	25. C	29. E	33. A	37. B
2. B	6. C	10. C	14. D	18. D	22. D	26. C	30. B	34. C	38. A
3. D	7. D	11. D	15. B	19. C	23. B	27. C	31. A	35. E	39. D
4. B	8. A	12. B	16. D	20. D	24. D	28. D	32. B	36. A	40. C

EXPLAINED ANSWERS

Reading

1. **D** The paragraph describes how careful shopping can result in lower prices.
2. **E** The author is trying to raise AIDS awareness and not to present any particular fact.
3. **C** The passage explains that AIDS is transmitted through blood and other bodily fluids.
4. **D** The sentence for this choice best describes the message the author is trying to convey.
5. **D** The retired basketball player mentions youth basketball as one of the reasons why today's players were better athletes. The passage also mentions an increased focus on training. However, the question does not ask for all the factors the retired player mentioned.
6. **C** This writer believes that generals should be judged by results. Even if you do not agree, that is the view of this writer.
7. **C** The author writes that the question still cannot be answered. The author does not say that the question can never be answered.
8. **B** The author never questions or attacks Adjustment Boards.
9. **C** The passage gives an example of a person who both supported and did not support requested exemptions.
10. **B** The author is writing about a local issue.
11. **D** In the last paragraph the author uses these words to describe Boards of Adjustment.
12. **C** The author gives several examples in which people support or don't support exemptions based on their own needs.
13. **A** Strategies I and II, together, assure the student that she will be chosen and give her a chance to get into a sorority she wants.
14. **B** List II is the only list that meets all the requirements.
15. **C** The rate, alone, does not provide enough information. You must also know the starting point.
16. **B** You should question any growth rate when only the percentage is given.

17. **C** Choice C is correct. A sentence can state both a fact and an opinion. "(2) alone states an opinion" means that it is the only sentence that states an opinion.
18. **D** This choice gives the fundamental reason why the schools' programs are copied. The other reasons grow out of the decision to provide extra resources.
19. **C** The author objects to using these programs with students who don't know mathematics.
20. **C** This is the only question that can be answered from information in the passage. The answer is that it can be used when students already understand equations and graphing.
21. **B** Only the information listed next to II can be found in the passage.
22. **B** The author mentions liking this aspect in the middle of the first paragraph.
23. **B** Choice B replicates the intent of the original sentence.
24. **B** The author presents this information in the first sentence of the second paragraph.
25. **A** This is the only choice that has a plausible explanation of why potentially weaker spots appear stronger.
26. **B** The author's view is that all children should be treated the same.
27. **C** Choice C describes the problem. All the students who might have been admitted early this year will be admitted next year along with the other kindergarten students.
28. **B** Only this choice is a logical conclusion.
29. **C** When there are three lanes for passenger cars, school buses, school vans, and school cars can all use the lane for cars with two or more passengers.
30. **B** Only this choice meets all the rules.
31. **B** The context tells us that the answer is the tenor (direction, tendency) of the times.
32. **E** Of the listed sentences, only "This cycle is more akin. . ." contains an opinion.
33. **B** The author is being a little dramatic to emphasize the length of the time span.

34. **C** Hemlines move without apparent reason, which is this author's point about educational practices.

35. **D** The character visited the school and so is certainly curious. The character's reaction to the custodian shows respectfulness.

36. **C** The author discusses childhood from each of the perspectives described in C. Choice D is incorrect because the meaning of fantasy play is never discussed.

37. **B** This sentence juxtaposes adulthood and childhood and provides a transition to discussing adulthood.

38. **B** The author says that these childhood experiences would have occurred regardless of the location.

39. **C** The description of going toe to toe inside a ring reminds us of a boxing match.

40. **C** The author is not lying, but the story is obviously not meant to be taken seriously.

Writing

Usage

1. **E** This sentence does not contain an error.

2. **C** The word *effected* is incorrect. It should be replaced by the word *affected*.

3. **E** This passage also contains no errors. *Townspeople* is an appropriate word.

4. **B** You can't print people. The underlined section should be *names of the people*.

5. **D** The word *Asia* is capitalized.

6. **B** The correct verb is *were*.

7. **C** The contraction *they're* (they are) is used incorrectly. *Their* is the correct word.

8. **C** The phrase *than to* is incorrectly used here. *But to* is the correct phrase.

9. **E** There are no underlined errors in this sentence.

10. **D** The conjunction *or* is incorrectly used here. The correct conjunction is *and*.

11. **C** There is no reason to use the word *individually*. Each citizen is an individual. The word *individually* should be removed.

12. **E** The passage contains no errors in underlined parts.

13. **C** The word *they* creates confusion because it could mean that there is one driver for both of them. A better usage is *each often has*.

14. **A** *Making* is the wrong verb. *Made* is the correct choice.

15. **B** The words *and now* should read *and which now*, in order to clarify just what faces anonymity.

16. **E** This sentence contains no underlined errors.

17. **D** This part of the sentence does not follow a parallel development. The correct usage is *reduced inflammation*.

18. **B** The correct replacement for *would be surprised* is *will be surprised*.

19. **C** The word *like* is incorrectly used here. The correct replacement is *such as*.

20. **C** The correct replacement for *so short supply* is *such short supply*.

21. **D** These words do not continue a parallel development. The correct replacement is *of their talent*.

22. **B** The word *how* is used inappropriately here. The correct choice is *that*.

23. **C** The word *therefore* is used incorrectly here because the second part of this sentence does not follow from the first part.

24. **C** The word *clear* is used incorrectly here. The correct word is *clearly*.

25. **A** The phrase *would have* is used incorrectly here. The correct choice is *had*.

Sentence Correction

26. **A** The underlined portion is appropriate.

27. **A** The underlined portion is appropriate.

28. **D** The rewording in D clarifies that the papers are in sealed envelopes—not in the house.

29. **C** This choice is the best wording from among the five choices available.

30. **B** This choice creates an agreement in number between nouns and pronoun.

31. **C** This choice replaces the wordy *in the event that* with *if*.

32. **D** This wordy expression is replaced by *can*.

33. **A** The underlined portion is appropriately worded.

34. **C** This choice appropriately replaces the double negative underlined in the original sentence.

35. **C** Adding the word *by* creates the desired parallel development in the sentence.

36. **A** The sentence is correct. The pronoun *his* agrees with the antecedent *Tom*.

37. **B** *Who* correctly shows the subjective case.

38. **E** *Have learned* is the correct present plural verb.
39. **D** *Office World* is singular and takes the singular verb *claims*.
40. **A** The sentence is correct. The conjunction *and* shows that the two clauses are equally important.
41. **C** Use a comma before the conjunction that joins these two independent clauses. An independent clause can stand on its own as a sentence.
42. **D** Punctuation before a quote goes outside the quotation marks, while punctuation following a quote goes inside the quotation marks.
43. **C** Change *it's* to *its* to show the possessive.
44. **A** The sentence is correct. The word *lead* in the original sentence is correct.
45. **D** A future opinion is one that *might be held*.

Essay

Show your essay to an English professor or teacher for evaluation using this scale.

Rating Scale

6 This essay is extremely well written. It is the equivalent of an A in-class assignment. The essay addresses the question and provides clear supporting arguments, illustrations, or examples. The paragraphs and sentences are well organized and show a variety of language and syntax. The essay may contain some minor errors.

5 This essay is well written. It is the equivalent of a B+ in-class assignment. The essay addresses the question and provides some supporting arguments, illustrations, or examples. The paragraphs and sentences are fairly well organized and show a variety of language and syntax. The essay may contain some minor mechanical or linguistic errors.

4 This essay is fairly well written. It is the equivalent of a B in-class assignment. The essay adequately addresses the question and provides some supporting arguments, illustrations, or examples for some points. The paragraphs and sentences are acceptably organized and show a variety of language and syntax. The essay may contain mechanical or linguistic errors but is free from an identifiable pattern of errors.

3 This essay may demonstrate some writing ability, but it contains obvious errors. It is the equivalent of a C+ in-class assignment. The essay may not clearly address the question and may not give supporting arguments or details. The essay may show problems in diction including inappropriate word choice. The paragraphs and sentences may not be acceptably developed. There will be an identifiable pattern or grouping of errors.

2 This essay shows only the most limited writing ability. It is the equivalent of a C in-class assignment. It contains serious errors and flaws. This essay may not address the question, it may be poorly organized, or it may provide no supporting arguments or detail. It usually shows serious errors in diction, usage, and mechanics.

1 This essay does not demonstrate minimal writing ability. It is the equivalent of a D or F on an in-class assignment. This essay may contain serious and continuing errors, or it may not be coherent.

Mathematics

1. **A** We know from the circle graph that $0.3 \cdot 12{,}000 = 3{,}600$ of the students are freshmen and $0.19 \cdot 12{,}000 = 2{,}280$ are seniors.

   There are $3{,}600 - 2{,}280 = 1{,}320$ more freshmen than seniors.

2. **B** To find what percent 520 is of 1300, divide 520 by 1300 to get the decimal representation of percent. Then multiply by 100 to get the answer into percent form.

3. **D** A is not true because none of the windows are squares. All of the windows are rectangles, so B, C, and E are not true. Choice D meets both of the requirements.

4. **B** The larger square has seven of the smaller squares along each side. The area of the smaller square is 4 in^2, so each side of the smaller square is 2 in. The length of one side is $2 \text{ in} \cdot 7 = 14 \text{ in}$.

5. **E** 5.3794 is the only number between 1 and 10.

6. **C** Person 5 had 3 more awards than person 3. Therefore person 5 had $3 \cdot 20 = 60$ more awards than person 3.

7. **D** $A \cdot B + C = -4 \cdot 2 + 11 = -8 + 11 = 3$

8. **A** The sum of the ages is 394, and then we divide this number by 10 to get the mean.

9. **C** None of the other choices cut into four equal pieces have two pieces containing crust.

10. **C** Use the formula for the area of a circle.
$$A = \pi r^2 = \pi \cdot (5 \text{ cm})^2 = 25\pi \text{ cm}^2$$

11. **D** There are a total of $5 + 2 = 7$ animals, 5 of which are cats. Therefore the answer is $\frac{5}{7}$.

12. **B** $\frac{4}{9} = 0.444\ldots$, which is less than 0.45.

13. **E** $45{,}000 \cdot 0.00001 = .45$

14. **D** $(0, 1)$ shows an x-intercept of 1.

$(1, 0)$ shows a y-intercept of 1.

15. **B** The decimal equivalents of each answer choice are:

A. $0.\overline{4}$

B. $0.4\overline{8}$

C. $0.\overline{4}$

D. $0.\overline{4}$

E. $0.\overline{4}$

Answer choices A, C, D, and E are equal.

16. **D** The formula for the area of a trapezoid is $A = \frac{h}{2}(b_1 + b_2)$.

However, in the new trapezoid the length of each base is doubled; therefore, the formula is

$$A = \frac{h}{2}(2b_1 + 2b_2) =$$

$$\frac{h}{2} \cdot 2(b_1 + b_2) =$$

$$h(b_1 + b_2)$$

17. **B** Follow the steps.
$$5 \cdot 5 = 25$$
$$25 + 5 = 30$$
$$30 - 4 = 26$$
$$26 \div 2 = 13$$

18. **D** Jack's lowest weight is 170 pounds and Jack's highest weight is 190 pounds.

$$170 \div 190 \approx 0.89 \approx 89\%$$

19. **C** 6:45 P.M. is 11 hours after 7:45 A.M.

Add the other 15 minutes to get 7:00 P.M.

20. **D** The trapezoid, choice D, has only one pair of congruent sides.

21. **B** Each diameter in choice B is part of the perimeter. When answering this question, consider only the perimeter and not any segments within a figure.

22. **D** A. $3^4 \times 9 \times 12 = 3^4 \times 9 \times 4 \times 3 = 3^5 = \times 4 \times 9$
This is choice E.

B. $3^3 \times 27 \times 12 = 3^3 \times 9 \times 3 \times 4 \times 3 = 3^5 = \times 4 \times 9$
This is choice E.

C. $3^5 \times 36 = 3^5 \times 4 \times 9$
This is choice E.

D. $3^3 \times 9^3 \times 4 = 3^3 \times 3^2 \times 9^2 \times 4 = 3^5 \times 4 \times 9^2 \neq 3^5 \times 4 \times 9$
This is **not** choice E.

23. **B** $45{,}250 + 78{,}375 + 52{,}540 + 62{,}325 = 238{,}490 \approx 238{,}000$

24. **D** The y-value (vertical axis) moves up as the x-value (horizontal axis) moves right.

25. **C** $65\% = 0.65$ $(0.65) \cdot 400 = 260$

26. **C** $\dfrac{1}{2} = \dfrac{6}{12}, \dfrac{2}{3} = \dfrac{8}{12}, \dfrac{5}{12}$

$$\left(\dfrac{6}{12} + \dfrac{8}{12} + \dfrac{5}{12}\right) \div 3 =$$

$$\dfrac{19}{12} \div 3 =$$

$$\dfrac{19}{12} \cdot \dfrac{1}{3} = \dfrac{19}{36}$$

27. **C** In a standard deck of cards there are 12 "face cards"—4 kings, 4 queens, and 4 jacks out of 52 possible cards.

P(face card) $= \dfrac{12}{52} = \dfrac{3}{13}$

28. **D** $2.3 \times 10^5 = 230,000$

$11,500 \times 20 = 230,000$

29. **E**

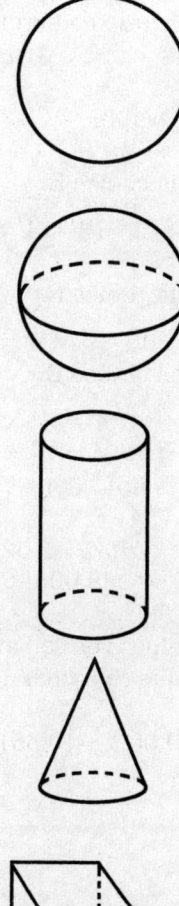

These figures show the circle in a circle, a sphere, a cylinder, and a cone. A cube does not contain a circle.

30. **B** Each mark on the scale represents two degrees.

31. **A** $6(2) + 2(-1) = 12 - 2 = 10$

32. **B** There are 18 tickets and you can buy 16 of the tickets for $120 ($4 \times \$30$) and the remaining two tickets at $16.

$120 + \$16 = \$136$

33. **A**

$$4A + 6 = 2(B - 1)$$

Divide by 2 on both sides:

$$2A + 3 = B - 1$$

Add 1 to both sides:

$$2A + 4 = B$$

$$B = 2A + 4$$

34. **C** Use this chart

Kilo	Hecto	Deka	Unit	Deci	Centi	Milli
1,000	100	10	1	0.1	0.01	0.001

Given below is each answer choice in meters.

A. 230 meters
B. 230 meters
C. 23 meters
D. 230 meters
E. 230 meters

Choice C is not equal to the others.

35. **E** $101 + 4 = 105 = 7 \cdot 15$

36. **A** $5 - 3\frac{1}{5} = 1\frac{4}{5}$, which is a little less than 2 miles.

37. **B** If Barbara earns $17 every 2 hours, she earns $\frac{\$17}{2} = \$8.50$ per hour. In 45 hours she earns $8.50 $\cdot$ 45 = $382.50.

38. **A** There are 4 pictures of computers in January and 6 pictures of computers in December; $\frac{6}{4} = 1.5$. It does not matter how many computers each picture represents, the answer will still be the same.

39. **D** The interest rate is based on the principal amount, and does not increase. Since the principal invested is $20,000, the interest rate is 5.75%. The time (T) is 7 years.

$I = \$20,000 \cdot .0575 \cdot 7 = \$8,050$

40. **C**
A. $V = \dfrac{4}{3}\pi r^3 = \dfrac{4}{3}\pi(6)^3 = 288\pi$

B. $V = \pi r^2 h = \pi(6)^2(6) = 216\pi$

C. $V = \dfrac{1}{3}\pi r^2 h = \dfrac{1}{3}\pi(6)^2(6) = 72\pi$

D. $V = \pi r^2 h = \pi(6)^2(3) = 108\pi$

E. $V = \dfrac{1}{3}\pi r^2 h = \dfrac{1}{3}\pi(3)^2(6) = 36\pi$

7 PRACTICE PPST 2

TEST INFO BOX		
Reading	40 items	50 minutes
Writing Multiple Choice	45 items	50 minutes
Writing Essay	1 essay	30 minutes
Mathematics	40 items	50 minutes

Take this test in a realistic, timed setting. You should not take this practice test until you have completed practice PPST 1.

The setting will be most realistic if another person times the test and ensures that the test rules are followed exactly. If another person is acting as test supervisor, he or she should review these instructions with you and say "Start" when you should begin a section and "Stop" when time has expired.

Use the multiple-choice answer sheet on page 259.

Use a pencil to mark the answer sheet. The actual test will be machine scored, so completely darken in the answer space.

Once the test is complete, review the answers and explanations for each item as you correct the test.

ANSWER SHEET FOR PRACTICE PPST 2

Reading—50 minutes

1 Ⓐ Ⓑ Ⓒ Ⓓ	9 Ⓐ Ⓑ Ⓒ Ⓓ	17 Ⓐ Ⓑ Ⓒ Ⓓ	25 Ⓐ Ⓑ Ⓒ Ⓓ	33 Ⓐ Ⓑ Ⓒ Ⓓ
2 Ⓐ Ⓑ Ⓒ Ⓓ	10 Ⓐ Ⓑ Ⓒ Ⓓ	18 Ⓐ Ⓑ Ⓒ Ⓓ	26 Ⓐ Ⓑ Ⓒ Ⓓ	34 Ⓐ Ⓑ Ⓒ Ⓓ
3 Ⓐ Ⓑ Ⓒ Ⓓ	11 Ⓐ Ⓑ Ⓒ Ⓓ	19 Ⓐ Ⓑ Ⓒ Ⓓ	27 Ⓐ Ⓑ Ⓒ Ⓓ	35 Ⓐ Ⓑ Ⓒ Ⓓ
4 Ⓐ Ⓑ Ⓒ Ⓓ	12 Ⓐ Ⓑ Ⓒ Ⓓ	20 Ⓐ Ⓑ Ⓒ Ⓓ	28 Ⓐ Ⓑ Ⓒ Ⓓ	36 Ⓐ Ⓑ Ⓒ Ⓓ
5 Ⓐ Ⓑ Ⓒ Ⓓ	13 Ⓐ Ⓑ Ⓒ Ⓓ	21 Ⓐ Ⓑ Ⓒ Ⓓ	29 Ⓐ Ⓑ Ⓒ Ⓓ	37 Ⓐ Ⓑ Ⓒ Ⓓ
6 Ⓐ Ⓑ Ⓒ Ⓓ	14 Ⓐ Ⓑ Ⓒ Ⓓ	22 Ⓐ Ⓑ Ⓒ Ⓓ	30 Ⓐ Ⓑ Ⓒ Ⓓ	38 Ⓐ Ⓑ Ⓒ Ⓓ
7 Ⓐ Ⓑ Ⓒ Ⓓ	15 Ⓐ Ⓑ Ⓒ Ⓓ	23 Ⓐ Ⓑ Ⓒ Ⓓ	31 Ⓐ Ⓑ Ⓒ Ⓓ	39 Ⓐ Ⓑ Ⓒ Ⓓ
8 Ⓐ Ⓑ Ⓒ Ⓓ	16 Ⓐ Ⓑ Ⓒ Ⓓ	24 Ⓐ Ⓑ Ⓒ Ⓓ	32 Ⓐ Ⓑ Ⓒ Ⓓ	40 Ⓐ Ⓑ Ⓒ Ⓓ

Writing—50 minutes

1 Ⓐ Ⓑ Ⓒ Ⓓ	10 Ⓐ Ⓑ Ⓒ Ⓓ	19 Ⓐ Ⓑ Ⓒ Ⓓ	28 Ⓐ Ⓑ Ⓒ Ⓓ	37 Ⓐ Ⓑ Ⓒ Ⓓ
2 Ⓐ Ⓑ Ⓒ Ⓓ	11 Ⓐ Ⓑ Ⓒ Ⓓ	20 Ⓐ Ⓑ Ⓒ Ⓓ	29 Ⓐ Ⓑ Ⓒ Ⓓ	38 Ⓐ Ⓑ Ⓒ Ⓓ
3 Ⓐ Ⓑ Ⓒ Ⓓ	12 Ⓐ Ⓑ Ⓒ Ⓓ	21 Ⓐ Ⓑ Ⓒ Ⓓ	30 Ⓐ Ⓑ Ⓒ Ⓓ	39 Ⓐ Ⓑ Ⓒ Ⓓ
4 Ⓐ Ⓑ Ⓒ Ⓓ	13 Ⓐ Ⓑ Ⓒ Ⓓ	22 Ⓐ Ⓑ Ⓒ Ⓓ	31 Ⓐ Ⓑ Ⓒ Ⓓ	40 Ⓐ Ⓑ Ⓒ Ⓓ
5 Ⓐ Ⓑ Ⓒ Ⓓ	14 Ⓐ Ⓑ Ⓒ Ⓓ	23 Ⓐ Ⓑ Ⓒ Ⓓ	32 Ⓐ Ⓑ Ⓒ Ⓓ	41 Ⓐ Ⓑ Ⓒ Ⓓ
6 Ⓐ Ⓑ Ⓒ Ⓓ	15 Ⓐ Ⓑ Ⓒ Ⓓ	24 Ⓐ Ⓑ Ⓒ Ⓓ	33 Ⓐ Ⓑ Ⓒ Ⓓ	42 Ⓐ Ⓑ Ⓒ Ⓓ
7 Ⓐ Ⓑ Ⓒ Ⓓ	16 Ⓐ Ⓑ Ⓒ Ⓓ	25 Ⓐ Ⓑ Ⓒ Ⓓ	34 Ⓐ Ⓑ Ⓒ Ⓓ	43 Ⓐ Ⓑ Ⓒ Ⓓ
8 Ⓐ Ⓑ Ⓒ Ⓓ	17 Ⓐ Ⓑ Ⓒ Ⓓ	26 Ⓐ Ⓑ Ⓒ Ⓓ	35 Ⓐ Ⓑ Ⓒ Ⓓ	44 Ⓐ Ⓑ Ⓒ Ⓓ
9 Ⓐ Ⓑ Ⓒ Ⓓ	18 Ⓐ Ⓑ Ⓒ Ⓓ	27 Ⓐ Ⓑ Ⓒ Ⓓ	36 Ⓐ Ⓑ Ⓒ Ⓓ	45 Ⓐ Ⓑ Ⓒ Ⓓ

Mathematics—50 minutes

1 Ⓐ Ⓑ Ⓒ Ⓓ	9 Ⓐ Ⓑ Ⓒ Ⓓ	17 Ⓐ Ⓑ Ⓒ Ⓓ	25 Ⓐ Ⓑ Ⓒ Ⓓ	33 Ⓐ Ⓑ Ⓒ Ⓓ
2 Ⓐ Ⓑ Ⓒ Ⓓ	10 Ⓐ Ⓑ Ⓒ Ⓓ	18 Ⓐ Ⓑ Ⓒ Ⓓ	26 Ⓐ Ⓑ Ⓒ Ⓓ	34 Ⓐ Ⓑ Ⓒ Ⓓ
3 Ⓐ Ⓑ Ⓒ Ⓓ	11 Ⓐ Ⓑ Ⓒ Ⓓ	19 Ⓐ Ⓑ Ⓒ Ⓓ	27 Ⓐ Ⓑ Ⓒ Ⓓ	35 Ⓐ Ⓑ Ⓒ Ⓓ
4 Ⓐ Ⓑ Ⓒ Ⓓ	12 Ⓐ Ⓑ Ⓒ Ⓓ	20 Ⓐ Ⓑ Ⓒ Ⓓ	28 Ⓐ Ⓑ Ⓒ Ⓓ	36 Ⓐ Ⓑ Ⓒ Ⓓ
5 Ⓐ Ⓑ Ⓒ Ⓓ	13 Ⓐ Ⓑ Ⓒ Ⓓ	21 Ⓐ Ⓑ Ⓒ Ⓓ	29 Ⓐ Ⓑ Ⓒ Ⓓ	37 Ⓐ Ⓑ Ⓒ Ⓓ
6 Ⓐ Ⓑ Ⓒ Ⓓ	14 Ⓐ Ⓑ Ⓒ Ⓓ	22 Ⓐ Ⓑ Ⓒ Ⓓ	30 Ⓐ Ⓑ Ⓒ Ⓓ	38 Ⓐ Ⓑ Ⓒ Ⓓ
7 Ⓐ Ⓑ Ⓒ Ⓓ	15 Ⓐ Ⓑ Ⓒ Ⓓ	23 Ⓐ Ⓑ Ⓒ Ⓓ	31 Ⓐ Ⓑ Ⓒ Ⓓ	39 Ⓐ Ⓑ Ⓒ Ⓓ
8 Ⓐ Ⓑ Ⓒ Ⓓ	16 Ⓐ Ⓑ Ⓒ Ⓓ	24 Ⓐ Ⓑ Ⓒ Ⓓ	32 Ⓐ Ⓑ Ⓒ Ⓓ	40 Ⓐ Ⓑ Ⓒ Ⓓ

Answers on pages 293–296

✂ Remove answer sheet by cutting on dotted line

PRACTICE PPST READING TEST

You should not take this practice test until you have completed practice PPST 1.

The test rules allow you exactly 50 minutes for this test.

Keep the time limit in mind as you work. Answer the easier questions first. Be sure you answer all the questions. There is no penalty for guessing. You may write on the test booklet and mark up the questions.

Each question or statement on the multiple-choice portions of the test has five answer choices. Exactly one of these choices is correct. Mark your choice on the answer sheet provided for this test.

Your score is based on the spaces you fill in on the answer sheet. Make sure that you mark your answer on the answer sheet in the correct space next to the correct question number.

Once the test is complete, review the answers and explanations for each item as you correct the test.

When instructed, turn the page and begin.

READING

40 items   50 minutes

You will read selections followed by one or more questions with five answer choices. Select the best answer choice based on what the selection states or implies and mark that letter on the answer sheet.

1. Cellular phones, once used by the very rich, are now available to almost everyone. With one of these phones, you can call just about anywhere from just about anywhere. Since the use of these phones will increase, we need to find legal and effective ways for law enforcement agencies to monitor calls.

   Which of the following choices is the best summary of this passage?
   (A) Criminals are taking advantage of cellular phones to avoid legal wiretaps.
   (B) The ability to use a cellular phone to call from just about anywhere makes it harder to find people who are using the phones.
   (C) The increase in cellular phone use means that we will have to find legal ways to monitor cellular calls.
   (D) Cellular phones are like regular phones with a very long extension cord.
   (E) Since cellular phones are more available to everyone, they are certainly more available to criminals.

2. The moon takes about 28 days to complete a cycle around the earth. Months, 28 days long, grew out of this cycle. Twelve of these months made up a year. But ancient astronomers realized that it took the earth about 365 days to make one revolution of the sun. Extra days were added to some months and the current calendar was born.

   The passage indicates that the current calendar
   (A) describes the moon's movement around the earth.
   (B) is based on the sun's position.
   (C) is based on the earth's rotation and position of the moon.
   (D) combines features of the moon's cycle and the earth's revolution.
   (E) was based on the number 12.

3. Occasionally, college students will confuse correlation with cause and effect. Correlation just describes the degree of relationship between two factors. For example, there is a positive correlation between poor handwriting and intelligence. However, writing more poorly will not make you more intelligent.

   The author's main reason for writing this passage is to
   (A) explain the difference between correlation and cause and effect.
   (B) encourage improved penmanship.
   (C) explain how college students can improve their intelligence.
   (D) make those with poor penmanship feel more comfortable.
   (E) describe a cause-and-effect relationship.

Questions 4–6

It is striking how uninformed today's youth are about Acquired Immune Deficiency Syndrome. Because of their youth and ignorance, many young adults engage in high-risk behavior. Many of these young people do not realize that the disease can be contracted through almost any contact with an infected person's blood and bodily fluids. Some do not realize that symptoms of the disease may not appear for ten years or more. Others do not realize that the danger in sharing needles to inject intravenous drugs comes from the small amounts of another's blood injected during this process. A massive education campaign is needed to fully inform today's youth about AIDS.

4. The main idea of this passage is
   (A) previous education campaigns have failed.
   (B) AIDS develops from the HIV virus.
   (C) the general public is not fully informed about AIDS.
   (D) people should not share intravenous needles.
   (E) young people are not adequately informed about AIDS.

5. Which of the following is the best summary of the statement about what young people don't realize about how AIDS can be contracted?
   (A) The symptoms may not appear for ten years or more.
   (B) AIDS is contracted because of ignorance.
   (C) AIDS is contracted from intravenous needles.
   (D) AIDS is contracted through contact with infected blood or bodily fluids.
   (E) You will not contract AIDS if you know what to avoid.

6. Which of the following best describes how the author views young people and their knowledge of AIDS?
   (A) Stupid
   (B) Unaware
   (C) Dumb
   (D) Unintelligible
   (E) Reluctant

7. When Lyndon Johnson succeeded John F. Kennedy, he was able to gain congressional approval for programs suggested by Kennedy but never implemented. These programs, called Great Society programs, included low-income housing and project Head Start. To some, this made Johnson a better president.

Based on this statement, Johnson
(A) was a better president than Kennedy.
(B) gained approval for programs proposed by Kennedy.
(C) was a member of a Great Society.
(D) was president before Kennedy.
(E) originally lived in low-income housing.

Questions 8–9

I think women are discriminated against; however, I think men are discriminated against just as much as women. It's just a different type of discrimination. Consider these two facts: Men die about 6 years earlier than women, and men are the only people who can be drafted into the armed forces. That's discrimination!

8. What is the author's main point in writing this passage?
   (A) Men are discriminated against more than women are.
   (B) Both sexes are discriminated against.
   (C) Women are not discriminated against.
   (D) On average, men die earlier than women.
   (E) Men are not discriminated against.

9. Which of the following could be substituted for the word *drafted* in the next to last sentence?
   (A) Inducted against their will
   (B) Signed up
   (C) Pushed in by society
   (D) Drawn in by peer pressure
   (E) Serve in a foreign country

<u>Questions 10–11</u>

Alice in Wonderland, written by Charles Dodgson under the pen name Lewis Carroll, is full of symbolism, so much so that a book titled *Understanding Alice* was written containing the original text with marginal notes explaining the symbolic meanings.

10. By symbolism, the author of the passage above meant that much of *Alice in Wonderland*
    (A) was written in a foreign language.
    (B) contained many mathematical symbols.
    (C) contained no pictures.
    (D) had a figurative meaning.
    (E) was set in a special type.

11. What does the author mean by the phrase "marginal notes" found in the last sentence?
    (A) Explanations of the musical meaning of the text
    (B) Notes that may not have been completely correct
    (C) Notes written next to the main text
    (D) Notes written by Carroll but not included in the original book
    (E) An explanation of the text by Alice Liddell, the real Alice

12. Following a concert, a fan asked a popular singer why the songs sounded so different in person than on the recording. The singer responded, "I didn't record my emotions!"

Which of the following statements is suggested by this passage?
    (A) The singer was probably not in a good mood during that performance.
    (B) The fan was being intrusive, and the performer was "brushing her off."
    (C) The performance was outdoors where sound quality is different.
    (D) The fan didn't realize the controls available for studio recordings.
    (E) The performance may vary depending on the mood of the performer.

Questions 13–18

The War of 1812 is one of the least understood conflicts in American history. However,
many events associated with the war are among
Line the best remembered from American History.
5 The war began when the United States invaded
British colonies in Canada. The invasion failed,
and the United States was quickly put on the
defensive. Most Americans are not aware of how
the conflict began. During the war, the *USS*
10 *Constitution* (Old Ironsides) was active against
British ships in the Atlantic. Captain William
Perry, sailing on Lake Erie, was famous for
yelling to his shipmates, "Don't give up the
ship." Most Americans remember Perry and his
15 famous plea, but not where or in which war he
was engaged.
Most notably, British troops sacked and
burned Washington, D.C. during this conflict.
Subsequent British attacks on Fort McHenry
20 near Baltimore were repulsed by American
forces. It was during one of these battles that
Francis Scott Key wrote the "Star Spangled
Banner" while a prisoner on a British ship.
The "rockets red glare, bombs bursting in
25 air" referred to ordnance used by the British
to attack the fort. Many Americans mistakenly
believe that the "Star Spangled Banner" was
written during or shortly after the Revolutionary
War.

13. All the following statements can be implied
from the passage EXCEPT:
(A) The British did not start the war.
(B) Francis Scott Key was not at Fort
McHenry when he wrote the "Star
Spangled Banner."
(C) The rockets referred to in the "Star
Spangled Banner" were part of a cele-
bration.
(D) The British army entered Washington,
D.C., during the war.
(E) The nickname for the *USS Constitution*
was Old Ironsides.

14. Which of the following words is the most
appropriate replacement for "sacked" in
line 17?
(A) Entered
(B) Ravished
(C) Invaded
(D) Enclosed
(E) Encapsulated

15. Which of the following statements best summarizes the difference referred to in the
passage between Perry's involvement in the
War of 1812 and the way many Americans
remember his involvement?
(A) Perry was a drafter of the Constitution
and later served on the *Constitution* in
the Atlantic, although many Americans
don't remember that.
(B) Perry served in the Great Lakes, but
many Americans don't remember that.
(C) Perry served in Washington, D.C.,
although many Americans don't remember that.
(D) Perry served on the *Constitution* at
Fort McHenry during the writing of the
"Star Spangled Banner," although many
Americans do not remember that.
(E) Perry served on the *Constitution* in the
Atlantic, but many Americans don't
remember that.

16. What can be inferred about Francis Scott
Key from lines 21–23 of the passage?
(A) He was killed in the battle.
(B) All his papers were confiscated by the
British after the battle.
(C) He was released by or escaped from the
British after the battle.
(D) He returned to Britain where he settled
down.
(E) He was a British spy.

17. Based on the passage, which of the follow-
ing words best describes the United States'
role in the War of 1812?
(A) Colonizer
(B) Neutral
(C) Winner
(D) Loser
(E) Aggressor

18. What main point is the author making in
this passage?
(A) The Americans fought the British in the
War of 1812.
(B) The Revolutionary War continued into
the 1800s.
(C) The British renewed the Revolutionary
War during the 1800s.
(D) Many Americans are unaware of events
associated with the War of 1812.
(E) Americans should remember the
treachery of the army that invaded
Washington during this war.

Questions 19–24

Computer-based word processing programs have spelling checkers and even a thesaurus to find synonyms and antonyms for highlighted words. To use the thesaurus, the student just types in the word, and a series of synonyms and antonyms appears on the computer screen. The program can also show recommended spellings for misspelled words. I like having a computer program that performs these mechanical aspects of writing. However, these programs do not teach about spelling or word meanings. A person could type in a word, get a synonym and have not the slightest idea what either meant.

Relying on this mindless way of checking spelling and finding synonyms, students will be completely unfamiliar with the meanings of the words they use. In fact, one of the most common misuses is to include a word that is spelled correctly but used incorrectly in the sentence.

It may be true that a strictly mechanical approach to spelling is used by some teachers. There certainly is a place for students who already understand word meanings to use a computer program that relieves the drudgery of checking spelling and finding synonyms. But these computer programs should never and can never replace the teacher. Understanding words—their uses and meanings—should precede this more mechanistic approach.

19. What is the main idea of this passage?
    (A) Mechanical spell checking is one part of learning about spelling.
    (B) Programs are not effective for initially teaching about spelling and synonyms.
    (C) Teachers should use word processing programs as one part of instruction.
    (D) Students who use these programs won't learn about spelling.
    (E) The programs rely too heavily on a student's typing ability.

20. Which of the following information is found in the passage?
    I. The type of computer that runs the word processor
    II. The two main outputs of spell-checking and thesaurus programs
    III. An explanation of how to use the word-processing program to teach about spelling and synonyms
    (A) I only
    (B) II only
    (C) I and II only
    (D) II and III only
    (E) I, II, and III

21. Which aspect of spell checking and thesaurus programs does the author like?
    (A) That you just have to type in the word
    (B) That the synonyms and alternative spellings are done very quickly
    (C) That the difficult mechanical aspects are performed
    (D) That you don't have to know how to spell to use them
    (E) That they can't replace teachers

22. Which of the following questions could be answered from the information in the passage?
    (A) When is it appropriate to use spell checking and thesaurus programs?
    (B) How does the program come up with recommended spellings?
    (C) What type of spelling learning experiences should students have?
    (D) Why do schools buy these word processing programs?
    (E) Which word program does the author recommend?

23. Which of the following statements could be used in place of the first sentence of the last paragraph?
    (A) It may be true that some strict teachers use a mechanical approach.
    (B) It may be true that a stringently mechanical approach is used by some teachers.
    (C) It may be true that inflexible mechanical approaches are used by some teachers.
    (D) It may be true that the mechanical approach used by some teachers is too rigorous.
    (E) It may be true that some teachers use only a mechanical approach.

24. According to this passage, what could be the result of a student's unfamiliarity with the meanings of words or synonyms?
    (A) Using a program to display the alternative spellings
    (B) Relying on mindless ways of checking spelling and finding synonyms
    (C) Strictly mechanical approaches
    (D) Using microcomputers to find synonyms for highlighted words
    (E) Being able to just type in a word

Questions 25–28

As a child he read the *Hardy Boys* series of books and was in awe of the author, Franklin Dixon. As an adult, he read a book entitled the *Ghost of the Hardy Boys*, which revealed that there was no Franklin Dixon and that ghost writers had authored the books. The authors were apparently working for a large publishing syndicate.

25. Which of the following is the likely intent of the author of this passage?
   (A) To describe a book-publishing practice
   (B) To contrast fiction and fact
   (C) To contrast childhood and adulthood
   (D) To correct the record
   (E) To dissuade children from reading the Hardy Boys books

26. Which of the following does the word *syndicate* in the last sentence most likely refer to?
   (A) A business group
   (B) An illegal enterprise
   (C) An illegal activity
   (D) A large building
   (E) A large number of books

27. What does the word *Ghost* in the title of the second mentioned book refer to?
   (A) A person who has died or was dead at the time the book was published
   (B) A person who writes books without credit
   (C) A person who influences the way a book is written
   (D) The mystical images of the mind that affect the way any author writes
   (E) A person who edits a book after the author has submitted it for publication

28. Which of the following would NOT be an acceptable replacement for the word *awe* in the first sentence?
   (A) Wonder
   (B) Admiration
   (C) Esteem
   (D) Aplomb
   (E) Respect

Questions 29–32

The Iroquois nation consisted of five main tribes—Cayuga, Mohawk, Oneida, Onondaga, and Seneca. Called the Five Nations or the League of Five Nations, these tribes occupied much of New York State. Since the tribes were arranged from east to west, the region they occupied was called the long house of the Iroquois.

The Iroquois economy was based mainly on agriculture. The main crop was corn, but they also grew pumpkins, beans, and fruit. The Iroquois used wampum (hollow beads) for money, and records were woven into wampum belts.

The Iroquoian Nation had a remarkable democratic structure, spoke a common Algonquin language, and were adept at fighting. These factors had made the Iroquois a dominant power by the early American colonial period. In the period just before the Revolutionary War, Iroquoian conquest had overcome most other Indian tribes in the northeastern United States as far west as the Mississippi River.

During the Revolutionary War, most Iroquoian tribes sided with the British. At the end of the Revolutionary War the tribes scattered, with some migrating to Canada. Only remnants of the Seneca and Onondaga tribes remained on their tribal lands.

29. Which of these statements best explains why the Iroquois were so successful at conquest?
 (A) The Iroquois had the support of the British.
 (B) The Iroquois had a cohesive society and were good fighters.
 (C) All the other tribes in the area were too weak.
 (D) There were five tribes, more than the other Indian nations.
 (E) The Iroquois had developed a defensive structure called the long house.

30. Which of the following best describes the geographic location of the five Iroquoian tribes?
 (A) The northeastern United States as far west as the Mississippi River
 (B) Southern Canada
 (C) Cayuga
 (D) New York State
 (E) The League of Nations

31. Which of the following best describes why the area occupied by the Iroquois was called the long house of the Iroquois?
 (A) The tribes were arranged as though they occupied different sections of a long house.
 (B) The Iroquois lived in structures called long houses.
 (C) The close political ties among tribes made it seem that they were all living in one house.
 (D) The Iroquois had expanded their original tribal lands through conquest.
 (E) It took weeks to walk the trail connecting all the tribes.

32. According to the passage, which of the following best describes the economic basis for the Iroquoian economy?
 (A) Wampum
 (B) Corn
 (C) Agriculture
 (D) Conquest
 (E) Warfare

Questions 33–38

Europeans had started to devote significant resources to medicine when Louis Pasteur was born December 7, 1822. By the time he died in the fall of 1895, he had made enormous contributions to science and founded microbiology. At 32, he was named professor and dean at a French university dedicated to supporting the production of alcoholic beverages. Pasteur immediately began work on yeast and fermentation. He found that he could kill harmful bacteria in the initial brewing process by subjecting the liquid to high temperatures. This finding was extended to milk in the process called pasteurization. This work led him to the conclusion that human disease could be caused by germs. In Pasteur's time, there was a widely held belief that germs were spontaneously generated. Pasteur conducted experiments that proved germs were always introduced and never appeared spontaneously. This result was questioned by other scientists for over a decade. He proved his theory of vaccination and his theory of disease during his work with anthrax, a fatal animal disease. He vaccinated some sheep with weakened anthrax germs and left other sheep unvaccinated. Then he injected all the sheep with a potentially fatal dose of anthrax bacteria. The unvaccinated sheep died while the vaccinated sheep lived. He developed vaccines for many diseases and is best known for his vaccine for rabies. According to some accounts, the rabies vaccine was first tried on a human when a young boy, badly bitten by a rabid dog, arrived at Pasteur's laboratory. The treatment of the boy was successful.

33. What is topic of this passage?
    (A) Microbiology
    (B) Pasteur's scientific discoveries
    (C) Germs and disease
    (D) Science in France
    (E) Louis Pasteur

34. What does the process of pasteurization involve?
    (A) Inoculating
    (B) Experimenting
    (C) Hydrating
    (D) Heating
    (E) Fermenting

35. Which of the following statements could most reasonably be inferred from this passage?
    (A) The myth of spontaneous generation was dispelled immediately following Pasteur's experiments on the subject.
    (B) The pasteurization of milk can aid in the treatment of anthrax.
    (C) Pasteur's discoveries were mainly luck.
    (D) Even scientists don't think scientifically all the time.
    (E) Injecting sheep with fatal doses of anthrax is one way of vaccinating them.

36. Which of the following statements can be implied from this passage?
    (A) That germs do not develop spontaneously was already a widely accepted premise when Pasteur began his scientific work.
    (B) Scientists in European countries had made significant progress on the link between germs and disease when Pasteur was born.
    (C) Europe was ready for scientific research on germs when Pasteur conducted his experiments.
    (D) Most of Pasteur's work was the replication of other work done by French scientists.
    (E) The theory that germs could cause human disease was not yet accepted at the time of Pasteur's death.

37. Which of the following choices best characterizes the reason for Pasteur's early work?
    (A) To cure humans
    (B) To cure animals
    (C) To help the French economy
    (D) To study germs
    (E) To be a professor

38. According to this passage, the rabies vaccine
    (A) was developed after Pasteur had watched
        a young boy bitten by a rabid dog.
    (B) was developed from the blood of a
        rabid dog, which had bitten a young
        boy.
    (C) was developed from the blood of a
        young boy bitten by a rabid dog.
    (D) was developed in addition to the vac-
        cines for other diseases.
    (E) was developed in his laboratory where a
        young boy had died of the disease.

<u>Questions 39–40</u>

I believe that there is extraterrestrial life—probably in some other galaxy. It is particularly human to believe that our solar system is the only one that can support intelligent life. But our solar system is only an infinitesimal dot in the infinity of the cosmos and it is just not believable that there is not life out there—somewhere.

39. What is the author of this passage proposing?
   (A) That there is other life in the universe
   (B) That there is no life on earth
   (C) That humans live on other planets
   (D) That the sun is a very small star
   (E) That we should explore other galaxies

40. The words *infinitesimal* and *infinite* are best characterized by which pair of words below?
   (A) Small and large
   (B) Very small and very large
   (C) Very small and limitless
   (D) Large and limitless
   (E) Small and very large

PRACTICE PPST WRITING TEST

Take this test in a realistic, timed setting. You should not take this practice test until you have completed practice PPST 1.

The test rules allow exactly 50 minutes for this section.

Keep the time limit in mind as you work. Answer the easier questions first. Be sure you answer all the questions. There is no penalty for guessing. You may write on the test booklet and mark up the questions.

Each question or statement has five answer choices. Exactly one of these choices is correct. Mark your choice on the answer sheet provided for this test.

Your score is based on the spaces you fill in on the answer sheet. Make sure that you mark your answer on the answer sheet in the correct space next to the correct question number.

When instructed, turn the page and begin.

WRITING

45 items   30 minutes

USAGE

(Use about 30 minutes)

> You will read sentences with four parts underlined and lettered. Determine whether one of the underlined parts contains grammatical, word use, or punctuation errors. If so, mark the letter of that part on your answer sheet. If there are no errors, mark E.

1. A professional golfer told the <u>new golfer</u>
                                    (A)
that <u>professional instruction</u> or more
         (B)
practice <u>improve</u> most golfers' <u>scores.</u>
           (C)   (D)
<u>No error.</u>
   (E)

2. It was <u>difficult for</u> the farmer
             (A)
<u>to comprehend</u> the unhappiness he
      (B)
<u>encountered among</u> so many of the rich
       (C)
<u>produce buyers</u> in the city. <u>No error</u>.
       (D)   (E)

3. No goal is <u>more noble</u>—no feat more
                  (A)
<u>revealing</u>—<u>as the</u> exploration <u>of space</u>.
   (B)   (C)   (D)
<u>No error</u>.
   (E)

4. The soccer player's <u>slight</u> strain from the
                          (A)
<u>shot</u> on goal led to a <u>pulled</u> muscle,
 (B)   (C)
<u>resulted</u> in the player's removal from the
  (D)
game. <u>No error</u>.
        (E)

5. The <u>young college graduate</u> had
             (A)
no family to help her but

<u>she was fortunate</u> to get a job with a
        (B)
<u>promising school district superintendent</u>
                    (C)
and <u>eventually became a superintendent</u>
                    (D)
herself. <u>No error</u>.
            (E)

6. He <u>was concerned</u> about crossing the
           (A)
bridge, <u>but the officer</u> said <u>that it</u> was
             (B)   (C)
<u>all right</u> to cross. <u>No error.</u>
   (D)   (E)

7. As the students <u>prepared to take</u> the
                          (A)
test, they <u>came to realize</u> that it was not
                (B)
only what they knew <u>and also</u> how well
                         (C)
they <u>knew how to</u> take tests. <u>No error.</u>
         (D)   (E)

8. As <u>many</u> as a ton of bananas may have
         (A)
<u>spoiled</u> when the <u>ship</u> was <u>stuck</u> in the
   (B)   (C)   (D)
Panama Canal. <u>No error.</u>
                     (E)

9. Employment agencies <u>often place</u>
                        (A)
   newspaper advertisements <u>when no</u>
                             (B)
   jobs <u>exist</u> to get the names of <u>potential</u>
        (C)   (D)
   employees on file. <u>No error.</u>
                       (E)

10. Visitors <u>to New York can</u> expect
             (A)
    <u>to encounter people</u>, noise, and
     (B)
    <u>finding themselves in traffic</u> just
     (C)
    <u>about any day of the</u> week. <u>No error,</u>
     (D)   (E)

11. It <u>was obvious</u> to Kim that neither
       (A)
    her family <u>or her friends</u> could
                (B)
    <u>understand why</u> the study <u>of science was</u>
     (C)   (D)
    so important to her. <u>No error.</u>
                          (E)

12. While <u>past safaris</u> had entered the jungle
          (A)
    to hunt <u>elephants with rifles</u>, this safari
            (B)
    had only a <u>single armed</u> guard to protect
               (C)
    <u>the tourists as</u> they took photographs.
     (D)
    <u>No errors.</u>
     (E)

13. <u>Buddhism is an</u> interesting <u>religion</u>
     (A)   (B)
    because Confucius <u>was born</u> in India,
                       (C)
    but the religion never <u>gained lasting</u>
                            (D)
    popularity there. <u>No error.</u>
                       (E)

14. John Dewey's <u>progressive</u> philosophy
                  (A)
    <u>influenced</u> thousands of teachers;
     (B)
    however, Dewey was often <u>displeased</u>
                              (C)
    with <u>there</u> teaching methods. <u>No error</u>.
         (D)   (E)

15. <u>While only</u> in the school for
     (A)
    <u>a few weeks</u>, the gym teacher
     (B)
    <u>was starting</u> to <u>felt comfortable</u> with
     (C)   (D)
    the principal. <u>No error</u>.
                    (E)

16. The <u>carnival</u>, which <u>featured</u> a wild
        (A)   (B)
    animal act was due to <u>arrive</u> in town
            (C)   (D)
    next week. <u>No error</u>.
                (E)

17. <u>While</u> the bus <u>driver</u> <u>waited</u>, the motor
     (A)   (B)   (C)
    runs and uses <u>expensive</u> gasoline.
                   (D)
    <u>No error</u>.
     (E)

18. <u>Having needed</u> to eat <u>and earn</u> money,
     (A)   (B)
    the college <u>graduate decided</u> it was
                 (C)
    <u>time to</u> look for a job. <u>No error</u>.
     (D)   (E)

19. The salesman <u>spent the day</u> calling
                  (A)
    contacts <u>with which</u> he had
              (B)
    <u>previously had</u> <u>business dealings</u>.
     (C)   (D)
    <u>No error</u>.
     (E)

20. <u>Thomas, the only player</u> to go
        (A)
    <u>undefeated through</u> the preliminary round,
        (B)
    <u>giving him</u> the highest <u>position for the</u>
        (C)   (D)
    tournament final. <u>No error</u>.
                        (E)

21. Because his <u>father was a wonderful</u>
                    (A)
    student, Jim's <u>teachers expected</u> him
                    (B)
    <u>to be a good</u> student just as his sister
        (C)
    Beth <u>did</u>. <u>No error</u>.
        (D)   (E)

22. We were <u>enjoying our</u> trip through the
                (A)
    <u>west, but</u> the car broke down much
        (B)
    <u>more frequent</u> than <u>we had</u> expected.
        (C)   (D)
    <u>No error</u>.
        (E)

23. Lynne <u>didn't like</u> bullfights so she was
                (A)
    <u>even</u> more uncomfortable sitting near
        (B)
    the <u>bulls'</u> <u>entrance</u> to the ring. <u>No error</u>.
        (C)   (D)   (E)

24. Anthropologists <u>appear</u> to agree that
                        (A)
    <u>there</u> can be no bond stronger than the
        (B)
    <u>bond</u> between a mother <u>with</u> her child.
        (C)   (D)
    <u>No error</u>.
        (E)

25. As <u>fast as</u> the pretzel <u>machine made</u>
            (A)   (B)
    pretzels, it was not faster <u>than person</u> it
                                (C)
    was <u>designed to</u> replace. <u>No error</u>.
            (D)   (E)

SENTENCE CORRECTION

You will read sentences with some or all of the sentence underlined, followed by five answer choices. The first answer choice repeats the underlined portion and the other four present possible replacements. Select the answer choice that best represents standard English without altering the meaning of the original sentence. Mark that letter on the answer sheet.

26. The dean was famous for delivering grand sounding <u>but otherwise unintelligible speeches.</u>
    (A) but otherwise unintelligible speeches.
    (B) but in every other way speeches that could not be intelligible.
    (C) but speeches which were not that intelligent.
    (D) but otherwise speeches that could be understood.
    (E) but speeches that could be unintelligible.

27. <u>The hiker grew tired greater</u> as the day wore on.
    (A) The hiker grew tired greater
    (B) The hiker grew tired more
    (C) The hiker grew greater tired
    (D) The hiker's tired grew greater
    (E) The hiker grew more tired

28. The man knew that <u>to solve the problem now can be easier</u> than putting it off for another day.
    (A) to solve the problem now can be easier
    (B) to solve the problem now is easier
    (C) to solve the problem now can be less difficult
    (D) solving the problem now can be easier
    (E) to try to solve the problem now

29. Lee's <u>mother and father insists that</u> he call if he is going to be out after 8:00 P.M.
    (A) mother and father insists that
    (B) mother and father insist that
    (C) mother and father insists
    (D) mother and father that insist
    (E) mother and father that insists

30. The weather forecaster said that people living near the shore should be prepared <u>in the event that</u> the storm headed for land.
    (A) in the event that
    (B) if the event happened and
    (C) the event
    (D) if
    (E) and

31. After years of observation, the soccer coach concluded that women soccer players were more aggressive than <u>men who played soccer.</u>
    (A) men who played soccer.
    (B) men soccer players.
    (C) soccer playing men.
    (D) those men who played soccer.
    (E) men.

32. The stockbroker advised her client to sell the stock before it <u>could no longer be popular.</u>
    (A) could no longer be popular.
    (B) could be popular no longer.
    (C) may be popular no longer.
    (D) could become unpopular.
    (E) was no longer popular.

33. Bringing in an outside consultant usually means that it will take too long for the consultant to understand what's going on, <u>the functioning of the office will be impaired</u> and, because a new person has been introduced into the company, it will create dissension.
    (A) the functioning of the office will be impaired
    (B) the impairment of office functioning will follow
    (C) caused impairment in office functioning
    (D) office functioning impairment will occur
    (E) it will impair the functioning of the office

34. The primary election was very <u>important because winning could give the candidate a much more</u> clearer mandate.
    (A) important because winning could give the candidate a much more
    (B) important because winning there could give the candidate a much more
    (C) important because a win there could give the candidate a
    (D) important because winning could give the candidate a
    (E) important because a loss there would be devastating

35. She had become a doctor with the noble purpose of saving lives; however, <u>the process of applying for medical benefits and the responsibilities for managing the office had become her primary and overriding concern.</u>
    (A) the process of applying for medical benefits and the responsibilities for managing the office had become her primary and overriding concern.
    (B) applying for medical benefits and managing the office had become her main concerns.
    (C) applying for medical benefits, and the responsibilities for managing the office had become her primary and overriding concern.
    (D) applying for medical benefits and office work had become her main concern.
    (E) she soon found out that being a doctor was not noble.

36. Among the most popular television programs are those that critics classify <u>is soap operas.</u>
    (A) is soap operas.
    (B) are soap operas.
    (C) as soap operas.
    (D) in soap operas.
    (E) with soap operas.

37. If a person <u>has the ability in music</u>, then he should try to develop this ability by taking music lessons.
    (A) has the ability in music
    (B) has musical ability
    (C) can play an instrument
    (D) is a talented musician
    (E) is interested in music

38. <u>The players on the national team were supposed by some of their countrymen to have almost superhuman ability.</u>
    (A) The players on the national team were supposed by some of their countrymen to have almost superhuman ability.
    (B) The players on the national team had superhuman ability, according to some of their countrymen.
    (C) The players in the national team were better at the sport than most of their countryman.
    (D) Suppose the players on the national team were not good enough, thought some of their countrymen.
    (E) Some of their countrymen thought that the players on the national team had almost superhuman ability.

39. Mr. Littler had managed to stay popular with the students, even though any serious breach of discipline <u>inevitably brought</u> them to his office.
    (A) inevitably brought
    (B) brought inevitably
    (C) was inevitable
    (D) considerably brought
    (E) inevitably bring

40. No matter how much she tried, she could never convince her father <u>that he should stop</u> smoking cigarettes.
    (A) that he should stop
    (B) he should stop
    (C) should stop
    (D) to stop
    (E) about stopping

41. The main error <u>of superhighway driving is to forget</u> what the speedometer reads.
    (A) of superhighway driving is to forget
    (B) driving is to forget on superhighways
    (C) is speeding on superhighways
    (D) people make when they drive on superhighways is to forget
    (E) is forgetting on superhighways to drive

42. People who set fires are frequently captured, <u>and it is common</u> at the scene of the crime.
    (A) and it is common
    (B) and common
    (C) in common at the
    (D) and
    (E) commonly

43. It was easy for the sailor to spot his boat on the river because of <u>it's collapsible mast.</u>
    (A) it's collapsible mast.
    (B) it's mast being collapsible.
    (C) its collapsible mast.
    (D) its mast being collapsible.
    (E) it's mast, which was collapsible.

44. The woods were beautiful but he was from the city and the sounds of animals often <u>aroused him up</u> from his sleep.
    - (A) aroused him up
    - (B) roused up
    - (C) roused him
    - (D) roused him up
    - (E) aroused him

45. <u>Contrary to the belief held in the distant past</u>, the earth is not at the center of our solar system.
    - (A) Contrary to the belief held in the distant past
    - (B) In contrast to the belief held in the distant past
    - (C) Contrary to that held in the distant past
    - (D) Unlike the view held in the distant past
    - (E) Unlike the distant past

PRACTICE PPST ESSAY

Take this test in a realistic, timed setting. You should not take this practice test until you have completed practice PPST 1.

Write an essay on the topic found on the next page. Write on this topic only. An essay written on another topic, no matter how well done, will receive a 0. You have 30 minutes to complete the essay.

Use the space provided to briefly outline your essay and to organize your thoughts before you begin to write. Use this opportunity to demonstrate how well you can write but be sure to cover the topic.

Write your essay on the lined paper provided. Write legibly and do not skip any lines. Your entire essay must fit on these pages.

Once the test is complete, ask an English professor or English teacher to evaluate your essay holistically using the rating scale on page 34.

When instructed, turn the page and begin.

ESSAY

You have 30 minutes to complete this essay question. Use the lined pages to write a brief essay based on this topic.

Choose a memorable moment in your life. Write an essay in the space provided, on the topic "My Most Memorable Moment."

Write a brief outline here.

PRACTICE PPST MATHEMATICS TEST

Take this test in a realistic, timed setting. You should not take this practice test until you have completed practice PPST 1.

The test rules allow you exactly 50 minutes for this section.

Keep the time limit in mind as you work. Answer the easier items first. Be sure you answer all the items. There is no penalty for guessing. You may write on the test booklet and mark up the items.

Each item has five answer choices. Exactly one of these choices is correct. Mark your choice on the answer sheet provided for this test.

Your score is based on the spaces you fill in on the answer sheet. Make sure that you mark your answer in the correct space next to the correct item number.

When instructed, turn the page and begin.

MATHEMATICS
40 items   50 minutes

Each item below includes five answer choices. Select the best choice for each item and mark that letter on the answer sheet.

1. A representative of the magazine advertising department is responsible for 9 to 10 full-page ads, 12 to 14 half-page ads, and 15 to 20 quarter-page ads per issue. The minimum and maximum numbers of ads that each representative is responsible for are
   (A) 9 and 20
   (B) 9 and 15
   (C) 15 and 20
   (D) 36 and 44
   (E) 10a and 20

2. 7.17 is between
   (A) 7.0 and 7.2
   (B) 7.02 and 7.10
   (C) 7.5 and 7.9
   (D) 7.00 and 7.04
   (E) 7.012 and 7.102

3. Which of the following expresses the relationship between x and y shown in the table?

x	y
0	1
3	7
6	13
7	15
9	19

   (A) $y = 3x - 2$
   (B) $y = 2x + 1$
   (C) $y = x + 3$
   (D) $y = 2x - 2$
   (E) $y = 2x + 3$

4. It took Liz 12 hours to travel by train from New York to North Carolina at an average speed of 55 miles per hour. On the return trip from North Carolina to New York, Liz traveled by bus and averaged 45 miles per hour. How many hours did the return trip take?
   (A) $13\frac{2}{3}$
   (B) 14
   (C) $14\frac{2}{3}$
   (D) 15
   (E) 16

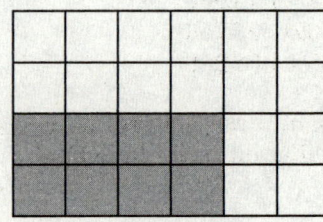

5. In the figure, what percent of the region is shaded?
   (A) $66\frac{2}{3}$ percent
   (B) 50 percent
   (C) 25 percent
   (D) 60 percent
   (E) $33\frac{1}{3}$ percent

6. 5×10^5 is equal to
   (A) 250
   (B) one-half million
   (C) 5 million
   (D) 50,000
   (E) 0.00005

7. Which of the following could be the length of a couch?
   (A) 75 cm
   (B) 4 meters
   (C) 150 mm
   (D) 1.2 decimeters
   (E) 0.5 kilometers

8. C is 5 more than half of B. Which of the following expressions states this relationship?
   (A) $C + 5 = B/2$
   (B) $C = \frac{1}{2}B + 5$
   (C) $C + 5 = 2B$
   (D) $C + 5 > B/2$
   (E) $C + 5 < B/2$

9. If your commission for this month is 15% of $500, which of the following commissions is more than yours?
   (A) 20% of $380
   (B) 10% of $500
   (C) 1% of $1000
   (D) 10% of $750
   (E) 25% of $280

10. Which of these figures has a perimeter measure different from the others?

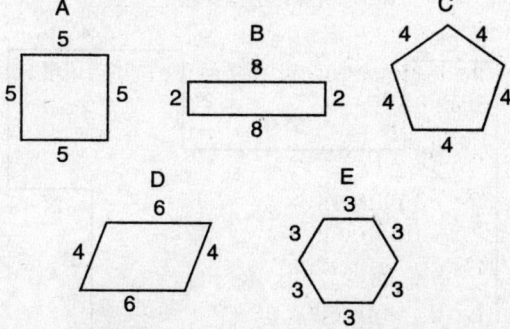

Time	8 A.M.	9 A.M.	10 A.M.	11 A.M.	12 NOON
Temp	50°	55°	60°	60°	70°
Time	1 P.M.	2 P.M.	3 P.M.	4 P.M.	
Temp	75°	75°	70°	65°	
Time	5 P.M.	6 P.M.	7 P.M.	8 P.M.	
Temp	55°	50°	50°	45°	

11. The above table shows the temperature tracked for a 12-hour period of time. Which graph best illustrates this information?

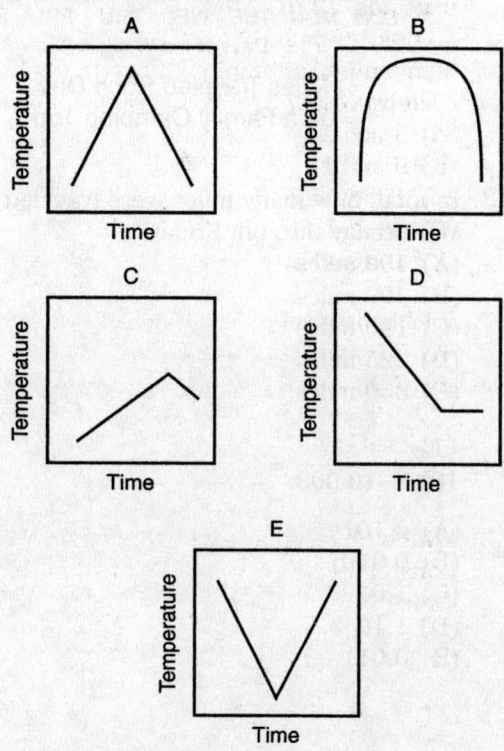

12. A rectangular garden measures 23 feet by 63 feet. What is the greatest number of nonoverlapping 5-foot square plots that can be ruled off in this garden?
   (A) 48
   (B) 57
   (C) 58
   (D) 289
   (E) 290

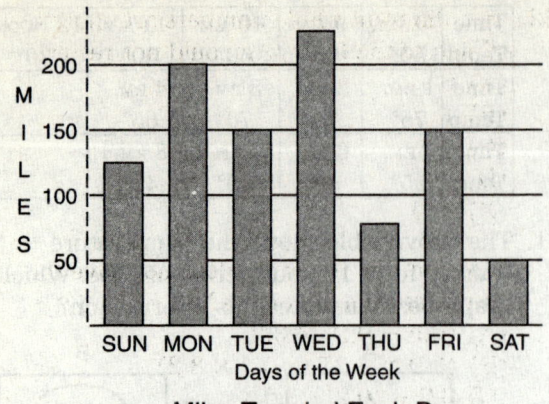

Miles Traveled Each Day
on a Family Camping Trip

13. In total, how many miles were traveled
    Wednesday through Friday?
    (A) 450 miles
    (B) 400 miles
    (C) 150 miles
    (D) 225 miles
    (E) 350 miles

14. $\dfrac{1}{100} + \dfrac{1}{10,000} =$

    (A) 0.101
    (B) 0.0101
    (C) 1.01
    (D) 1.10
    (E) 0.011

15. A junior high school has a teacher-student
    ratio of 1 to 15. If there are 43 teachers,
    how many students are there?
    (A) 645
    (B) 430
    (C) 215
    (D) 630
    (E) 600

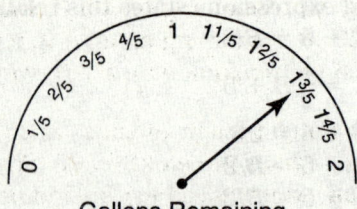

Gallons Remaining

16. On the gauge, the arrow points to
    (A) $1\dfrac{1}{2}$

    (B) $1\dfrac{3}{5}$

    (C) 1.5

    (D) $1\dfrac{3}{4}$

    (E) 1.75

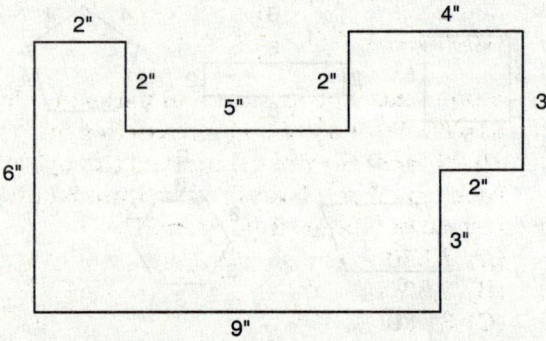

17. A floor plan is drawn with a scale of 5 feet
    per inch. If the diagram represents the floor
    plan, what is the actual perimeter of the
    house?
    (A) 38 inches
    (B) 38 feet
    (C) 200 feet
    (D) $7\dfrac{2}{5}$ feet
    (E) 190 feet

18. Mary must make tablecloths for 12 banquet tables. She needs a piece of cloth 5 ft. by 8 ft. for each tablecloth. Each cloth must be made from the same bolt and cannot be sewn. Of the five bolts listed here, which one must be eliminated due to insufficient material?
    (A) 25 yd. remaining on an 8-ft. wide bolt
    (B) 33 yd. remaining on a 6-ft. wide bolt
    (C) 25 yd. remaining on a 5-ft. wide bolt
    (D) 20 yd. remaining on an 8-ft. wide bolt
    (E) 36 yd. remaining on a 7-ft. wide bolt

19. Blaire bought a pair of shoes at 25 percent off the regular price of $40.00. She had a coupon, which saved her an additional 15 percent off the sale price. What price did she pay for the shoes?
    (A) $24.00
    (B) $15.00
    (C) $25.50
    (D) $11.25
    (E) $27.50

20. Points L, M, N, and O are on the same line. Which could NOT be values for LM and NO?
    (A) $LM = 15$; $NO = 10$
    (B) $LM = 12$; $NO = 9$
    (C) $LM = 3$; $NO = 2$
    (D) $LM = 0.75$; $NO = 0.5$
    (E) $LM = 1$; $NO = \dfrac{2}{3}$

21. Store A has videocassettes in packs of 3 for $15.60. Store B sells videocassettes for $6.00 each. How much is saved (if any) on each tape if you buy six tapes from Store A instead of 6 tapes from Store B?
    (A) $3.40
    (B) $.80
    (C) $1.80
    (D) $2.40
    (E) There is no saving.

22. Two different whole numbers are multiplied. Which of the following could not result?
    (A) 0
    (B) 1
    (C) 7
    (D) 19
    (E) 319

23. Which of the following does not have the same value as the others?
    (A) $(0.9 + 0.2) \times 3.2$
    (B) $(0.9 \times 3.2) + (0.2 \times 3.2)$
    (C) $0.9 + (0.2 \times 3.2)$
    (D) $3.2 \times (0.2 + 0.9)$
    (E) $3.2 \times (1.1)$

24. In the figure, if the first cube represents a weight of 100 grams, which of the other cubes most likely represents 25 grams?

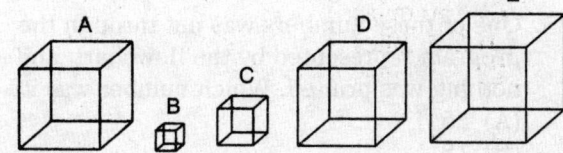

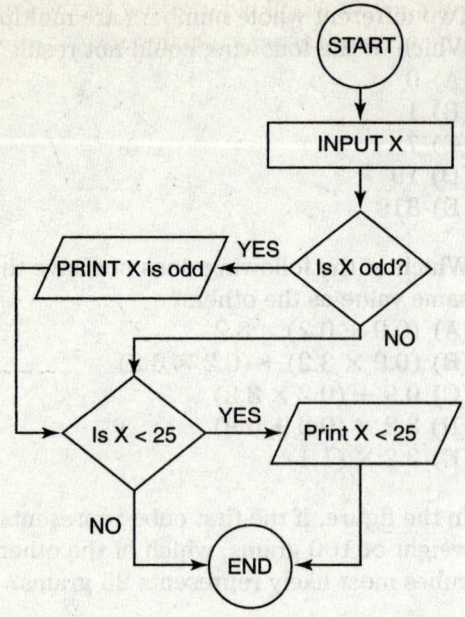

25. One of these numbers was put through the program represented by the flowchart, and nothing was printed. Which number was it?
    (A) 25
    (B) 18
    (C) 13
    (D) 38
    (E) 27

26. A calculator displays a multiple-digit wholc number ending in 0. All the following statements must be true about the number EXCEPT:
    (A) it is an even number.
    (B) it is a multiple of 5.
    (C) it is a power of 10.
    (D) it is a multiple of 10.
    (E) it is the sum of 2 odd numbers.

27. Some values of Y are more than 50. Which of the following could not be true?
    (A) 60 is not a value of Y.
    (B) 45 is not a value of Y.
    (C) There are Y values more than 50.
    (D) All values of Y are 50 or less.
    (E) Some values of Y are more than 50.

28. A pedometer shows distance in meters. A distance of 0.5 kilometers would have a numerical display that is
    (A) 100 times as great.
    (B) twice as great.
    (C) half as great.
    (D) 1000 times as great.
    (E) $\frac{1}{10}$ times as great.

29. Which fraction is the greatest?
    (A) $\frac{5}{4}$
    (B) $\frac{99}{100}$
    (C) $\frac{25}{24}$
    (D) $\frac{12}{13}$
    (E) $\frac{17}{16}$

30. Two dice are rolled. What is the probability that the sum of the numbers is even?
    (A) $\frac{1}{2}$
    (B) $\frac{16}{36}$
    (C) $\frac{3}{4}$
    (D) $\frac{1}{12}$
    (E) $\frac{5}{6}$

31. If the product of P and 6 is R, then the product of P and 3 is
    (A) $2R$
    (B) $R/2$
    (C) $\frac{1}{2}P$
    (D) $2P$
    (E) $P/6$

32. The multiplication and division buttons on a calculator are reversed. A person presses ÷ 5 = and the calculator displays 625. What answer should have been displayed?
    (A) 125
    (B) 625
    (C) 25
    (D) 50
    (E) 250

33. If V, l, w, and h are positive numbers and $V = l \times w \times h$, then $l =$
    (A) $\frac{1}{3} whv$

    (B) $\frac{v}{hw}$

    (C) $\frac{lw}{v}$

    (D) vlw
    (E) $w(v + h)$

34. If 0.00005 divided by $X = 0.005$, then $X =$
    (A) 0.1
    (B) 0.01
    (C) 0.001
    (D) 0.0001
    (E) 0.00001

35. The product of two numbers is 900. One number is tripled. In order for the product to remain the same, the other number must be
    (A) multiplied by 3.
    (B) divided by $\frac{1}{3}$.

    (C) multiplied by $\frac{1}{3}$.

    (D) subtracted from 900.
    (E) quadrupled.

36. Which of the following could be the face of the cross section of a cylinder?

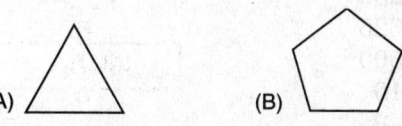

(A) (B)

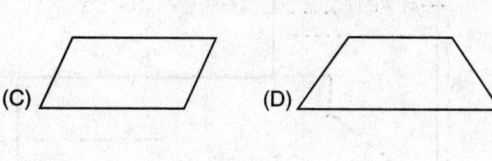

(C) (D)

(E)

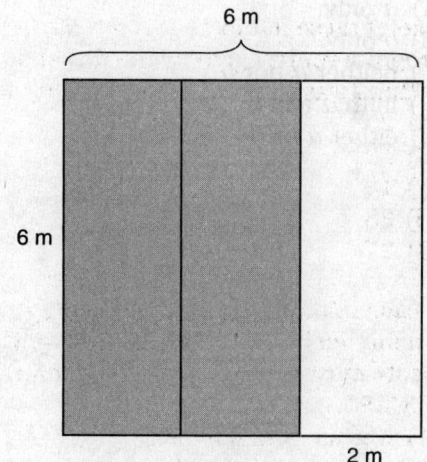

37. What is the area of the shaded portion of the figure?
    (A) 12 square meters
    (B) 22 square meters
    (C) 20 square meters
    (D) 36 square meters
    (E) 24 square meters

38. Estimate the answer for $124 \times \dfrac{49}{24}$.
    (A) 200
    (B) 250
    (C) 325
    (D) 500
    (E) 10

40. Deena finished the school run in 52.8 seconds. Lisa's time was 1.3 seconds faster. What was Lisa's time?
    (A) 51.5 seconds
    (B) 54.1 seconds
    (C) 53.11 seconds
    (D) 65.8 seconds
    (E) 52.93 seconds

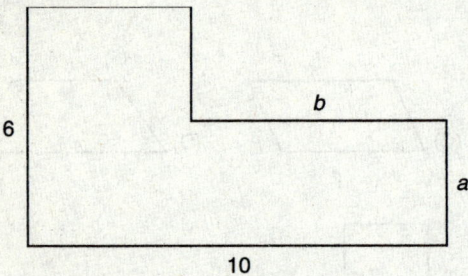

39. Which of the following dimensions would be needed to find the area of the figure?
    (A) a only
    (B) b only
    (C) neither a nor b
    (D) both a and b
    (E) either a or b

PPST 2 ANSWER KEYS

Reading

1. C	5. D	9. A	13. C	17. E	21. C	25. D	29. B	33. B	37. C
2. D	6. B	10. D	14. B	18. D	22. A	26. A	30. D	34. D	38. D
3. A	7. B	11. C	15. B	19. B	23. E	27. B	31. A	35. D	39. A
4. E	8. B	12. E	16. C	20. B	24. B	28. D	32. C	36. C	40. C

Writing

Usage

1. C	4. D	7. C	10. C	13. E	16. C	19. B	22. C	25. C
2. E	5. C	8. A	11. B	14. D	17. C	20. C	23. E	
3. C	6. E	9. E	12. B	15. D	18. A	21. D	24. D	

Sentence Correction

26. A	28. D	30. D	32. E	34. D	36. C	38. E	40. D	42. E	44. C
27. E	29. B	31. B	33. E	35. B	37. B	39. A	41. D	43. C	45. A

Mathematics

1. D	5. E	9. A	13. A	17. E	21. B	25. D	29. A	33. B	37. E
2. A	6. B	10. E	14. B	18. C	22. B	26. C	30. A	34. B	38. B
3. B	7. B	11. A	15. A	19. C	23. C	27. D	31. B	35. C	39. D
4. C	8. B	12. A	16. B	20. B	24. C	28. D	32. C	36. E	40. A

EXPLAINED ANSWERS

Reading

1. **C** This choice paraphrases the last sentence of the passage.
2. **D** The passage identifies both the moon's cycle and the earth's revolution as factors contributing to the development of the current calendar.
3. **A** The author explains the difference with the description and an example.
4. **E** The passage is about youth and constantly refers to what they do not know about AIDS.
5. **D** This choice paraphrases the third sentence in the paragraph.
6. **B** The passage uses many synonyms of this word to describe young people's knowledge of AIDS.
7. **B** This choice paraphrases the first sentence in the passage.
8. **B** The author says, and then gives an example to show, that men are discriminated against just as much as women.
9. **A** Drafted, in the sense used here, means to be inducted into the armed forces against one's will.
10. **D** *Alice in Wonderland*, a fanciful story about a young girl's adventures underground, has underlying figurative meanings.
11. **C** The content reveals that marginal means the area of a page to the left and right of the text.
12. **E** Music is more than notes and varies with the mood of the performer.
13. **C** The passage states that rockets refer to ordnance or weapons used by the British.
14. **B** *Ravished* is the best choice and describes what happens when a town is sacked.
15. **B** The last sentence of the first paragraph says that most Americans remember Perry, but not where he served.
16. **C** Francis Scott Key must have been able to distribute his "Star Spangled Banner" in America, so he must have been released by or escaped from the British.
17. **E** The second sentence in the paragraph identifies the United States as the aggressor.
18. **D** The author signals this main point in the first sentence of the passage.

19. **B** The next to the last sentence in the first paragraph indicates that these programs do not teach about spelling or word meanings.
20. **B** The type of computer used and teaching methods are not mentioned in the passage.
21. **C** The fourth sentence in the first paragraph explains that the author likes having a program to perform the mechanical aspects.
22. **A** This question can be answered from information in the passage's last paragraph.
23. **E** This choice paraphrases the first sentence in the last paragraph.
24. **B** This information is found in the first sentence of the first paragraph.
25. **D** The author wants to share what he or she learned about the Hardy Boys books.
26. **A** The word *syndicate* can have many meanings. The context reveals that this word *syndicate* means a business group.
27. **B** A ghost writer is someone who writes books but does not receive credit.
28. **D** Every other choice is an acceptable replacement for the word *awe*.
29. **B** The second sentence in the third paragraph supports this choice.
30. **D** This information is contained in the first sentence of the first paragraph.
31. **A** This choice is supported by the last sentence in the first paragraph.
32. **C** The first sentence of the second paragraph provides this information.
33. **B** This paragraph is about Pasteur's scientific discoveries and not about Pasteur the person.
34. **D** This answer can be found in lines 9–14 of the passage.
35. **D** The passage contains examples of scientists who opposed Pasteur's theories even though Pasteur had proven his theories scientifically.
36. **C** The first sentence indicates that Europeans had already started to devote resources to medicine when Pasteur was born, and theories about germs existed when Pasteur began his work.

37. **C** The passage mentions that his early work was at a university dedicated to supporting an important product of the French economy.
38. **D** The third from last sentence in the passage mentions that Pasteur developed vaccines for many diseases.
39. **A** This choice paraphrases the first sentence in the paragraph.
40. **C** *Infinitesimal* means very small, and *infinite* means without limit.

Writing

Usage
1. **C** This singular verb should end in *s*.
2. **E** This sentence contains no errors.
3. **C** The phrase *as the* should be replaced by the word *than*.
4. **D** *Resulted* should be replaced by *resulting*.
5. **C** It is not possible to tell whether the school district or the superintendent is promising.
6. **E** This sentence contains no errors.
7. **C** Replace *and also* with *but also*.
8. **A** Replace *many* with *much*.
9. **E** This sentence contains no errors.
10. **C** Remove *finding themselves in* to maintain the parallel development of this sentence.
11. **B** Replace *or* with *nor*.
12. **B** This phrase makes it seem that elephants are armed with rifles.
13. **E** This sentence contains no errors.
14. **D** Replace *there* with *their*.
15. **D** Replace *felt* with *feel*.
16. **C** A comma is missing.
17. **C** Replace *waited* with *waits*.
18. **A** Replace *having needed* with *needing*.
19. **B** Replace *which* with *whom*.
20. **C** Replace *giving him* with *earned* or *had*.
21. **D** Replace *did* with *was*.
22. **C** Replace *frequent* with *frequently*.
23. **E** This sentence contains no errors.
24. **D** Replace *with* with *and*.
25. **C** Include *the* between *than* and *person*.

Sentence Correction
26. **A** The underlined portion is acceptable as written.
27. **E** Use this replacement for the awkward wording in the original sentence.
28. **D** Use this replacement for the awkward wording in the original sentence.
29. **B** The plural verb does not end in *s*.
30. **D** Use the word *if* in place of the wordy underlined phrase.
31. **B** This wording is clearer and more understandable than the original wording in the sentence.
32. **E** The correct verb is *was*, rather than *could . . . be*.
33. **E** Use this replacement to maintain the parallel structure of the sentence.
34. **D** The words *much more* in the original sentence are not needed. Choice C is not correct because it unnecessarily changes the sentence.
35. **B** Use this more direct wording to replace the underlined portion of the sentence.
36. **C** Replace *is* with *as*.
37. **B** Use this more direct wording to replace the underlined portion of the sentence.
38. **E** Use this more direct wording to replace the underlined portion of the sentence.
39. **A** The underlined portion of the sentence is acceptable as written.
40. **D** *To stop* is more effective and compact than the original underlined wording.
41. **D** While this choice is longer than the underlined wording, it is much easier to understand.
42. **E** Use *commonly* to replace the awkward and wordy *and it is common*.
43. **C** Replace *it's* with *its*.
44. **C** This choice is more compact and clearer than the original wording.
45. **A** The original underlined wording is acceptable.

Essay
Ask an English professor or teacher to rate your essay using the scale on page 34.

Mathematics

1. **D** Add the three smaller numbers and then the three larger numbers to find this answer.
2. **A** 7.1_ is always between 7.0 and 7.2
3. **B** Multiply x by 2 and then add 2 to find y.
4. **C** Multiply 12 times 55 = 660 to find the total length of the trip. Divide 660 by 45 = 14.66_ to find the number of hours for the return trip.

5. **E** One third or $33\frac{1}{3}$% of the region is shaded.

6. **B** $10^5 \times 100,000$, so $5 \times 100,000 = 500,000$ or $\frac{1}{2}$ million.

7. **B** Four meters, or about 12 feet, is the only plausible answer.

8. **B** This equation correctly expresses the relationship.

9. **A** $0.15 \times 500 = 75$; $0.20 \times 380 = 76$.

10. **E** All the other figures have a perimeter of 20 except this hexagon, which has a perimeter of 18.

11. **A** This graph best represents the steady movement up and then down of the temperatures.

12. **A** $5\overline{)23} = 4$ R 3; $5\overline{)63} = 12$ R 3; $4 \times 12 = 48$.

13. **A** Add 225, 75, and 150 to find the answer.

14. **B** This is the correct decimal representation for the sum of the fractions.

15. **A** Write the proportion $\frac{1}{15} = \frac{43}{x}$, so $x = 645$.

16. **B** The gauge is marked in fifths of a gallon.

17. **E** Add the perimeters to find the total of 38 inches; $5 \times 38 = 190$.

18. **C** Choice C yields a piece 75 feet by 5 feet. Mary needs a piece 96 feet by 5 feet.

19. **C** $0.25 \times \$40 = \$10$; $\$40 - \$10 = \$30$; $0.15 \times \$30 = \$4.50$; $\$30 - \$4.50 = \$25.50$.

20. **B** The ratio of LM to NO is 3:2. Choice B does not reflect this ratio.

21. **B** Three tapes cost $15.60 at Store A and $18.00 at Store B. The saving for all three tapes is $2.40. The saving on one tape is $0.80.

22. **B** The product of two whole numbers is 1 only if both whole numbers are 1.

23. **C** The value of each of the other choices is 3.52.

24. **C** This choice is closest to one-quarter of the first cube.

25. **D** The flowchart prints numbers that are odd or less than 25.

26. **C** Powers of 10 are 1, 10, 100, 1000. The calculator could be displaying 20, which is not a power of 10.

27. **D** If some of the values of Y are more than 50, then all of the values of Y could not be less than 50.

28. **D** The display would show 500, which is 1000 times (0.5).

29. **A** $\frac{5}{4}$ is greater than 1, so (B) and (D) cannot be correct. Cross multiply to see that $\frac{5}{4}$ is greater than choices (C) and (E).

30. **A** There are 36 possible outcomes. Half of these outcomes are even and half are odd.

31. **B** $6 \cdot P = R$. Divide both sides by 2 to get $3 \cdot P = R/2$.

32. **C** Every time the $\boxed{=}$ key is pressed, the calculator multiplies: $125 \times 5 = 625$, which correlates to $125 \div 5 = 25$, the correct answer.

33. **B** $V = l \times w \times h$. Divide both sides by $w \times h$ to get $V/w \times h = 1$.

34. **B** Dividing by 0.01 is the same as multiplying by 100.

35. **C** Multiplying by $\frac{1}{3}$ is the same as dividing by 3.

36. **E** Imagine a cylinder with a height equal to its diameter. The vertical cross section of this cylinder is a square.

37. **E** The area of the figure is 36 square meters. Two-thirds of the figure is shaded, so $\frac{2}{3} \times 36 = 24$.

38. **B** Use 125×2 to estimate. The answer is about 250.

39. **D** Both dimensions are needed to find the area of the right-hand rectangle in the figure.

40. **A** Faster times are represented by smaller numbers. Subtract $52.8 - 1.3$ to find Lisa's time.

 **PRACTICE CBT**

TEST INFO BOX	
READING	30 items 95 minutes
WRITING Multiple Choice	35 items 30 minutes
WRITING Essay	1 essay 40 minutes
MATHEMATICS	40 items 65 minutes

You will need a simple four-function calculator with a square root key for the mathematics test and a word processor for the essay.

Take this test in a realistic timed setting. You should not take this practice test until you have completed Practice PPST 2.

The setting will be most realistic if another person times the test and ensures that the test rules are followed. If another person is acting as test supervisor, he or she should review these instructions with you and say "Start" when you should begin and "Stop" when time has expired.

You use your pencil on this test as you will use a mouse and a keyboard on the actual CBT. Answer the items on the test page. Answer each item as you come to it. You may not change an answer. Do not skip an item without answering; you may not come back to that item.

Once the test is complete, review the answers and explanations for each item as you correct the test.

Once instructed, turn the page and begin.

PRACTICE CBT READING TEST

You should not take this test until you have completed both Practice PPST Reading Tests.

The test rules allow you 95 minutes for this test.

On the actual CBT you will click on the screen to make your choices. Keep the time limit in mind as you work. Be sure to answer all the items. There is no penalty for guessing. Remember, you can't change an answer or return to an item.

This test consists of passages and items. You may be asked to select a correct answer or answers, to check items in a table, to put events in order, or to select portions of the passage. Mark your answers on the test page.

Once the test is complete, review the answers and explanations for each item.

When instructed, turn the page and begin.

READING

30 items   95 minutes

line

There was very little oxygen in the Earth's atmosphere about 3.5 billion years ago. We know that molecules (much smaller than a cell) can develop spontaneously in this type of environment. This is how life probably began on Earth about 3.4 billion years ago.

5   Eventually these molecules linked together to form complex groupings of molecules. These earliest organisms must have been able to ingest and live on non-organic compounds. Over a period of time these organisms adapted and began using the sun's energy. The organisms began to use photosynthesis, which released oxygen into the oceans and the atmosphere. The stage was set for more
10   advanced life forms.

The first cells were prokaryotes (bacteria), which created energy (respired) without oxygen (anaerobic). Next these cells developed into blue-green algae prokaryotes, which were aerobic (create energy with oxygen) and used photosynthesis. The advanced eukaryotes were developed from these primitive cells.

15   Algae developed about 750 million years ago. Even this simple cell contained an enormous amount of DNA and hereditary information. It took about 2.7 billion years to develop life to this primitive form. This very slow process moved somewhat faster in the millennia that followed as animal and plant forms slowly emerged.

20   Animals developed into vertebrate (backbone) and invertebrate (no backbone) species. Mammals became the dominant vertebrate species and insects became the dominant invertebrate species. As animals developed, they adapted to their environment. The best adapted survived. This process is called natural selection. Entire species have vanished from Earth.

25   Mammals and dinosaurs co-existed for over 100 million years. During that time, dinosaurs were the dominant species. When dinosaurs became extinct 65 million years ago, mammals survived. Freed of dinosaurian dominance, mammals evolved into the dominant creatures they are today. Despite many years of study, it is not known what caused the dinosaurs to become extinct or why mammals survived.

---

1. Which of the following statements is the best description of the main idea of the second paragraph (lines 5–10)?

☐ Molecules can only ingest nonorganic compounds.

☐ Evolution is based on adaptation.

☐ Photosynthesis allowed organisms to exist without the need of sunlight.

☐ Oxygen is more important to life than the sun's energy.

2. From the list below, check two true statements, according to the information in the passage.

☐ The prokaryote cells developed with the help of the sun's energy.

☐ The Earth was formed about 3.5 billion years ago.

☐ The early development of animals depended on photosynthesis.

☐ The extinction of dinosaurs led to the development of mammals.

☐ Other reptiles survived the dinosaurs; so entire species have not vanished from the Earth.

3. The list below names events discussed in the article. At the bottom of the screen are two events from this article, with one missing event in between. Choose the event from the top of the screen that goes in this space.

<u>Events to Choose From</u>

Eukaroytes
Respiration with Oxygen
Oxygen release
Development of molecules
700 million years ago

DEVELOPMENT OF LIFE ON EARTH

Ingestion of inorganic compounds

↓

[ ]

↓

Anerobic respiration

4. This passage suggests

☐ that mammals were the more intelligent species.

☐ how life evolved on Earth.

☐ that mammals and dinosaurs are natural enemies.

☐ that the environment did not affect evolution.

5. Circle the sentence in the passage that describes the dominance of mammals.

line

The Vietnam War stretched across the 12 years of the Kennedy and Johnson presidencies and into the presidency of Richard Nixon. While the war officially began with Kennedy as president, its actual beginnings stretch back many years.

5 Before the war, Vietnam was called French Indochina. During WW II the United States supported Ho Chi Minh in Vietnam as he attacked Japan. After the war, the United States supported the French over Ho Chi Minh as France sought to regain control of its former colony.

Fighting broke out between the French and Ho Chi Minh with support from Mao Ze-dong (Mao Tse Tung), the leader of Mainland China. Even with substantial

10 material aid from the United States, France could not defeat Vietnam. In 1950 the French were defeated at Dien Bien Phu.

Subsequent negotiations in Geneva divided Vietnam into North and South with Ho Chi Minh in control of the North. Ngo Dinh Diem was installed by the United States as a leader in the south. Diem never gained popular support in the south.

15 Following a harsh crackdown by Diem, the Viet Cong organized to fight against him. During the Eisenhower administration, 2,000 American "advisors" were sent to South Vietnam.

When Kennedy came to office, he approved a CIA coup to overthrow Diem. When Johnson took office he was not interested in compromise. In 1964 Johnson

20 started a massive buildup of forces in Vietnam until the number ultimately reached over 500,000. The Gulf of Tonkin Resolution, passed by Congress, gave Johnson discretion in pursuing the war.

Living and fighting conditions were terrible. Although American forces had many victories, neither that nor the massive bombing of North Vietnam led to vic-

25 tory. In 1968, the Viet Cong launched the Tet Offensive. While ground gained in the offensive was ultimately recaptured, the offensive shook the confidence of military leaders.

At home, there were deep divisions. War protests sprung up all over the United States. Half a million people protested in New York during 1967 while the tension

30 between hawks and doves increased throughout the country.

Richard Nixon was elected in 1970 in the midst of this turmoil. While vigorously prosecuting the war, he and Secretary of State Henry Kissinger were holding secret negotiations with North Vietnam. In 1973 an agreement was finally drawn up to end the war. American prisoners were repatriated, although there were still a num-

35 ber Missing in Action (MIA), and U.S. troops withdrew from Vietnam.

The war cost 350,000 American casualties. The $175 billion spent on the war could have been used for Great Society programs.

---

6. In this passage the author expresses a bias against

☐ the Eisenhower administration   ☐ the military

☐ the French people   ☐ hawks

7. The passage implies which of the following?

☐ The Vietnam War was a glorious war.

☐ Kennedy laid the foundation for the war.

☐ The United States paid a great price for this war.

☐ The people of the United States gave united support for the war effort.

8. Circle the word or phrase that has the same meaning as *popular* (line 14).

☐ widespread ☐ complete ☐ well liked ☐ major ☐ famous

9. Circle the sentence that describes Kennedy's role in the actual beginning of the war.

10. Those mentioned in the article who were carrying on negotiations were

☐ Ho Chi Minh and Mao Ze-dong

☐ The United States and North Vietnam

☐ France and Japan

☐ South Vietnam and the Viet Cong

11. For each item in the list on the left, check a box in the column to show whether it was associated with North Vietnam or South Vietnam.

	NORTH VIETNAM	SOUTH VIETNAM
VIET CONG		
NGO DINH DIEM		
HO CHI MINH		
CIA		

line

We use language, including gestures and sounds, to communicate. Humans first used gestures, but it was spoken language that opened the vistas for human communication. Language consists of two things. First we have the thoughts that language conveys and then the physical sounds, writing and structure of the language itself.

Human speech organs (mouth, tongue, lips etc.) were not developed to make sounds but they uniquely determined the sounds and words humans could produce. Human speech gradually came to be loosely bound together by unique rules for grammar.

Many believe that humans developed their unique ability to speak with the development of a specialized area of the brain called Broca's area. If this is so, human speech and language probably developed in the past 100,000 years.

12. What is the main idea of this passage?

☐ Language consists of thoughts and physical sounds.

☐ Human communication includes gestures.

☐ Human speech and language slowly developed through the years.

☐ Broca's area of the brain controls speech.

13. What is the first component of language development?

☐ gestures

☐ thoughts

☐ sound

☐ writing

14. Circle the sentence in the passage that explains how grammar developed.

line

Information can be retrieved from books, magazines, and other print sources by simply picking up the reading materials and turning and flipping through the pages. The book, newspaper, or periodical remains one of the most efficient ways to access print information.

5   Print materials are also found in libraries or other storage locations on microfilm and microfiche. Microfilms are 35 mm films of books, while microfiche are flat and can contain hundreds of pages of text material. Microfilm and microfiche are read with specialized readers.

Other information can be retrieved on or through the computer. Written materials can be entered on a computer, usually with a word processor. This information can be accessed directly through the computer's hard disk. Special features of most word processors and other utilities permit the user to search electronically for words and phrases. Sound, graphics, and animation may also be stored on a computer's hard disk. These sounds and images may be accessed using specialized computer programs.

15

Print materials, images, sounds and animation may also be stored on CD-ROMs designed for computer use. Information on these CD-ROMs may be accessed through a CD ROM player that is connected to the computer. Images and sounds on videotapes, audio tapes, music CD-ROMs, and videodisk may also be accessed through the computer.

20

Computers can be connected to telephone lines using a modem. Modems allow the computer user to retrieve information from other computers and bulletin boards. Almost all periodical and newspaper information can be retrieved through these sources. For example Lexis/Nexis, primarily designed for lawyers, has almost every newspaper and periodical article for the past several years. Other bulletin boards and information retrieval services contain a full range of text, graphics, sound, and animation and ways of searching for and retrieving this information.

25

15. The author's purpose for writing this passage was to?

☐ persuade   ☐ narrate   ☐ inform   ☐ entertain

16. Circle the word or words in the second paragraph that means repositories.

17. Circle the sentence in the passage that includes a fact about images and sounds.

18. What is the topic of this passage?

☐ Computers and survival in the 21st century.

☐ Computer animation in the next decade.

☐ Computers past and present.

☐ Who needs a computer.

19. Draw a line around the portion of the passage that discusses animation and speech recognition.

20. From the list below, check two true statements about home computers, according to the information in the passage.

☐ Home computers are more powerful than any computer was 20 years ago.

☐ Home computers are more powerful than computers that used to fill whole buildings.

☐ If you don't know how to use a home computer you will be unemployed.

☐ Home computers are now fast and affordable.

☐ Home computers will be adding word processing and number crunching.

21. Circle the audience that this article is intended for.

elementary school students   those on unemployment

computer programmers   business executives

the general public   computer manufacturers

line

Eliza, a runaway slave, made her desperate retreat across the river just in the
dusk of twilight. The gray mist of evening, rising slowly from the river, enveloped
her as she disappeared up the bank, and the swollen current and floundering
masses of ice presented a hopeless barrier between her and her pursuer. Haley,
5 the pursuer, therefore slowly and discontentedly returned to the little tavern, to
ponder further what was to be done. Haley sat him down to meditate on the
instability of human hopes and happiness in general.

"What did I want with the little cuss, now," he said to himself, "that I should
have got myself treed like a coon, as I am, this yer say?"

10 He was startled by the loud and dissonant voice of a man who was apparently
dismounting at the door. He hurried to the window.

"By the land! if this yer an't the nearest, now, to what I've heard folks call Providence," said Haley. "I do b'lieve that ar's Tom Loker."

Haley hastened out. Standing by the bar, in the corner of the room, was a
15 brawny, muscular man, full six feet in height and broad in proportion. In the head
and face every organ and lineament expressive of brutal and unhesitating violence
was in a state of the highest possible development. Indeed, could our readers fancy
a bull-dog come into man's estate, and walking about in a hat and coat, they would
have no unapt idea of the general style and effect of his physique. He was accom-
20 panied by a traveling companion, in many respects an exact contrast to himself.
The large man poured out a big tumbler half full of raw spirits, and gulped it down
without a word. The little man stood tiptoe, and putting his head first to one side
and then to the other, and snuffing considerately in the directions of the various
bottles, ordered at last a mint julep, in a thin and quivering voice, and with an air
25 of great circumspection.

"Wall, now, who'd a thought this yer luck 'ad come to me? Why, Loker, how are
ye?" said Haley, coming forward, and extending his hand to the big man.

"The devil" was the civil reply. "What brought you here, Haley?"

The mousing man, who bore the name of Marks, instantly stopped his sipping . . .

30 "I say, Tom, this yer's the luckiest thing in the world. I'm in a devil of a hobble,
and you must help me out."

Haley began a pathetic recital of his peculiar troubles. Loker shut up his mouth,
and listened to him with gruff and surly attention.

---

22. The list below names events discussed in the passage. At the bottom of the
screen are two events from this article, with one missing event in between.
Choose the event from the top of the screen that goes in this space.

Events to Choose From
Haley hastens out
The little man stood tiptoe
Haley recites his troubles
Tom Loker is recognized
Ice presents a barrier between the slave and her pursuer

UNCLE TOM'S CABIN
Brawny man standing by the bar
↓

↓
The last mint julep is ordered

23. According to the passage, Haley

☐ looked like a bulldog   ☐ was a little man

☐ meditated about human hopes   ☐ drank mint juleps

24. Circle the portion of the passage in which Haley indicates that he is in a difficult position.

25. According to the passage, the runaway slave

☐ crossed the river just before sunrise   ☐ was not captured

☐ was brought back to the tavern   ☐ was carrying a baby

26. From the list below, check two true statements about Tom Loker, according to the information in the passage.

☐ He stood by the bar in the corner of the room.   ☐ He met Haley outside the tavern.

☐ Haley saw him through the tavern window.   ☐ He was a pursuer.

☐ His real name was Marks.

27. Which of the following is the best explanation of how the shaded sentence functions in the paragraph.

☐ The sentence provides a transition.   ☐ The sentence gives a comparison.

☐ The sentence gives a description.   ☐ The sentence provides a contradiction.

line

About two hundred yards from the tree a small brook crossed the road and ran into a marshy and thickly wooded glen, known by the name of Wiley's swamp. On that side of the road where the brook entered the wood, a group of oaks and chestnuts, matted thick with wild grapevines, threw a cavernous gloom over it. To pass this bridge was the severest trial. It was at this identical spot that the unfortunate André was captured, and under the covert of those chestnuts and vines were the sturdy yeomen concealed who surprised him. This has ever since been considered a haunted stream, and fearful are the feelings of the schoolboy who has to pass it alone after dark.

As he approached the stream his heart began to thump; he summoned up, however, all his resolution, gave his horse half a score of kicks in the ribs, and attempted to dash briskly across the bridge; but instead of starting forward, the perverse old animal made a lateral movement and ran broadside against the fence. Ichabod, whose fears increased with the delay, jerked the reins on the other side, and kicked lustily with the contrary foot; it was all in vain; his steed started, it is true, but it was only to plunge to the opposite side of the road into a thicket of brambles and alder bushes. The schoolmaster now bestowed both whip and heel upon the starveling ribs of old Gunpowder, who dashed forward, snuffling and snorting, but came to a stand just by the bridge with a suddenness that had nearly sent his rider sprawling over his head. Just at this moment a plashy tramp by the side of the bridge caught the sensitive ear of Ichabod. In the dark shadow of the grove, on the margin of the brook, he beheld something huge, misshapen, black and towering. It stirred not, but seemed gathered up in the gloom, like some gigantic monster ready to spring upon the traveler.

---

28. Circle one of the sentences in which the author describes how Ichabod got his horse to go faster.

---

29. From the list of topics below, check two that are discussed in the first paragraph.

☐ Andre's capture

☐ The thing that frightened Ichabod

☐ How trees affected the road

☐ The sounds a horse makes

☐ Ichabod nearly being thrown from his horse

☐ Ichabod's increasing fears

30. Circle one of the sentences in which the author uses a synonym for *horse*.

31. For each item in the list on the left, check a box in the column to show whether it was associated with a description of the area or with Ichabod's horse.

	Area Description	Ichabod's Horse
Wooded glen		
Into a thicket		
Lateral movement		
Cavernous gloom		

32. Suppose that the sentence shown below was once in the passage. Write "32" in the passage to show where this sentence belongs.

A few rough logs, laid side by side, served for a bridge over this stream.

line
Early, advanced civilizations developed in the Indus Valley. The inhabitants were called Dravidians. Around 2500 B.C. a series of floods and foreign invasions appears to have all but destroyed these civilizations. Between 2500 B.C. and 1500 B.C. the Dravidians were forced into southern India by a nomadic band with Greek and Persian roots.

The conquerors brought a less sophisticated civilization to India. It was this latter group the formed the Indian civilization. An early caste system was established with the Dravidians serving as slaves.

After a time, the society developed around religious, nonsecular concerns. The Mahabarata became a verbal tradition around 1000 B.C. It describes a war hero, Krishna. The Mahabarata's most significant impact was the frequent descriptions of correct conduct and belief. The Mahabarata also describes how the soul remains immortal through transmigration—the successive occupation of the soul of many bodies.

Buddha was born in India about 580 B.C. His teachings developed the Buddhist religion. Buddha preached nirvana—a rejection of worldly and material concerns and a surrender of individual consciousness. During his lifetime, his ideas spread throughout India.

From about 750 B.C. the caste system became fixed and it was almost impossible for a person to move out of their caste. The priests, or Brahmans, were at the top of the caste system. Next were rulers and warriors and then farmers and tradesmen, then near the bottom were workers. Then there were those who had no caste at all—outcastes—who could not participate in society.

The Marryan Dynasty ruled India from about 320 B.C. to 220 B.C. During this time, Buddhism was spread throughout Asia, China and Indochina. The Andrhan Dynasty ruled India proper from 220 B.C. to 220 A.D. Buddhism became less popular in India during this period while Brahmans gained more prominence.

After disorder following the collapse of the Andhran Dynasty, the Gupta Dynasty ruled from about 320 A.D. to 500 A.D. Arts, literature, and mathematics flourished during this period. Indian mathematicians used the decimal system and probably introduced the concept of zero. Hinduism developed from earlier religions and became the dominant religion in India. Most people in India worshipped many gods including Brahma (creator), Vishnu (preserver), and Shiva (destroyer).

The Gupta Dynasty declined with the invasion of the Huns in the 5th century A.D. Successors of these invaders, called Rajputs, intermarried, joined Hindu society, and dominated Northern India until 1200 A.D. Other kingdoms were established in central and southern India.

By this time, Hindu was the religion of India and Buddhism had all but disappeared. The caste system and the power of Brahman priests were dominant throughout India.

Around 1200, Moslems (Turks and Afghans) invaded India from the north. The invaders controlled all but the southern part of India by about 1320. The Delhi Sultanate lasted in a state of intrigue until about 1530. Moslem sultans oppressed Hindus while their supporters killed and "converted" many Hindus. Remnants of this strife between Moslems and Hindus can be seen to this day.

33. The events in the list below are taken from this passage. List the events in the time line below, from earliest to latest, to correctly reflect the sequence in the passage.

> The Marryan Empire rules India
> Fixed caste system is established
> The belief in successive reincarnation is established
> The Huns invade India
> Buddha is born
> Hinduism becomes the dominant religion

TIME LINE

```
┌─────────────────────────────────────┐
│                                       │
└─────────────────────────────────────┘
                 ↓
┌─────────────────────────────────────┐
│                                       │
└─────────────────────────────────────┘
                 ↓
┌─────────────────────────────────────┐
│                                       │
└─────────────────────────────────────┘
                 ↓
┌─────────────────────────────────────┐
│                                       │
└─────────────────────────────────────┘
                 ↓
┌─────────────────────────────────────┐
│                                       │
└─────────────────────────────────────┘
                 ↓
┌─────────────────────────────────────┐
│                                       │
└─────────────────────────────────────┘
```

34. According to this passage, which of the following groups was forced from power in India, leading to an inferior civilization?

☐ Dravidians   ☐ Greeks   ☐ The Gupta Dynasty   ☐ The Rajputs

35. Which of the following best describes the relationship between the two highlighted sentences in the passage?

☐ The first sentence gives a general statement, while the second sentence gives a specific statement.

☐ Each sentence describes what happened after the conflict.

☐ Each sentence describes a cultural heritage.

☐ The first sentence gives an insight, while the second sentence gives an example.

36. Circle one of the sentences in the passage that describes a class that ruled India for about 400 years.

CBT ENGLISH PRACTICE TEST

You should not take this test until you have completed both Practice PPST English Tests.

Each item consists of a sentence with three underlined parts. Look for the underlined part that is inappropriate in well-written English. If you find one, circle that portion. If there are no errors, circle No error. A sentence will not have more than one error.

On the actual CBT you will click on the underlined portion of your choice.

The test rules allow you 30 minutes for this test. Keep the time limit in mind as you work. Be sure to answer all the items. There is no penalty for guessing. Remember, you can't change an answer or return to an item.

Once the test is complete, review the answers and explanations for each item.

When instructed, turn the page and begin.

CBT WRITING

35 items   30 minutes

---

1. Most people <u>would</u> <u>enjoying</u> four <u>weeks</u> vacation last year. <u>No error</u>.

---

2. The tugboat <u>strains against</u> the ship, revved up its engines, <u>and was able</u>

to <u>maneuver</u> the ship into the middle of the channel. <u>No error</u>.

---

3. A newspaper columnist <u>promised</u> <u>to print</u> the story about the secret

negotiations concerning the sports stadium in <u>their</u> next column. <u>No error</u>.

---

4. The flower shop is <u>pleasant</u> and <u>possess</u> an aroma that <u>welcomes</u> its customers.

<u>No error</u>.

---

5. The <u>incredible</u> <u>intense</u> seminar held all the participants in a <u>hypnotic</u> trance.

<u>No error</u>.

---

6. <u>His</u> boat was badly damaged after the <u>manufacturers</u> warranty expired when its

propeller struck a rock. <u>No error</u>.

---

7. Many students <u>prefer to</u> gain <u>life experience</u> outside <u>college. Such</u> as the Peace

Corps. <u>No error</u>.

8. Weather conditions have a controlling affect on our air traffic. No error.

9. Europeans had started to devote significant resources to medicine, when Louis Pasteur was born December 7, 1822. No error.

10. The final stage of the construction is successful. No error.

11. Because of their immaturity and ignorance. Many young people engage in high-risk behavior. No error.

12. These same questions was asked by other lawyers for decades after the trial ended. No error.

13. Amanda wanted to write a letter about her faulty sunglasses but she knew not who to send it to. No error.

14. It may be true that a strictly mechanical approach is used by some teachers, however, there is certainly a way for their students to develop more difficult concepts. No error.

15. Computer graphing programs are <u>capable</u> of graphing almost any equations <u>including</u> advanced equations from <u>calculus the</u> student just types in the equation and the graph appears on the screen. <u>No error</u>.

16. The Board of Adjustment can <u>exempt</u> a person from the requirements of a <u>particular</u> land-use <u>ordnance</u>. <u>No error</u>.

17. The <u>laboratory</u> was sterile and was highly <u>regarded</u> by <u>them</u> in the industry. <u>No error</u>.

18. Roseanna, Lisa, and <u>Jenn, are</u> preparing for the coming <u>summer camp</u> <u>session</u> with great expectations. <u>No error</u>.

19. <u>Succulent</u> crab, <u>plentiful</u> shrimp, and meaty lobster are the <u>mainly</u> dishes advertised by the Lobster Hut. <u>No error</u>.

20. Charles Monroe III and his family <u>enjoys</u> yachting, swimming, and polo, <u>when</u> <u>on holiday</u>, <u>delighting</u> in the South of France. <u>No error</u>.

21. The teacher asked all <u>her students</u> to bring in <u>his</u> permission slips <u>to go on</u> the Washington trip. <u>No error</u>.

22. The <u>shower dripped</u> for an hour after each person <u>bathed</u> until finally a repairman <u>had been call</u> to fix it. <u>No error</u>.

23. They will not be able to understand how to <u>create</u> a sculpture from ice or to <u>understands</u> the <u>basis</u> for the more complicated sculptures. <u>No error</u>.

24. Erik <u>walks</u> three miles every day and he <u>rubbed</u> the dirt off his sneakers as he <u>went</u>. <u>No error</u>.

25. I <u>have talked</u> to my daughter about <u>telling</u> the truth countless times over the <u>past</u> few weeks. <u>No error</u>.

26. A <u>masive</u> <u>education campaign</u> <u>is needed</u> to fully inform today's youth about AIDS. <u>No error</u>.

27. The <u>dairy farm</u> is maintained by the support of sixty new <u>cows in</u> addition there are thirty-five original <u>cows who</u> still supply some milk. <u>No error</u>.

28. I am going to visit <u>my</u> aunt so <u>I</u> left a message for <u>whoever</u> may need to locate me. <u>No error</u>.

29. The <u>retired</u> baseball player haggled <u>unexpectedly</u> with the younger child over who played <u>good</u>. <u>No error</u>.

30. Bill <u>hope</u> to <u>receive</u> the <u>most</u> votes in the election. <u>No error</u>.

31. <u>At 41 she was</u> named <u>president</u> and CEO at a large technology <u>company</u> dedicated to providing fast access to stock quotes. <u>No error</u>.

32. The mechanic <u>immediate</u> <u>began</u> <u>work</u> on the car that had just been towed in. <u>No error</u>.

33. The pesticide expert found that <u>she could kill</u> harmful insects during the <u>initial</u> development <u>period, by</u> using a low dose. <u>No error</u>.

34. A little over 100 years ago experiments led scientists to the <u>conclusion that</u> human <u>disease</u> could be <u>caused of germs</u>. <u>No error</u>.

35. The professor <u>explained that</u> there <u>were always causes</u> for human behavior and that behavior never appeared <u>spontaneously</u>. <u>No error</u>.

PRACTICE CBT ESSAY

Take this test in a realistic, timed setting.

Write an essay on the topic found on the next page. Write on this topic only. An essay on another topic, no matter how well done, will receive a 0. You have 40 minutes to complete the essay. Keep the time limit in mind as you work.

Use the space provided to briefly outline your essay and to organize your thoughts before you begin to write. Use this opportunity to demonstrate how well you can write but be sure to cover the topic.

Type your essay on a word processor. Do not use the spelling checker or the grammar checker.

Once the test is complete, ask an English professor or English teacher to evaluate your essay holistically using the rating scale on page 34.

ESSAY

You have 40 minutes to complete this essay question. Type your essay on a word processor. Do not use the spelling checker or the grammar checker.

In your opinion, should a college offer an entire degree program over the Internet, without students ever coming to the campus?

Be specific as you support your point of view with reasons from your own interpretations, experiences, and reading.

Write a brief outline here.

PRACTICE CBT MATHEMATICS TEST

Use a simple four-function calculator with a square root key with this practice test. You may also use a ruler.

You should not take this practice test until you have completed both Practice PPST Mathematics Tests.

The test rules allow you exactly 65 minutes for this test. Since the actual test is administered on a computer, it will likely take more time than this paper and pencil version.

Use a pencil to circle the correct answer(s), to write in answers, and to represent the answer. On the actual test, you will use a mouse and a keyboard.

Once the test is complete, review the answers and explanations for each item.

When instructed, turn the page and begin.

CBT MATHEMATICS

29 items   65 minutes

---

1. The bar graph below shows the number of birds sold in a pet store over a 12-month period. In how many months, other than March, was the number of birds sold less than or equal to the number of birds sold in March?

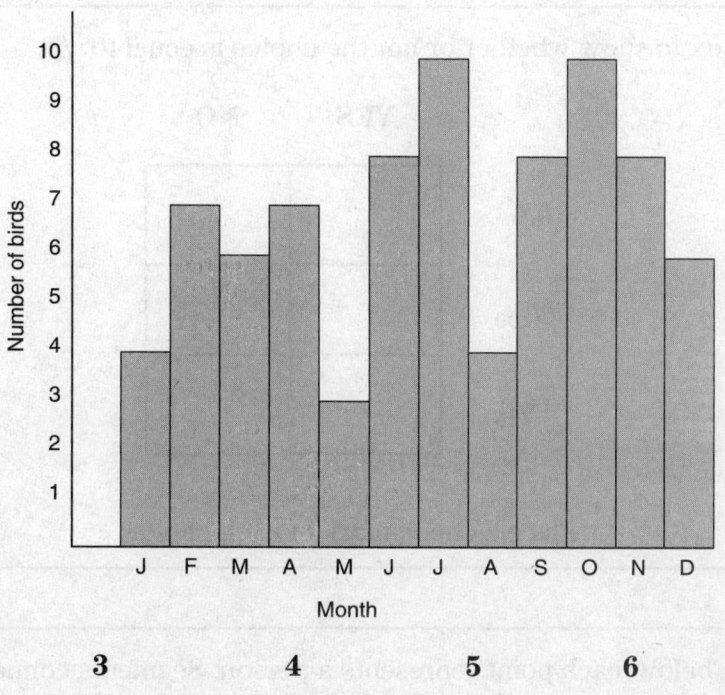

3   **4**   **5**   **6**

Circle your choice(s).

---

2. The radius and height are needed to calculate the volume of which of the following figures?

Cone

Sphere

Cube

Cylinder

Circle your choice(s).

3. Jane has three brothers, two of whom are twins. The sum of the ages of the brothers is 25, and the brother who is not a twin is 9 years old. How old is each of the twins?

Write your answer(s) in the box.

4. Check the box to show whether or not the choice is equal to $3/5$.

	YES	NO
0.6		
$6/100$		
$15/25$		

Place a check mark in each choice.

5. In the graph below, each point represents a person. Segments connect to points if the two people know each other. Who does not know Steve?

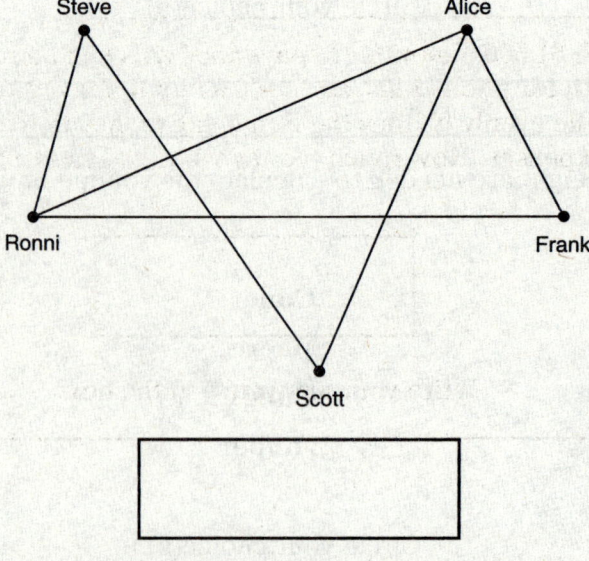

Write your answer(s) in the box.

6. Which of the shaded regions below represents $2/3$?

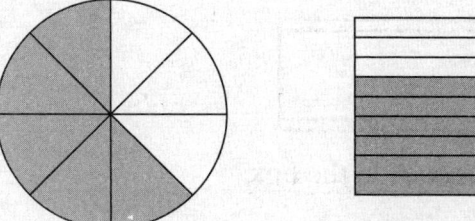

Circle your selection(s).

7. The high temperature on a certain day was 86°, and the low was 54°. Mark the thermometer below to show the average temperature for this day.

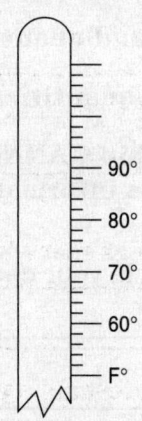

90°

80°

70°

60°

F°

8. Chad takes home $1,500 a month. He pays $550 a month on rent, $300 a month for food, $50 a month for phone bills, and $100 a month for utility bills. After Chad pays these bills, he evenly divides the remaining money between savings and miscellaneous expenses. How much money will Chad save after one year?

Write your answer(s) in the box.

9. Greg is 18 years old and twice as old as Todd. What is the sum of Greg and Todd's ages?

Write your answer(s) in the box.

10. Compare the two quantities:

$$\frac{4}{9} \qquad \frac{7}{17}$$

Which of the following statements is true?

- **The left-hand quantity is GREATER**
- **The right-hand quantity is GREATER**
- **The two quantities are EQUAL**
- **The relationship CANNOT be determined from the information given**

Circle your choice(s).

11. The original price of a pair of pants was $30, but they are now on sale for $21. The sale price is what percent of the original price?

Write your answer(s) in the box.

12. Use the figure below. Check next to each statement to show whether or not the statement is true.

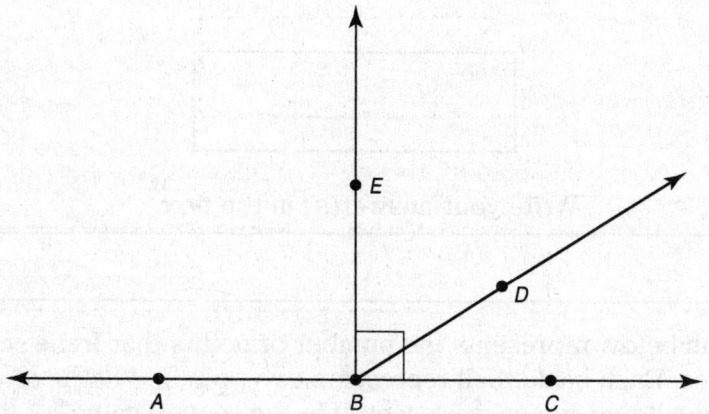

	YES	NO
∠*EBD* and ∠*DBC* are complementary angles		
∠*EBD* and ∠*DBC* are supplementary angles		
m∠*EBD* + m∠*DBC* = 90°		

13. Compare the two numbers.

$$3^4 \qquad 9^3$$

Which of the following statements is true?

- **The left-hand quantity is GREATER**

- **The right-hand quantity is GREATER**

- **The two quantities are EQUAL**

- **The relationship CANNOT be determined from the information given**

Circle your choice(s).

14. On Monday, Wednesday, and Friday, Joanie ran a total of 26 miles. On Wednesday, Joanie ran 3 more miles than she did on Monday, and on Friday, she ran 2 more miles than she ran on Wednesday. How many miles did Joanie run on Friday?

Write your answer(s) in the box.

15. The pictograph below represents the number of points that Irene scored in 5 different games. Each basketball represents two points. What percent of the points Irene scored in all five games were scored in the second game?

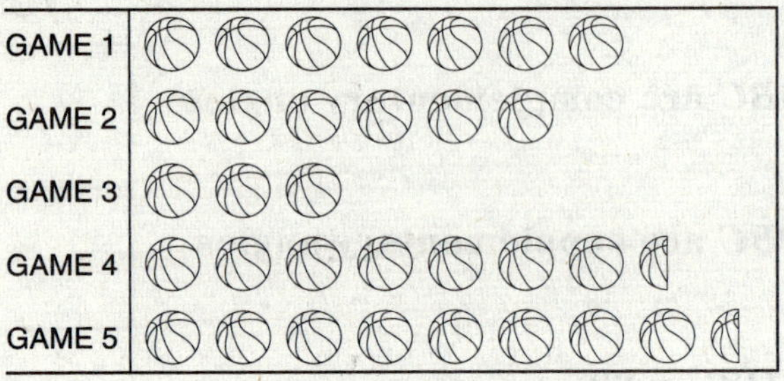

GAME 1
GAME 2
GAME 3
GAME 4
GAME 5

Write your answer(s) in the box.

16. In a cookie jar there are 3 chocolate chip cookies, 5 oatmeal cookies, 4 sugar cookies, and 2 gingerbread cookies. If a person pulls out a cookie without looking, what is the probability of not choosing a gingerbread cookie?

$6/7$

$3/14$

$1/7$

$9/14$

Circle your choice(s).

17. Jack works 8 hours a day. If Jack has already worked 270 minutes, what percent of work time does Jack have remaining?

Write your answer(s) in the box.

18. Which of the following is not equal to the others?

$$\sqrt{(16)}$$

$$2^2$$

$$2 + 2$$

$$1^4$$

Circle your choice(s).

19. A car traveling at a constant speed went 197.4 miles in 3 hours. At this speed, what is the total distance traveled in the 6 hours?

Write your answer(s) in the box.

20.

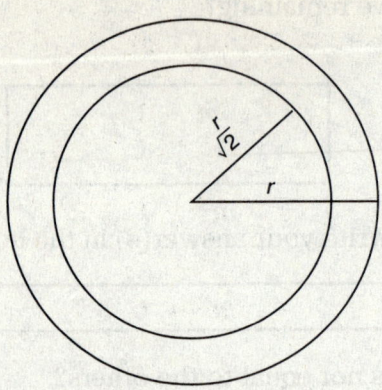

Compare the two values:

Area of inner circle   **Area between inner circle and outer circle**

Which of the following statements is true?

- **The left-hand quantity is GREATER**
- **The right-hand quantity is GREATER**
- **The two quantities are EQUAL**
- **The relationship CANNOT be determined from the information given**

Circle your choice(s).

---

21. Select the two values that are equal.

0°F

32°C

0°C

32°F

Circle your choice(s).

22. Which of the following represents the nth term of the sequence

$$2, 5, 10, 17, 26, 37, \ldots$$

$$2n - 1$$

$$n^2 - 1$$

$$n^2 + 1$$

$$2n + 1$$

Circle your choice(s).

23. What is the volume $(V = {}^{4}/_{3}(\pi r^3))$, in cubic inches, of the sphere shown below?

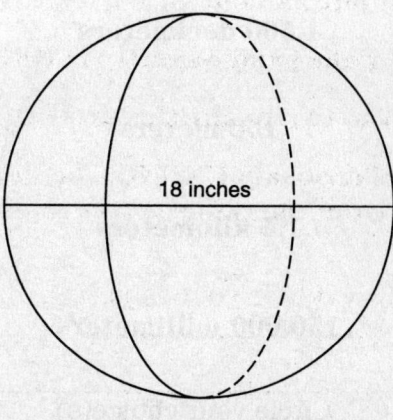

18 inches

Write your answer(s) in the box.

24. In a class of 20 students, 40% got an A, 20% got a B, 10% got a C, and 30% got a D. Construct a bar graph on the outline below that displays the number of students that received each grade.

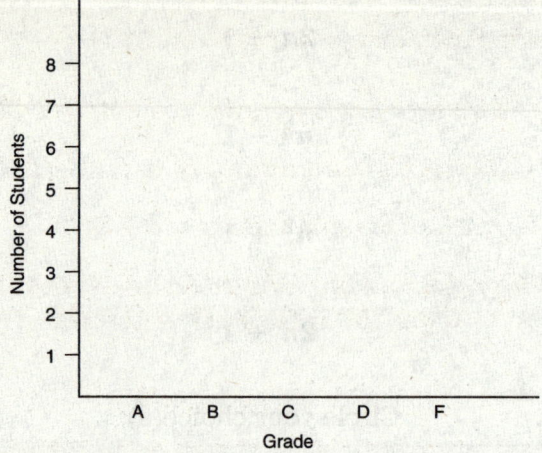

25. Which of the measurements does not equal the others?

1,500 decimeters

150 meters

1.5 kilometers

150,000 millimeters

Circle your choice(s).

26. A 24-year-old person is approximately how many minutes old?

7,568,600 minutes

12,614,400 minutes

1.2614 × 10⁸ minutes

7.5686 × 10⁸ minutes

Circle your answer.

27. Compare the two values.

$$0.02 \qquad (0.02)^2$$

Which of the following statements is true?

- **The left-hand quantity is GREATER**

- **The right-hand quantity is GREATER**

- **The two quantities are EQUAL**

- **The relationship CANNOT be determined from the information given**

Circle your choice(s).

28. John has $360 to get his car fixed. The table below is an itemized list of the charges, including taxes.

SERVICE CHARGES

Oil	**$20**
Brakes	**$80**
2 Tires	**$60 per tire**
4 Spark plugs	**$4 per spark plug**
2 hours labor	**$60 per hour**

A car wash costs ten dollars. Find how much money John will have LEFT after he pays for the service and the car wash or how much more he NEEDS for the service and the car wash.

Write your answer(s) in the box.

29. Ken hit more home runs than Joe, but fewer home runs than Sam. Mark hit more home runs than Ken. Decide whether or not each choice can be concluded with the given information.

	YES	NO
Mark hit the most home runs		
Sam hit more home runs than Ken		
Joe hit the least home runs		

Place a check in the appropriate box.

CBT ANSWERS

Reading

1.

■ Molecules can only ingest nonorganic compounds.

☐ Evolution is based on adaptation.

☐ Photosynthesis allowed organisms to exist without the need of sunlight.

☐ Oxygen is more important to life than the sun's energy.

2.

■ The prokaryote cells developed with the help of the sun's energy.

☐ The Earth was formed about 3.5 billion years ago.

■ The early development of animals depended on photosynthesis.

☐ The extinction of dinosaurs led to the development of mammals.

☐ Other reptiles survived the dinosaurs; so entire species have not vanished from the Earth.

3.

DEVELOPMENT OF LIFE ON EARTH

Ingestion of inorganic compounds

↓

Oxygen release

↓

Anerobic respiration

4.

☐ that mammals were the more intelligent species.

■ how life evolved on Earth.

☐ that mammals and dinosaurs are natural enemies.

☐ that the environment did not affect evolution.

5.

Mammals and dinosaurs co-existed for over 100 million years. During that time, dinosaurs were the dominant species. When dinosaurs became extinct 65 million years ago, mammals survived. Freed of dinosaurian dominance, mammals evolved into the dominant creatures they are today. Despite many years of study, it is not known what caused the dinosaurs to become extinct or why mammals survived.

6.

☐ the Eisenhower administration   ☐ the military

☐ the French people   ■ hawks

7.

☐ The Vietnam War was a glorious war.

☐ Kennedy laid the foundation for the war.

■ The United States paid a great price for this war.

☐ The people of the United States gave united support for the war effort.

8.

■ widespread   ☐ complete   ☐ well liked   ☐ major   ☐ famous

9.

The Vietnam War stretched across the 12 years of the Kennedy and Johnson presidencies and into the presidency of Richard Nixon. While the war officially began with Kennedy as president, its actual beginnings stretch back many years.

10.

☐ Ho Chi Minh and Mao Ze-dong

■ The United States and North Vietnam

☐ France and Japan

☐ South Vietnam and the Viet Cong

11. For each item in the list on the left, check a box in the column to show whether it was associated with North Vietnam or South Vietnam.

	NORTH VIETNAM	SOUTH VIETNAM
VIET CONG	✓	
NGO DINH DIEM		✓
HO CHI MINH	✓	
CIA		✓

12.

☐ Language consists of thoughts and physical sounds.

☐ Human communication includes gestures.

■ Human speech and language slowly developed through the years.

☐ Broca's area of the brain controls speech.

13.

☐ gestures   ■ thoughts   ☐ sound   ☐ writing

14.

Human speech organs (mouth, tongue, lips etc.) were not developed to make sounds but they uniquely determined the sounds and words humans could produce. Human speech gradually came to be loosely bound together by unique rules for grammar.

15.

☐ persuade   ☐ narrate   ■ inform   ☐ entertain

16.

Print materials are also found in libraries or other storage locations on microfilm and microfiche. Microfilms are 35 mm films of books, while microfiche are flat and can contain hundreds of pages of text material. Microfilm and microfiche are read with specialized readers.

17.

Other information can be retrieved on or through the computer. Written materials can be entered on a computer, usually with a word processor. This information can be accessed directly through the computer's hard disk. Special features of most word processors and other utilities permit the user to search electronically for words and phrases. Sound, graphics, and animation may also be stored on a computer's hard disk. These sounds and images may be accessed using specialized computer programs.

18.

☑ Computers and survival in the 21st century.

☐ Computer animation in the next decade.

☐ Computers past and present.

☐ Who needs a computer.

19.

Are you ready?—it's computer time. That's right. Everyone will need to be able to use a computer to just survive in the next century. If you can't use a computer watch out. You may find yourself on the unemployment line. In less than 20 years computers have gone from being slow, wimpy and unavailable to fast, powerful and affordable. Why you can buy a computer for your home that is more powerful than computers that filled buildings less than 40 years ago. Computers enable you to communicate all over the world, to see animation, hear sounds, and recognize speech—all in addition to word processing and number crunching. Face it—you're going to live in a world in which computer competence will be required.

20.

- ☐ Home computers are more powerful than any computer was 20 years ago.
- ☑ Home computers are more powerful than computers that used to fill whole buildings.
- ☐ If you don't know how to use a home computer you will be unemployed.
- ☑ Home computers are now fast and affordable.
- ☐ Home computers will be adding word processing and number crunching.

21.

- ☐ elementary school students
- ☐ computer programmers
- ☑ the general public

- ☐ those on unemployment
- ☐ business executives
- ☐ computer manufacturers

22.

UNCLE TOM'S CABIN

Brawny man standing by the bar

↓

The little man stood tiptoe

↓

The last mint julep is ordered

23.

- ☐ looked like a bulldog
- ☑ meditated about human hopes

- ☐ was a little man
- ☐ drank mint juleps

24.

"Wall, now, who'd a thought this yer luck 'ad come to me? Why, Loker, how are ye?" said Haley, coming forward, and extending his hand to the big man.

"The devil" was the civil reply. "What brought you here, Haley?"

The mousing man, who bore the name of Marks, instantly stopped his sipping.

"I say, Tom, this yer's the luckiest thing in the world. I'm in a devil of a hobble, and you must help me out."

Haley began a pathetic recital of his peculiar troubles. Loker shut up his mouth, and listened to him with gruff and surly attention.

25.

- ☐ crossed the river just before sunrise
- ☐ was brought back to the tavern
- ☑ was not captured
- ☐ was carrying a baby

26.

- ☐ He stood by the bar in the corner of the room.
- ☑ Haley saw him through the tavern window.
- ☐ He met Haley outside the tavern.
- ☑ He was a pursuer.
- ☐ His real name was Marks.

27.

- ☑ The sentence provides a transition.
- ☐ The sentence gives a description.
- ☐ The sentence gives a comparison.
- ☐ The sentence provides a contradiction.

28.

As he approached the stream his heart began to thump; he summoned up, however, all his resolution, gave his horse half a score of kicks in the ribs, and attempted to dash briskly across the bridge; but instead of starting forward, the perverse old animal made a lateral movement and ran broadside against the fence. Ichabod, whose fears increased with the delay, jerked the reins on the other side, and kicked lustily with the contrary foot; it was all in vain; his steed started, it is true, but it was only to plunge to the opposite side of the road into a thicket of brambles and alder bushes. The schoolmaster now bestowed both whip and heel upon the starveling ribs of old Gunpowder, who dashed forward, snuffling and snorting, but came to a stand just by the bridge with a suddenness that had nearly sent his rider sprawling over this head. Just at this moment a plashy tramp by the side of the bridge caught the sensitive ear of Ichabod. In the dark shadow of the grove, on the margin of the brook, he beheld something huge, misshapen, black and towering. It stirred not, but seemed gathered up in the gloom, like some gigantic monster ready to spring upon the traveler.

29.

- ■ Andre's capture

- ☐ The thing that frightened Ichabod

- ■ How trees affected the road

- ☐ The sounds a horse makes

- ☐ Ichabod nearly being thrown from his horse

- ☐ Ichabod's increasing fears

30.

As he approached the stream his heart began to thump; he summoned up, however, all his resolution, gave his horse half a score of kicks in the ribs, and attempted to dash briskly across the bridge; but instead of starting forward, the perverse old animal made a lateral movement and ran broadside against the fence. Ichabod, whose fears increased with the delay, jerked the reins on the other side, and kicked lustily with the contrary foot; it was all in vain; his (steed) started, it is true, but it was only to plunge to the opposite side of the road into a thicket of brambles and alder bushes. The schoolmaster now bestowed both whip and heel upon the starveling ribs of old Gunpowder, who dashed forward, snuffling and snorting, but came to a stand just by the bridge with a suddenness that had nearly sent his rider sprawling over this head. Just at this moment a plashy tramp by the side of the bridge caught the sensitive ear of Ichabod. In the dark shadow of the grove, on the margin of the brook, he beheld something huge, misshapen, black and towering. It stirred not, but seemed gathered up in the gloom, like some gigantic monster ready to spring upon the traveler.

31.

	Area Description	Ichabod's Horse
Wooded glen	✓	
Into a thicket		✓
Lateral movement		✓
Cavernous gloom	✓	

32.

⃝32

  About two hundred yards from the tree a small brook crossed the road and ran into a marshy and thickly wooded glen, known by the name of Wiley's swamp. On that side of the road where the brook entered the wood, a group of oaks and chestnuts, matted thick with wild grapevines, threw a cavernous gloom over it. To pass this bridge was the severest trial. It was at this identical spot that the unfortunate André was captured, and under the covert of those chestnuts and vines were the sturdy yeomen concealed who surprised him. This has ever since been considered a haunted stream, and fearful are the feelings of the schoolboy who has to pass it alone after dark.

33.

TIME LINE

The belief in successive reincarnation is established

↓

Buddha is born

↓

Fixed caste system is established

↓

The Marryan Empire rules India

↓

Hinduism becomes the dominant religion

↓

The Huns invade India

34.

▨ Dravidians   ☐ Greeks   ☐ The Gupta Dynasty   ☐ The Rajputs

35.

☐ The first sentence gives a general statement, while the second sentence gives a specific statement.

▨ Each sentence describes what happened after the conflict.

☐ Each sentence describes a cultural heritage.

☐ The first sentence gives an insight, while the second sentence gives an example.

36.

> The Marryan Dynasty ruled India from about 320 B.C. to 220 B.C. During this time, Buddhism was spread throughout Asia, China and Indochina. The Andrhan Dynasty ruled India proper from 220 B.C. to 220 A.D. Buddhism became less popular in India during this period while Brahmans gained more prominence.

English Multiple Choice

1. Most people would enjoying four weeks vacation last year. No error.

would enjoy   have enjoyed

Use the correct verb tense.

2. The tugboat strains against the ship, revved up its engines, and was able

to maneuver the ship into the middle of the channel. No error.

strained against

The past tense *strained* agrees with the other verbs.

3. A newspaper columnist promised to print the story about the secret

negotiations concerning the sports stadium in their next column. No error.

his or her

These pronouns agree with the antecedent *columnist*.

4. The flower shop is pleasant and possess an aroma that welcomes its customers.

No error.

possesses

***Flower shop* is singular and takes the singular verb possesses.**

5. The incredible intense seminar held all the participants in a hypnotic trance.

No error.

incredibly

Use the adverb *incredibly* to modify the adjective intense.

6. His boat was badly damaged after the manufacturers warranty expired when its

propeller struck a rock. No error.

manufacturer's

Use *manufacturer's* to show possession.

7. Many students prefer to gain life experience outside college. Such as the Peace

Corps. No error.

college such

Such as the Peace Corps is not a sentence.

8. Weather conditions have a controlling affect on our air traffic. No error.

effect

The correct word is *effect*.

9. Europeans had started to devote significant resources to medicine, when Louis

Pasteur was born December 7, 1822. No error.

medicine when

When the main clause is followed by a dependent clause, no comma is necessary.

10. The final stage of <u>the construction</u> is <u>successful</u>. <u>No error</u>.

was

Use the verb *was* to show past tense.

11. Because of their <u>immaturity</u> and <u>ignorance. Many</u> young people <u>engage</u> in high-risk behavior. <u>No error</u>.

ignorance many

***Because the their immaturity and ignorance* is not a sentence.**

12. <u>These same questions</u> was <u>asked</u> by <u>other lawyers</u> for decades after the trial ended. <u>No error</u>.

This same question

This change agrees with the singular verb *was*.

13. Amanda <u>wanted to write</u> a letter about her <u>faulty</u> sunglasses but she knew not <u>who</u> to send it to. <u>No error</u>.

whom

Use the objective case *whom*. *Amanda* is the subject of the sentence, while the person she wants to send the letter to is the object.

14. It may be <u>true that</u> a strictly mechanical approach is used by some <u>teachers, however,</u> there is certainly a way for <u>their students</u> to develop more difficult concepts. <u>No error</u>.

teachers; however,

Set off the independent clause with a semicolon.

15. Computer graphing programs are <u>capable</u> of graphing almost any equations

    <u>including</u> advanced equations from calculus the student just types in the equation

    and the graph appears on the screen. <u>No error</u>.

    calculus. The

    Correct the run-in sentence.

16. The Board of Adjustment can <u>exempt</u> a person from the requirements of a

    <u>particular</u> land-use <u>ordnance</u>. <u>No error</u>.

    ordinance

    Use the correct word.

17. The <u>laboratory</u> was sterile and was highly <u>regarded</u> by them in the industry.

    <u>No error</u>.

    those

    Use the correct word.

18. Roseanna, Lisa, and <u>Jenn, are</u> preparing for the coming <u>summer camp</u> <u>session</u>

    with great expectations. <u>No error</u>.

    Jenn are

    The comma is unnecessary.

19. <u>Succulent</u> crab, <u>plentiful</u> shrimp, and meaty lobster are the mainly dishes

    advertised by the Lobster Hut. <u>No error</u>.

    main

    Use the adjective *main*.

20. Charles Monroe III and his family enjoys yachting, swimming, and polo, when

on holiday, delighting in the South of France. No error.

enjoy

The subject is plural and takes the plural verb *enjoy*.

21. The teacher asked all her students to bring in his permission slips to go on the

Washington trip. No error.

their

The substitution is *their*, which agrees with the antecedent.

22. The shower dripped for an hour after each person bathed until finally a repairman

had been call to fix it. No error.

had been called

The past tense *called* is correct.

23. They will not be able to understand how to create a sculpture from ice or to

understands the basis for the more complicated sculptures. No error.

understand

The plural subject *They* takes the plural verb *understand*.

24. Erik walks three miles every day and he rubbed the dirt off his sneakers as

he went. No error.

walked

Use the past tense to agree with the other verbs.

25. I <u>have talked</u> to my daughter about <u>telling</u> the truth countless times over the <u>past</u> few weeks. <u>No error</u>.

    No error.

    The verbs are correct.

26. A <u>masive</u> <u>education campaign</u> <u>is needed</u> to fully inform today's youth about AIDS.

    <u>No error</u>.

    massive

    Use the correct spelling.

27. The <u>dairy farm</u> is maintained by the support of sixty new <u>cows in</u> addition there are thirty-five original <u>cows who</u> still supply some milk. <u>No error</u>.

    cows. In

    Correct the run-in sentence.

28. I am going to visit <u>my</u> aunt so <u>I</u> left a message for <u>whoever</u> may need to locate me.

    <u>No error</u>.

    No error.

    All the pronouns are correct.

29. The <u>retired</u> baseball player haggled <u>unexpectedly</u> with the younger child over who played <u>good</u>. <u>No error</u>.

    well

    Use the adverb *well* to modify the verb *played*.

30. Bill <u>hope</u> to <u>receive</u> the <u>most</u> votes in the election. <u>No error</u>.

    hopes

    ***Bill* is a singular noun and takes a singular verb.**

31. At 41 she was named president and CEO at a large technology company dedicated

to providing fast access to stock quotes. No error.

At 41, she was

Set off the introductory phrase *At 41* with a comma.

32. The mechanic immediate began work on the car that had just been towed in.

No error.

immediately

Use the verb *immediately* to modify the verb *began*.

33. The pesticide expert found that she could kill harmful insects during the initial

development period, by using a low dose. No error.

period by

The comma is not necessary.

34. A little over 100 years ago experiments led scientists to the conclusion that human

disease could be caused of germs. No error.

caused by germs

Use the correct preposition.

35. The professor explained that there were always causes for human behavior and

that behavior never appeared spontaneously. No error.

No error.

The original sentence is correct.

English Essay

Ask an English professor or English teacher to rate your essay using the scale on page 34.

Mathematics

1.

3   4   5   6

There were four months in which the store either sold fewer birds or the same number of birds in March.

2.

Cone   Sphere   Cube   Cylinder

The formula for volume of a cone is $V = \frac{1}{3}\pi r^2 h$.

The formula for volume of a sphere is $V = \frac{4}{3}\pi r^3$.

The formula for volume of a cube is $V = s^3$.

The formula for volume of a cylinder is $V = \pi r^2 h$.

3.

8 years old

Use t for the age of each twin.

Then:

$2t + 9 = 25$

$2t = 16$

$t = 8$

The twins are each 8 years old.

4.

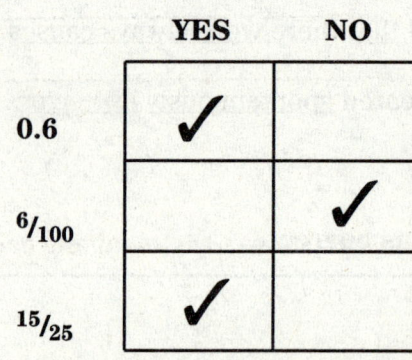

$0.6 = \frac{3}{5}$ $\frac{6}{100} = \frac{3}{50}$ $\frac{15}{25} = \frac{3}{5}$

5.

Alice and Frank

There is no segment connecting Steve and Alice, and there is not a segment joining Steve and Frank.

6.

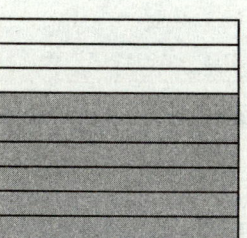

7.

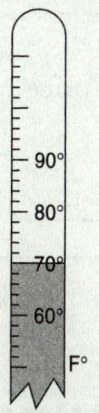

The average temperature is 70°.

8.

$3,000

$1,500 − ($550 + $300 + $50 + $100) = $500 remaining each month.

$500 ÷ 2 = $250 saved each month.

$250 × 12 = $3,000 saved in a year.

9.

27

Greg is 18 years old and he is twice as old as Todd which means Todd is 9 years old.

The sum of their ages is $18 + 9 = 27$.

10.

- **The left-hand quantity is GREATER**
- **The right-hand quantity is GREATER**
- **The two quantities are EQUAL**
- **The relationship CANNOT be determined from the information given**

Cross multiply to find that $\frac{4}{9} > \frac{7}{17}$.

11.

70%

Divide the sale price by the original price.

$\frac{\$21}{\$30} = 0.70$

$0.70 = 70\%$

12.

	YES	NO
$\angle EBD$ and $\angle DBC$ are complementary angles	✓	
$\angle EBD$ and $\angle DBC$ are supplementary angles		✓
$m\angle EBD + m\angle DBC = 90°$	✓	

From the figure we can see that $\angle EBD$ and $\angle DBC$ are complementary angles.

Therefore $\angle EBD$ and $\angle DBC$ are not supplementary angles.

$m\angle EBD + m\angle DBC = 90°$ because the angles are complementary.

13.

- **The left-hand quantity is GREATER**
- **The right-hand quantity is GREATER**
- **The two quantities are EQUAL**
- **The relationship CANNOT be determined from the information given**

$3^4 = 3 \cdot 3 \cdot 3 \cdot 3 = 9 \cdot 9 = 9^2$

$9^2 < 9^3$

14.

11

Let m represent the number of miles that Joanie ran on Monday.

Then $m + (3 + m) + (5 + m) = 26$.

$3m + 8 = 26$

$3m = 18$

$m = 6$

The miles run on Friday = $m +'' 5$.

Joanie ran 6 miles on Monday, so she ran 11 miles on Friday.

15.

18.75%

Count the numbers of balls found in the Game 2 row and divide by the total number of balls in the pictograph. (You don't need to consider what each ball represents.)

We get $^6/_{32} = 0.1875$.

$0.1875 = 18.75\%$ of the points were scored in Game 2.

16.

$^{6}/_{7}$ $^{3}/_{14}$ $^{1}/_{7}$ $^{9}/_{14}$

There are 14 cookies in the cookie jar, of which $14 - 2 = 12$ are not gingerbread cookies.

The probability of not picking a gingerbread cookie is $^{12}/_{14} = {}^{6}/_{7}$.

17.

43.75%

8 hours is $8 \cdot 60$ minutes $= 480$ minutes.

If Jack already worked 270 minutes, he has $480 - 270 = 210$ minutes of work left.

Divide the work time remaining by the total work time. $^{210}/_{480} = 0.4375$.

$0.4375 = 43.75\%$ of work remaining.

18.

$\sqrt{(16)}$ 2^2 $2 + 2$ 1^4

$\sqrt{(16)} = 4$ $2^2 = 4$ $2 + 2 = 4$ $1^4 = 1$

1^4 is not equal to the others.

19.

394.8 miles

Divide to find the speed per hour. $\frac{197.4}{3} = 65.8$ miles per hour

Multiply to find the total distance. $65.8 \times 6 = 394.8$ miles

20.

- **The left-hand quantity is GREATER**

- **The right-hand quantity is GREATER**

- **The two quantities are EQUAL**

- **The relationship CANNOT be determined from the information given**

The area of the inner circle is $A_1 = \pi\left[\dfrac{5}{\sqrt{2}}\right]^2 = \dfrac{\pi r^2}{2}$.

The area between the inner circle and the outer circle is the difference of the area of the two circles.

Therefore $A_2 = \pi r^2 - \dfrac{\pi r^2}{2} = (2\pi r^2 - \pi r^2) \div 2 = \dfrac{\pi r^2}{2}$.

The areas are equal.

21.

| **0°F** | **32°C** | **0°C** | **32°F** |

0°C and 32°F each represent the freezing point of water.

22.

| **$2n - 1$** | **$n^2 - 1$** | **$n^2 + 1$** | **$2n + 1$** |

To find a term, square the number of the term and add 1. The nth term is $n^2 + 1$.

23.

972π

$V = {}^4/_3\pi r^3$.

Since the length of the diameter is 18 inches, the length of the radius is 9 inches.

$V = {}^4/_3\pi(9)^3 =$

${}^4/_3\pi \times 729 =$

${}^4/_3(729)\pi =$

972π

Leave the answer in pi form.

24.

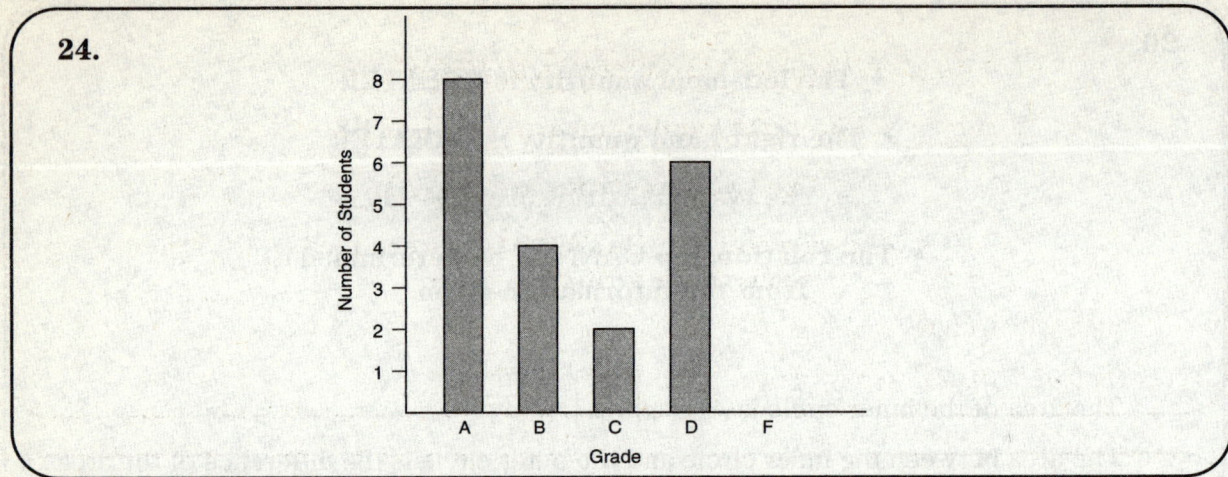

25.

1,500 decimeters

150 meters

1.5 kilometers

150,000 millimeters

1,500 decimeters = 150 meters

150,000 millimeters = 150 meters

1.5 kilometers equals 1,500 meters, and is the measurement not equal to the others.

26.

7,568,600 minutes

12,614,400 minutes

1.2614 × 10⁸ minutes

7.5686 × 10⁸ minutes

There are about 365 days in a year, 24 hours in a day, and 60 minutes in an hour.

Find the number of minutes in a day.   24 × 60 minutes = 1440 minutes

Find the approximate number of minutes in a year.   365 × 1440 = 525,600 minutes

Find the approximate number of minutes in 24 years.   24 × 525,600 = 12,614,400

A 24-year-old person is about 12,614,400 minutes old.

Notice that $1.26144 \times 10^8 = 126,144,000$.

27.

> • **The left-hand quantity is GREATER**
>
> • **The right-hand quantity is GREATER**
>
> • **The two quantities are EQUAL**
>
> • **The relationship CANNOT be determined from the information given**

$(0.02)^2 = 0.0004$

So $0.02 > (0.02)^2$

28.

NEEDS $6

Compute the cost of the service and the car wash.
$20 + $80 + 2($60) + 4($4) + 2($60) + $10 = $366.
John has $360, which is less than the cost.
John needs $366—$360 = $6.

John NEEDS $6 for the service and the car wash.

29.

	YES	NO
Mark hit the most home runs		✓
Sam hit more home runs than Ken	✓	
Joe hit the least home runs	✓	

M—Number of Mark's home runs
K—Number of Ken's home runs
J—Number of Joe's home runs
S—Number of Sam's home runs

Create inequalities. $J < K < S$
$\qquad\qquad\qquad K < M$

We can't tell if Mark or Sam hit the most home runs.
We can conclude that Sam hit more home runs than Ken.
We can conclude that Joe hit the fewest home runs.

PART IV

Scores and Careers

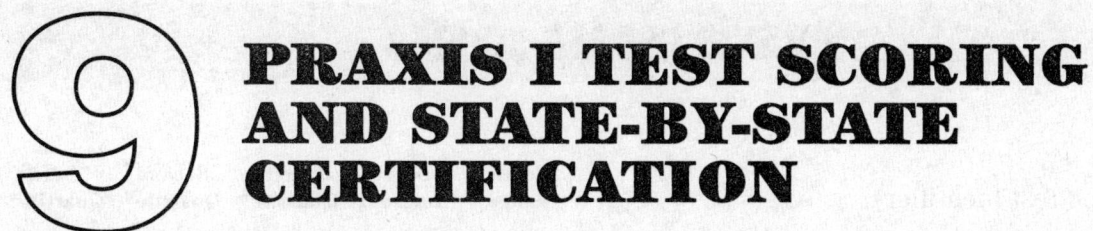

PRAXIS I TEST SCORING AND STATE-BY-STATE CERTIFICATION

PRAXIS I TEST SCORING

RAW SCORES AND SCALE SCORES

Your raw score is the number of items you answer correctly, or the number of points you actually earn. Your scale score converts your raw score to a score that can be compared to those of every one else who has taken that test.

It works this way. Test items, test sections, and different forms of the test have different difficulty levels. For example, an item on one form might be harder than a comparable item on another form. To make up for this difference in difficulty, the harder item might earn a 0.9 scale point, while the easier item might earn a 0.8 scale point. A scale score can be compared to the scale score on all forms of a test.

This is the fair way to do it. To maintain this fairness, Praxis I scores are given as scale scores. All the scores discussed here are scale scores.

Praxis I Scale Scoring

The scoring for each Praxis I test is summarized on the following pages. The tables show the scale score range and score interval for each test, along with the scale scores at the first quartile, second quartile, and third quartile. An explanation of quartiles is given below.

	Percent of test-takers who scored <u>at or below</u> this scale score.	Percent of test-takers who scored <u>above</u> this scale score.
First quartile	25%	75%
Second quartile	50%	50%
Third quartile	75%	25%

PPST scores range from 150 to 190, while CBT scores range from 300 to 335, for about 40 scale points and 35 scale points, respectively. You can't be sure that a scale score of 160 is twice as "good" as a scale score of 130. And you don't really care. The only thing that matters is if your scale score is at or above the score required by your certification state(s). If it is, you pass.

PRAXIS I SCALE SCORES

Test Name (Test Identifier)	Score Range	Score Interval	First Quartile*	Second Quartile*	Third Quartile*
CBT/PPST					
CBT: Mathematics (0731)	300 – 335	1	319	324	329
CBT: Reading (0711)	300 – 335	1	324	328	331
CBT: Writing (0721)	300 – 335	1	320	323	326
Pre-Professional Skills Test: Mathematics (0730)	150 – 190	1	173	179	184
Pre-Professional Skills Test: Reading (0710)	150 – 190	1	175	179	182
Pre-Professional Skills Test: Writing (0720)	150 – 190	1	173	175	178

*Explanation of Quartiles:

First quartile About 25% of the scale scores are below this score.
About 75% of the scale scores are above this score.

Second quartile About 50% of the scale scores are below this score.
About 50% of the scale scores are above this score.

Third quartile About 75% of the scale scores are below this score.
About 25% of the scale scores are above this score.

PASSING SCORES

No one can be sure what the passing raw score will be. That's because there are many different forms of each test, and the same raw score will earn a different scale score on each form. Besides, the best approach is to just relax and do your best.

You can get an idea of how difficult it is to pass the test in your certification state. Look up the passing score for a test in your certification state. Then compare that score to the quartile scores above.

Examples

PPST Reading Test for Virginia

Virginia Passing Score	1st quartile	2nd quartile	3rd quartile
178	175	179	182

The passing score is just below the second quartile. That means that about 50 percent of test-takers pass.

CBT Mathematics Test for Connecticut

Connecticut Passing Score	1st quartile	2nd quartile	3rd quartile
319	319	324	332

The passing score is at the first quartile. That means that about 75% of test-takers pass.

STATE-BY-STATE CERTIFICATION

This section lists all the state education departments, and shows the Praxis I tests and passing scores required in each state as well as contact information.

This listing is current and has been carefully checked. However, certification requirements change constantly. Go to *www.teachingandlearning.org/licensure/praxis*. Click on state-by-state requirements for the most recent testing requirements and contact information.

ALABAMA

Alabama Department of Education
Division of Professional Service
5108 Gordon Parsons Building
Montgomery, AL 36130-3901
(205) 242-9977
www.alsde.edu

ALL CERTIFICATES

Praxis I: Academic Skills

☐ PPST—Mathematics   ☐ CBT—Mathematics
☐ PPST—Reading   ☐ CBT—Reading
☐ PPST—Writing   ☐ CBT—Writing

ALASKA

Alaska Department of Education
Teacher Education and Certification Office
801 West 10th Street Suite 100
Juneau, AK 99801-1894
(907) 465-2831
www.educ.state.ak.us

ALL CERTIFICATES WITH PASSING SCORES

Praxis I: Academic Skills

173 PPST—Mathematics   318 CBT—Mathematics
175 PPST—Reading   322 CBT—Reading
174 PPST—Writing   321 CBT—Writing

Take either the PPST or the CBT, *not both*.

ARIZONA

Arizona Department of Education
Teacher Certification Unit
1535 West Jefferson
Phoenix, AZ 85002
(602) 542-4368
www.ade.state.az.us

ALL CERTIFICATES

Praxis I: Academic Skills

☐ PPST—Mathematics   ☐ CBT—Mathematics
☐ PPST—Reading   ☐ CBT—Reading
☐ PPST—Writing   ☐ CBT—Writing

ARKANSAS

Arkansas Department of Education
Office of Professional Licensure
4 Capital Mall, Rooms 106B/107B
Little Rock, AR 72201
(501) 682-4342
www.arkedu.state.ar.us

ALL CERTIFICATES WITH PASSING SCORES

Praxis I: Academic Skills

171 PPST—Mathematics   316 CBT—Mathematics
172 PPST—Reading   319 CBT—Reading
173 PPST—Writing   319 CBT—Writing

Take either the PPST or the CBT, *not both.*

CALIFORNIA

California Commission on Teacher Credentialing
1812 Ninth Street
Sacramento, CA 94244-7000
(916) 445-7254
www.ctc.ca.gov

ALL CERTIFICATES

Praxis I: Academic Skills

☐ PPST—Mathematics   ☐ CBT—Mathematics
☐ PPST—Reading   ☐ CBT—Reading
☐ PPST—Writing   ☐ CBT—Writing

See Barron's *How to Prepare for CBEST* and *How to Prepare for the MSAT*

COLORADO

Colorado Department of Education
Teacher Education and Certification
201 East Colfax Avenue
Denver, CO 80203
(303) 866-6628
www.cde.state.co.us

ALL CERTIFICATES

Praxis I: Academic Skills

☐ PPST—Mathematics   ☐ CBT—Mathematics
☐ PPST—Reading   ☐ CBT—Reading
☐ PPST—Writing   ☐ CBT—Writing

CONNECTICUT

Bureau of Certification and Teacher Preparation
Connecticut State Department of Education
PO Box 150471-Room 243
Hartford, CT 06115-0471
(860) 566-5201
FAX: (860) 566-8929
www.state.ct.us/sde/cert

ALL CERTIFICATES WITH PASSING SCORES

Praxis I: Academic Skills

☐ PPST—Mathematics   319 CBT—Mathematics
☐ PPST—Reading   324 CBT—Reading
☐ PPST—Writing   318 CBT—Writing

Take only the CBT.

DELAWARE

Delaware Department of Public Instruction
Division of Professional Development and Certification
Townsend Building, Box 1402
Dover, DE 19903
(302) 739-4686
www.doe.state.de.us

ALL CERTIFICATES WITH PASSING SCORES

Praxis I: Academic Skills

174 PPST—Mathematics   319 CBT—Mathematics
175 PPST—Reading   322 CBT—Reading
173 PPST—Writing   319 CBT—Writing

Take either the PPST or the CBT, *not both.*

You are exempt from the Reading Test if you submit an SAT I Verbal score of at least 560, or a GRE Verbal score of at least 490. You are exempt from the Mathematics test if you submit an SAT I Mathematics score or a GRE quantative score of at least 540.

DISTRICT OF COLUMBIA

Educational Credentialing and Standards Branch
District of Columbia Public Schools
825 North Capitol Street, NE
Washington, DC 20002
(202) 442-5377
www.K12.dc.us

ALL CERTIFICATES WITH PASSING SCORES

Praxis I: Academic Skills

174 PPST—Mathematics   319 CBT—Mathematics
172 PPST—Reading   319 CBT—Reading
171 PPST—Writing   316 CBT—Writing

Take either the PPST or the CBT, *not both.*

FLORIDA

Florida Department of Education
Bureau of Teacher Certification
325 West Gaines, Room 201
Tallahassee, FL 32399-0400
(850) 488-2317
(800) 445-6739 (in state)
www.firn.edu/doe

ALL CERTIFICATES WITH PASSING SCORES

Praxis I: Academic Skills

175 PPST—Mathematics   317 CBT—Mathematics
172 PPST—Reading   321 CBT—Reading
171 PPST—Writing   318 CBT—Writing

Take either the PPST or the CBT, *not both.*

See Barron's *How to Prepare for the CLAST.*

GEORGIA

Georgia Department of Education
Division of Teacher Certification
1452 Twin Towers East
Atlanta, GA 30334
(404) 657-9000
(800) 869-7775
www.gapsc.com

ALL CERTIFICATES WITH PASSING SCORES

Praxis I: Academic Skills

176 PPST—Mathematics	321 CBT—Mathematics
176 PPST—Reading	322 CBT—Reading
174 PPST—Writing	321 CBT—Writing

Take either the PPST or the CBT, *not both.*

You are exempt from the Praxis I requirement if you submit: an SAT I total of 1000 with at least 480V and 520M, or a GRE total of 1030 with at least 490V and 540Q, or an ACT total of 22 with at least 21V and 22M.

HAWAII

Hawaii Department of Education
Office of Personnel Services
Certification Section
Box 2360
Honolulu, HI 96804
(808) 586-3276
(808) 586-3420 for certification packet
www2.k12.hi.us

ALL CERTIFICATES WITH PASSING SCORES

Praxis I: Academic Skills

176 PPST—Mathematics	321 CBT—Mathematics
175 PPST—Reading	322 CBT—Reading
171 PPST—Writing	316 CBT—Writing

Take either the PPST or the CBT, *not both.*

IDAHO

Idaho Department of Education
Teacher Certification Division
Len B. Jordan Building
Boise, ID 83720-3650
(208) 334-3475
www.sde.state.id.us

ALL CERTIFICATES

Praxis I: Academic Skills

☐ PPST—Mathematics   ☐ CBT—Mathematics
☐ PPST—Reading   ☐ CBT—Reading
☐ PPST—Writing   ☐ CBT—Writing

ILLINOIS

Illinois State Certification and Placement Section
100 North First Street
Springfield, IL 62777
(800) 845-8749
www.isbe.state.il.us

ALL CERTIFICATES

Praxis I: Academic Skills

☐ PPST—Mathematics   ☐ CBT—Mathematics
☐ PPST—Reading   ☐ CBT—Reading
☐ PPST—Writing   ☐ CBT—Writing

ILLINOIS CERTIFICATION TESTING SYSTEM

Basic Skills Test

The Basic Skills Test is very similar to Praxis I and is required for all teaching certificates.

Basic Skills Test   5 hours

Grammar
Reading
Mathematics
Essay

All questions, except the essay, are multiple choice.

Preparation Strategy
Follow the Praxis I study plan.

INDIANA

Indiana Department of Education
Professional Standards Board
251 East Ohio Street, Room 201
Indianapolis, IN 46204-2133
(317) 232-9010
www.ideanet.doe.state.in.us

ALL CERTIFICATES WITH PASSING SCORES

Praxis I: Academic Skills

175 PPST—Mathematics   320 CBT—Mathematics
176 PPST—Reading   323 CBT—Reading
172 PPST—Writing   318 CBT—Writing

Take either the PPST or the CBT, *not both.*

IOWA

Iowa Department of Education
Board of Educational Examiners
Grimes Office Building
Des Moines, IA 50319-0147
(515) 281-3245
www.state.ia.us/educate/

ALL CERTIFICATES

Praxis I: Academic Skills

- ☐ PPST—Mathematics
- ☐ PPST—Reading
- ☐ PPST—Writing

- ☐ CBT—Mathematics
- ☐ CBT—Reading
- ☐ CBT—Writing

KANSAS

Kansas Department of Education
Division of Teacher Education and Accreditation
120 West Tenth Street
Topeka, KS 66612-1182
(913) 296-2288

ALL CERTIFICATES WITH PASSING SCORES

Praxis I: Academic Skills

- 174 PPST—Mathematics
- 173 PPST—Reading
- 172 PPST—Writing

- ☐ CBT—Mathematics
- ☐ CBT—Reading
- ☐ CBT—Writing

Take only the PPST.

KENTUCKY

Kentucky Department of Education
Division of Teacher Education and Certification
Capital Plaza Tower, 18th Floor
Frankfort, KY 40601
(502) 564-4606
www.kde.state.ky.us.

ALL CERTIFICATES WITH PASSING SCORES

Praxis I: Academic Skills

173 PPST—Mathematics   318 CBT—Mathematics
173 PPST—Reading   320 CBT—Reading
172 PPST—Writing   318 CBT—Writing

Take either the PPST or the CBT, *not both.*

LOUISIANA

Louisiana Department of Education
Bureau of Higher Education and Teacher Certification
Box 94064
Baton Rouge, LA 70804-9064
(504) 342-3490
www.doe.state.la.us

ALL CERTIFICATES WITH PASSING SCORES

Praxis I: Academic Skills

170 PPST—Mathematics   315 CBT—Mathematics
172 PPST—Reading   319 CBT—Reading
171 PPST—Writing   316 CBT—Writing

Take either the PPST or the CBT, *not both.*

The PPST is not currently offered in Louisiana. You may submit a combination of PPST and CBT scores. Check the *Louisiana Praxis Registration Bulletin.*

MAINE

Maine Department of Education
Division of Certification and Placement
State House, Station 23
Augusta, ME 04333
(207) 287-5944
www.janus.state.me.us/education

ALL CERTIFICATES WITH PASSING SCORES

Praxis I: Academic Skills

172 PPST—Mathematics   317 CBT—Mathematics
173 PPST—Reading   320 CBT—Reading
168 PPST—Writing   312 CBT—Writing

Take either the PPST or the CBT, *not both.*

MARYLAND

Maryland Department of Education
Department of Certification
200 West Baltimore Street
Baltimore, MD 21201
(410) 767-0412
www.msde.state.md.us

ALL CERTIFICATES WITH PASSING SCORES

Praxis I: Academic Skills

177 PPST—Mathematics   322 CBT—Mathematics
177 PPST—Reading   325 CBT—Reading
173 PPST—Writing   319 CBT—Writing

Take either the PPST or the CBT, *not both.*

MASSACHUSETTS

Massachusetts Department of Education
Office of Teacher Certification
350 Main Street
Malken, MA 02148
(617) 770-7517
www.doe.mass.edu

ALL CERTIFICATES

Praxis I: Academic Skills

- ☐ PPST—Mathematics
- ☐ PPST—Reading
- ☐ PPST—Writing
- ☐ CBT—Mathematics
- ☐ CBT—Reading
- ☐ CBT—Writing

MICHIGAN

Michigan Department of Education
Teacher Preparation and Certification Services
Box 30008
Lansing, MI 48909
(517) 373-3310
www.mde.state.mi.us

ALL CERTIFICATES

Praxis I: Academic Skills

- ☐ PPST—Mathematics
- ☐ PPST—Reading
- ☐ PPST—Writing
- ☐ CBT—Mathematics
- ☐ CBT—Reading
- ☐ CBT—Writing

MICHIGAN TESTS FOR TEACHER CERTIFICATION

Basic Skills Examination

The Basic Skills Examination is very similar to the reading, mathematics, and essay portions of Praxis I and is required for all teaching certificates.

Basic Skills Examination   4 hours

Writing (essay)
Reading
Mathematics

All questions, except the essay, are multiple choice.

Preparation Strategy
Follow the Praxis I study plan.

MINNESOTA

Minnesota Department of Children, Families, and Learning
Personnel Licensing Team
1500 Highway 36 West
Roseville, MN 55113-4266
(651) 582-8691
www.educ.state.mn.us

ALL CERTIFICATES WITH PASSING SCORES

Praxis I: Academic Skills

169	PPST—Mathematics	314	CBT—Mathematics
173	PPST—Reading	320	CBT—Reading
172	PPST—Writing	318	CBT—Writing

Take either the PPST or the CBT, *not both*.

MISSISSIPPI

Mississippi Department of Education
Division of Teacher Certification
Box 771
Jackson, MS 39205-0771
(601) 359-3483
www.mde.k12.ms.us

ALL CERTIFICATES WITH PASSING SCORES

Praxis I: Academic Skills

169 PPST—Mathematics
170 PPST—Reading
172 PPST—Writing

314 CBT—Mathematics
316 CBT—Reading
318 CBT—Writing

MISSOURI

Missouri Department of Elementary
  and Secondary Education
Box 480
Jefferson City, MO 65102
(314) 751-0051
www.dese.state.mo.us

ALL CERTIFICATES

Praxis I: Academic Skills

☐ PPST—Mathematics
☐ PPST—Reading
☐ PPST—Writing

☐ CBT—Mathematics
☐ CBT—Reading
☐ CBT—Writing

MONTANA

Montana Office of Public Instruction
Teacher Education and Certification
Box 202501
Helena, MT 59620-2501
(406) 444-3150
www.metnet.state.mt.us

ALL CERTIFICATES WITH PASSING SCORES

Praxis I: Academic Skills

170 PPST—Mathematics   315 CBT—Mathematics
170 PPST—Reading   316 CBT—Reading
170 PPST—Writing   314 CBT—Writing

Take either the PPST or the CBT, *not both.*

NEBRASKA

Nebraska Department of Education
Division of Teacher Certification
301 Centennial Mall South
Box 94987
Lincoln, NE 68509-4987
(402) 471-2496
www.nde4.nde.state.ne.us

ALL CERTIFICATES WITH PASSING SCORES

Praxis I: Academic Skills

171 PPST—Mathematics   316 CBT—Mathematics
170 PPST—Reading   316 CBT—Reading
172 PPST—Writing   318 CBT—Writing

Take either the PPST or the CBT, *not both.*

NEVADA

Nevada Department of Education
Teacher Licensure and Education
State Mail Room
1820 East Sahara Suite 205
Las Vegas, NV 89104-3746
(702) 486-6455
www.nsn.k12.nv.us.nvdoe

ALL CERTIFICATES WITH PASSING SCORES

Praxis I: Academic Skills

170 PPST—Mathematics
172 PPST—Reading
172 PPST—Writing

315 CBT—Mathematics
319 CBT—Reading
318 CBT—Writing

Take either the PPST or the CBT, *not both.*

NEW HAMPSHIRE

New Hampshire Department of Education
Bureau of Teacher Education and Professional Standards
State Office Park South
101 Pleasant Street
Concord, NH 03301
(603) 271-2407
www.state.nh.us/doe/

ALL CERTIFICATES WITH PASSING SCORES

Praxis I: Academic Skills

172 PPST—Mathematics
174 PPST—Reading
172 PPST—Writing

317 CBT—Mathematics
321 CBT—Reading
318 CBT—Writing

NEW JERSEY

New Jersey Department of Education
Office of Licensing and Academic Credentials
CN 500
Trenton, NJ 08625-0500
(609) 292-2070
www.state.nj.us

ALL CERTIFICATES

Praxis I: Academic Skills

☐ PPST—Mathematics   ☐ CBT—Mathematics
☐ PPST—Reading   ☐ CBT—Reading
☐ PPST—Writing   ☐ CBT—Writing

NEW MEXICO

New Mexico Department of Education
Director, Professional Licensure Unit
Education Building
300 Don Gaspar
Santa Fe, NM 87501-2786
(505) 827-6587
www.sde.state.nm.us

ALL CERTIFICATES

Praxis I: Academic Skills

☐ PPST—Mathematics   ☐ CBT—Mathematics
☐ PPST—Reading   ☐ CBT—Reading
☐ PPST—Writing   ☐ CBT—Writing

NEW YORK

New York Department of Education
Office of Teaching
Cultural Education Center
Empire State Plaza
Albany, NY 12230
(518) 474-6440
www.nysed.gov/tcert

ALL CERTIFICATES

Praxis I: Academic Skills

☐ PPST—Mathematics
☐ PPST—Reading
☐ PPST—Writing

☐ CBT—Mathematics
☐ CBT—Reading
☐ CBT—Writing

See Barron's *How to Prepare for the LAST and ATS-W.*

NORTH CAROLINA

North Carolina Department of Public Instruction
Licensure Section
North Carolina Education Building
301 North Wilmington Street
Raleigh, NC 27601-2825
(919) 733-4125
www.dpi.state.nc.us

ALL CERTIFICATES WITH PASSING SCORES

Praxis I: Academic Skills

173 PPST—Mathematics
176 PPST—Reading
173 PPST—Writing

318 CBT—Mathematics
323 CBT—Reading
319 CBT—Writing

Take either the PPST or the CBT, *not both.*

NORTH DAKOTA

North Dakota Department of Public Instruction
Director of Certification
Bismarck, ND 58505-0440
(701) 224-2264
www.dpi.state.nd.us

ALL CERTIFICATES

Praxis I: Academic Skills

☐ PPST—Mathematics   ☐ CBT—Mathematics
☐ PPST—Reading   ☐ CBT—Reading
☐ PPST—Writing   ☐ CBT—Writing

OHIO

Ohio Department of Education
Department of Teacher Education and Certification
65 South Front Street, Room 1012
Columbus, OH 43266-0308
(614) 466-3593
www.ode.state.oh.us

ALL CERTIFICATES

Praxis I: Academic Skills

☐ PPST—Mathematics   ☐ CBT—Mathematics
☐ PPST—Reading   ☐ CBT—Reading
☐ PPST—Writing   ☐ CBT—Writing

OKLAHOMA

Oklahoma Department of Education
Division of Professional Standards
2500 North Lincoln Blvd., Room 211
Oklahoma City, OK 73105
(405) 521-3337
www.sde.state.ok.us

ALL CERTIFICATES WITH PASSING SCORES

Praxis I: Academic Skills

171 PPST—Mathematics	316 CBT—Mathematics
173 PPST—Reading	320 CBT—Reading
172 PPST—Writing	318 CBT—Writing

Take either the PPST or the CBT, *not both.*

OREGON

Oregon Teacher Standards and Practices Commission
630 Center Street NE, Suite 200
Salem, OR 97310
(503) 378-3586
www.ode.state.or.us

ALL CERTIFICATES WITH PASSING SCORES

Praxis I: Academic Skills

175 PPST—Mathematics	320 CBT—Mathematics
174 PPST—Reading	321 CBT—Reading
171 PPST—Writing	317 CBT—Writing

Take either the PPST or the CBT, *not both.*

See Barron's *How to Prepare for the MSAT.*

PENNSYLVANIA

Pennsylvania Department of Education
Bureau of Teacher Preparation and Certification
333 Market Street
Harrisburg, PA 17126-0333
(717) 787-3356
(717) 772-2846 TTY
www.pde.psu.edu

ALL CERTIFICATES WITH PASSING SCORES

Praxis I: Academic Skills

173 PPST—Mathematics   ☐ CBT—Mathematics
172 PPST—Reading   ☐ CBT—Reading
172 PPST—Writing   ☐ CBT—Writing

Take only the PPST.

RHODE ISLAND

Rhode Island Department of Education
Office of Teacher Certification
Roger Williams Building
22 Hayes Street
Providence, RI 02908
(401) 277-2675
www.mstruct.ride.ri.net

ALL CERTIFICATES

Praxis I: Academic Skills

☐ PPST—Mathematics   ☐ CBT—Mathematics
☐ PPST—Reading   ☐ CBT—Reading
☐ PPST—Writing   ☐ CBT—Writing

SOUTH CAROLINA

South Carolina Department of Education
Teacher Certification Section
Rutledge Building, Room 1015
Columbia, SC 29201
(803) 734-8466
www.state.sc.us/sde/

ALL CERTIFICATES WITH PASSING SCORES

Praxis I: Academic Skills

172 PPST—Mathematics	317 CBT—Mathematics
175 PPST—Reading	322 CBT—Reading
173 PPST—Writing	319 CBT—Writing

SOUTH DAKOTA

South Dakota Department of Education
Office of Certification
Kneip Office Building
700 Governors Drive
Pierre, SD 57501-2291
(605) 773-3553
www.state.sd.us

ALL CERTIFICATES

Praxis I: Academic Skills

☐ PPST—Mathematics	☐ PBT—Mathematics
☐ PPST—Reading	☐ PBT—Reading
☐ PPST—Writing	☐ PBT—Writing

TENNESSEE

Tennessee Department of Education
Office of Teacher Licensing
Fifth Floor, Andrew Johnson Tower
710 James Robertson Parkway
Nashville, TN 37243-0377
(615) 532-4880
www.state.tn.us

ALL CERTIFICATES WITH PASSING SCORES

Praxis I: Academic Skills

173 PPST—Mathematics	318 CBT—Mathematics
174 PPST—Reading	321 CBT—Reading
173 PPST—Writing	319 CBT—Writing

Take either the PPST or the CBT, *not both.*

TEXAS

Texas Education Agency
Division of Teacher Certification
William B. Travis State Office Building
1701 North Congress Avenue
Austin, TX 78701-1494
(512) 463-8976
www.sbec.state.tx.us

ALL CERTIFICATES WITH PASSING SCORES

Praxis I: Academic Skills

171* PPST—Mathematics	☐ CBT—Mathematics
172* PPST—Reading	☐ CBT—Reading
173* PPST—Writing	☐ CBT—Writing

Take only the PPST.
*Alternate Certification Route

UTAH

Utah Board of Education
Certification and Personnel Development
250 East 500 South Street
Salt Lake City, UT 84111
(801) 538-7740

ALL CERTIFICATES

Praxis I: Academic Skills

☐ PPST—Mathematics   ☐ CBT—Mathematics
☐ PPST—Reading   ☐ CBT—Reading
☐ PPST—Writing   ☐ CBT—Writing

VERMONT

Vermont Department of Education
Licensing Office
120 State Street
Montpelier, VT 05602-2703
(802) 828-2445
www.state.vt.us/educ/

ALL CERTIFICATES

Praxis I: Academic Skills

175 PPST—Mathematics   322 CBT—Mathematics
177 PPST—Reading   327 CBT—Reading
174 PPST—Writing   322 CBT—Writing

Take either the PPST or the CBT, *not both*.

VIRGINIA

Virginia Department of Education
Office of Professional Licensure
Box 2120
Richmond, VA 23216-2120
(804) 225-2022
www.per.k12.va.us

ALL CERTIFICATES WITH PASSING SCORES

Praxis I: Academic Skills

178 PPST—Mathematics
178 PPST—Reading
176 PPST—Writing

323 CBT—Mathematics
326 CBT—Reading
324 CBT—Writing

WASHINGTON

Washington State Superintendent of Public Instruction
Director of Professional Certification
Old Capitol Building, Box 47200
Olympia, WA 98504-7200
(206) 753-6773
www.k12.wa.us

ALL CERTIFICATES

Praxis I: Academic Skills

☐ PPST—Mathematics
☐ PPST—Reading
☐ PPST—Writing

☐ CBT—Mathematics
☐ CBT—Reading
☐ CBT—Writing

WEST VIRGINIA

Office of Professional Preparation
West Virginia Department of Education
Building 6, Room 252
1900 Kanawha Blvd. East
Charleston, WV 25305-0330
(800) 982-2378
(304) 558-7826
www.wvde.state.wv.us

ALL CERTIFICATES WITH PASSING SCORES

Praxis I: Academic Skills

172	PPST—Mathematics	317	CBT—Mathematics
174	PPST—Reading	321	CBT—Reading
172	PPST—Writing	318	CBT—Writing

Take either the PPST or the CBT, *not both.*

WISCONSIN

Department of Public Instruction
Bureau of Teacher Education, Licensing and Placement
Box 7841
125 South Webster Street
Madison, WI 53707-7841
(608) 266-1788
www.dpi.state.wi.us

ALL CERTIFICATES WITH PASSING SCORES

Praxis I: Academic Skills

173	PPST—Mathematics	318	CBT—Mathematics
175	PPST—Reading	322	CBT—Reading
174	PPST—Writing	320	CBT—Writing

Take either the PPST or the CBT, *not both.*

WYOMING

Wyoming Department of Education
Professional Teaching Standards Board
Hathaway Building, 2nd Floor
Cheyenne, WY 82002
(307) 777-7291
www.k12.wy.us

ALL CERTIFICATES

Praxis I: Academic Skills

☐ PPST—Mathematics ☐ CBT—Mathematics
☐ PPST—Reading   ☐ CBT—Reading
☐ PPST—Writing   ☐ CBT—Writing

DEPARTMENT OF DEFENSE SCHOOLS

4040 North Fairfax Drive
Arlington, VA 22203
(703) 696-3033
www.ode.dodea.edu

ALL CERTIFICATES WITH PASSING SCORES

Praxis I: Academic Skills

175 PPST—Mathematics   320 CBT—Mathematics
177 PPST—Reading   325 CBT—Reading
174 PPST—Writing   320 CBT—Writing

Take either the PPST or the CBT, *not both.*

You are exempt from the test requirement if you have a state-issued teaching certificate.

U.S. VIRGIN ISLANDS

44-46 Kongens Gade
Charlotte
U.S. Virgin Islands 00802
(340) 774-0100
www.usui.org/education

ALL CERTIFICATES WITH PASSING SCORES

Praxis I: Academic Skills

170	PPST—Mathematics	315	CBT—Mathematics
175	PPST—Reading	322	CBT—Reading
174	PPST—Writing	320	CBT—Writing

Take either the PPST or the CBT, *not both*.

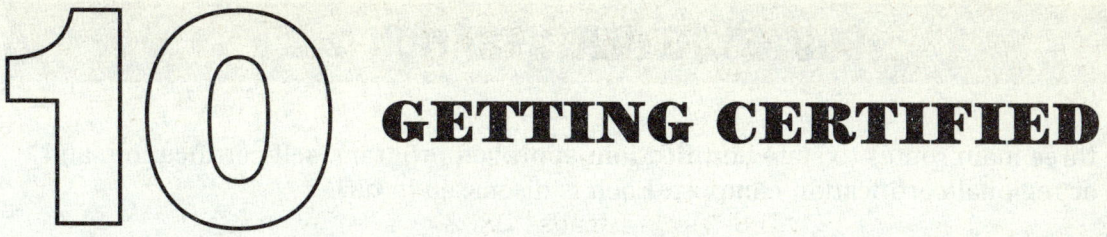

10 GETTING CERTIFIED

CERTIFICATION REQUIREMENTS

Every state requires teachers to be certified. Most teacher certification requirements include a bachelors degree, a certification test, and required education and liberal arts courses. However, the types of certificates, tests, and required courses vary widely from state to state.

Decide in which states you will seek certification and contact the state certification offices directly to get the teacher certification regulations. Chapter 9 contains the address and phone number for each state certification office.

When you contact the state certification office, find out about any local or regional certificates within that state. For example, a city or county may have certification regulations that vary somewhat from the state regulations. There may also be exemptions or extra requirements for certain certificates.

Some states offer special certificates for students who have the bachelors degree but have not completed all the certification requirements. In some states or localities, a school district that wants to hire you can get you an emergency certificate, even if you haven't finished all the certification requirements.

Keep on asking questions until you have a complete understanding of the certification rules, regulations, and special routes for the certificates you are pursuing. These rules and regulations can change frequently depending on the need for teachers, actions by state legislatures and state boards of education (regents), and the policies of the chief education officer for a state.

In this chapter you'll learn about the administrative details of teacher certification—that is, the steps you should follow to get certified. This writer has helped thousands of students as they worked toward teacher certification, and tells you what works and what to look out for. A lot of it will seem like common sense, but then most of life's successes are available to those who apply common sense and follow through on what they know they should do.

In one way, these steps are the least important part of becoming a teacher. Your work in college classes and with students in the schools is far more important in helping you become the kind of teacher you want to be. But in another way these steps are the most important. You certainly don't want to go through a whole college career, or an entire set of courses, and not be eligible for a teaching certificate.

Remember, you are a consumer. You will be spending money on tuition, books, certification fees, and the like. Good consumers are always aware of their options, making sure they are getting their money's worth, never making a decision without all the facts, and never assuming anything.

ROUTES TO CERTIFICATION

There are three main routes to state certification: approved program, self-certification, and interstate or regional certification compact. Each is discussed in turn.

APPROVED PROGRAM CERTIFICATION

The approved program certification route takes you to certification via a college's approved certification program. This is the best way to pursue certification because it removes any uncertainty about certification requirements. It's worth making an extra effort to get into one of these programs.

Most states approve certification programs offered through colleges and universities at both the bachelors degree and masters degree levels. Call the state certification office to find out which colleges offer approved programs for which certificates.

When you enter an approved program at the college or university, the catalog or an advisor will inform you about the study plan and required tests that lead to certification. But don't take anything for granted. This is your life we're talking about. The details of the approved certification program should appear in the college catalog, which is usually considered a legal contract between you and the college or university.

Beware if no one is willing to absolutely promise that meeting the requirements means certification. Ask questions. Find out. You can do all of this in a very friendly way. After all, you have a right to know what's going on and to be sure that you will receive your certificate.

You may have to take Praxis I tests for admission to a teacher certification program. Once in an approved program, you must follow the program exactly. Usually, the catalog in effect when you enter or matriculate at a college is your contract with that school. So hang onto that catalog and follow its guidelines, checking things off as you go. Go to see an advisor every term. This will keep you up to date about any impending changes and will establish contacts in the college you can talk to when you have questions.

You may take Praxis I tests during your certification program. Undergraduates will probably do best at the end of their sophomore year. Graduate students should take the tests immediately.

Don't rely on the college to obtain any needed test scores, records, or transcripts. As the time for graduation and certification draws near, check your certification file or folder and make sure that everything is up to date. If something is missing or incomplete, take the responsibility of bringing your folder or file up to date. Your goal should be to have all paperwork and requirements completed prior to graduation.

SELF-CERTIFICATION

The self-certification route takes you to certification through the state education department and to the same teaching certificates as an approved program. While self-certification almost always involves more work and more responsibility than an approved program, it may be the best route to certification.

Self-certification is often most appropriate when you have completed your undergraduate study and need a few courses or some tests to get certified. Perhaps you attended several colleges and you do not qualify for the approved program in the college you are attending now. If so, self-certification may be the best way for you to be certified.

There is one ironclad rule to follow: Get everything in writing. No matter how honest or well-meaning, unwritten responses can't be counted on. There are countless horror stories of students who didn't get written responses to self-certification. Some have had to spend up to an additional year in school. Get it in writing!

Follow these steps.

1. Begin by contacting the state education department in your certification state(s) and get the certification regulations and a certification application. Try to make the contact by phone and ask questions about the certification regulations as they apply to your particular background. Remember, though, that this phone advice is not binding on the state certification office, and similar questions asked of different certification representatives may yield different responses.

2. Look over the regulations and identify the courses, competencies, tests, and experience required for the certification(s) in which you are interested.

3. Gather together all the information you have about yourself. Use the checklist below. Take these steps right now.

   Get a transcript for every college course you have ever taken. Don't worry if the transcript includes poor grades or negative comments about your status in school. Get them all.

   Get notes documenting all the important competencies you possess. Some states require particular competencies such as knowledge about substance abuse or local history. If you attained one of these competencies in a course or on the job, but it's not evident from the course title or job description, you need documentation. Get a note from a college or employer documenting that you have indeed attained each competency.

   Get reports for all the certification and other relevant tests you have taken. Gather reports for all the teacher certification tests you have taken. Don't worry if the tests include poor scores or if the tests are not specifically required by the state in which you are seeking certification. Also get together reports for all advanced placement tests and tests you took to earn college credit.

   Get notes documenting all your education-related experience. Whether it was years of experience as a teacher aide or assistant or just some volunteer work with children at the local boys or girls club, get a note documenting each education-related experience. The note should be on the school or organization letterhead, be signed by the supervisor, and tell what you did and for how long you did it in an honest but complimentary way.

4. Once you have gathered all this information, you are ready to apply for your certificate. That's right, even if you are just at the beginning of your work toward certification you're going to apply. In this way you will find out exactly what you have to do to be certified and you won't take unnecessary courses.

   Fill out the certification application. Then submit the application along with the certification fee and copies of all your documentation, neatly organized, to the state certification office.

   You are strongly advised to submit the application in person. Many states provide in-person service at the certification office or regional centers. There's nothing like talking to someone in person. You can answer questions and fill in details during the meeting. It's usually worth the time and effort to have an in-person meeting.

If the state does not offer in-person meetings with certification officers, or if you absolutely can't make a meeting, you'll have to submit your application and documentation by mail. Make sure that you send the application to the correct address and enclose a brief cover letter that includes your phone number. Make sure you have proof that the application was delivered.

5. Following an evaluation of your materials, you should receive written notification of the requirements you still have to meet. If they list requirements you think you've met, submit additional documentation. The notification may be a checklist or a letter. This response is now your most important certification document. The state certification office has put in writing how you can get certified.

   Do not accept an informal or verbal response to your application. The certification officer may not remember talking to you or he may move on to another job or, well, there are lots of possibilities. Insist, nicely, on a written response. Anything less is not useful.

6. Take the required courses and tests and get the experience noted on the response to your application. You may have to check back from time to time to be sure that a particular course or experience will meet their requirements. If you're not sure about something, find out. Get that in writing, too.

7. When you've met all the requirements, send documentation for these courses, tests, and experiences to the state education department along with a copy of their original response to your application. In most states, you will have to file another application and pay another fee.

INTERSTATE OR REGIONAL CERTIFICATION COMPACT

Those seeking certification via the interstate or regional certification compact route already have a certificate in another state. Most states belong to the Interstate Certification Compact, which means that they generally accept comparable certificates from other states. There are also regional certification organizations that serve the same function.

However, just because the state you are certified in and the state you want to be certified in belong to the Interstate Certification Compact or one of the regional organizations, you have no guarantee that you will automatically be certified in the "new" state. States usually still insist that you meet their particular testing or other requirements.

Get a certification application from the state in which you want to be certified. Follow steps 1–7 in the self-certification section. In some cases, states may give previously certified teachers a temporary certificate while they meet the additional requirements. Find out about these special arrangements during your investigations.

11 GETTING A TEACHING JOB

It is never too early to start preparing to get a teaching job. You might as well start now.

There are specific steps you can follow to increase your chances of getting the teaching job you want. There are no guarantees, mind you. But you can definitely improve the odds. Let's begin with a discussion of job opportunities.

WHERE ARE THE TEACHING JOBS?

There are teaching jobs everywhere! This writer served on the board of education in a small suburban town with about 80 teachers in a K–8 school district. It was the kind of place most people would like to teach. There were between two and five teaching openings each year, for six years. But you could hardly find an advertisement or announcement anywhere.

About the only people who knew about the jobs were administrators and teachers in the district and surrounding districts, the few people who read a three-line ad that ran once in a weekly paper, and those who called to inquire about teaching jobs. Keep this information in mind. It is your first clue about how to find a teaching job.

The *Occupational Outlook Handbook*, released by the federal government, predicts that teaching opportunities for elementary and secondary school teachers will increase faster than all occupations as a whole during the next 10 years. The book predicts a much faster increase in jobs for special education teachers.

Other sources predict an increased need for mathematics, science, and bilingual teachers during this same period. Experience indicates that the opportunities for teachers certified in more than one area will grow much faster than average as well.

Some publications predict that the population of elementary age school children will increase about 10 percent by 2005. If the number of teachers were to increase at this rate overall, the number of teachers in the United States would grow from about 3,250,000 to about 3,560,000. Teachers are apportioned approximately as follows: elementary school, 1,600,000; secondary school, 1,300,000; and special education, 360,000.

Well over half of American teachers are over 40. The number of retirements during the next decade will probably be larger than we have seen in the last 20 years. Knowledgeable sources predict that as many as 2,500,000 people will be teaching in 2010 who are not now teaching.

The growth in the school age population and the increased retirement rate will produce a large number of teaching jobs during the next decade. You need only one.

HOW CAN I FIND A JOB?

Before discussing this question, let's talk about rejection. Remember, you need only one teaching job. If you are interested in 100 jobs, you should be extremely happy with a success rate of 1%. A success rate of 2% is more than you need, and a very high success rate of 5% will just make it too hard to decide which job to take.

Rejection and failure are part of the job search process. Be ready; everyone goes through it.

OKAY, I'M READY TO BEGIN. HOW DO I FIND A JOB?

Start now even if you won't be looking for a job for several years.

Begin by deciding on the kind of teaching jobs you want and the geographic areas you are willing to teach in. There is no sense pursuing jobs you don't want in places you don't want to go.

Write your choices here.

These are the kind of teaching positions I'm interested in.

_____   _____

_____   _____

These are the places or locales I'm willing to teach in.

_____   _____

_____   _____

You can change your mind as often as you like. But limit your job search to these choices.

Follow the guidelines presented below. You must actually do the things outlined here. Reading, talking, and thinking about them will not help.

    Make and use personal contacts
    Find out about every appropriate teaching position
    Apply for every appropriate teaching position go to every interview
    Develop a good resume
    Use the placement office

MAKE AND USE PERSONAL CONTACTS

You will not be surprised to learn that many, if not most, jobs are found through personal contacts. You must make personal contacts to maximize your chances of finding the job you want. Take things easy, one step at a time, and try to meet *at least* one new person each month.

Find a way to get introduced to teachers, school administrators, board of education members, and others who will know about teaching jobs and may influence hiring decisions. The more people you meet and talk to, the better chance you will have of getting the job you want.

Get a mentor. Get to know a superintendent or principal near where you want to teach, and ask that person to be your mentor. Tell them immediately that you are not asking for a job in their district. (That will not stop them from offering you one if they want to.) Explain that you are just beginning your teaching career and that you need help learning about teaching jobs in surrounding communities and about teaching in general. Ask your mentors to keep their eyes and ears open for any openings for which you are qualified. You can have as many mentors as you want. Listen to their advice.

You already have a lot of contacts through your friends and relatives. Talk to them all. Tell them you will be looking for a teaching job and ask them to be alert for any possibilities. Ask them to mention your name and your interest in a teaching position to everyone they know.

FIND OUT ABOUT EVERY APPROPRIATE TEACHING POSITION

The contacts you have and are making each month will help you keep abreast of some teaching opportunities. Follow these additional steps. Look in every paper every day distributed in the places you want to teach. Don't forget about weekly papers.

Call all the school districts where you want to teach. Ask the administrative assistant or secretary in the superintendent's or principal's office if there are current or anticipated job openings in the district. If you are in college or a recent graduate, visit or contact the placement office every week and ask your professors if they know about any teaching opportunities.

Find out about jobs now even if you won't be teaching for several years. This information may help you decide where you want to student teach.

DEVELOP A RESUME

Start working on your resume right away. Just thinking about a resume will help you develop skills and choose experiences that will look good on a resume.

A good resume is a one-page advertisement. A good resume highlights the things you have done that prospective employers will be interested in. A good resume is not an exhaustive listing of everything you have done. A good resume is not cluttered.

For example, say you worked as a teacher assistant and spent most of your time on lunch duty and about 10% of your time conducting whole language lessons. What goes on the resume? The whole language experience.

Your resume should include significant school-related experience. It should also include other employment that lasted longer than a year. Omit noneducation-related short-term employment. Your resume should list special skills, abilities, and interests that make you unique.

An example of a resume using a format that has proven successful appears in this chapter. This resume combines the experience of more than one person and is for demonstration purposes only.

An outline of a resume you can copy, to begin to develop your own resume, is also included in this chapter. If you are interested in two different types of teaching positions, you may have two resumes. Go over your final resume and cover letters with a placement officer or advisor.

CREATE A PORTFOLIO

A resume helps get you an interview. A portfolio is what you bring to an interview to show a prospective employer what you have done. Start working on a portfolio right away.

Your portfolio should include the things you do in college classes, in practica, in student teaching, and in any other activity related to teaching. Include lesson plans, unit plans, letters and other communication from teachers, administrators, and parents, examples of students' work, pictures of you working with students, pictures of bulletin boards, documentation of teaching-related activities, and anything else that relates to your work with or about children.

Keep everything in a big folder. Make copies and keep them in a safe place. When you are ready to go on interviews you can decide what to include and put those materials under acetate covers in a professional loose-leaf book.

Some employers will want to see your portfolio, and some will not. But you've got to be ready. Check with your advisor, your professor, your mentor, as well as other teachers and administrators, for more advice about preparing your portfolio.

Derek Namost
33 Ann Street
Kearning, NJ 99999
(555) 555-5555

Objective:	Elementary School Teacher Special Education Teacher Secondary History Teacher
Education:	BS History—Collegiate College (minor in education) 1994 MS in Education at Long Key College in progress
Certification:	Teacher of Special Education Teacher of Elementary Education

Experience: **Lincoln School District**,2000–present
Elementary School Teacher Fifth Grade
- Teach in a student-centered elementary school
- Prepare and teach individualized lessons geared to student needs
- Use computer software and CD-ROMs to teach mathematics and motivate students
- Prepare and implement whole language instruction
- Integrate instruction in science, language arts, and social studies

Southern Pines School District   1994–2000
Secondary School Special Education Teacher
- Planned and taught modified classes for classified students
- Modified the curriculum to meet the individual needs of students
- Taught modified science and social studies courses to classified students
- Assisted students with class assignments, self-management, and study skills
- Collaborated with class and subject matter teachers

Watson School   Spring 1994
Student Teacher, Preschool Class
- Collaborated in teaching a class of preschool students

Honors:	Kappa Delta Pi, Phi Delta Kappa
Coaching/ Advising:	Coach, varsity soccer team 1996–1999 Advisor, mathematics team 1997–1999 Interested in coaching and advising after-school activities
Special Skills:	Extensive experience using computers, including Macintosh and IBM computers, multimedia, and CD-ROMs.
References:	References are available on request

_____

_____

_____

_____

( ) _____ _____

Objective:

Education:

Certification:

Experience:

Honors:

**Coaching/
Advising:**

**Special
Skills:**

References:

APPLY FOR EVERY APPROPRIATE TEACHING POSITION— GO TO EVERY INTERVIEW

When it is time, apply for every teaching position that is of the type and in the location you listed. No exceptions! Direct application for a listed position is probably the second most effective way to get a job. The more appropriate the jobs you apply for, the more likely you are to get one. It is not unusual for someone to apply for more than 100 teaching positions.

Go to every interview you are invited to. Going to interviews increases your chances of getting a job. If you don't get the job, it was worth going just for the practice.

Your application should include a brief cover letter and a one-page resume. The cover letter should follow this format: The first brief paragraph should identify the job you are applying for. The second brief pragraph should be used to mention a skill or ability you have that matches a district need. The third brief paragraph should indicate an interest in a personal interview. Every cover letter should be addressed to the person responsible for hiring in the school district.

USE THE PLACEMENT OFFICE

If you are a college student or a college graduate, use your school's placement office. Set up a placement file that includes recommendation letters from professors, teachers, and supervisors. It's handy to have these references on file. If a potential employer wants this information, you can have them sent out from the placement office instead of running around.

College placement offices often give seminars on job hunting and interviews. Take advantage of these.

WHAT TIME LINE SHOULD I FOLLOW?

Let's say you are looking for a job in September and you will be certified three months earlier, in June. You should begin working on your personal contacts by September of the previous year. You should start looking for advertisements and tracking down job possibilities during the previous January. Have your placement file set up and a preliminary resume and portfolio done by February. You can amend them later if you need to. Start applying for jobs in February.

ANY LAST ADVICE?

Stick with it. Follow the steps outlined here. Start early and take things one step at a time. Remember the importance of personal contacts. Remember that you need only one teaching job. Let people help you.